A DICTIONARY
OF GESTURES

by
Betty J. Bäuml
and
Franz H. Bäuml

The Scarecrow Press, Inc.

Metuchen, N.J. 1975

Library of Congress Cataloging in Publication Data

Bäuml, Betty J
  A dictionary of gestures.

    Bibliography: p.
    Includes index.
    1. Gesture--Dictionaries. 2. Nonverbal communi-
cation--Dictionaries. I. Bäuml, Franz H., joint
author. II. Title.
BF591.B3   152.3'84   75-23144
ISBN 0-8108-0863-3

To
ROSE ZEIDNER
and the memory
of
WALTER ZEIDNER

CONTENTS

v

INTRODUCTION

This dictionary contains primarily non-codified, non-arbitrary, culturally transmitted (semiotic) gestures. It does not include sign languages, gestures used in narrative dances, military gestures, or such fragmentary sign languages as the occupationally determined gestures of truck drivers, railroad men, or monks, nor is it primarily concerned with autistic gestures. The reason for the exclusion of these types of gestural activity is the fact that in function as well as in structure they differ basically from culturally transmitted gestures.

However, the boundaries between culturally transmitted gestures and codified gesture systems or sign languages as well as autistic gestures cannot be drawn sharply. Between them lies a shadowy area of overlap, in which considerable exchange takes place among the various systems. A well-known example is the liturgical gesture of the (major) sign of the cross, i. e. the right hand moved from the forehead to the chest, then from the left to the right shoulder (Roman rite), which frequently occurs also beyond the limits of the liturgy. For this reason we have chosen to base the denotations of many Roman Catholic liturgical gestures on the somewhat popular manual of the Benedictine Convent of Perpetual Adoration rather than on more scholarly sources which concentrate on the liturgical history of the gestures.

Rather than sacrifice potentially useful information in the interest of methodological consistency, we have often chosen to violate this interest and include material related to culturally transmitted gestures but which lies beyond the limits of this category.

The currency of gestures, unlike that of languages, does not offer natural delimitations: no national, linguistic, or chronological boundaries arise from the material itself that can be applied to delimit and classify it. One can, of course, superimpose boundaries on a chosen set of gestural

activities for practical purposes, a procedure that has been
followed hitherto. But whether the limits chosen are chronological, as in the classic work by Carl Sittl, Die Gebärden
der Griechen und Römer, or geographical, as in the recent
study by Robert L. Saitz and Edward J. Cervenka, Handbook
of Gestures: Colombia and the United States, or a combination of both, as in the work of Andrea de Jorio, La mimica
degli antichi investigata nel gestire napoletano, patterns of
distribution and evolution remain partly or entirely obscured
precisely because forms of gestural communication transcend
such limits. In choosing not to make such delimitations, on
the other hand, one surrenders any hope for exhaustiveness,
which in any case is only achievable by diachronic and/or
typologically limited studies such as those of Gerhart B. Ladner on the gestures of prayer in papal iconography of the
thirteenth and early fourteenth centuries and Archer Taylor
on the Shanghai gesture.

A dictionary comprising every gesture in existence and
every gesture once existing is unthinkable. We have limited
our collection to descriptions or depictions of gestures in
verifiable sources. No gestures of solely our own observa-
tion are included. If, therefore, the description in this Dictionary of a gesture is inadequate for the purpose of the
reader, its original description, depiction, or context can
readily be consulted.

Since it would be impossible as well as pointless to
register every recorded occurrence of any given gesture we
have attempted to proceed typologically in our selection of
entries, by listing variants of types and identifying them geo-
graphically and chronologically, either explicitly or by indication of the source. It goes without saying that many of these
geographical and chronological identifications of gestures could
be increased practically ad infinitum: merely because a gesture is listed with a nineteenth-century Hungarian source does
not imply that this gesture is not also common elsewhere and
at other times.

The contents of this Dictionary may be approached from
two directions: the starting point may be the part(s) of the
body primarily involved in the execution of a gesture, or it
may be the significance of the gesture. The main alphabetical sequence of the Dictionary, i.e., the main entries, are
the executing parts of the body, under which are then sub-
arranged, likewise in alphabetical order, the significance(s)
of the gesture. An Index of Significances refers the reader
to all the parts of the body under which the gestures of a
given significance are listed.

A heading combining two or more parts of the body
may signify that all designated parts are involved in executing
one gesture, that a cluster of gestures is executed by a number of the parts, or that one part of the body executes the
gesture and another "receives" it (e. g., kissing someone's
foot). Since it is often a matter of opinion what part of the
body is significant in the execution of a gesture, we have
chosen to give duplicate listings (i. e., inverted alphabetical
entries) in questionable cases in order to keep cross references within reasonable limits. Occasionally matter is included which may not be considered a gesture proper--in one
instance the absence of a non-gesture (carefree laughter or
a smile) is considered to be a gesture (signifying humility);
we have preferred to err on the side of inclusiveness rather
than adhere to an excessively narrow definition of gesture.
Manifestations of an emotion, for instance, can also serve
as gestures conveying that emotion.

Variations of a gesture sometimes include parts of the
body not used in its basic form. In these cases, the gesture
is listed under the body parts used to execute its basic form.
The occurrence of apparent synonyms of significances is often
due to the necessity for listing gestures under the meaning
given them in the source rather than risk a possible misin-
terpretation by listing them under a category of our own de-
vising. Similarly, descriptions of gestures are given under
the parts of the body with which the gestures are associated
in the source; occasionally these differ from the parts of the
body with which the gesture is most familiarly executed.

In order not to overburden the entries with bibliographical detail, in most cases only authors' names, and where
necessary with title abbreviations, and page numbers (or their
equivalent), are used in citing sources. (An Abbreviations
key, a Source List/Bibliography, and a list of Works of Art
Cited follow this Introduction; for very common sources--
e. g., Shakespeare and books of the Bible--a simple abbrevi-
ation is given without recourse to a key.) Immediately preceding such a citation is a brief geographical or cultural note
of the provenience of a gesture. For example, under ARM,
Prayer, will be found "Embracing the altar. Anc. Gk. ? and
Rom. Sittl, p. 179." In Carl Sittl, Die Gebärden der Griechen und Römer, page 179, will be found the exact references
to the works of Plautus, Ovid, and Apuleius where the act of
embracing an altar is described (the question mark after
"Gk. " indicates uncertainty over its application). Occasionally a self-explanatory reference is given for which no expanded citation was deemed necessary--e. g., in the second

entry of the Dictionary, simply "Terence, Andria 3, 2."

Regarding the references in the text two details should
be noted.   First, whenever a reference to Jerald R.
Green,
A Gesture Inventory for the Teaching of Spanish, is preceded
by the notation "Span., Lat. Am.," the "Lat. Am." indicates
that the Spanish gesture was understood by at least two-thirds
of a panel of six Latin American informants representing five
Latin American countries (Green, p. 8).

Secondly, Robert A. Barakat has labelled each item
in his collection of Arabic gestures as autistic, culture-induced, technical, or semiotic.   Without necessarily agreeing
with his definitions we regard this practice as very useful
and have therefore included these classifications in our citations from Barakat.   In order to prevent misunderstandings,
however, it is necessary for the reader to abide by Barakat's definitions: "autistic gestures are those bodily movements that are highly personal in nature, or unique to a particular person....   Closely related to autistic gestures are
culture-induced gestures....   Unlike autistic gestures, however, [they] are learned like any symbolic code such as
speech...; that is, individuals of a specific culture learn
these gestures through imitation and practice....   [Technical
gestures] are characterized by their arbitrariness, their required prior verbal agreement for meanings and their rather
limited use among a select group of professional classes."
... "Semiotic, or folk, gestures ... are substitutes for speech,
arbitrary in meaning and require prior verbal agreement from
the members of a community to standardize meaning with that
group.   ...Semiotic gestures are also handed down from generation to generation as part of a culture's store of traditions..." (Barakat, pp. 766, 767-768).

Many of our friends and colleagues have taken an interest in the compilation of our dictionary, and we owe them
our gratitude for their encouragement.   Preeminent among
them was the late Professor Archer Taylor of the University
of California, Berkeley, to whose suggestion, made some
seventeen years ago, this Dictionary owes its existence, and
who kept us richly supplied with bibliographical advice while
lending a resolutely deaf ear to our complaints of the magnitude of our task.   We are likewise grateful to Professor
Herbert Fischer of the University of Graz, Austria, and Professors Wayland D. Hand, University of California, Los
Angeles, Mary Ritchie Key, University of California, Irvine,
and John H. R. Polt, University of California, Berkeley,

from whose friendship, advice and contributions of material
the dictionary as well as we have benefitted.

B. J. B.

F. H. B.

ABBREVIATIONS

ABA	Abhandlungen der bayerischen Akademie der Wissenschaften, 23 (1905)
AGA	Archiv des Vereins für Geschichte und Altertümer der Herzogtümer Bremen und Verden
DAK	Denkmäler alter Sprache und Kunst
DAS	Dictionary of American Slang
DEP	Dictionary of English Proverbs, 2d ed.
DRA	Grimm, J. and W. Deutsche Rechtsaltertümer
DWb	Grimm, J. and W. Deutsches Wörterbuch
HDA	Handwörterbuch des deutschen Aberglaubens
HDM	Handwörterbuch des deutschen Märchens
HDV	Handbuch der deutschen Volkskunde
IJAL	International Journal of Anthropology and Linguistics
JAF	Journal of American Folklore
KHM	Grimm, J. and W. Kinder- und Hausmärchen
NQ	Notes and Queries
OED	Oxford English Dictionary
PG	Patrologia Graeca, ed. Migne
PL	Patrologia Latina, ed. Migne
SAV	Schweizer Archiv für Volkskunde
SFQ	Southern Folklore Quarterly
WF	Western Folklore
ZDR	Zeitschrift für deutsches Recht
ZV	Zeitschrift für Volkskunde

SOURCE LIST (BIBLIOGRAPHY)

d'Abreu Brás, Luis. Portugal Medica. Coimbra, 1726.
Achelis, H. Das Christentum in den ersten drei Jahrhunderten. Leipzig, 1912.
Ades, Raphael. "My First Encounter with the Spanish of Medellín," Hispania, 36 (1953), 325-327.
Aimoinus monachus historiae Francorum libri, 5. Paris, 1567.
Alas, Leopoldo. Las dos cajas. Madrid, 1886.
_____. Pipá. Madrid, 1886.
Allingham, Margery. The Tiger in the Smoke. London, 1952.
Alós, Concha. Los enanos. Barcelona, 1963.
Alpharts Tod. In Deutsches Heldenbuch, II, ed. E. Martin. Berlin, 1866-73.
Alsop, Stewart. "How to Speak French Without Saying a Word," Saturday Evening Post (Dec. 24-31, 1960), 26-29.
Altdeutsche Gedichte, ed. Keller. Tübingen, 1846-80.
Ambrosius. Hexaemeron, ed. R. O. Gilbert. Leipzig, 1840.
Amira, Karl von. "Die Handgebärden in den Bilderhandschriften des Sachsenspiegels." Abhandlungen der bayerischen Akademie der Wissenschaften, 23 (1905), 161-264.
Amis, Kingsley. That Uncertain Feeling. New York, 1971.
Anderson, C. J. Lake Ngami. London, 1856.
Anderson, J. D. "The Language of Gesture," Folk-Lore, 31 (1920), 70-71.
Anrich, G. Das antike Mysterienwesen in seinem Einfluss auf das Christentum. Göttingen, 1894.
Apollonius Rhodius. Argonautica, ed. R. C. Seaton. London, 1912.
Arce, Manuel. Oficio de muchachos. Barcelona, 1963.
Archäologische Zeitung.
Ariosto, Ludovico. Orlando Furioso. Turin, 1923-29.
Arndt, Ernst Moritz. Gedichte. Leipzig, 1840.
Arnobius. Adversus nationes, ed. A. Reifferscheid. In Corpus Scriptorum Ecclesiasticorum Latinorum 4.

d'Artois, Le livre du très chevalereux Comte.   Paris, 1837.
Athanasius. In Patrologia Graeca, 25-27, ed. Migne.
Aubert, Charles. The Art of Pantomime.   New York, 1927.
Augustinus, Aurelius (St. Augustine). De Doctrina Christi-
    ana. In Patrologia Latina, 34, ed. Migne.
    _____. Confessiones, ed. v. Raumer. Stuttgart, 1856.
d'Aulnoy, Condesa. Un Viaje por España en 1679. Madrid,
    n. d.
Austin, Mary. "Gesture in Primitive Drama, " Theatre Arts
    Magazine, 11 (1927), 594-605.

Babelon, Ernest. Description historique et chronologique des
    monnaies de la République Romaine. Paris, 1885-86.
Baden, T. "Bemerkungen über das komische Gebärdenspiel
    der Alten nach den Originalen, " Neue Jahrbücher für
    Philologie, Supplementband I (1832), 447-56.
Bäumer, S. "Kreuzzeichen, " Kirchenlexikon, 7/2, 1135-41.
Baker, Frank. "Anthropological Notes on the Human Hand, "
    American Anthropologist, 1 (1888), 51-75.
Ball, C. J. Light from the East.   London, 1899.
*Barakat, Robert A. "Arabic Gestures, " Journal of Popular
    Culture, 6 (1973), 749-87.
Barbazon, E. de, and D. M. Méon.   Fabliaux et Contes.
    Paris, 1808.
Bartholmae, Chr. Die Gathas des Awesta.   Strassburg, 1905.
Bas, Philippe le see Le Bas, Philippe
Basile, Giambattista. Pentamerone, ed. Penzer. London,
    1932.
Basto, Cláudio. "A linguagem dos gestos em Portugal, "
    Revista Lusitana, 36 (1938), 5-72.
Bastow, A. "Peasant Customs and Superstitions in 13th-
    century Germany, " Folk-Lore, 47 (1936), 313-28.
Batchelor, J. The Ainu of Japan.   London, 1892.
Baudoin de Sebourc, Li Romans de.   Valenciennes, 1841.
Bauer, L. Volksleben im Lande der Bibel.   Leipzig, 1903.
Baumeister, A. Denkmäler des klassischen Altertums zur
    Erläuterung des Lebens der Griechen und Römer in Re-
    ligion, Kunst und Sitte.   Munich and Leipzig, 1885-88.
Bee, Jon. Sportsman's Slang; A New Dictionary of Terms
    used in the Affairs of the Turf, the Ring, the Chase,
    and the Cock-Pit; with those of Bon-ton, and the Vari-

_____

*To best understand any reference to the Barakat work, see
the penultimate paragraph of the Introduction to this Dictionary.

eties of Life, ed. altera. London, n.d.
Beitl, Richard. Deutsche Volkskunde. Berlin, 1933.
Belloc, Hilaire. "Advice on Wine, Food, and other Matters,"
    Gourmet, 22 (Jan. 1962), 12-3.
Belon, Pierre. Les observations des plusiers singularitez
    et choses mémorables, trouvées en Grèce, Asie, Iudée,
    Egypte. Anvers, 1555.
Benndorf, O. Griechische und sicilische Vasenbilder. Ber-
    lin, 1869-83.
Beowulf, ed. F. Klaeber. Boston and New York, 1922.
Berceo, G. de. Vida de Santo Domingo de Silos, ed. Fitz-
    gerald. Paris, 1904.
Bergemann, Bernhard. Das höfische Leben nach Gottfried
    von Strassburg. Halle, 1876.
Bergmann, J. "Folkloristische Beiträge," Monatsschrift für
    Geschichte und Wissenschaft des Judentums, 79 (1935),
    329-32.
Bertau, Karl. Deutsche Literatur im Europäischen Mittel-
    alter. Munich, 1972.
Birdwhistell, R. L. Introduction to Kinesics. Louisville,
    1952.
_____. "Background to Kinesics," ETC., 13 (1955), 10-
    18.
_____. "Do Gestures Speak Louder than Words?" Col-
    lier's (March 4, 1955), 56-57.
_____. Time, 70 (July 15, 1957), 68.
_____. Kinesics and Context. Philadelphia, 1970.
Bischoff, Erich. Die Elemente der Kabbalah. Berlin, 1913.
Biterolf und Dietleib, ed. Jänicke. In Deutsches Heldenbuch,
    I. Berlin and Zürich, 1963.
Blasco Ibáñez, Vicente. "En la boca del horno," in Enrique
    Anderson-Imbert and Lawrence B. Kiddle, eds., Veinte
    Cuentos Españoles del Siglo XX. New York, 1961.
Bloch, Marc. Les rois thaumaturges. Strasbourg, 1924.
Boccaccio, Giovanni. Decamerone. Milan, 1951.
Boehm, F. De symbolis Pythagoreis. Diss. Berlin, 1905.
Boggs, R. S. "Gebärde," Handwörterbuch des deutschen
    Märchens, II, 318-322. Berlin, 1934.
Boileau-Despréaux, Nicolas. Satires. Paris, 1932.
Boissonade, J. F. Marini vita Procli. Amsterdam, 1966.
Bolte, J. L. K. "Bilderbogen des 16. und 17. Jahrhunderts,"
    Zeitschrift für Volkskunde, 19 (1909), 51-82.
_____, and G. Polivka. Anmerkungen zu den Kinder-
    und Hausmärchen der Brüder Grimm. Leipzig, 1913-
    1932.
Bonnanini, Philippe. Museum Kircherianum. Rome, 1709.
Bonnet, H. Reallexikon der aegyptischen Religionsgeschichte.
    Berlin, 1952.

Borchard, W. and G. Wustmann. Die sprichwörtlichen Re-
densarten im deutschen Volksmund. Leipzig, 1925.
Boucher, Anthony. Nine Times Nine. New York, 1962.
Bowers, F. "Encounters in Moscow, " New Yorker, 33
(Feb. 15, 1958), 102-114.
Bowers, R. H. "Gesticulation and Elizabethan Acting, "
Southern Folklore Quarterly, 12 (1948), 267-277.
Brant, Sebastian. Das Narrenschiff, ed. F. Bobertag. In
Deutsche National-Litteratur, 16. Berlin and Stuttgart,
n. d.
Branwen, Daughter of Llyr. In Mabinogion, tr. Gwyn and
Thomas Jones. London, 1950.
Brault, Gerard J. "Kinesics and the Classroom: Some
Typical French Gestures, " The French Review, 36
(1963), 374-82.
Bresciani, A. Dei costumi dell'isola di Sardegna. Naples,
1850.
_____. L'ebreo di Verona. Milan, 1858.
_____. Don Giovanni. Milan, 1863.
_____. Edmondo. Milan, 1872.
Brissonius, B. De formulis et sollemnibus populi romani
verbis. Mainz, 1649.
Brunner, H. Deutsche Rechtsgeschichte. Leipzig, 1887-92.
Buck, M. R. Medizinischer Volksglauben und Volksaberglau-
ben aus Schwaben. Ravensburg, 1865.
Bulwer, John. Chirologia. London, 1644.
Burke, T. A. Polly Peablossom's Wedding and Other Tales.
Philadelphia, 1851.
Buschan, G. Uber Medizinzauber und Heilkunst im Leben
der Völker. Berlin, 1941.
Butler, Samuel. Hudibras, ed. A. R. Waller. Cambridge,
1905.

Caballero Bonald, J. M. Dos Días de Setiembre. Barcelona,
1962.
Cadalso, José. Cartas Marruecas. Madrid, 1789 [reprinted
1956].
Cameron, V. L. Across Africa. London, 1877.
Cange, Charles du see du Cange, Charles...
Cantar del Mio Cid, ed. R. Menéndez Pidal. Madrid, 1908-
11. Tr. L. B. Simpson. Berkeley and Los Angeles,
1957.
Carr, John Dickson. The Case of the Constant Suicides.
New York, 1941.
_____. Hag's Nook. New York, 1963.
_____. To Wake the Dead. New York, 1965.

Cascudo, Luis da Câmera. Diccionario do Folclore Brasil-
    lero. Rio de Janeiro, 1962.
Catholic Encyclopaedia. New York, 1907-12.
Catullus, Gaius Valerius. [Works] ed. E. Baehrens. Leip-
    zig, 1885.
Cela, Camilo José. Viaje a la Alcarria. Barcelona, 1954.
La Celestina, tr. L. B. Simpson. Berkeley and Los Ange-
    les, 1959.
Cervantes, Miguel de. Don Quijote, ed. F. Rodríguez
    Marín. Madrid, 1943.
_____. La Galatea, ed. J. D. Avalle-Arce. Madrid,
    1961.
_____. Novelas Ejemplares, vol. 2, ed. Rodríguez
    Marín. Madrid, 1943.
Chanson de Roland, ed. J. Bédier. Paris, 1937.
Chauvé, P. R. G. in North Indian Notes and Queries, 5
    (1895), 125.
Chevalerie Vivien, ed. A.-L. Terracher. Paris, 1923.
Chevalier, Abbé L. Naples, le Vésuve et Pompei. Tours,
    1871.
Li Chevaliers as deus espees, ed. Foerster. Halle, 1877.
Chrétien de Troyes. Erec und Cligès, ed. W. Foerster.
    Halle, 1884-1932.
Chronicon Petershusanum see under Petershusanum
Cleomadès, Li Romans de; p. Adenés li Rois. Bruxelles,
    1865.
Codex Iustinianus, ed. Krüger. Berlin, 1877.
Codrington, R. H. The Melanesians. Oxford, 1891.
Coincy, Gautier de. Du riche homme à cui le Diable servi
    por vii ans. Les Miracles de la Sante Vierge. Paris,
    1857.
Comrie, P. "Anthropological Notes on New Guinea, "
    Journal of the Anthropological Institute, 6 (1877, 102ff.
Concilium IV aurelianense. Can. 16 in Mansi sacrorum
    conciliorum nova et amplissima collectio. Florence
    and Venice, 1759-98.
Conrad, Joseph. The Rover. New York, 1923.
Conybeare, F. C. Rituale Armenorum. Oxford, 1905.
Cook, Arthur. "CYKOΦANTHC, " Classical Review, 21
    (1907), 133-136.
Cook, James. Voyages. London, 1809.
Coulton, G. G. The Chronicler of European Chivalry.
    Creative Art, 1930.
Custine, Marquis de. L'Espagne sous Ferdinand VII. Paris,
    1838.
Cuvelier, Jean (?). Chronique de Bertrand du Guesclin.
    Paris, 1839.

d'Abreu Brás   see under   Abreu Brás
Dante Alighieri.   The Divine Comedy, tr. L. G. White.   New York, 1948.
Danzel, Th. W.   Kultur und Religion des primitiven Menschen.   Stuttgart, 1924.
d'Artois   see under   Artois
Darwin, Charles R.   Expression of the Emotions in Man and Animals.   New York, 1955.
d'Aulnoy   see under   Aulnoy
David-Neel, A.   Meister und Schüler.   Leipzig, 1934.
Davidson, Levette J.   "Some Current Folk Gestures and Sign Languages, " American Speech, 25 (1950), 3-9.
Dawson, W. R.   The Bridle of Pegasus.   London, 1930.
Defoe, Daniel.   Moll Flanders.   Oxford, 1927.
de Jorio   see under   Jorio
Denkmäler alter Sprache und Kunst.   Bonn, 1823-27.
Despériers, Bonaventure.   Oevres Françoises.   Paris, 1856.
Deutsches Wörterbuch   see   Grimm, Jacob and Wilhelm
Dickens, Charles.   Oliver Twist.   New York, 1910.
_____ .   Little Dorrit.   London, 1911.
_____ .   The Pickwick Papers.   London, 1932.
Didron, A. N.   Christian Iconography, tr. E. I. Millington.   New York, 1851.
Dietrichs Flucht, ed. E. Martin.   In Deutsches Heldenbuch, II.   Dublin and Zürich, 1963.
Dracontius, Blossius Aemilius.   [Poems] ed. F. J. E. Raby.   In Christian Latin Poetry.   Oxford, 1953.
Duby, Georges.   Foundations of a New Humanism 1280-1440, tr. P. Price.   Geneva, 1966.
Du Cange, Charles Du Fresne.   Glossarium mediae et infimae latinitatis.   Graz, 1954.
Duchenne, G. B.   Mécanisme de la physionomie humaine.   Paris, 1876.
Duchesne, L. M. O.   Christian Worship.   London, 1903.
du Fail, Noël.   Propos Rustiques.   Paris, 1842.
_____ .   Oevres Facétieuses.   Paris, 1874.

Ebert, M. ed.   Reallexikon der Vorgeschichte.   Berlin, 1924-32.
Efron, David.   Gesture and Environment.   A tentative study of some of the spatio-temporal and "linguistic" aspects of the gestural behavior of Eastern Jews and Southern Italians in New York City, New York, 1941.
Eichler, Lillian.   The Customs of Mankind.   New York, 1924.
Eike von Repgowe.   Sachsenspiegel, ed. K. A. Eckhardt.

Göttingen, 1955.
Eilhart von Oberge. Tristrant, ed. F. Lichtenstein. Strass-
    burg, 1877.
Elie de St. Gille, ed. G. Raynaud. Paris, 1879.
Eliot, George. The Mill on the Floss. New York, n. d.
Ellis, W. Polynesian Researches. London, 1832.
Elworthy, F. T. The Evil Eye. London, 1832.
_____. Horns of Honour. London, 1900.
Encyclopaedia Judaica. Berlin, 1928-34.
Endres, J. A. and A. Ebner. "Ein Königsgebetbuch des 11.
    Jahrhunderts, " St. Elises-Festschrift zum elfhundert-
    jährigen Jubiläum des deutschen Campo Santo in Rom.
    Freiburg, 1897.
Ermisch. Das sächsische Bergrecht des Mittelalters. Leip-
    zig, 1887.
Ernoul, La Chronique d', et de Bernard le Trésorier. Paris,
    1971.
Eschenbach see Wolfram von Eschenbach
Eyrbyggja Saga, ed. N. M. Petersen. Copenhagen, 1925.

Fail, Noël du see du Fail, Noël
Feijóo, P. "Sabiduria aparente, " in A. del Rio, Antología
    general de la literatura española. New York, 1960.
Ferres, Antonio. Los Vencidos. Paris, 1965.
Fielding, Henry. Joseph Andrews. London, 1742.
Fierabras. Paris, 1860.
Fischer, Herbert. "Heilgebärden, " Antaios, 2 (1960), 318-
    47.
_____. "Leben und Tod in alter Mittelfingersymbolik, "
    Basler Nachrichten (Oct. 30, 1960). Beilage.
_____. "Die kosmurgische Symbolik der Sonnen-Erde-
    Stellung, " Symbolon, 3 (1962), 89-107.
Fischer, R. Osterreichisches Bauernleben. Vienna, 1903.
Flachskampf, Ludwig. "Spanische Gebärdensprache, "
    Romanische Forschungen, 52 (1938), 205-258.
Flaubert, Gustave. Bouvard et Pécuchet. Paris, 1881.
Folengo, Teofilo. Orlandino. Venice, 1842.
Foz, Braulio. Vida de Pedro Saputo. Zaragozza, 1955.
Frazer, James G. The Golden Bough. London, 1911.
Urkundenbuch der Stadt Freiberg, ed. Ermisch. Leipzig,
    1891.
Freiberg, H. Afrika ruft. Berlin, 1936.
Frezzi, Federigo. Il Quadriregio o Poema de' quattro regni.
    Foligno, 1725.
Frobenius, L. Kulturgeschichte Afrikas. Zürich, 1935.

Ganzinger, K. Apothekenaltertümer in Osterreich. Stuttgart, 1951.

García de Pruneda, Salvador. La encrucijada de Carabanchel. Madrid, 1965.

Gardiner, A. H. The Tomb of Huy. London, 1926.

Gaskell, Mrs. Cranford and Other Tales. In Works, vol. 2, London, 1906.

Gaudentius. De Evangeli lectione. In Patrologia Latina, 2, ed. Migne.

George, S. S. "Gesture of Affirmation Among the Arabs, " American Journal of Psychology, 27 (1916), 320-23.

Gerhard, E. Etruskische und Kampanische Vasenbilder des kgl. Museums zu Berlin. Berlin, 1843.

Gessner, S. Der Tod Abels in fünf Gesängen. Zürich, 1758.

Gesta Franconum, ed. L. Brehier. Paris, 1924.

Goar, Jacques. Εὐχολόγιον... Venice, 1730.

Godefroy de Paris, Chronique métrique de Philippe-Bel. Paris, 1856.

Gogol, Nikolai. Betrachtungen über die göttliche Liturgie, tr. R. v. Walter. Freiburg, 1954.

Goldziher, I. "Die Entblössung des Hauptes, " Der Islam, 4 (1915-16), 304ff.

_____ . "Über Gebärden und Zeichensprache bei den Arabern, " Zeitschrift für Völkerpsychologie und Sprachwissenschaft, 16 (1886), 369-86.

_____ . "Zauberelemente im islamischen Gebet, " Orientalische Studien. Festschrift Nöldeke, p. 303-29, Giessen, 1906.

Gottfried von Strassburg. Tristan, ed. F. Ranke. Berlin, 1965.

Gougand, L. Dévotions et pratiques ascétiques du moyen âge. Collection "Pax, " 21. Paris, 1925.

Gowing, Lawrence. "Brueghel's World, " Art News Annual, 36 (1970), 12.

Graf Rudolf, ed. P. Ganz. Berlin, 1964.

Graham, Janet. "A Handful of Italian, " Gourmet (May 1969), 24ff.

Grajew, Felix. Untersuchungen über die Bedeutung der Gebärden in der griechischen Epik. Diss. Berlin, 1934.

*Green, J. R. A Gesture Inventory for the Teaching of

---

*The use of "Spain, Lat. Am. " as indicator of provenience of a gesture in conjunction with citations to Green's book means that it was understood by at least four of a six-member panel of Latin American informants (representing five countries).

Spanish. Philadelphia, 1968.
Gregorius Magnus. Dialogi, ed. U. Moricca. Rome, 1924.
Gregorius of Nazianzus. In Patrologia Graeca, 36, ed.
    Migne.
Gregory of Tours. Vitae Patrum. In Patrologia Latina, 71, ed.
    Migne.
Grimm, Jacob. Deutsche Rechtsaltertümer. Darmstadt,
    1955.
_____. Weistümer. Darmstadt, 1957.
_____, and Wilhelm. Deutsches Wörterbuch. Leipzig,
    1854-1954.
_____. Kinder- und Hausmärchen. Wiesbaden, Berlin,
    n. d.
Grønbech, V. P. Mystikere i Europa og Indien. Copenhag-
    en, 1925.
Guys, P. A. Voyage littéraire de la Grece. Paris, 1783.

Hahn, J. G. von. Griechische und albanesische Märchen.
    Leipzig, 1864.
Handbuch der deutschen Volkskunde, ed. W. Pessler and A.
    Bach et al. Potsdam, 1934- .
Handwörterbuch des deutschen Aberglaubens, ed. H. Bächtold-
    Stäubli. Berlin and Leipzig, 1921-42.
Handwörterbuch des deutschen Märchens, ed. Lutz Mackensen.
    Berlin and Leipzig, 1930-40.
Harou, Alfred. Revue des Traditions Populaires, 13 (1898),
    192, and 14 (1899), 384.
Hartmann von Aue. Iwein, ed. G. F. Benecke and K. Lach-
    mann. Berlin, 1965.
Haseloff, Arthur. Eine thüringisch-sächsische Malerschule
    des 13. Jahrhunderts. Strassburg, 1897.
Hastings, James, ed. Dictionary of the Bible. New York,
    1923.
_____, ed. Encyclopaedia of Religion and Ethics. New
    York, 1926.
Hawthorne, N. The Marble Faun. New York, 1925.
Hayes, Francis. "Gestures: A Working Bibliography, "
    Southern Folklore Quarterly, 21 (1957), 219-317.
Heiler, E. Das Gebet. Munich, 1920.
Heinrich der Löwe. Urkunden, ed. K. Jordan. Stuttgart,
    1949-57.
Heinrich von Freiberg. Tristan, ed. R. Bechstein. Leip-
    zig, 1877.
Helbig, W. Untersuchungen über die campanische Wandma-
    lerei. Leipzig, 1873.
Heliant, ed. O. Behaghel. Tübingen, 1965.

Hellwig, A. "Mystische Meineidzeremonien," Archiv für
       Religionswissenschaft, 12 (1909), 46-66.
Hemingway, Ernest. For Whom the Bell Tolls. New York,
       1940.
Herwegen, J. "Germanische Rechtssymbolik in der römis-
       chen Liturgie," Deutschrechtliche Beiträge, 8 (1913),
       Heft 4.
Herzog Ernst, ed. K. Bartsch. Vienna, 1869.
Hildburgh, W. L. "Psychology Underlying the Employment
       of Amulets in Europe," Folk-Lore, 62 (1951), 231-51.
His, R. Das Strafrecht der Friesen im Mittelalter. Leip-
       zig, 1901.
Hone, William. Year Book of Daily Recreation and Infor-
       mation. London, 1832.
Hovorka, O. von and A. Kronfeld. Vergleichende Volksme-
       dizin. Stuttgart, 1908-09.
Howard, Maureen. Not a Word About Nightingales. New
       York, 1962.
Hrabanus Maurus. De Institutione Clericorum. In Patro-
       logia Latina, 107, ed. Migne.
Hupel, A. W. Topographische Nachrichten von Lief-und
       Ehstland. Riga, 1777.
Huxley, Aldous. Crome Yellow. New York, 1922.

Immermann, K. Münchhausen. Düsseldorf, 1841.
Irenaeus. Quaestiones et Responsiones ad Orthodoxos, ed.
       A. Stieren, fragm. vii. Leipzig, 1848-53.
Iustinianus, Codex, ed. Krüger. Berlin, 1877.

Jahn, O. "Uber den Aberglauben des bösen Blicks bei den
       Alten," Berichte über die Verhandlungen der sächsischen
       Gesellschaft der Wissenschaften, 7 (1855), 28ff.
James, E. O. Primitive Ritual and Belief. London, 1917.
Jean, Ch. F. La religion sumerienne. Paris, 1931.
Jeremias, A. Handbuch der altorientalischen Geisteskultur.
       Berlin and Leipzig, 1929.
Jerome, St. Vita S. Pauli primi eremitae. In Patrologia
       Latina, 23, ed. Migne.
Jiménez, A. Picardía Mexicana. Mexico, 1962.
Johannes Damascenus. In Patrologia Graeca, 94, ed. Migne.
Johnson, S. Camping Among Cannibals. London, 1883.
Johnston, H. H. The Uganda Protectorate. London, 1904.
de Jorio, A. La mimica degli antichi investigata nel gestire
       Napoletano. Naples, 1832.
Jungmann, J. A. Die Frohbotschaft und unsere Glaubens-

verkündigung. Regensburg, 1936.
Juvenalis, Decimus Iunius. Saturae, ed. A. E. Housman. Cambridge, 1931.

Kamrisch [Kramrisch], Stella. Indische Kunst. London, 1955.
Kany, Charles E. American-Spanish Euphemisms. Berkeley and Los Angeles, 1960.
Kaufringer, Heinrich. Gedichte, ed. Euling. In Stuttgart Litterarischer Verein, 182. Tübingen, 1888.
Kaulfers, W. V. "Curiosities of Colloquial Gestures," Hispania, 14 (1931), 249-64.
Kelly, Amy. Eleanor of Aquitaine. New York, 1957.
Kelly, Jonathan F. The Humors of Falconbridge. Philadelphia, 1856.
Kemelman, Harry. Friday the Rabbi Slept Late. New York, 1966.
Kenyatta, Jomo. "Kikuyu Religion, Ancestor-worship and Sacrificial Practices," Africa, 10 (1937), 310ff.
Key, Mary Ritchie. "Gestures and Responses: A Preliminary Study among Some Indian Tribes of Bolivia," Studies in Linguistics, [University of Buffalo], 16 (1962), no. 3-4.
Kindlinger, V. N. Geschichte der ältern Grafen bis zum 13. Jahrhundert. Münster, 1793.
King, W. S. "Hand Gestures," Western Folklore, 8 (1949), 263-64.
Kleinpaul, Rudolf. Das Leben der Sprache und ihre Weltstellung. Leipzig, 1888-93.
Klitgaard, C. "Skaelsord og foragtelig gestus," Danske Studier, (1934), 88-9.
Konrad von Würzburg. Otte mit dem Barte. In Erzählungen und Schwänke, ed. H. Lambel. Leipzig, 1883.
_____. Partonopier und Meliur, ed. Bartsch. Vienna, 1871.
Kramrisch see Kamrisch
Krapf, J. L. Travels, Researches and Missionary Labours during an Eighteen Years Residence in Eastern Africa. London, 1860.
Kraus, F. X., ed. Realenzyclopädie der christlichen Altertümer. Freiburg, 1882-86.
Krauss, F. S. Sitte und Brauch der Südslaven. Vienna, 1885.
Kroeber, Theodora. Ishi in two Worlds: A Biography of the last Wild Indian in North America. Berkeley and Los Angeles, 1961.
Kroll, H. H. Rogues' Company. Indianapolis, 1943.

Krout, M. H.   Autistic Gestures.   In Psychological Mono-
    graphs, 46 (1935), 1-126.
Krukenberg, Eberhard Freiherr von.   Schwurgebärde und
    Schwurfingerdeutung.   Die Rechtswahrzeichen.   Frei-
    burg, 1941.
Kudrun, ed. Bruno Boesch.   Tübingen, 1954.
Kunz, George.   The Magic of Jewels and Charms.   Philadel-
    phia, 1915.

Lacroix, Paul.   Moers, usages et costumes au moyen âge
    et à l'époque de la renaissance.   Paris, 1874.
Lactantius.   De passione domini, ed. S. Brandt and G. Laub-
    mann.   In Corpus Scriptorum Ecclesiasticorum Lati-
    norum, 27.
Ladner, Gerhart B.   "The Gestures of Prayer in Papal
    Iconography of the Thirteenth and Early Fourteenth
    Centuries, " Didascaliae.   Studies in Honor of Anselm
    M. Albareda.   New York, 1961.
Laiglesia, A. de.   La Rueda.   Madrid, n. d.
Lammeus, H.   L'Islam.   Beyreuth, 1926.
Lampedusa, Giuseppe di.   The Leopard, tr. Colquhoun.   New
    York, 1961.
Lane, E. W.   Manners and Customs of the Modern Egyptians.
    London, 1846.
Larivey, Pierre.   "Les Laquais, " Ancien théâtre français,
    5.
Lathen, Emma.   Ashes to Ashes.   New York, 1971.
Le Bas, Philippe.   France.   Dictionnaire encyclopaedique.
    Paris, 1840-45.
Legrand d'Aussy, P. J. B.   Histoire de la vie privée des
    Français.   Paris, 1815.
Lehmann, Chr.   Chronica der freyen Reichsstadt Speyer.
    Frankfurt, 1698.
Leite de Vasconcellos, Pereira de Mello, J.   A Figa.
    Porto, 1925.
Leuzinger, E.   Afrika.   [Kunst der Welt.   Kunst der Ne-
    gervölker].   Baden-Baden, 1959.
Levi, Carlo.   Words Are Stones, tr. T. A. Davidson.   New
    York, 1958.
Lex Alamannorum.   In Monumenta Germanica, Legum Sect.
    I.   Hannover, 1888.
Lex Ripuaria.   In P. Georgisch, Corpus juris germanici
    antiqui.   Halle, 1738.
Liebrecht, Felix.   Zur Volkskunde.   Alte und neue Aufsätze.
    Heilbronn, 1879.
Liell, H. F. J.   Die Darstellungen der allerseligsten

Jungfrau und Gottesgebärerin Maria. Freiburg, 1887.
Liutprand. Relatio de legatione Constantinopolitane, ed. J.
    Becker in Scriptores rerum germanicarum. 1915.
Livingstone, D. Missionary Travels and Researches in
    South Africa. London, 1857.
Löfgren, O. "Die beiden äthiopischen Anaphoren des heiligen
    Cyrillus," tr. S. Euringer, in Orientalia Christiana,
    30 (1933), 44-86.
Lomas, Juan. Teoria y Practica del Insulto Mexicano.
    Mexico, n. d.
Lommatzsch, Eduard. System der Gebärden, dargestellt auf
    Grund der mittelalterlichen Literatur Frankreichs.
    Diss. Berlin, 1910.

Mabillon, J. De re diplomatica. Supplementum. Paris,
    1709.
McCord, Charlotte. "Gestures [at the University of Califor-
    nia, Berkeley], Western Folklore, 7 (1948), 290-92.
MacDonald, Philip. The List of Adrian Messenger. New
    York, 1959.
McHale, Tom. Farragan's Retreat. New York, 1971.
MacInnes, Helen. Decision at Delphi. New York, 1965.
Macrobius, Ambrosius Theodosius. Saturnalia, ed. J. Willis.
    Leipzig, 1963.
Mai und Beaflor, ed. F. Pfeiffer. Leipzig, 1848.
Maimon, Solomon. Autobiography. New York, 1947.
Mallery, Garrick. Greetings by Gesture. New York, 1891.
Malory, Sir Thomas. Le Morte d'Arthur. London, 1897.
Man, E. H. "On the Aboriginal Inhabitants of the Andaman
    Islands," Journal of the Anthropological Institute, 12
    (1883), 69ff, 117ff, 327ff.
Mantegazza, Paolo. Physiognomik und Mimik, tr. R. Löwen-
    feld. Leipzig, 1890.
Manzoni, A. I Promessi Sposi. Milan, 1922.
Marques-Rivière, Jean. Amulettes, Talismans, et Pantacles.
    Les Traditions orientales et occidentales. Paris, 1950.
Marsh, Ngaio. Died in the Wool. London, 1947.
Martial d'Auvergne. Aresta Amorum. Lyon, 1533.
Martialis, Marcus Valerius. Epigrammaton libri, ed. L.
    Friedländer, 1886.
Maspero, G. Popular Stories of Ancient Egypt. London,
    1915.
Mass, Treasures of the. Benedictine Convent of Perpetual
    Adoration, Clyde, Missouri. 1949.
Mathéolus, Les Lamentations de. Paris, 1892-1905.
Medieval Frescoes from Yugoslavia. An exhibition organized

by the Gallery of Frescoes, Belgrade. Smithsonian Institution, Publ. No. 4594. 1966.

Medio, Dolores. Diario de una maestra. Barcelona, 1961.

Meichelbeck, C. Historia Frisingensis. Augsburg, 1724.

Meier, John. "Der blaue Stein zu Köln, " Zeitschrift für Volkskunde, 40 (1931), 29-40.

_____. "Älter Rechtsbrauch im Bremischen Kinderlied, " Festschrift zur 400-Jahrfeier des Alten Gymnasiums zu Bremen 1520-1928, 219-44.

Meier, Jonas. De Gladiatura Romana. Bonn, 1881.

Mencken, J. B. The Charlatanry of the Learned, ed. H. L. Mencken. New York, 1937.

Mérimée, Prosper. Colomba. Paris, 1854.

Meschke, Kurt. "Gebärde, " Handwörterbuch des deutschen Aberglaubens, 3, (cols. 329-337), Berlin, 1927-42.

Meyer, E. Geschichte des alten Ägyptens. Berlin, 1887.

Michel, Francisque. Histoire des races maudites. Paris, 1847.

Mitton, A. "Le langage par gestes, " Nouvelle Revue des Traditions Populaires, 1 (1949), 138-51.

Möller, E. v. Die Rechtssitte des Stabbrechens. Weimar, 1900.

Mone, F. J. Anzeiger für Kunde der deutschen Vorzeit. 1835.

Montfaucon, B. de. Les Monuments de la monarchie françoise. Paris, 1729-33.

Monumenta Boica. Munich, 1763-1916.

Moser, O. "Zur Geschichte und Kenntnis der volkstümlichen Gebärden, " Carinthia, 1 (1954), 735-774.

Muggeridge, Malcolm. "Dolce Vita in a Colder Climate, " Esquire, 60 (Nov. 1963), 97.

Müllenhoff, K. and W. Scherer, eds. Denkmäler deutscher Poesie und Prosa aus dem VIII.-XII. Jahrhundert. Berlin, 1892.

Müller, G. "Über die geographische Verbreitung einiger Gebärden im östlichen Mittelmeergebiet und dem nahen Osten, " Zeitschrift für Ethnologie, 71 (1939), 99ff.

Müller, W. Der schauspielerische Stil im Passionsspiel des Mittelalters. Diss. Greifswald, 1927.

Mystères inédits du XVe siècle. Paris, 1837.

Nabokov, Vladimir. Pnin. New York, 1957.

Neckel, G. Über eine allgemeine Geste des Schmerzes, " Archiv für das Studium der neueren Sprachen, 167 (1935), 64ff.

Nettesheim, H. C. Agrippa von. Magische Werke. Berlin,

1916.
Newman, J. H. Essays on Various Subjects. London, 1853.
Nibelungenlied. Ed. Bartsch and De Boor. Wiesbaden, 1956.
Niebuhr, Carsten. Reisebeschreibung nach Arabien und
    andern umliegenden Ländern. Copenhagen, 1778.
Notscher, F. Biblische Altertumskunde. Bonn, 1940.
Nykl, A. R. Hispano-Arabic Poetry and Its Relations with
    the Old Provençal Troubadours. Baltimore, 1946.

———. Der Bilderkreis zum Welschen Gast. Heidelberg,
    1890.
Odilonis, Vita Sancti, Abbatis. In Patrologia Latina, 142,
    ed. Migne.
Odo of Cluny. Vita Sancti Geraldi. In Patrologia Latina,
    133, ed. Migne.
Oechelhäuser, A. von. Die Miniaturen der Universitäts-
    Bibliothek zu Heidelberg. Heidelberg, 1887-95.
Ohm, Thomas. Die Gebetsgebärden der Völker und das
    Christentum. Leiden, 1948.
Onians, R. B. The Origins of European Thought about the
    Body. Cambridge, 1951.
Opie, Iona and Peter. The Lore and Language of School-
    children. Oxford, 1959.
Orendel, ed. A. E. Berger. Bonn, 1888.
Ortnit, ed. A. Holtzmann. Heidelberg, 1865.
Østrup, D. J. Orientalische Höflichkeit. Formen und
    Formeln im Islam. Leipzig, 1929.
Otfrid. Liber Evangeliorum. Ed. O. Erdmann. 1882.
Otto, A. Die Sprichwörter und sprichwörtlichen Redensarten
    der Römer. Leipzig, 1890.
Otto, W. G. A. Handbuch der Archaeologie. Munich, 1939-
    54.
Otto von Freising. Gesta Frederici. Berlin, 1965.
Ovid [Publius Ovidius Naso]. Metamorphoses, ed. Miller.
    Cambridge, Mass., 1957-60.

Palaye, S. Mémoire sur l'ancienne chevalerie. Paris, 1759.
Palladius. Historia Lausiaca, ed. P. R. Coleman-Norton.
    1958.
Panchatantra, tr. A. W. Ryder. Calcutta and Bombay, 1949.
Pardo Bazán, Emilia. La madre naturaleza. In Obras
    completas, 4. Madrid, n. d.
Paso, Alfonso. Cosas de Mamá y Papá. In Teatro Español.
    Madrid, 1962-63.
Das Passional, ed. K. A. Hahn and F. K. Köpke. Frank-

furt, 1845 (1, 2), Quedlinburg and Leipzig, 1852 (3).

Paulinus of Petricordia. Vita Sancti. Martini episc. libri vi, ed. E. F. Corpet. Paris, 1852.

Pauly and Wissowa, eds. Realenzyklopaedie der klassischen Altertumswissenschaft. Stuttgart, 1894-1963.

Percy, Thomas. Reliques of Ancient English Poetry. Edinburgh, 1927.

Pereda, José María de. La Puchera. Madrid, 1889.

Pérez Galdós, Benito. Fortunata y Jacinta. Madrid, 1950.

Persius Flaccus, Aulus. Saturae, ed. F. Villeneuve. Paris, 1918.

Petermann, H. Reisen im Orient. Leipzig, 1860.

Petershusanum, Chronicon. In Prodromus Germaniae Sacrae, ed. Ussermann, Sanblasien, 1790.

Petrus Damiani. De bono suffragorum. In Patrologia Latina, 145, ed. Migne.

Pitrè, Giuseppe. Usi e costumi del popolo siciliano. Palermo, 1889.

Plautus, Titus Maccius. Asinaria, ed. Havet and Freté. Paris, 1925.

Plutarch, L. Mestrius. Lives, tr. Dryden. New York, n. d.

Pollock, F. and F. W. Maitland. The History of English Law Before the Time of Edward I. Cambridge, 1923.

Pollux, Julius. Onomasticon, ed. Bethe. Leipzig, 1900-37.

Possart, P. A. F. K. Die russischen Ostseeprovinzen. Kurland, Livland und Esthland. Teil 2. Stuttgart, 1846.

Potter, Charles. "Gesture, " Standard Dictionary of Folklore. New York, 1949.

Pound, Ezra. Lustra. New York, 1917.

Prutz, H. Staatengeschichte des Abendlandes im Mittelalter. Berlin, 1885-87.

Quasten, J. Musik und Gesang in den Kulten der Heiden. Antike und christliche Frühzeit. Münster, 1930.

Quintilianus, Marcus Fabius. Institutio Oratoria, ed. M. Niedermann. Neuchâtel, 1947.

Rabelais, F. Oevres, ed. A. Lefranc. Paris, 1923- .

Rabener, G. W. Satiren. Leipzig, 1759.

Rajna, Pio. Le fonti dell'Orlando Furioso. Florence, 1900.

Randolph, Vance. We Always Lie to Shanguo. New York, 1951.

Receual géneral et complet des Fabliaux. Paris, 1872-83.

Recke, E. v. d. Tagebuch einer Reise durch einen Teil

Deutschlands und durch Italien in den Jahren 1804-06,
    ed., Böttiger. Berlin, 1815-17.
Reinecke Fuchs. In K. Simrock, Die Deutschen Volksbücher, I.
    Basel, 1887.
Reinke de Vos, ed. F. Prien. Halle, 1925.
Renart le Nouvel, ed. H. Roussel. Paris, 1961.
Révész, G. Ursprung und Vorgeschichte der Sprache. Bern,
    1946.
_____. "Die Psychologie des Händedrucks und der Welt-
    sprache der Hände, " Universitas, 11 (1956), 143-48.
Rheinisches Wörterbuch, ed. J. Müller, Bonn, 1928.
Richardson, Samuel. Clarissa Harlowe. London, 1902.
Ripuaria, Lex see Lex Ripuaria
Ritter, K. B. "Das liturgische Gebet. Die liturgische Ge-
    bärdensprache," Christentum und Leben, 11 (1936),
    373-76.
Robertson, D. W. Preface to Chaucer. Princeton, 1962.
Robinson, Robert. Landscape with Dead Dons. New York,
    1956.
Röhrich, Lutz. Gebärde-Metapher-Parodie. Düsseldorf,
    1967.
Rolandslied, ed. K. Bartsch. Leipzig, 1874.
Le Roman de Renart, ed. M. Roques. Paris, 1951-60.
Rose, H. A. "The Language of Gesture, " Folk-Lore, 30
    (1919), 312-15.
Rosenberg, A. "Die Kreuzmeditation." In Bitter, W.,
    Meditation in Religion und Psychotherapie. Stuttgart,
    1958.
Roth, H. Ling. "On Salutations, " Journal of the Anthropo-
    logical Institute, 19 (1890), 164ff.
Rother, ed. de Vries. Heidelberg, 1922.
Rousseau, J.-J. Confessions. Paris, 1927.
    _____. Emile. Paris, 1957.
Ruesch, Jurgen and Weldon Kees. Nonverbal Communication.
    Berkeley and Los Angeles, 1956.
Ruíz, Juan. Libro de buen amor, ed. Cejador. Madrid, 1955.

Sachau, E. Reise in Syrien und Mesopotamien. Leipzig,
    1883.
Saitz, Robert L. and Edward J. Cervenka. Handbook of
    Gestures: Colombia and the United States. The Hague
    and Paris, 1972 (Approaches to Semiotics 31).
Sammlung Sabouroff der Kunstdenkmäler aus Griechenland,
    ed. Furtwängler. Berlin, 1883-
Schjelderup, Kr. Die Askese. Berlin and Leipzig, 1928.
Schmidt, Leopold. "Die volkstümlichen Grundlagen der

Gebärdensprache." Beiträge zur sprachlichen Volksü-
berlieferung, pp. 233-49. Berlin, 1953.
Schmidt, O. Die gotischen Skulpturen des Freiburger
Münsters. Frankfurt a. M., 1926.
Schmidt-Pauli, E. v. Kolumbus und Isabella. Salzburg,
1901.
Schmitz, H. J. Die Bussbücher und die Bussdisziplin der
Kirche. Mainz, 1883.
Schrader, Hermann. Der Bilderschmuck der deutschen
Sprache. Berlin, 1886.
Schreiber, Th. Die Sirenen. Berlin, 1868.
Schreiber, W. L. and Paul Heitz. Die deutschen "Accipies"
und "Magister cum Discipulis" Holzschnitte. Kehl,
1957. (Studien zur deutschen Kunstgeschichte 100.)
Schroeder, H. R. P. Geschichte des Lebensmagnetismus
und des Hypnotismus. Leipzig, 1899.
Schulberg, Budd. Waterfront. New York, 1955.
Schultz, Alwin. Das höfische Leben zur Zeit der Minne-
sänger. Leipzig, 1889.
Schulze, F. Bilderatlas zur deutschen Kulturgeschichte.
Leipzig, 1936.
Schwäbischen Idiotikons, Versuch eines, ed. Schmid. Berlin,
Stettin, 1795.
Schwäbisches Wörterbuch, ed. H. v. Fischer. Tübingen,
1904-36.
Schweizer Archiv für Volkskunde, 21 (1917).
Schweizerisches Idiotikon, ed. F. Staub and L. Tobler.
Frauenfeld, 1881-1961.
Sebourc, Baudoin de see Baudoin de Sebourc
Seemann, Otto. Die gottesdienstlichen Gebräuche der Grie-
chen und Römer. Leipzig, 1888.
Seiler, Friedrich. Deutsche Sprichwörterkunde. Munich,
1922.
Seligmann, Siegfried. Der böse Blick und Verwandtes. Ber-
lin, 1910.
Sercambi, Giovanni. Novelle inédite. Torino, 1889.
Seroux d'Agincourt, J. B. L. G. Histoire de l'art par les
monuments depuis sa décadence au IVe siècle jusqu'à
son renouvellement au XVIe. Paris, 1823.
Servii Grammatici Qui feruntur in Vergilii carmina commen-
tarii recensuerunt G. Thilo et H. Hagen. Leipzig, 1881-
87.
Seton, Ernest Thompson. Sign Talk. Garden City, N.Y.,
1918.
Siccama, S. T. Lex Frisionum. Leipzig, 1730.
Simenon, Georges. Maigret Abroad. New York, 1940.
Simms, W. G. Southward Ho! New York, 1882.
Simrock, K. Handbuch der deutschen Mythologie. Bonn,
1874.

Sittl, Carl. Die Gebärden der Griechen und Römer. Leipzig, 1890.

Siuts, Heinrich. Bann und Acht und ihre Grundlagen im Totenglauben. Berlin, 1959.

Slick, Jonathan (Mrs. Ann S. Stephens). High Life in New York. London, 1844.

Smith, M. Studies in the Early Mysticism in the Near and Middle East. London, 1901.

Snow, C. P. The Affair. London, 1962.

Snow, W. P. "The Wild Tribes of Tierra del Fuego, " Transactions of the Ethnological Society, 1 (1860), 263.

Soest. Gerichtsordnung. In: Westphalen monumenta inedita. Leipzig, 1730-45.

Speke, J. H. Journal of Discovery of the Source of the Nile. London, 1863.

Stegmann von Pritzwald, K. "Der Sinn einiger Grussformeln im Lichte kulturhistorischer Parallelen, " Wörter und Sachen, 10 (1927), 23ff.

Stephani, L. Compte rendu de la commission archéologique de l'academie de St. Petersbourg. 1861.

Stoebe, K. "Altgermanische Grussformen, " Beiträge zur Geschichte der deutschen Sprache und Literatur, 37 (1910), 173ff.

Surtees, R. S. Plain or Ringlets. London, 1860.

Swete, H. B. Church Services and Service Books. London, 1905.

Swift, Jonathan. Polite Conversation, ed. Partridge. London, 1963.

"Syr Isenbras. " In Select Pieces of Early Popular Poetry. London, 1817.

Taylor, Archer. "The Shanghai Gesture, " Folklore Fellows Communications, 166 (1956).

Temesvary, R. Volksbräuche und Aberglauben in der Geburtshilfe und der Pflege des Neugebornen in Ungarn. Leipzig, 1900.

Tepl, Johann v. Der Ackermann aus Böhmen, ed. Hammerich and Jungbluth. Copenhagen, 1951.

Tey, Josephine. The Singing Sands. New York, 1960.

Thackeray, William M. The Virginians. London, 1911.

Theocritus. [Works] ed. J. M. Edmonds. London, 1912.

Thomas, P. Hindu Religion, Customs and Manners. Bombay, n. d.

Thomasin von Circlaria. Der welsche Gast, ed. Rückert. Quedlinburg, 1852.

Thousand Nights and a Night, tr. R. F. Burton. London, n. d.

Thümmel, M. A. v. Reise in den mittäglichen Provinzen
    von Frankreich im Jahre 1785-86. Leipzig, 1791-1805.
Tibullus, Albius. [Works] ed. F. W. Lenz. Leipzig, 1937.
Tieck, Ludwig. Der blonde Eckbert. In Schriften, 4. Ber-
    lin, 1828-54.
Treasures of the Mass see Mass, ...
Trissino, G. G. L'Italia liberata. Orleans, 1787.
Trollope, Anthony. Can You Forgive Her? London, 1948.

Ulloa, Alfonso. Delle lettere dell'ill.^re signore Don Antonio
    di Guevara. Venice, 1585.
Urtel, Hermann. Beiträge zur portugiesischen Volkskunde.
    Hamburg, 1928.

Vergilius Maro, Publius. Aeneid, tr. J. Conington. Lon-
    don, 1870.
Vielhauer, A. "Heidentum und Evangelium im Grasland
    Kameruns, " Evangelische Missions-Zeitschrift, 3
    (1942), 150.
Vierordt, C. F. De iunctarum in precando manum origine
    Indo-Germanico. Karlsruhe, 1851.
Vinogradoff, P. Outlines of Historical Jurisprudence. Lon-
    don, 1920.
Vita Sancti Odilonis see under Odilonis
Vogt, M. In Geschichte des Sports aller Völker und Zeiten,
    ed. G. A. E. Bogeng. Leipzig, 1926.
Völgyesi, F. A. Die Seele ist alles. Von der Dämonologie
    bis zur Heilhypnose. Zürich, 1948.
Voullième, E. Quomodo veteres adoraverint. Diss. Halle,
    1887.

Wächter, Theodor. Reinheitsvorschriften im griechischen
    Kult. Giessen, 1910.
Walahfrid Strabo. De rebus eccles. In Patrologia Latina,
    114, ed. Migne.
Wallnöfer, H. and A. v. Rottauscher. Der goldene Schatz
    der chinesischen Medizin. Stuttgart, 1959.
Weinert, H. Der geistige Aufstieg der Menschheit. Stutt-
    gart, 1940.
Weise, G. and G. Otto. Die religiösen Ausdrucksgebärden
    des Barock und ihre Verbreitung durch die italienische
    Kunst der Renaissance. Stuttgart, 1938.
Weissel, L. Der Mönch von Montaudon. Basel, 1882.
Wensinck, A. J. "Uber das Gebetsweinen in den mono-

theistischen Religionen Vorderasiens, " Enzyklopädie des Islams, 4. Leipzig, 1910-1938.

Wentworth, H. and S. B. Flexner. Dictionary of American Slang. New York, 1960.

Wéyland, W. G. Áspero intermedio. Buenos Aires, 1949.

Winkelmann, J. J. Herkulaneische Entdeckungen. In Sämtliche Werke, 2. Donauöschingen, 1825-29.

Winkler, H. "Der alte Orient und die Geschichtsforschung. " In Mitteilungen der vorderasiatischen Gesellschaft, 9 (1909).

Wirnt von Gravenberg. Wigalois, ed. J. M. N. Kapteyn. Bonn, 1926.

Wocel, Johann Erasmus. Welislaws Bilderbibel aus dem 13. Jahrhundert. Prague, 1871.

Wodehouse, P. G. Fish Preferred. New York, 1929.

Wolff-Hurden, Philipp. "Die Lichtgebärde und die grosse Hand, " Basler Nachrichten (Dec. 22, 1957).

Wolfram von Eschenbach. Parzival, ed. K. Bartsch. Leipzig, 1875.

Wundt, Wilhelm. Völkerpsychologie. Leipzig, 1911.

Würzburg, Konrad von see Konrad von Würzburg

Wuttke, A. Der deutsche Volksaberglaube der Gegenwart. Berlin, 1900.

Wynne, Marianne. "Hagen's Defiance of Kriemhild, " Mediaeval German Studies Presented to Frederick Norman, pp. 104-14. London, 1965.

Zappert, G. "Uber den Ausdruck des geistigen Schmerzes im Mittelalter, " Denkschriften der Akademie der Wissenschaften zu Wien, 5 (1854), 73.

Zeller, Paul. Die täglichen Lebensgewohnheiten im altfranzösischen Karlsepos. Marburg, 1885.

Zigler und Klipphausen, H. A. von. Die asiatische Banise. In DNL, 36.

Zoëga, G. Abhandlungen. Göttingen, 1817.

Zola, Emile. "Le Forgeron, " in French Short Stories, ed. D. L. Buffum. New York, 1933.

WORKS OF ART CITED

Barcelona. Museo de Arte de Cataluña. Mural from the church of Tosas. Rm. 14.

Breughel, Pieter. "Le Fête des Fous" (1560), in René Bastelaer, Les Estampes de Pieter Bruegel (Brussels, 1908), no. 195.

Chantilly. Musée Condé. Les Très Riches Heures du duc de Berry (New York, 1969).

Cranach, Lucas, the Elder. "The Mocking of Christ" (1538). Los Angeles County Museum of Art.

Dürer, Albrecht. "Christ at the Pillar," in Franz Juraschek, Albrecht Dürer (Vienna and Leipzig, 1936), no. 68.

Gallego, Fernando. (1466-1507.) "Calvary." Prado. Madrid.

Giacomo, Niccolò di. "Annunciation and Marriage of the Virgin." Milan. Ambrosiana Ms. B 42 inf. In A Book of Miniatures, ed. Formaggio and Basso (London, 1962), p. 23.

Hamburg. Wingpanel of the altarpiece of St. Peter's. Master Bertram, "Creation of the Animals." Kunsthalle. In German Painting: The Late Middle Ages (Geneva, 1968), p. 31.

Hanover. Master Bertram, "The Agony in the Garden." Center panel of the altarpiece of the Passion. Niedersächsische Landesgallerie. In German Painting: The Late Middle Ages (Geneva, 1968), p. 32.

Heidelberg. Universitätsbibliothek, Cpg. 848 (Heidelberger Liederhandschrift C).

Istanbul. Book of Accomplishments. Topkapi Palace Museum.

London. Harley Ms. 4379, f. 135v. The British Library. In Maximilian's Triumphal Arch (New York, 1972).

New York. Guennol Collection. The book of Hours of Catherine of Cleves. Fol. 53. In The Hours of Catherine of Cleves (New York, n. d.), plate 19.

_____. Metropolitan Museum. "Noli me tangere." Late

11th-century Spanish ivory panel. In Pedro de Palo
and Max Hirmer, Early Medieval Art in Spain (New
York, n. d.), plate 79.

Oxford. Bodl. Ms. Douce 6. Psalter, Flemish, ca. 1300.

Pacher, Michael. "Prayer of St. Wolfgang. " Wing panel of
the altarpiece of the Church Fathers. Alte Pinakothek.
In German Painting: The Late Middle Ages (Geneva,
1968), p. 142.

Paolo, Giovanni di. "Salomé presents the head. " Chicago
Art Institute.

Paris. Bibliotheque Nationale. Ms. lat. 919. In The
Grandes Heures of Jean, Duke of Berry (New York,
1971).

Perugia. Biblioteca Augusta ms. 1238. In La Vita medioe-
vale italiana nella miniatura, ed. Volpe et al. (Rome,
1960), p. 14.

Polack, Jan. "Ecce Homo" (1492). Panel of the Franciscan
altarpiece. Bayr. Nationalmuseum. In German Painting: The Late Middle Ages (Geneva, 1968), p. 119.

Prague. National Gallery. Master of Vysebròd, "Resurrection. " In Georges Duby, Foundations of a New Humanism (Geneva, 1966), p. 75.

Schermann, Johannes. "Christus. " Graz, 1959.

Sitten. Switzerland. Ceiling carving in the Jörg Supersax
house. After 1500. In Schweiz, No. 6 (1961), cover.

Venice. Biblioteca Marciana. Ms. lat. 1, 100, 2089. In
A Book of Miniatures, ed. D. Formaggio and C. Basso
(London, 1962), p. 13.

_____. Biblioteca Marciana. Ms. lat. III, 120, 2478.
Missale Fratrum Servorum S. Mariae. Ibid. , p. 29.

THE DICTIONARY

ABDOMEN
Anger: Standing up, pushing out abdomen. If the adversary is small, he may be pushed with the abdomen. Portugal. Basto, p. 7.

ABDOMEN, CHEST, HAND
Innocence (protestation of): Chest and abdomen protruded, hands extended forward. Terence, Andria 3, 2; Baden, p. 450.

ABDOMEN, FINGER
Insult: Tips of right forefinger and thumb touch, forming the equivalent of an anal passage or vagina, holding this configuration in front of the abdomen; other fingers folded into palm. Obscenity. Lebanon, Syria. Semiotic. Barakat, no. 48.

ABDOMEN, HAND
Appreciation: Patting the abdomen. Amer. schoolchildren. Seton, p. xxiii; Krout, 24.
    Disbelief: Half-closed hand placed in front of abdomen, then turned slightly indicates that the person addressed is a liar. Saudi Arabia. Semiotic. Barakat, no. 215.
    Eating: Open hand, palm down, strikes sideways against gesticulator's belt or waist. Argentina. Kany, p. 89. Open hand rubbed back and forth across abdomen. Colombia, U.S. Saitz and Cervenka, p. 56.
    Frustration: Pressing the open hand, fingers slightly bent, against abdomen. Span, Lat. Am. Green, p. 45.
    Greeting: Among the Uvinza, after an elaborate exchange of courtesies, the parties slap their sides and pat their stomachs. Tanganyika. Cameron, I, p. 226. In the Marianas they stroke the abdomen. Mallery, p. 4.
    Hunger: Tips of joined fingers press abdomen. Palestine. Bauer, p. 223. Right palm pressed on abdomen, then the hand is moved in a circle while still in contact. Jordan, Lebanon, Libya, Syria, Saudi Arabia. Culture-induced, or semiotic. Barakat, no. 26. Both fists held against abdomen; mouth open. Rural Colombia. Saitz and Cervenka, p. 57.
    Medico-magical: "...then he grasps the hands of the patient, puts them over his stomach and leads him around the fire, calling out the names of helping demonic animals." Tlinkit Indians. Danzel, p. 34.
    Pregnancy: Right hand is moved in half circle from lower

1

chest to abdomen. Indicates that a certain woman is pregnant.
Lebanon, Jordan, Syria. Semiotic. Barakat, no. 195.

Satisfaction: Striking the abdomen affectionately with the open
fingers and palm of one hand. Span, Lat. Am. Green, pp. 31-
32. Colombia, U. S. Saitz and Cervenka, p. 58.

Sick: Hands clasped across abdomen indicates stomach ache.
Amer. schoolchildren. Seton, p. xxi.

ANIMAL, HAND

Oath: (cf. s. v. HAND, Oath). Swearing an oath by touching sacrificial animal. Medieval Scand. Grimm, DRA II, p. 552.
Swearing an oath by touching roast peacock. Council of Orléans,
900: the king or the most honored knight carved the peacock and,
his hand upon the bird, swore some brave oath, then passed the
dish and everyone who received it did likewise. Palaye, I, pp.
184, 187, 244, 246; II, p. 394; Legrand, pp. 365-367; Grimm,
DRA II, p. 553.

Sacrifice: Jews as well as pagans laid hand on sacrificial
animal. Sittl, p. 192. Sacrifice is extended with the right hand,
left is raised. Altaic, anc. Rom. Sittl, p. 189. Right hand
raised. Rare. Sittl, p. 189, n. 3.

ARM

Adoration: Arms extended horizontally to the side. (Solar ritual
gesture.) Fischer, Symbolon III, p. 91. Arms extended as for
an embrace (Venus ritual). Ibid. Arms raised (solar ritual gesture). Bogomil grave, Yugoslavia, 13th-14th century. Ibid., p.
95.

Affection: Embrace--with one arm if the gesticulator wore a
tunic. Anc. Gk. Sittl, p. 31. Two-armed. Anc. Gk. and Rom.
Sittl, p. 32; Medieval German. Kudrun, st. 1251, 1; Shakesp.,
Othello IV, 1, 139, and often; Smollett, Peregr. Pickle, ch. ci,
"clasping him in his arms"; Dickens, Pickw., I, p. 165, "hugged
the old lady with filial cordiality"; modern Gk. when one refers to
the other as "brother"; Sittl, p. 31, no. 9; Boggs, col. 320:
"love is commonly expressed by an embrace."

Amusement: Extended and rigid arm raised from a position
of rest at the side of the body to approximately the level of the
shoulder; normally raised to the side rather than the front. Rare
among women. Social context: "¡Os encapricháis del primer
hombre en la oficina!" Spain. Green, pp. 55-56.

Anger: "For I may never left an angry arm against his min-
ister" Shakesp., Richard II, I, ii, 40. Accompaniment to an expression of anger: raising arm vertically from a neutral position
to the side of the head, then dropping it to its original position.
Span., Lat. Am. Green, p. 74.

Apotropy: Arms crossed as protection against witches. Röhrich, p. 29, and pl. 25: woodcut, ca. 1500.

Approach: Waving by raising the arm and moving it towards
oneself indicates that he toward whom one waves is to approach.
Grimm, KHM, nos. 181, 182; Boggs, col. 322. "...spread her
arms..." Birdwhistell, Intro., p. 30.

Assistance: In battle, the warrior asks for help and defense

by stretching his arms out to his comrade. Anc. Gk. and Rom.
Sittl, p. 148. Cf. s. v. ARM, Plea.

Attention: Among orientals the extended arm is a familiar
sign of animation and action. During excitement and discussion
it is an understood prelude to speech, implying possession of
something that ought to be heard. Hastings, Dict. I, p. 151.
General desire for attention. Univ. of Calif., Berkeley. Mc-
Cord, p. 291.

Authority: Extended arm as sign of power. Biblical. Hastings, Dict. I, p. 151. Arm outstretched with hand in motion;
the various movements of the fingers express the particular action
which is commanded, e. g. coming, going. Anc. Rom., Neapol.
De Jorio, pp. 86-87.

Baby: Hands and arms across front as if holding infant,
rocking from side to side. Colombia. Saitz and Cervenka, p.
24.

Blessing: Arms raised and extended. Biblical. Ohm, p.
265.

Confession: Spreading of arms during baptism. In Coptic
ritual the neophyte spreads out his arms in the form of a cross
after disrobing. The deacon then takes his right hand, raises it
and the neophyte, turning West, renounces the devil and, turning
east, confesses his faith in Christ. Ohm, p. 257.

Congratulation: Embrace. Anc. Gk. Sittl, p. 32.

Death: One arm extended, palm down and elbow bent in front
of speaker--a sharp movement from side to side. Spain. Green,
p. 317. Both arms extended, palms down, elbows bent, in front
of the speaker, then arms drawn away from one another sharply
--accompanies expressions of death, failure, ruin, disappearance.
Madrid, Lat. Am. Green, p. 86.

Defiance: Arms crossed over chest. Medieval German, medieval French. Lommatzsch, p. 94. 19th cent. Corsica. Méri-
mee, p. 123. "She put her arms akimbo, as much to say she
defied me." Mrs. Gaskell, p. 155. (Cf. s.v. ARM, BREAST,
Defiance.)

Disbelief: Raising arm vertically from neutral position to
side of head, then dropping it to original position. Accompanies
expressions of incredulity. Span., Lat. Am. Green, p. 75.

Emphasis: "'Sir,' said Mr. Ben Allen...working his right
arm vehemently up and down, 'you--you ought to be ashamed of
yourself.'" Dickens, Pickw., II, p. 382.

Encouragement: "...and the motion of his arm, which he
was waving violently towards the postilions, denoted that he was
encouraging them to increased exertion." Dickens, Pickw., I,
p. 141.

Enthusiasm: Spectators or auditors embrace one another.
Anc. Gk., Rom. Sittl, p. 63.

Etiquette: "Then drawing his arm through that of the obse-
quious Mr. Cushton, Lord Mutanhed walked away." Dickens,
Pickw., II, p. 122.

Farewell: Embrace. Acts 20, 1. Anc. Gk. and Rom. only
among good acquaintances. Sittl, p. 31. Repeatedly, in Sidoni-
us Apollin., Epist. (about two French bishops). Sittl, p. 36.

Fear: Forearms raised diagonally. Anc. Gk. Sittl, p. 46.
Lowering of the arms. Anc. Gk. Sittl, p. 46.
Flattery: Embrace. Anc. Gk. Sittl, p. 31.
Friendship: "He marcheth with us arm in arm." Shakesp.,
II Henry IV, I, 1, 57. " 'I shall be very happy, I am sure,'
said Mr. Pickwick. 'So shall I,' said Mr. Alfred Jingle, draw-
ing one arm through Mr. Pickwick's, and another through Mr.
Wardle's, as he whispered confidentially in the ear of the form-
er gentleman...." Dickens, Pickw., I, p. 113. "...they were
drinking auf Bruderschaft [sic], which is performed by inter-
twining arms with one's co-drinker...." Nabokov, p. 180.
Gratitude: Embrace. Anc. Rom. Sittl, p. 31. Medieval
Germ. Wolfram v. Eschenbach, Parz., bk. IV, 199.
Greeting: Embrace. Gen. 29, 13; 33, 4; 48, 10, etc.
Ancient Egypt: when the gods receive the dead king (later all
the dead) to be one of them, they take him into their arms.
The desire to embrace became polite epistolary formula. Daw-
son, p. 86. Anc. Gk. Only close acquaintances or relatives.
Sittl, p. 31. Spanish. Only masculine and executed only by
close friends, sometimes to seal an agreement. Also Lat. Am.
Green, p. 34. Cf. Cid, I: El Cid receives his vassal Martín
Antolínez with open arms. Medieval German: Passional, 165;
Altdt. Ged., p. 194, 20; Grimm, DWb, IV/2. Fullest form of
embrace, the hug, is not of wide distribution. E.g. W. P.
Snow, p. 263 (Tierra del Fuego); Roth, p. 169 (Central Asia,
Polynesia, Austral. aborig.); Dawson, p. 92. Silent passing of
the person greeted, arms lowered to knees as sign of submis-
sion (anc. Egypt). Herodot. 2, 80; Stegmann v. Pritzwald,
p. 26.
Innocence (protestation of): Accompanying disclaimer of
blame, arms are raised to the side of the speaker, palms up.
Spain, Lat. Am. Green, p. 84.
Interrogation: Arms raised to the side, palms up. Spain,
Lat. Am. Green, pp. 81-82.
Joy: Embrace. Anc. Gk. and Rom. Sittl, p. 32.
Judgment: Judge raises both arms vertically to legitimize
a piece of recently acquired land. Fischer, Antaios, II, p. 343.
Magnitude: Shortness: lowering slightly bent arm in front
of gesticulator, palm down. Spain, Lat. Am. Tallness: hand
raised, palm down, to level referred to verbally. Spain, Lat.
Am. Green, 32-33. Magnitude of distance: outstretched arm
moved vertically. Ital. Manzoni, ch. xviii; Sittl, p. 111.
Size: Arms extended horizontally on both sides. Anc. Rom.
Sittl, p. 111.
Marriage: Bride is carried on arms to the church. Lor-
raine. Grimm, DRA I, 598. Bride is lifted thrice. Estonia.
Grimm, ibid.
Medico-magical: One arm extended forward, the other
drawn back, as if aiming an arrow. Chinese. Wallnöfer and
Rottauscher, p. 147, fig. 64; Fischer, Antaios II, fig. 5. With
one arm extended horizontally to side, the Asclepios priest puts
patient in incubation. Völgyesi, p. 20, fig. 8; Fischer, ibid.,
fig. 16 and p. 334. Right arm extended vertically upward, left

arm extended vertically downward. Nicobars. Buschan, p. 208; Fischer, ibid. , fig. 13. Left arm extended vertically, right arm bent at right angle, lower arm horizontally across body. Chinese. Vogt, p. 119, fig. 91; Fischer, ibid. , fig. 6. 4. Right arm extended forward, left arm drawn back as if aiming arrow. Chinese. Vogt, p. 119, fig. 91; Fischer, ibid. , fig. 6. Both arms raised vertically above the head, fingers of one hand folded over, fingers of the other extended. Dogon. Leuzinger, p. 70, fig. 6; Celtic, Austria. Moser, pp. 144, 740, fig. 2; Fischer, ibid. , fig. 14 and p. 336. Patient stretches arms out to each side to gain the necessary harmony and basis for improvement of his condition. Rosenberg, p. 35ff. ; Fischer, ibid. , p. 337.

Melancholy: Crossed arms. Shakesp., Jul. Caes., II, i, 239.

Mourning: Embracing the grave. Anc. Gk. and Rom. Sittl, p. 74. "...at the feet of the statue, embraces the stone knees and weeps..." Boggs, p. 319.

Negation: With verbal expressions of inability the bent arms are pushed forward, palms facing one another, then suddenly and sharply the arms are raised behind body. Shoulders are shrugged while executing movement. Spain, Lat. Am. Green, pp. 85-86.

Oath: After Christianization of the Roman empire, the arm is raised in calling upon God. Athanas., Apol. ad Const.; Sittl, p. 145. Arms crossed over breast. Neapol. De Jorio, p. 168.

Pacification: Apollo pacifies fighting Lapiths and Centaurs with arm outstretched toward them. West gable of temple of Zeus, Olympia; Fischer, Antaios II, fig. 15.

Plea: Embrace. Only children or close relatives. Anc. Rom. Sittl, pp. 31-32. Crossing arms on breast: "loosening upon my breast the cross formed by my arms in mortal agony" Dante, Purg. V, 126-127. "He...made a desperate attempt to articulate. It was unavailing--he extended his arm towards them, and made another violent effort." Dickens, Pickw., I, p. 48. Extending arms to side of gesticulator, palms up. Spain, Lat. Am. Green, p. 83. Both arms extended in front of body, elbows close to side, palms facing one another. Spain, Lat. Am. Green, pp. 82-83.

Pointing: "The old gentleman untucked his arm from his side, and having pointed to one of the oaken presses, immediately replaced it in its old position." Dickens, Pickw., I, p. 231. " 'Let us take this as a hypothetical case,' said the don, waving in the direction of the naked men." Robinson, p. 229. Right arm uplifted to demonstrate stars in sky, fingers extended. Woodcut, Brant, p. 168.

Praise: Swinging one or both arms in applause. Anc. Gk. and Rom. Sittl, p. 62.

Prayer: Arms raised. Babylon. Frequently the patron god stands before deity, holding hand of supplicant, both patron god and supplicant raising arm toward deity. Heiler, p. 102. Arms bared. Assyrian requirement in hymnal recitation. Heiler, p. 104. Raised arm. Anc. Egypt. Heiler, p. 102. Arms spread in front. Indian, Persian, Anc. Egypt., Sumerian,

Babylonian, Assyr., Aegean, Etruscan. Ohm, pp. 253-254.
On some anc. Gk. depictions of sacrifice, the sacrificial bowl
is held with extended right arm, while the left is raised. Sittl,
p. 189; Heiler, p. 102. Embracing the altar. Anc. Gk. ? and
Rom. Sittl, p. 179. Arms extended toward heaven or where-
ver the deity was thought to reside. The more urgent the
prayer, the more energetic the gesture. Anc. Gk. and Rom.
Sittl, pp. 187-188. Extending arms toward heaven. Anc. Gk.
and Rom. Sittl, pp. 174-175, 187. Arms raised. Early
Christian. Duchesne, p. 107. Medieval: Très Riches Heures,
pl. 73-74. The old orans-gesture (arms extended) is still the
priest's basic attitude for the Collect, the Secret Prayers, the
Preface, the Canon, the Pater Noster. In the late Middle Ages
a crucifix-like extension of arms and hands was used for the
Unde et Memores oration. Ladner, p. 271. Cf. s.v. ARM,
HAND, Prayer. Prostration with arms extended. Medieval
German. Kudrun, st. 1170, 2; König Rother, 376; Rolandslied
6895.

Pregnancy: Arms extended, forming circle, fingertips of
one hand touching those of the other. Neapol. De Jorio,
p. 172.

Pride: Arms extended, father lifts infant over his head.
Spain. Rare in America. Green, p. 92.

Protection: "Upon this, the women...flung their arms round
them to preserve them from danger." Dickens, Pickw., II,
p. 72.

Refusal: Crossing of arms over breast signals refusal of a
witness to give evidence. Medieval German. Künssberg,
Sachsenspiegel, fig. 88; also Shakesp., Hamlet, I, v, 174:
"with arms encumb'red thus." W. Müller, p. 17.

Rejection: Outstretched arms crossed in front of speaker
at level of waist. Madrid, Lat. Am. Green, p. 87.

Resignation: Arms raised and dropped sharply at sides of
gesticulator. Spain. Green, p. 88. "For answer, Francine
went to the chair he had previously drawn out for her, and sat
down in it with the air of one who folds her arms." Carr, To
Wake the Dead, p. 63. Arms raised to head level, head suddenly cocked to the right: "Que voulez vous? C'est comme ça!"
French. Brault, p. 380.

Rest: No participation in action is indicated in medieval
miniatures by arms hanging relaxed, hands clasped or crossed.
Medieval German. Oechelhäuser, Miniaturen I, p. 57; medieval
French. Lommatzsch, pp. 33-34.

Satisfaction: Arms raised. Zola, p. 259.

Series: Arms extended in front of gesticulator, palms down,
one hand above the other. Spain, Lat. Am. (Can also indicate
levels.) Green, p. 60.

Sincerity: Arms raised to side to level of shoulders, palms
up at conclusion. Spain, Lat. Am. Green, pp. 78-79.

Sorrow: Arms crossed over breast. Shakesp., Lucr.,
793, 1662; Tit. Andr., III, ii, 7; Jul. Caes. II, i, 240, etc.

Stop: Arm extended vertically, palm raised and directed
towards the person intended to stop. Anc. Rom., Neapol. De

Jorio, p. 152.
Strength: Arm stretched out, clenched fist. Anc. Rom.
Sittl, p. 115.
Submission: Arms crossed on chest. Ohm, p. 278.
Surprise: Both arms raised. Anc. Gk. and Rom. Sittl,
p. 272. Mod. French. Mitton, p. 146.
Surrender: In surrendering a city the women and children
stretch their arms out toward the victors. Anc. Rom. Sittl,
p. 148. Letting gesticulating arms sink. Doré's illustr. to
Rabelais' Gargantua, bk. I, ch. xviii; Röhrich, p. 11 and pl. 2.
In surrendering, the warrior stretches out his arms to his sides.
Anc. Gk. and Rom. Sittl, p. 147.
Understanding: Poking someone in the ribs as sign of com-
plicity. Spain and Amer. Green, p. 44.
Victory: Victor in a fight moves arms up and down and
crows (in imitation of cockfight). Demosth. Sittl, p. 114.
Voting: Cf. s.v. HAND, Voting.
Welcome: Embrace. Shakesp., Henry VIII, I, iv, 63.

ARM, BREAST
Adoration: Cf. s.v. Prayer. Arms crossed on breast. Niccolò di Giacomo, "Annunciation, " Ambrosiana, Milan; in For-
maggio and Basso, p. 23; also "Coronation of the Virgin, "
Missale Fratrum Serv. S. Mariae, Venice, ibid., p. 29; Très
Riches Heures, pl. 40, 59, 65, 102, 128 (see illustrations 1 and
2).
Affection: Shakesp., Love's Lab. Lost, IV, iii, 131: "lay
his wreathed arms athwart his loving bosom. "
Alarm: Beating shield against chest, calling "to arms, to
arms!" Statius. Sittl, p. 215.
Defiance: Arms crossed over chest. Medieval. Oechelhäuser, Miniaturen I, p. 15; Lommatzsch, p. 94. Corsica.
Mérimée, p. 123. (Cf. s.v. ARM, Defiance.)
Humility: Arms crossed upon the breast so that hands lie
on shoulders while executing a deep bow. Oriental. Ohm,
p. 277.
Oath: While crossing arms over chest, the following is
said: "Cross cross the Bible, never tell a lie. If I do my
mother will die. " Children. Aberystwyth. Opie, p. 123.
Passion: Arms crossed over breast. Appears in Byzant.
religious art in the tenth and eleventh centuries and in western
religious art since the thirteenth century. Ohm, p. 277; Weise
and Otto, pp. 28-47.
Plea: Crossing arms on breast: "loosening upon my breast
the cross formed by my arms in mortal agony. " Dante, Purg.
v, 126-127.
Prayer: Arms crossed on chest. Anc. Egypt., Roman,
Buddhist; Luzon (Aëtas), Bali. Ohm, p. 277. Christian: Ceiling carving of the Nativity, Haus Supersax, Sitten, Switzerland
(after 1500). Cf. s.v. ARM, HAND, Prayer.
Refusal: Cf. s.v. ARM, Refusal.
Sorrow: Arms crossed over breast. Shakesp., Lucr.,
793, 1662; Tit. Andr., III, ii, 7; Jul. Caes., II, i, 240, etc.

Submission: Arms crossed on chest.   Roman Cath., Prot.,
Russ. Orth.   Ohm, p. 278.

ARM, BREAST, KNEE
Prayer: Arms crossed over breast while kneeling on one knee.
Très Riches Heures, pl. 84.

ARM, BREAST, SHOULDER
Oath: Crossing arms across whole chest, touching shoulders.
Children.   Oxford.   Opie, p. 124.

ARM, ELBOW
Encouragement: Someone is encouraged to speak by being
punched in the side by the elbow of person(s) next to him.   Anc.
Gk. and Rom.   Sittl, p. 222.
Warning: A careless speaker is warned to be careful by
being punched in the side with elbow of someone standing next
to him.   Anc. Gk.   Sittl, p. 221.

ARM, FACE
Prayer: Embracing feet of statue and pressing face upon them.
Anc. Rom.   Sittl, p. 179.

ARM, FINGER
Accusation: Cf. s.v. Guilt.
Assistance: Request for a ride (hitchhiking).   A forward
swing of the forearm, bent at the elbow and held upright or
horizontal with the thumb extended.   Univ. of Calif., Berkeley.
McCord, p. 291.
Denial: Index finger shaken from side to side, arm ex-
tended forward, palm outward.   Aubert, p. 92, fig. 139.   Cf.
s.v. FINGER, Negation.
Egotism: Flexing arm with finger.   Krout, p. 23.
Enmity: Grasp little fingers of both hands, moving arms
in sawing motion.   Jordan, Saudi Arabia.   Semiotic.   Barakat,
no. 191.
Enthusiasm: Cf. s.v. ARM, HAND, Enthusiasm.
Greed: "He put out his good arm and rubbed his fingers
together to make the ancient sign of greed for money."   Schul-
berg, p. 83.   Cf. s.v. FINGER, Money and Pay.
Guilt: Right arm and forefinger extended in accusation.
Woodcut, Brant, p. 61.
Hesitation: Lower arm raised, fingers half cupped.   Anc.
Gk.   Sittl, p. 273.

---

1 and 2 [opposite].   Left: David kneeling on one knee, arms
crossed, to invoke God.   Pl. 84 of the Très riches heures du duc
de Berry.   Right: The Ascension.   Pl. 128 of the Très riches
heures....   Both illustrations reproduced by permission of the
Musée Condé, Chantilly, and George Braziller, Inc., New York
(see ARM, BREAST--Adoration).

Medico-magical: Nosebleed is stilled by raising the arm on the side of the bleeding nostril vertically, the other arm extends vertically downward, and each hand is a clenched fist with middle finger extended. Thuringia. Wuttke, p. 347, no. 518; Fischer, Antaios II, p. 324.

Mockery: Left arm extended toward another person, fist closed except for index, which is extended. Woodcut, Brant, p. 45. Cf. s.v. FINGER, Mockery.

Money: Forearm raised, palm forward, fingers repeatedly curled one after another or together. Colombia. Saitz and Cervenka, p. 88.

Peace: Cf. s.v. FINGER, Peace.

Pointing: Arm and index extended. Boggs, col. 322; Grimm, KHM, nos. 96, 182. Right arm raised to point to stars in sky, fingers extended. Woodcut, Brant, p. 168.

Pride: Thumbs under armpits, other fingers spread wide, chest thrust out: braggart, or expression of pride. Saudi Arabia, Bahrein. Autistic or culture-induced. Barakat, no. 188. U.S., Colombia. Saitz and Cervenka, p. 96.

Threat: Right arm raised, fingers extended upward. Woodcut, Brant, p. 32. Cf. s.v. FINGER, Threat.

ARM, FINGER, HAND

Affirmation: Right hand clenched, index extended, forearm extended horizontally forward, elbow at waist, forearm waved rapidly vertically. Spain. Kaulfers, p. 251.

Anger: Arm extended forward, fingers extended, palm up. Anc. Gk. and Rom. Sittl, pp. 288-289. Cf. s.v. FINGER, Anger.

Approach: Arm extended, palm down, four fingers extended, then repeatedly folded down to touch palm. Italy, Balkans, Aegean Islands, Turkey, North Africa, Iraq, Iran, India. Müller, p. 99. Cf. s.v. HAND, Approach.

Begin: Forearm raised, hand extended and thumb pointing upward. Spain. Flachskampf, p. 226. Anc. Rom.: forearm raised, thumb and index extended. In postclassical art the middle finger is added. In painting the index is often raised alone. Sittl, p. 285.

Blessing: Fingers of right hand extended and joined, moving from forehead to chest and from left to right shoulder (Roman rite). Ohm, p. 294. Cf. s.v. HAND, Blessing.

Command: Arm energetically extended forward, two or three or all fingers extended. Anc. Gk. and Rom. Sittl, p. 288.

Direction: Hand and arm extended, index pointing in specific direction. Ruesch and Kees, p. 77.

Finished: Crossing arms at waist level and extending them in an arc, fingers extended, palms down (specifically used by referee at prize fights). Calif. King, p. 264.

Mockery: Thumb and index extended, other fingers folded into palm, left arm extended toward object of mockery. Woodcut, Brant, p. 106.

Money: Cf. s.v. ARM, HAND, Money.

Negation: Right hand clenched, index extended, forearm extended horizontally forward, elbow at waist, forearm waved rapidly back and forth horizontally in an arc of 90°. Spain. Kaulfers, p. 250.

Prayer: Arms extended, fingers spread apart. Anc. Gk. Sittl, pp. 189-190.

ARM, HAND

Accusation: Upper arm low, bent at elbow, forearm raised, hand raised, all fingers except little finger extended. Woodcut, Brant, p. 240.

Anger: Both arms extended toward the offender, fingers extended, palms parallel, hands shaking vigorously at the side of the listener's face. Spain, Lat. Am. Green, p. 75.

Apology: "...spread his arms with his hands held open... raised one hand, turning it slightly outward...raised his other hand, and turned it palm-side up...dropped both hands and held them, palms forward, to the side and away from his thighs." Birdwhistell, Intro., p. 30.

Assistance: (hitchhiking). Arm and hand extended, palm facing down. Fingers, hand or arm may be moved up and down. Colombia. Saitz and Cervenka, p. 130, cf. note to "Hitchhiking," p. 70.

Authority: Arms at side, bent at elbow, hands (fists) resting on hips. Medieval French. Lommatzsch, p. 90. Anc. Rom., Neapol., general. De Jorio, p. 199. Cf. s.v. ARM, Authority and Defiance.

Baby: Cf. s.v. ARM, Baby.

Cold: Each hand grasps opposite upper arm, shoulders hunched. U.S., Colombia. Saitz and Cervenka, p. 26.

Consolation (Maternal): Holding a child tightly or picking him up. Ruesch and Kees, p. 85.

Copulate: Extended forearms and fists are jerked backward and downward toward the body. Lat. Am. Kany, p. 187.

Crowd: Forearms raised, hands form teardrop shape, fingers extended; sometimes they are opened and shut several times, sometimes shaken. Colombia. Saitz and Cervenka, p. 30.

Defiance: "She put her arms akimbo, as much to say she defied me." Mrs. Gaskell, p. 155. Left arm raised slowly, right hand passed beneath it simultaneously as body turns slightly. Jordan, Lebanon. Semiotic. Barakat, no. 63. Cf. s.v. ARM, HEAD, Defiance.

Delicacy: Forearm is raised parallel to the ground with hand extended almost touching chest. Colombia. Saitz and Cervenka, p. 26.

Depart: Forearm horizontal to waist; fingers held together and extended, palm facing away from body; hand moves out sharply to side. Colombia. Saitz and Cervenka, p. 80. Edge of left hand is brought down smartly over the crook of the right elbow. ("Let's get the hell out of here--fast.") French. WW II. Alsop, p. 29.

Disagreement: Forearm at right angle to upper arm, fist

clenched and moved back and forth several times.   Impolite.
Colombia.   Saitz and Cervenka, p. 36.

Disbelief: Motion of using a shovel to throw bull manure
over one's shoulder.   Usually humorous.   Male.   U.S.   Saitz
and Cervenka, p. 42.

Effeminancy: Left forearm rests on the supporting open
palm of the right hand.   Lat. Am.   Kany, p. 181.

Enthusiasm: Vigorous vertical movement of forearm, snapping of middle finger against ball of thumb.   Mexico.   Kaulfers,
p. 251.

Etiquette: Greek women of good society were accompanied
in public each by two maids or two daughters, who--or at least
one of whom--assisted by supporting her arm.   Sittl, p. 161.
Men of princely rank appeared in public supported at the arm
by distinguished men.   Byzantine, and also the Greek Voyvods
of the Danubian principalities.   Sittl, p. 162.   At oriental
courts, the king was supported under the arm by his generals.
Sittl, p. 162.   Roman noblemen walked in public supported under
the arm by freedmen.   Sittl, ibid.

Farewell: Waving hand up and down.   Ruesch and Kees,
p. 77.   Cf. s.v. HAND, Farewell.

Finished: Arms crossed in front of body, palms down;
then arms move out to the sides, palms still down.   May serve
as general negation.   Colombia, U.S.   Saitz and Cervenka,
p. 137.

Friendship: Both arms extended full length at level of
shoulders, hands open, palms facing each other.   Aubert, p. 85.

Goad: Forearm extended parallel to ground; fist makes
twisting thrust.   Colombia.   Saitz and Cervenka, p. 42.

Greeting: Raising the hand with the palm outward and the
arm bent at the elbow.   Hand is occasionally waved from right
to left, but fingers are not waved.   Forearm may be waved if
the person is close by, the whole arm if he is at a distance.
Univ. of Calif. Berkeley.   McCord, p. 291.   Male grasps forearm or upper arm of another male, who grasps upper arm or
shoulder of the former.   Sometimes patting motion is used.
Women usually grasp one another's forearms.   This greeting
among women particularly in cities.   Colombia.   Saitz and
Cervenka, p. 66.

Homosexuality: Forearm raised, hand limp, palm facing
away from body; hand held like this for a moment or moved
forward.   Head usually inclined to the side.   Smile.   Colombia,
U.S.   Saitz and Cervenka, p. 119.

Insult: "He made 268 'figs' and 497 'sleeve cuts' at him"
Spain.   Foz, p. 97.   "Sleeve cut," Sp. "cortes de manga," is
executed by bending left arm at the elbow with clenched fist as
the edge of the right hand hits inside left elbow.   Also "mani-
chetto," or "armas de Saõ Francisco" (Portug.).   Bending the
left forearm vigorously upward with fist clenched or middle
finger extended, and thrusting the extended right hand into the
inner bend of the left arm.   Lat. Am.   Kany, pp. 174-175.
French.   Mitton, p. 151.   U.S.   Saitz and Cervenka, p. 114.

Interrogation: Arms raised to the side, palms up.   Spain,

Lat. Am. Green, pp. 81-82.

Invitation: Right arm extended toward victim, hand held out
limply. Woodcut, Brant, p. 258.

Leading: Women are forcefully led by the upper arm. Anc.
Gk. Benndorf, pl. 27; Sittl, p. 280. Bent arms moved back
and forth horizontally, elbows held close to the body, fingers
clenched, thumbs over curled indexes. Accompanying phrase:
"es un hombre que sabe conducirse." Madrid. Both hands
slightly closed, at chest level, fingers moved back and forth
rapidly so as to intertwine slightly. Accompanying phrase:
"era un hombre que sabía manejar elecciones." Madrid.
Green, p. 67.

Money: Forearm extended, palm up, thumb and index form
almost a complete circle, the remaining three fingers clenched
upon palm. Mexico. Kany, p. 95.

Mourning: Beating arms. Women. Anc. Rom. Sittl,
p. 26.

Nothing: Stiff left forearm, hand closed, palm of right hand
placed on inside of elbow. Sign that gesturer has nothing; performed angrily. Saudi Arabia. Semiotic. Barakat, no. 233.

Oath: In swearing an oath, the accused, kneeling, embraces
the altar. Anc. Rom. Tacitus, Ann. 16, 31; Sittl, p. 143.
"The Lord swore by his right hand and by the arm of his power." Isaiah 62, 8. Arms raised and spread. Daniel 12, 7;
Ohm, p. 265. Right arm moved from level of waist over right
shoulder with palm facing up during movement; head tilted backwards and eyes raised as hand moves up. Libya, Lebanon,
Syria. Semiotic. Barakat, no. 9.

Passion: Arms crossed over breast. Appears in Byzant.
religious art in the tenth and eleventh centuries and in western
religious art since the thirteenth century. Ohm, p. 277; Weise
and Otto, pp. 28-47.

Plea: "Hear the voice of my supplications... when I lift up
my hands...." Ps. 28, 2. Extending arms to side of gesticulator, palms up. Spain, Lat. Am. Green, p. 83. Both arms
extended in front of body, elbows close to side, palms facing
one another. Spain, Lat. Am. Green, pp. 82-83.

Pointing: Arm bent at elbow, palm up, forearm moves
back and forth in the direction indicated. Colombia. Saitz and
Cervenka, p. 34. Arm raised, hand extended, palm to side;
hand makes one or more sharp movements back and forth.
Colombia. Saitz and Cervenka, p. 35. "'Let us take this as
a hypothetical case,' said the don, waving in the direction of the
naked men." Robinson, p. 229.

Possession: Adopted child is lifted up by adopter's arms
and hands. Anc. Rom. Sittl, p. 130.

Prayer: Arms raised, hands holding sacrifice or object of
prayer. Anc. Gk. Sittl, p. 191. Hands raised, palms upward.
Anc. Rom. Sittl, p. 174. Arms outstretched, hands open and
bent back at the wrist. Arch. Ztg. 1880, pl. 12, 1; Sittl,
p. 291. Spreading of arms and hands upwards. Petroglyphs in
Morocco, the Sahara. Frobenius, pp. 129, 131; Weinert,
p. 190-191; Ohm, p. 252. Hands and arms extended toward

sides. Byzantine. Sittl, p. 175, no. 6. Hands raised three
times.   The vestal Quinta Claudia raises her hands three times
before prayer. No Gk. evidence; anc. Rom. Sittl, p. 190.
The Greeks prayed to the Olympian gods by spreading the arms,
hands turned back, palms turned outwards toward heaven.   Seemann, p. 41f.   The Romans lifted their hands while praying to
Jupiter. Macrob., Saturn. III, 9, 12. Kneeling and raising
arms toward heaven, once forbidden to Mohammedans, is now
common during the salāt and the du'ā'. At the du'ā' the palms
are turned toward the face. Ohm, p. 255. Spreading of arms,
raising of arms. Ps. 143, 6; 63, 5; Ex. 9, 29; 9, 33; etc.
Notscher, p. 348; Ohm, p. 256. The "orantes" of early Christian art are invariably depicted in catacomb frescoes with arms
extended or raised. Cath. Encycl. VI, pp. 423-427. Early
Christians (pre 500 A.D.) raised arms, but spread them somewhat to the side, approximating figure of the Cross. Euseb.,
Tertull., Minuc., Ambr.; but also later, cf. Kraus, I, pp. 538ff.,
Sittl, p. 198. Perhaps also Liutprandi leg.; Visio Tnugdali;
Dante, Purg. vi, 16; Mabillon, p. 61 (Bavarian women). Still
to be seen at shrines to which pilgrimages are undertaken.
Sittl, p. 198, n. 7 on p. 199, and still practiced by Dominican
nuns. Ohm, p. 266, and pl. 18. Cf. also the medieval Ger-
man Kudrun, st. 1170, 1. 2, and König Rother, 376. Crossing
of arms and hands over breast. Carthusians during the "Sup-
plices te rogamus." Ohm, p. 277. Benedictines during the
"Et non confundas me." Gongand, p. 65; Ohm, p. 278. Extending arms as symbolic of Trinity: according to the Armenian
Ritual, the neophyte is to turn west, spit three times against
Satan, then turn east, look towards heaven and spread his arms
"in avowal of the Trinity." Conybeare, p. 86; Ohm, p. 264.
Crossing of arms over breast during communion is common, especially among the Dominicans. Ohm, p. 278. In Russian
churches prayer with spread arms is still common, in the west
it is confined to a few orders, particularly the Capuchins and
Franciscans. Ohm, pp. 257-258. Arms raised. Medieval German. Otfrid I, 4, 16. Protestants sometimes cross arms and
hands over breast, e.g. during the silent prayer immediately preceding communion the officiating pastor executes this gesture.
Ritter, p. 375; Ohm, p. 278. Arms spread out to the side.
Yuin (Australia), Sioux, Massai (East Africa), Kikuyu (East
Africa). Heiler, p. 101; Ohm, pp. 252-253. In the grasslands
of Cameroon, open hands are turned toward the sun to show innocence. Vielhauer, p. 150; Ohm, p. 253. Arms spread out,
palms downward. Anc. Egypt., Roman. Prayer to terrestrial
and subterrestrial gods. Greeks went into the water with outstretched hands to pray to river and sea deities. Ohm, pp. 265-
266. Arms extended to the front, hands open, palms up. Sa-
maritan, Christian, Mohammedan, also known in Africa, India.
H. Freiberg, p. 12, pl. 2; Ohm, pp. 266-267. Jews in Jerusalem extended arms toward temple. Ps. 27 (28), 2; Sittl,
p. 190.
    Pride: Arms at side, bent at elbows, hands (fists) rest-
ing at hips. Medieval French. Lommatzsch, p. 92.

Refusal: Arms crossed at wrist, palms facing forward; then hands move apart. Colombia. Saitz and Cervenka, p. 33.

Reverence: Ancient Christians received the Eucharist with arms extended, hands crossed and open. Ohm, p. 279.

Series: Arms extended in front of gesticulator, palms down, one hand above the other. Spain, Lat. Am. Can also indicate levels. Green, p. 60.

Sorrow: "...and he stood momentarily arrested, one long hand outstretched, warding off realization.... To see him was like glimpsing a flame, an epitome of grief's impact." Allingham, p. 81.

Stop: Arm raised, hand upward, palm out. Anc. Rom., Neapol. Sittl, p. 86; De Jorio, pp. 87, 152.

Strength: Arm bent at elbow, fist clenched. U.S., Colombia. Saitz and Cervenka, p. 133. Arm extended, clenched fist. Anc. Rom. Sittl, p. 115.

Submission: Subordinates in ancient Egypt placed right hand on left shoulder, signifying peaceful intent. An extension of this gesture was the placing of the left hand on the right shoulder also. Ohm, p. 277. Head is placed between bound arms. Persian proskynesis, Egypt. Meyer, p. 313; Sittl, p. 151. One raised hand is grasped by the other at the wrist. Hittite. Arch. Ztg. 1885, pl. 13; Assyrian. Sybel, no. 6009; Sittl, p. 151.

Surrender: Arms raised, palms facing up. Anc. Gk. and Rom. Sittl, p. 147. Arms and hands raised as signal that warriors are unarmed. Anc. Gk. and Rom. Sittl, pp. 148, 219. Arms crossed over chest signify surrender to God. Schmidt-Pauli, p. 50.

Sympathy (false): Making the motions of playing a fiddle. Univ. of Calif., Berkeley. McCord, p. 291.

Teasing: Palm and back of right hand brushed back and forth over inside of left forearm several times like stropping a razor. Lebanon. Semiotic. Barakat, no. 128.

Threat: Arm bent at elbow, palm up, forearm moves back and forth toward the person threatened. Used by adult to child. Colombia. Saitz and Cervenka, p. 142. Cf. also s.v. HAND, Threat.

Victory: Arm of victor raised over his head, or arms raised and hands joined over his head. Spain, Lat. Am., North Am. Green, p. 48. Arm raised, index and middle finger spread apart, making a "V." Green, ibid. Cf. s.v. FINGER, Victory.

Volunteer: Hand raised. Anc. Rom. Sittl, p. 218.

Voting: Greeks raised right arm in voting, whereupon the raised arms were counted. Sittl, 217.

Warning: Head raised, fingers extended, sometimes waved rapidly. Columbia, U.S. Saitz and Cervenka, p. 148.

ARM, HAND, HEAD

Disbelief: Head of gesticulator turned away from the speaker; one arm raised, palm facing speaker; often the hand is then lowered briskly. U.S. Saitz and Cervenka, p. 40.

Pensiveness: Head cocked to one side, arms forward, fingers intertwined. Birdwhistell, Colliers (3/4/1955), p. 57.

ARM, HAND, MOUTH
Mockery: Forefinger of left hand in smiling mouth, right hand vertical with fingers outstretched, palm outward, forearm slightly raised. Woodcut, Brant, p. 70.

ARM, HAND, SHOULDER
Consolation: In friendly conversation, one woman puts arm around shoulders of the other. Anc. Gk. and Rom. Sittl, p. 281, fig. 32.
    Friendship: cf. s.v. Consolation.
    Frustration: Shoulders shrugged, both arms raised sharply, palms facing upward and fingers spread. Sometimes accompanied with expressions such as "Ya estoy harto!" Spain, Lat. Am. Green, p. 88.
    Indifference: Shrugging shoulders, head tilted, arms raised to side of body with elbows close to the body and palms facing up. Spain, Lat. Am. Can be exaggerated by arching the arms high above the shoulders with palms down. Spain. Green, p. 87.
    Oath: Witnesses grasp the arm or shoulder of the person for whose sake they are swearing. Medieval German. Grimm, DRA II, p. 551.
    Threat: Right hand, either open or closed, placed on left shoulder, right forearm raised to horizontal. Mexico. Kaulfers, p. 252.

ARM, HEAD
Confusion: Head thrown backwards, arms bent so that the waist is visible in the slight bend of the elbow. Quintilian xi, 3, 118; Baden, p. 451.
    Defiance: "And she tossed her head, and put her arms akimbo, with an air of confident defiance...." Trollope, Towers, ch. xxxiii. Cf. s.v. ARM, HAND, Defiance.
    Disbelief: Raising an arm vertically from its neutral position to the side of the head, then dropping it to its original position. Accompanies expressions of incredulity. Spain, Lat. Am. Green, p. 75.

ARM, HEAD, SHOULDER
Modesty: Shrugging shoulders, head tilted to the side, somewhat bent arms raised behind body. Spain, Lat. Am. Green, p. 49.

ARM, KNEE
Gratitude: Toward the end of antiquity, the touching of someone's knees can be an expression of gratitude. Gesture is performed kneeling. Anc. Gk. Sittl, p. 164. Arms extended toward someone's knees without touching them. Performed kneeling. Anc. Gk. and Rom. Sittl, ibid.
    Oath: In swearing an oath, the accused, kneeling, embraces

the altar. Anc. Rom. Sittl, p. 143.
    Plea: Embracing someone's knees while kneeling. Anc.
Gk. and Rom. Sittl, p. 163. One knee embraced while kneeling. Anc. Gk. Sittl, ibid. The poor man embraces the knees
of the rich man. Mamertin. paneg. Iulian.; Sittl, ibid. By
embracing knees, parties plead for mercy in court of law.
Apul.; Sittl, ibid. Roman soldiers embrace knees of their cap-
tors after a mutiny. Tacitus. Sittl, ibid. Roman soldiers
plead with their reluctant commander for continuation of the
war by embracing his knees. Tacitus. Sittl, ibid. During the
late empire, the office-seeker embraced the knees of his poten-
tial benefactor. Mamertin. paneg. Iulian.; Sittl, ibid. Pleading matron embraces knees of person to whom plea is directed.
Anc. Gk. Sittl, ibid. The pleader embraces the knees of the
person to whom the plea is directed--thus the knees are consecrated to Misericordia. Serv. Verg. Aen. Sittl, ibid. Arms
stretched out toward knees without touching them, while kneeling. Anc. Gk. and Rom. Sittl, p. 164.
    Prayer: Arms bent at right angle at elbow, lower arm ex-
tended to side of body. Appears during the twenty-first Egyptian
dynasty and continues to the Coptic period. Bonnet, p. 208.
Kneeling, arms spread apart. Anc. Gk. Sittl, p. 188. Kneeling on one knee, arms spread apart. Très Riches Heures, pl.
88.

ARM, LIP
    Affection: Embrace and kiss. Gen. 29, 13; 33, 4; etc. Medie-
val German. Kudrun 483, 4. In France the kiss on the lips is
used only between lovers. Before the nineteenth century it signified simply friendship. Mitton, p. 141.
    Greeting: Embrace and kiss. Kiss either on cheeks or
lips, together with embrace, was common greeting among Germanic warriors of friends or warriors of equal fame. Stoebe,
p. 188. Greeting of husband and wife. Odyss. Boggs, p. 320.
15th cent. Gk. Mazaris, p. 148; Sittl, p. 80. When two men
meet they embrace and kiss. Saudi Arabia. Semiotic or culture-induced. Barakat, no. 186.
    Seduction: "With kind embracements, tempting kisses."
Shakesp., Shrew, Induct. 1, 116.

ARM, MOUTH
    Vengeance: Pretending to bite one's elbow. ("I will do anything
to avenge myself--even the impossible, such as biting my elbows.") Ital. Graham, p. 26.

ARM, NECK
    Affection: Shakesp., Shrew, II, i, 300; Winter's Tale, V, iii,
112; etc. "So, throwing her arms round his neck and kissing
him affectionately...." Dickens, Pickw., II, p. 417; cf. also
Grimm, DWb, IV /2, cols. 243-4.
    Death: Rajah places sword on neck of follower, as if to
strike off head, symbolizing execution. North-East India.
Frazer, IV, p. 56.

Surrender: Neck is placed under the arm of the victor.
Aimoinus 3, 4; Grimm, DRA I, 190.

ARM, SHOULDER
Affection: Laying arm on someone's shoulder.   Triumphal arch
for Emperor Maximilian I, 1512-1515, pl. 20.   Cf. s.v. ARM,
HAND, SHOULDER, Friendship.
Mourning: According to the Talmud, it was customary
among the Palestinian Jews to bare the arm and shoulder as
sign of mourning. HDA, II, col. 849.
Negation: With verbal expressions of inability the bent arms
are pushed forward, palms facing one another, then suddenly and
sharply arms raised behind body.   Shoulders are shrugged while
executing movement. Spain, Lat. Am. Green, pp. 85-86.

ARM, WRIST
Contempt: Arm moved downward and to one side away from the
body with a flick of the wrist.   Univ. of Calif. Berkeley.
McCord, p. 291. Cf. s.v. HAND, Contempt.

BACK
Contempt: Turning one's back toward a person.   Anc. Rom.,
Neapol., General. De Jorio, p. 132.

BACK, BREAST, HAND, HEAD
Respect: "...he bows...and brings the right hand in a graceful
arc first to the ground, then to his chest and forehead...."
Palest. Bauer, 171.

BACK, HAND
Congratulation: "Whereupon Mr. Pickwick slapped him on the
back several times--with the compliments of the occasion."
Dickens, Pickw., II, p. 322.
Consolation: "With this consolation, old Wardle slapped Mr.
Tupman on the back and laughed heartily." Dickens, Pickw., I,
p. 297.
Greeting: Slapping the back of a person. Krout, p. 21.
Prayer: Hands placed or crossed behind back. Bushmen,
S. Africa. Ohm, p. 288.

BEARD
Sorrow: Beard cut off. Is. 15, 2.

BEARD, HAND
Adoption: The adoptive father touches the beard of the adopted
son. Canisius lect. ant. 2, 3 cap. 10: "ut Alaricus barbam
tangeret Clodovici effectus patrinus"; Aimoin. 1, 20: "et Alaricus
juxta morem antiquorum barbam Clodovei tangens adoptivus ei
fiebat pater." The Goths, Franks and Lombards often cut off
the beard as sign of adoption. Grimm, DRA I, pp. 201-202.
Affection: Grasping a person's beard. Anc. Gk. Sittl,

p. 33. Mullah Kashani, Iranian spiritual leader, stroked the beard of the assassin of Premier Ali Razma to show his affection and approbation. Cited by Hayes, p. 305 from Life (12/8/1952), p. 52.

Anger: Grasping beard. Medieval German. Haseloff, p. 307.

Boredom: Stroking an imaginary beard. Ital. Graham, p. 26.

Calmness: Scratching tip of nose with one hand and the beard with the other. du Fail, I, p. 13. Stroking beard. Shakesp., Much Ado, V, i, 15.

Despair: Hands grasp beard. Albanian. Hahn, II, p. 153; Sittl, p. 23.

Disbelief: Pulling an imaginary beard. Argentina. Kany, p. 70.

Embarrassment: Hand strokes chin or beard. Anc. Gk. and Rom. Sittl, p. 47.

Fear: Hands grasp beard. Albania. Hahn, II, p. 153; Sittl, p. 23.

Insult: " 'Never did man born of woman, Moor or Christian, pluck [my beard] as I did yours, o count, at the castle of Cabra! When I took Cabra and plucked your beard, there was no youth but took his share of it.' " Cid, c. iii. "Takes him by the beard" Shakesp., Henry V, IV, vi, 13; "Camest thou to beard me?" Hamlet, II, ii, 442; "Who calls me villain? breaks my pate across? Plucks off my beard, and blows it in my face? Tweaks me by the nose?" Hamlet, II, ii, 598; "Take our goodly aged men by the beards." Timon, V, i, 175; "Priest, beware your beard; I mean to tug it and to cuff you soundly." I Henry VI, I, iii, 47; "To pluck me by the beard." Lear, III, vii, 35; etc.

Mockery: Plucking someone's beard. Anc. Rom. Sittl, p. 105. Cf. s.v. Insult.

Mourning: Cf. s.v. HAND, Mourning.

Nervousness: Hand strokes chin or beard. Anc. Gk. and Rom. Sittl, p. 47.

Oath: Swearing by the beard. Konrad v. Würzb., 6-7; Rolandslied, 119 a; Grimm, DRA II, p. 549 cites medieval French as well as German sources. No occurrence of swearing by the beard in legal texts. The "judge" in the Münsterkirche at Kastl (Palatinate) holds his beard with the right hand, showing that he will keep his oath to judge impartially. Röhrich, p. 31. Touching of the beard or hair in swearing an oath. Frisian. Siccama, 12, 2: "tollat sinistra manu sinistros capilis capillos, eisque imponat dextrae manus duos digitos atque ita juret." Pulling hairs when swearing an oath. Schwäb. Id., p. 262. Also Cid: "Alzo la mano, a la barba se tomo" 2485, 2839, 3196.

Pensiveness: "Si duist sa barbe, afaitat sun germun." Chanson de Roland, 215. Plucking of beard or stroking of chin denote thoughtfulness, deliberation, doubt. Ghetto Jews. Efron, p. 146. Stroking beard. Shakesp., Troilus, I, iii, 165. Rhein. Wb., I, p. 478.

Plea: Grasping a person's beard. Anc. Gk. Sittl, p. 33.
Hand grasps beard and neck. Performed while kneeling. Anc.
Gk. Sittl, p. 165. Hand grasps beard. Performed while
kneeling. Anc. Gk. (sometimes with both hands). Sittl, p. 165.
Medieval German: Kudrun 386, 2.3 (chin).

Satisfaction: "What a great day in the court of the Campea-
dor when he wins the battle and slays King Búcar! My Cid
raised his hand and stroked his beard." Cid, c. iii.

Sorrow: Pulling one's beard. Biblical. Ohm, p. 230.
Anc. Gk. and Rom. Sittl, p. 274. Röhrich, pl. 36. Early
sixteenth century Europe. Röhrich, pl. 35; cf. also Röhrich,
p. 34. Malory, II, ch. vii; Shakesp., Much Ado, II, iii, 153;
Romeo, III, iii, 68.

Victory: Victors in battle cut off the beards of the vanquished: indicates victory, or that the vanquished are not virile.
Saudi Arabia. Semiotic. Barakat, no. 174.

BEARD, LIP
Affection: Kiss on beard. Quint. Smyrn. Sittl, p. 40.

BODY
Adoration: Squatting: lunar ritual gesture. Fischer, Symbolon
III, p. 91. "Joshua fell to the earth upon his face...." Josh.
7, 6. Mosaic of Honorius III (1216-1227) at St. Paul's in Rome
represents him prostrate at feet of Christ. He is bareheaded
and on his knees, the upper part of the body thrown forward,
extended hands almost touch foot of Christ. Ladner, pp. 249-
250. "Devoutly I threw myself at the holy feet." Dante, Purg.
c. 9. "He worshipped the Lord, bowing himself to the earth."
Gen. 24, 52.

Apology: " 'I am exceedingly sorry, Ma'am,' said Mr.
Pickwick, bowing very low." Dickens, Pickw., I, p. 380.

Applause: "After a speech in Russia, Bertrand Wolfe was
tossed in the air several times by several men as others stood
around and applauded." Hayes, p. 223.

Attention: "He gave the child a shake to make him obedient" Dickens, Pickw., II, p. 43.

Authority: In the service for Catechumens in the Russian
liturgy, the priest sits upon a raised seat while reading the
apostolic epistles. His being seated symbolizes his equality with
the apostles. Gogol, p. 25; Ohm, p. 335.

Blessing: "more than once he bowed toward the road by
which the young maid had come...." Wolfr. v. Eschenb., Bk.
vii, 1136-37.

Concentration: The position of the sitting Buddha: legs
crossed and lying one above the other, soles facing up, hands
resting on thighs, palms out, thumbs toward each other. The
"lotus position." Ohm, pp. 332-333.

Confidence: "The priest stands erect after his previous humble posture, to signify... that both he and the faithful are uplifted
and comforted by the firm hope of receiving forgiveness of their
sins." Mass, p. 18.

Defiance: To show an opponent that he is despised, the

duellant remains seated at his approach.   Medieval French.
Lommatzsch, p. 35; Rajna, p. 322.   Cf. Hagen remaining
seated, his (formerly Siegfried's) sword across his knees, at
Kriemhild's approach.   Nibelungenlied, st. 1781-1786.   Cf. also
Wynne, pp. 104-114.

Despair: Throwing oneself on the ground.   Anc. Gk. and
Rom.   Sittl, p. 23.

Disgust: "What, dost thou turn away and hide thy face? I
am no loathsome leper; look on me." Shakesp., II Henry VI,
III, ii, 74.

Enthusiasm: " 'tis he, I ken the manner of his gait; he
rises on the toe: that spirit of his in aspiration lifts him from
the earth." Shakesp., Troilus, IV, v, 14.

Etiquette: "She bow'd her to the people." Shakesp., Henry
VIII, IV, i, 86.   Bowing as an act of courtesy, such as bowing
when entering the presence of ladies, or leaving them, or after
an introduction.   Dickens, Pickw., I, pp. 23, 266, etc.

Farewell: Men rise when man or woman leaves room.
Women may or may not rise.   The more formal the occasion,
the more likely everyone is to rise.   Colombia, U.S.   Saitz
and Cervenka, p. 69.

Fear: Bowing to the ground.   Num. 22, 31; I Sam., 28,
14; Isaiah 21, 3; Luke 24, 5.   Shuddering.   Krout, p. 25.

Gratitude: Bowing.   II Kings, 4, 37; Gen., 23, 7, 12; etc.
Medieval German: "The lady rose and bowed." Wolfr. v.
Eschenb., Bk. iv, 196.   "Thereupon the knights bowed to her."
Kudrun, st. 64, 1.   Dickens, Pickw., II, p. 425: "for with a
humble, grateful bow to Mr. Pickwick." Cf. s.v. Greeting.

Greeting: Bowing.   Gen. 18, 2; 19, 1; 33, 3; etc.   Beowulf greets the king standing, Siegfried greets Gunther bowing;
cf. Stegmann v. Pritzwald, p. 42.   In greeting, the bow can
be executed at various angles: the lower the head, the humbler
the bower.   Stoebe, p. 184.   The whole body impulsively flung
to the ground.   Stoebe, pp. 184-185.   Bowing in gratitude shows
greater intensity of emotion than inclining the head.   Portug.
Basto, p. 8.   Men rise when a woman or man enters room,
women usually remain seated.   The more formal the occasion,
the more likely all are to rise.   Colombia, U.S.   Saitz and
Cervenka, p. 69.   Bow of head or upper part of body, standing
or walking, is of minimum courtesy.   Colombia.   The U.S.
male, when he does bow, does so with upper part of body rather
than head alone.   Saitz and Cervenka, p. 67.   Cf. s.v. BREAST,
HAND, Greeting.

Homage: Persons of low degree, captives and foreign vassals are usually depicted in ancient Egyptian paintings or reliefs
as prostrate.   Court officers usually stand up, but incline their
heads and bodies slightly.   Servants bend forward to a greater
degree and place one hand on the knee or kneel and raise both
hands before their faces.   Gardiner, pl. 17, 19, 27, etc.
Dawson, p. 86.

Humility: Woodmen prostrate themselves after felling a
tree to show humility so spirit will not chastise them as it es-
capes.   Greek (Island of Siphnos).   Frazer, II, p. 37.   At

commencement of Mass, the priest bows at the foot of the altar and presents himself as if laden with the sins of the people before God. Mass, p. 17.

Judgment: "Thereupon the chief rabbi rose from his seat (that what he said might not have the force of a judicial decision),..." Germany, 18th century. Maimon, ch. xxii.

Magical: Barren women roll on ground under solitary apple tree in order to obtain offspring. Kara-Kirghiz. Frazer, New Golden Bough, p. 138. Upon return from baptism with the infant, the midwife turns it upside down. Brandenburg. Kuhn and Schwartz, p. 430; HDA II, col. 414.

Mourning: Woman stands next to her husband's grave: indication that she will not remarry. Rwala Bedouin. Semiotic. Islamic custom. Barakat, no. 211.

Plea: Entire body on the ground, face down. (Not in republican Greece and Rome). Persian, Punic. Sittl, p. 157. "...and am enjoin'd by holy Lawrence to fall prostrate here, to beg your pardon" Shakesp., Romeo, IV, ii, 19. To cast oneself at someone's feet, seeking help or protection. Boggs, p. 322. Bowing "this feeble ruin to the earth." Shakesp., Tit. Andr., III, i, 208.

Prayer: (Cf. s.v. BODY, FACE, Prayer.) Prostration often precedes prayer, which is spoken standing or kneeling. In prostration, the ground is touched by the body, the hands and the face. It was common with the Sumerians, Babylonians, ancient Egyptians, Jews, Romans, Indians. Still customary in Chinese cults and it is one of the positions prescribed in Mohammedan prayers. Prostration is performed in passing, the actual prayer follows. Heiler, p. 100. Woman lying on ground, face almost touching the ground. Anc. Egypt. Papyrus of the 21st dynasty. Bonnet, p. 207. Ancient Egyptian priests' prescribed prayer positions: 1) worshipper must throw himself down, i.e. kneel and bend his upper body down; 2) he must throw himself upon the ground so that the entire body lies flat; 3) he must lower the head to the ground, "kiss the earth." Bonnet, p. 206. After this introductory proskynesis the worshipper rises and speaks standing to the deity, arms raised, slightly bent, palms open. Prostration. Biblical. Stegmann v. Pritzwald, p. 25, n. 2. Circular motion of upper body. Celtic, Anc. Rom., Yao (Kwantung). Voullième, pp. 11-13; Ohm, p. 322. Inclination of the body or head forwards can precede or accompany prayer. Sumerian, Babylonian, Jewish, Indian, Anc. Rom., tribal Germanic. Heiler, p. 101. Turning the body before prayer was common among Celts and anc. Romans. The Romans turned toward the right, the Gauls to the left. Possibly derived from circling a sacred object. Heiler, p. 101. Since, to the anc. Romans, standing was a sign of respect, a law of Numa prescribed that a worshipper, having ended his prayer, must sit down. Standing in prayer was usual among early Christians and was perhaps also common in pre-Christian Egypt. Sittl, p. 194. The following gestures of prayer before a statue of the Virgin in Regensburg (1519) are depicted in Beitl, p. 97: prostration, the face touching the ground; kneel-

ing, hands joined palm to palm; kneeling with raised and slightly
spread arms; prostration on the back, arms spread to the sides.
Anc. Gk. and Rom. mystery cults required nakedness.   Heiler,
p. 104.   The ancient Gks. prayed to the chtonic deities half
sitting, half kneeling, i.e. squatting.   Anc. Roman women were
permitted while praying to squat like mourners or supplicants
for protection.   Heiler, p. 100.   The men were required to
stand during prayer.   Ohm, p. 338.   In primitive Christianity
prostration before graves and reliques was common.   Heiler,
p. 100.   In praying during Mass, the priest bows.   Mass,
pp. 18, 36.   Also Biblical.   Ex. 4, 31; 12, 27; Gen. 24, 26;
24, 48; etc.   In Catholic liturgy the priest almost always turns
left toward the altar.   Ohm, p. 322.   Swaying of the body during prayer is common among Jews and Mohammedans.   Encycl.
Jud., VII, p. 130; Bergmann, p. 331.   Prostration in the form
of a cross ("in kriuzestal").   Kudrun, st. 1170, 1.2; König
Rother, 376.   Doña Ximena casts herself down on the steps of
the altar and prays.   Cid, c. i.

Recognition: "...and knocked gently at the door.   It was at
once opened by a woman, who dropped a curtsey of recognition..."
Dickens, Pickw., I, p. 361.

Respect: "And the king [Solomon] rose up to meet her, and
bowed down unto her" I Kings, 2, 19.   In an Assyrian hymn
"the great gods bowed in approval and prayer before him [Anu]
like sickles."   Østrup, p. 30; Ohm, pp. 340-341.   The gods
arose before Apollo.   Anc. Gk.   Sittl, p. 153.   A festive gathering at Olympia rose before Themistocles.   Pausan.   Sittl, ibid.
The judges rose before Sophocles when he finished reciting
Oedip. on Col.   Sittl, ibid.   Subjects rise when ruler enters.
Anc. Gk.   Sittl, p. 152.   According to Suetonius, the father of
the emperor Vitellius approached Caligula with covered head,
turning before him and prostrating himself.   Ohm, p. 322.   Subjects rise when Roman emperor or princes enter the theater.
Sittl, pp. 152-153.   Senators rose at entrance of Caesar.   Augustus desired them to remain seated at his entrance and exit
from the senate.   Suet.; Plut.; Sittl, p. 153.   One rose in the
presence of the highest Roman officials, including the tribunes.
Sittl, ibid.   Citizens rose in the presence of professors.   Lucian; Choricius; Sittl, p. 154.   Everyone, including senators,
rose when anyone wearing the citizen's crown entered the theater.
Anc. Rom.   Sittl, p. 153.   Someone riding or in a coach had to
rise and dismount in the presence of consul or praetor, on the
order of the lictor; only in the company of a lady is an exception made.   Sittl, p. 152.   Whenever a high personage rose before someone, it was viewed as an extraordinary honor.   Plutarch, Brut. 4; Sittl, p. 154.   If the emperor was present only
symbolically, as when an imperial message was read, one lis-
tened to it standing.   Sittl, p. 153.   "King Alfonso sees [the
Cid] enter and stands and...all the others of the court stand
also."   Cid, c. iii.   A knight had to dismount when he met a
lady walking.   Medieval German.   Zirclaere, 419; Schultz, II,
p. 181.   Among North American Indians, when two men met,
they sat down at approx. twenty yards distance from one another

and looked at each other for a few minutes without speaking.
They then rose and walked on together. When a person of importance approached, the other would remain seated while he
passed by. Eichler, p. 95. "Unmanner'd dog! stand thou, when
I command" Shakesp., Richard III, I, ii, 39. "The old gentleman bowed respectfully." Dickens, Twist, p. 88. Philippine
tribes, believing spirits of ancestors to be in trees, bow respectfully in passing and excuse themselves for disturbing their
repose. Frazer, II, p. 29ff. An Ethiopian takes the corner of
a stranger's robe and ties it about himself, so as to leave the
other almost naked. Eichler, p. 159. Maburiag boys (Africa)
are instructed to crouch in the presence of old men. Eichler,
p. 95. The Tahitians uncover the body down to the waist in the
presence of a king. Eichler, p. 159. Guests rise when an
esteemed person enters house or tent. Saudi Arabia, Syria,
Jordan, Lebanon, Kuwait, Iraq. Semiotic or culture-induced.
Barakat, no. 181. "Taipei, Formosa, Jan. 27. The Chinese
Nationalist government has ruled that any government employee
refusing to bow before a portrait of Sun Yat-sen, founder of the
Chinese republic, is liable to punishment--presumably dismissal
from his government job." Cited from the Tampa Morning
Tribune of Jan. 28, 1957 by Hayes, p. 231. Turning one's
back to someone. Japan. Life (Sept. 10, 1945), p. 33.

Self-importance: "Why, here he comes, swelling like a
turkey-cock." Shakesp., Henry V, V, i, 15. "Does he not
hold up his head, as it were, and strut in his gait?" Shakesp.,
Merry Wives, I, iv, 30.

Solemnity: "and then with a bow of mock solemnity to Mr.
Pickwick, and a wink to Mr. Weller, the audacious slyness of
which baffles all description, followed the footsteps of his hope-
ful master." Dickens, Pickw., I, p. 434.

Sorrow: "Therefore I will wail and howl, go stripped..."
Mic. 1, 8. "Wallow thyself in ashes,..." Jer. 6, 26. Sinking
to the ground, moaning. Odyss. iv, 719. Sitting on a stone.
Beowulf, 2417. Criminals sat on a stone before execution.
John Meier, pp. 219-44.

Submission: Bowing. II Sam. 9, 8; I Kings, 1, 53; Gen.
33, 6, 7; 43, 26; etc. Rolling on the ground. Anc. Gk. Sittl,
p. 161. Monks prostrated themselves in Egypt and Palestine.
Sittl, p. 160. Throwing oneself entirely on the ground appears
to have occurred only in extreme fear in the Roman empire.
Sittl, p. 161. Cf. HDV I, p. 318. "bowed three times before
him" Shakesp., Wint. Tale, III, iii, 24. "As low as to thy
foot doth Cassius fall." Shakesp., Jul. Caes., III, i, 56.
"...Pope Paul, shoeless and without his fisherman's ring, prostrated himself before a cross in the Basilica of St. Mary Major
in the Church's mournful Good Friday liturgy." L.A. Times,
3/28/1970.

Superiority: At Passover the Jews lay on their side, in
order to express and remember that they were no longer slaves,
but free since the exodus. Similarly, Christ and the apostles
lay at table (Mark 14, 18). Ohm, p. 339.

BODY, CHEEK, HAND
Sorrow: Body on the ground, face down, hands scratching cheeks. Anc. Rom. Men. Sittl, p. 25.

BODY, EYE, HAND
Reverence: Priest goes to center of the altar, "where raising his eyes to the Crucifix, and immediately lowering them again, he inclines profoundly, keeping his hands joined. " Mass, p. 28.

BODY, FACE
Adoration: Romans made a complete turn to the right so that kiss was thrown toward deity before or after the turn. Not Gk., but also Celtic; cf. Athen., 4, 152 d; Sittl, p. 194.
Fear: Falling or bowing with face to the ground. I Sam. 28, 14; Luke 24, 5; Lev. 9, 24; etc.; cf. s.v. BODY, Prayer and BODY, FACE, Prayer.
Gratitude: Falling down on one's face at the feet of one's benefactor. Luke 17, 16.
Greeting: Bowing, face to the ground. I Sam., 25, 41; 20, 41.
Plea: Falling down on one's face. Num. 14, 5; 16, 22; Luke 5, 12; etc.
Prayer: Prostration. Josh., 5, 14; 7, 6; Judg., 13, 20; I Kings 18, 39; Ezek. 1, 28; 3, 23; Matt. 26, 39; etc. Tertull. Iud. 11; Sittl, p. 199. Face touches floor. Portug. Basto, p. 12. Cf. s.v. Adoration above, and BODY, Prayer.
Respect: Prostration. Sandwich Islands. Eichler, p. 95.
Reverence: Prostration. Gen., 48, 16; 50, 18; I Sam., 24, 8; II Sam., 14, 33; 24, 20; etc.
Sorrow: Prostration. Num., 16, 4.

BODY, FINGER
Threat: Tips of right thumb, index and middle fingers joined; then this configuration moved rapidly in front of body. Saudi Arabia, Jordan. Semiotic or culture-induced. Barakat, no. 28.

BODY, FINGER, MOUTH
Pride: Blowing on fingernails of one hand, then rubbing them on front of body. Comic. U.S. Saitz and Cervenka, p. 96.

BODY, FOOT
Prayer: Anc. Gks. invoked the dead by sitting (or throwing themselves) on the ground and beating upon it with either hands or feet. Sittl, p. 191.

BODY, FOREHEAD
Submission: In Byzantine proskynesis the subjects throw themselves down so that the forehead touched the ground. Sittl, p. 160.

BODY, FOREHEAD, MOUTH
Sorrow: Vertically furrowed brow, mouth drawn down at corners, bent posture. Depressives. Krukenberg, p. 132.

BODY, HAND

Etiquette: "Here Job Trotter bowed with great politeness and laid his hand upon his heart." Dickens, Pickw., I, p. 433.
When guests enter the room, the ladies rise and bow, putting the hands together, then they sit down again. Medieval courtly. Schultz, I, p. 529. Cf. also Kudrun, st. 334; Dietrichs Flucht, 7411; Biterolf, 1301.

Finished: Cutting across the body with the open hand, fingers extended and palm inward from shoulder of one side to waist of the other. Spain. Green, p. 84.

Gratitude: Bowing and simultaneously swinging flat right hand, palm up, a little way down and to one side. Amer. schoolchildren. Seton, p. xxiv.

Greeting: " 'Moyo pochtenie (My respects),' said both men, bowing to each other over a powerful handshake." Nabokov, p. 126. "Pnin bowed deeply to them with an 'I am disarmed' spreading of the hands." Nabokov, p. 161.

Mourning: Body thrown on ground, hands beating ground. Men. Anc. Gk. Sittl, p. 26.

Possession: Wife expresses her belonging to a man by resting her hand on his knee or leaning against him. Sirionó Indians (Bolivia). Key, p. 97.

Prayer: Anc. Gks. invoked the dead by sitting (or throwing themselves) on the ground and beating upon it either with the hands or the feet. Sittl, p. 191.

Strike: Cutting across the body with the open hand, fingers extended and palm inward, from the shoulder of one side to the waist of the other. Spain. Green, p. 84.

Useless: Crossing the slightly cupped hand sharply across the body. The palm of the hand faces the shoulder at the beginning of the movement; at the conclusion, the palm faces outward. Spain, Lat. Am. Green, p. 85.

Virility: "Heavy back pounding after an athletic event often is an attempt to emphasize virility and sometimes reflects inner hostility." Birdwhistell, Colliers (3/4/1955), p. 56.

BODY, HAND, HEAD

Humility: The priest "joins his hands, bows his head and bends low to signify the profound humility of Christ hanging upon the Cross and praying for us, and to signify also his own humility." Mass, p. 65.

Reverence: Herero bow to omum borum bonga tree and place twigs or grass at its foot as reverence for it as source of life of all four-footed beasts. Frazer, II, p. 220.

Sorrow: Sinking to the ground, burying the face in the hands, weeping. Boggs, p. 319.

BODY, HEAD

Pride: Sideways movement of the head or body accompanying expression of affirmation. Amer. Journ. of Psych. XXVII (1916), p. 322.

Submission: Bowing head and entire body. Portug. Basto, p. 21.

Threat: Raising the head and assuming a vertical posture.
Krukenberg, p. 252.

BODY, HEAD, LIP
Arrogance: Raising the head, which is drawn slightly to the
rear, lips closed, stiff posture. Krukenberg, p. 256.

BREAST
Self-importance: Throw out chest. Amer. schoolchildren.
Seton, p. xxi.
Sorrow: Mothers open their clothes to show the breasts
which nourished their children as a means of attempting to stop
a son from departing. Anc. Gk. and Rom. Sittl, p. 173.

BREAST, CHEEK, HAIR, HAND
Mourning: Beating breast, tearing hair, scratching cheeks.
Sixteenth cent. Gk. Sittl, pp. 68-69.

BREAST, EYE, HAIR, HAND
Mourning: Beating breast, tearing hair, beating eyes. Men.
Anc. Rom. Sittl, p. 71.

BREAST, FINGER
Promise: Wet finger and make Sign of the Cross on one's
heart. Children. Yorkshire. Opie, p. 124. With right index
make little cross over the heart. Amer. schoolchildren. Seton,
p. 53.

BREAST, FOOT, HAND, LIP
Applause: Audience kisses chest, head, or foot of a rhetor
after a speech. Anc. Gk. Sittl, p. 166.

BREAST, FOREHEAD, HAND, MOUTH
Apotropy: Making a cross over forehead, mouth, and heart,
then the "large cross," touching forehead, chest and both sides,
whereupon a cross, made with thumb and index of right hand,
is kissed. Spain. Flachskampf, p. 243.
Greeting: Right hand reaches down as if to take dust from
the ground, then is raised to chest, mouth, and forehead. Arab.
Petermann, I, p. 172; Goldziher, Zeitschr., p. 370.
Prayer: Right hand touches breast, mouth, forehead in
prayer before graves of princes. Anc. Egypt. Ohm, p. 288.
"The priest makes the Sign of the Cross on the book at the beginning of the Gospel, then on his forehead, lips, and breast.
This is a prayer that the holy Gospel may be, first, on our
mind,...secondly, on our lips,...thirdly, in our heart." Mass,
p. 29.

BREAST, FOREHEAD, HAND, SHOULDER
Prayer: Crossing oneself. With the flat right hand, fingers
extended, touch forehead, then the breast, first the left side,
then the right. Roman Catholic. Ohm, p. 294. Same gesture,
but from right to left side of breast. Greek orthodox. Ohm,
p. 294.

BREAST, FOREHEAD, LIP
  Greeting: Under the Diocletian monarchy only the highest officials were permitted to kiss the chest of the emperor, who in
  return kissed their foreheads. Sittl, p. 166.

BREAST, HAIR, HAND
  Mourning: One hand beating breast, the other tearing the hair.
  Idealized. Anc. Gk. Schreiber, pp. 86-95; Sittl, p. 75.

BREAST, HAND
  Affection: Hand(s) of beloved pressed against one's chest.   Anc.
  Gk. and Rom. Sittl, p. 34.
  Affirmation: One hand laid upon the breast, the other ex-
  tended horizontally and somewhat to the side. Anc. Gk. and
  Rom., Baroque. Ohm, p. 288. Cf. s.v. Oath below.
  Alarm: Beating shield against chest, calling "to arms, to
  arms, to arms!" Statius. Sittl, p. 215.
  Anger: Beating one's breast in anger. Boggs, p. 321.
  Apotropy: Hermits beat their breast with fists to drive out
  evil thoughts. Early Christian. Sittl, p. 20.
  Assistance: Lightly patting one's heart with right palm indicates need for assistance. Saudi Arabia. Semiotic or culture-
  induced. Barakat, no. 187.
  Buxom: Both hands pretend to throw pendulous breasts back
  over shoulders. Colombia. Tracing form of breasts. Colombia, U.S. Saitz and Cervenka, p. 122.
  Congratulation: " 'If I were not a married man myself, I
  should be disposed to envy you, you dog, I should.' Thus expressing himself the little lawyer gave Mr. Winkle a poke in
  the chest, which that gentleman reciprocated; after which they
  both laughed." Dickens, Pickw., II, p. 322.
  Curse: "...goes by night in front of the house or on the
  roof, bares her breast toward the stars and, with the breast
  toward the heavens..." Palest. Bauer, p. 218.
  Dedication: In connection with the votum the hand touches
  the chest whenever the giver is referred to. Anc. Gk. Sittl,
  p. 196.
  Despair: Beating the breasts. Women. Anc. Gk. and Rom.
  Sittl, p. 19. Beating breast. Men. Early Christian. Sittl,
  p. 20.
  Disappointment: Beating the breast. Men. Anc. Rom.
  (The only anc. Gk. sources are Charito and the Vita Aesopi.)
  Sittl, p. 20.
  Disgust: Hand, palm down, placed horizontally in front of
  chest. Colombia, U.S. (Reported 1970 as not very common
  among young adults in U.S.) Saitz and Cervenka, p. 43.
  Distress: "beats her heart." Shakesp., Much Ado, II, iii,
  153; Hamlet, IV, v, 5; Ven. and Ad., 829.
  Eating: Cf. s.v. HAND, Eating.
  Emphasis: Cf. s.v. HAND, Emphasis.
  Enmity: Cf. s.v. HAND, Enmity.
  Excitement: Cf. s.v. HAND, Excitement.
  Gratitude: Left hand laid upon chest. Mod. Gk. Sittl,

p. 162. Right palm laid upon chest. Cf. Greeting below.

Greeting: Folding hands at chest and bowing down to the ground. High officials to maharajah. Thomas, p. 80. Right hand is brought to chest twice and head slightly bowed, saying "ram, ram." Among equals in Hindustan. Thomas, ibid. Folding the palms in front of the chest and saying "Namasti." Arya Samjists. Thomas, ibid. Left hand laid upon chest. Mod. Gk. Sittl, p. 162. Right palm pressed upon chest. Lebanon, Jordan, Syria, Saudi Arabia. Culture-induced or semiotic. Barakat, no. 25.

Humility: Arms crossed upon the breast so that hands lie on the shoulders while executing a deep bow. Oriental. Ohm, p. 277.

Identification: One or both hands, fingers spread, resting on chest. Colombia, U.S. Saitz and Cervenka, p. 113.

Insult: Hand is brought to the heart of the gesticulator. Feigned offense. Spain, Lat. Am., U.S. Green, p. 81.

Investiture: Cf. s.v. Oath, below.

Mourning: Striking chest with hands. Anc. Egypt., anc. Gk. and Rom., early Christian. Ohm, p. 281; Quasten, p. 217. Gesture prohibited by the third synod of Toledo (can. 22). Quasten, p. 221, n. 16. Beating breasts and mouth. Wall painting in Egypt. Tomb. Ball, p. 119; Hastings, Dict., I, p. 453. Beating breast. Men. Asiatic. Aeschyl., Pers.; Quint. Smyrn.; Hieron; Sittl, p. 25. Men. Anc. Rom. Sittl, ibid. Beating breast four times at cremation. Anc. Rom. Sittl, p. 73. Beating breast. Men. Hellenist. orient. Sittl, p. 67. Scratching breast. Women. Anc. Gk. and Rom., early Christian. Sittl, p. 27. Beating breast. Boggs, p. 319. "When women mourn, they swing or move one hand around the other... or they beat their breast alternately with the flat right and left hand." Palest. Bauer, pp. 218-219.

Oath: (Cf. s.v. HAND, Oath.) "He struck his hand upon his breast, and kist the fatal knife, to end his vow" Shakesp., Lucr., 1846. Women swearing an oath lay the hand upon their breast. Lex Alamannorum 56, 2 (54, 3): "tunc liceat illi mulieri jurare per pectus suum." Grimm, DRA II, p. 548. Men likewise swear lesser oaths with hand laid upon chest, particularly princes. In a deed of Bishop Florens of Münster (1372) (Kindlinger, I, p. 38) the gesture is described "as a bishop customarily swears." Women and clerics, in being invested with a fief, lay the hand upon the breast. Still common in asseveration in 19th century Germany. Grimm, DRA II, 249.

Obedience: Left hand placed on chest and held there, the anc. Gk. slave awaits the command of his master. Sittl, p. 162.

Penitence: Beating one's breast. Anc. Jews. Ohm, p. 281. Taken over by Christians, particularly popular among Catholics. Ohm, ibid.

Plea: French monk lays hand on chest. Sterne, ch. ii; Sittl, p. 162. Left hand placed on breast, right hand raised. Deïdamia on a Campania painting. Sittl, p. 162, n. 4. "The priest... places his left hand on the corporal while he strikes his breast with the right..." Mass, p. 68.   "The priest returns to the center of the altar, with his hands joined before his breast, and he implores mercy for himself and the people." Mass, p. 19.

Prayer: Hands crossed on breast.   Palest.   Bauer, p. 192; Dominicans; Russ. liturgy.   Ohm, p. 278.   Hands beating upon breast.   Bantu.   Ohm, p. 281.   Cf. s.v. HAND, Prayer.

Protest: "clenched both fists, pulled them with stress against his chest."   Birdwhistell, Backgr., p. 14; Intro. p. 27.

Regret: Smiting breast.   Luke 23, 48; 18, 13.

Relief: "she drew her hands, drawn into loose fists, up between her breasts."   Birdwhistell, Intro., p. 30.

Remorse: Smiting chest.   Anc. Jews.   Ohm, p. 281. Christians took the gesture from the Jews.   Walafrid Strabo, col. 932.   Catholics beat breast at "Confiteor," "Domine non sum dignus," "Agnus Dei."   Ohm, p. 281.

Resignation: Cf. s.v. HAND, Resignation.

Sacrifice: Beating chest.   Anc. Egypt.   Ohm, p. 281.

Satisfaction: Hands on belt, chest expanded.   Birdwhistell, Colliers (3/4/1955), p. 56.

Sincerity: "Moved, he lays her hand upon his heart." Stage direction in Kleist, II, 6; Neapol.   Critchley, p. 89.

Sorrow: Beating upon bare chest.   Anc. Egypt.   Ohm, p. 281.   Women.   Anc. Gk. and Rom.   Sittl, p. 19.   Scratching breasts.   Women.   Anc. Rom.   Sittl, p. 27.   Beating the breast.   Men.   Asiatic.   Sittl, p. 25.   Also anc. Rom.   Sittl, ibid.   The only anc. Gk. evidence is Charito 7, 1, 5.   Shakesp., Richard III, II, ii, 3; Bulwer, pp. 89-91.   Hands (arms crossed) on chest.   Medieval German.   Hamburg.   Stadt-bibl.   In scrinio 85, fol. 15a; Haseloff, p. 306.

Strength: One or both fists strike chest several times. Colombia, U.S.   Saitz and Cervenka, p. 133.

Teasing: Open hands moved over each other several times on chest.   Lebanon.   Semiotic.   Barakat, no. 36.

Truth: "lay hand on heart advise."   Shakesp., Romeo, III, v, 192.

BREAST, HAND, HEAD

Affection: Hands moved up the sides of the chest so that thumbs hit undersides of lapels; head is shaken slightly.   Unrequited love.   Hadhramaut, Saudi Arabia.   Semiotic.   Barakat, no. 203.

Gratitude: Palm of right hand placed on chest, head bowed, eyes closed.   Saudi Arabia.   Semiotic.   Barakat, no. 83.

Greeting: Tips of fingers of right hand touched to forehead, then chest and back to forehead while bowing slightly.   Jordan, Saudi Arabia.   Semiotic and culture-induced.   Barakat, no. 55.

Humility: In greeting one bows the head and lays the hand upon the chest as sign of humility and gratitude.   Arab.   Bauer, p. 224.

Mourning: After a death the female relatives uncover their heads, and often throw dust and earth upon them, "scratch their cheeks, tear their hair, blacken their faces with soot and beat their breasts."   Palest.   Bauer, p. 212.

BREAST, HAND, LIP
Respect: When greeting a dignitary, his right hand is shaken, then the person of lower rank kisses his own hand, places it on his chest and bows slightly. Saudi Arabia. Semiotic. Barakat, no. 138.

BREAST, LIP
Greeting: At the morning "salutatio" a client kissed the chest of a nobleman upon whom he is waiting. Rom. empire. Men. Sittl, p. 166. During the Diocletian monarchy the kiss on the chest is permitted only to high officials who, in turn, were kissed on the forehead by the emperor. Sittl, ibid.
Plea: Noblemen kissed the chest of their benefactor. Anc. Rom. Sittl, p. 166.

BREAST, LIP, SHOULDER
Affection: Kiss on shoulders and breast. Grandmother to grandson. Quint. Smyrn.; Sittl, p. 41.

BUTTOCKS
Apotropy: Vacating against the evil eye. Phrygian. Sittl, p. 124. Buttocks bared against the devil. Kleinpaul, p. 271; Sittl, p. 124. Italian seamen bare buttocks against unfavorable winds, since winds are ascribed to good or evil supernatural beings. Sittl, ibid. Naked Huzulian sorceresses bare their buttocks toward heaven against hail. Carpathians. HDA IV, col. 63. Baring the buttocks to ward off the evil eye was used primarily to protect children. Jutland. Meschke, col. 330. Baring the buttocks blunts the enemy's sword. Medieval Scand. Seligmann, I, p. 174. The Kafir sorcerer stands on his head, buttocks bared, in order to prevent rain. HDA II, col. 847. Belief in the apotropaic powers of the bared buttocks was especially common among French and Italian seamen, who believed the gesture to be a defence against storms. ZfVk. (1901), pp. 426ff.
Insult: Breaking wind. Romans at Jews. Horace. Merely ludicrous in anc. Gk., serious in mod. Gk. and Albanian. Sittl, p. 99. "Each morning, last January, an entire platoon of Chinese soldiers would march out on the ice, lower their trousers, and aim their buttocks toward the Soviet side of the border. This is the ultimate Chinese insult." Esquire (Jan. 1968), p. 55.
Magical: Baring the buttocks to call forth a storm. Upper Palatinate and Lapland. Meschke, col. 330. In Russia one calls up the spirit of the wood on St. John's eve by baring the buttocks. In Norse literature baring the buttocks blunts the enemy's sword. Seligmann, I, p. 174. Baring the buttocks attracts a dragon's treasure. Lapland. Meschke, col. 330. Exposure of female buttocks prevents the flight of bees. Pomerania. Meschke, col. 330.
Mockery: Breaking wind. Romans at Jews. Horace. Also modern Gk. and Albanian. Ludicrous in classical Gk. Sittl,

p. 99.
Shame: "... young and old, naked and barefoot, even with their buttocks uncovered..." Isaiah 20, 4.

BUTTOCKS, HAND
Contempt: "In a quarrel, particularly at the end of a quarrel, one sees, by way of final effect, one participant strike his buttocks with the words 'you are worth that' " Palest. Bauer, p. 220.
Encouragement: Hand strikes someone's buttocks once. Only on sports teams. U.S. Saitz and Cervenka, p. 48.
Insult: Open right hand moved at right side of buttocks while right side of buttocks is moved. Lebanon, Syria. Semiotic. Barakat, no. 49.
Meditation: Scratching the buttocks. Barb. and Méon, IV, pp. 143, 221.
Prayer: In calling upon the deities residing in the earth, one sat on the ground and beat upon it with the hands. Anc. Gk. and Rom. Sittl, p. 190.

BUTTOCKS, HAND, TONGUE
Mockery: Baring buttocks while sticking out tongue and making a "fig." Lucas Cranach the Elder, "The Mocking of Christ" (1538), L.A. County Mus. of Art.

CHEEK
Anger: Puffed up cheeks. Horace. Sittl, p. 14.
Indecision: Blowing up cheek. Krout, p. 22.
Submission: "He humbly puts his cheek on the ground before one reclining on a silken couch." Emir Al-Hakam in A. R. Nykl, pp. 20-21.

CHEEK, EYE
Embarrassment: Blushing and casting eyes down. Boggs, p. 321.

CHEEK, EYE, HAND
Fatigue: Eyes closed, head inclined laterally, cheek reposes on the back of one hand which is joined to the other palm to palm. French. Mitton, p. 148.

CHEEK, EYE, MOUTH
Disbelief: One corner of mouth drawn down, one cheek raised, partly closing an eye. Aubert, p. 149.
Uncertainty: One corner of mouth drawn down, one cheek raised, partly closing an eye. Aubert, p. 105.

CHEEK, EYEBROW
Surprise: Cheeks fill with air and eyebrows are raised. Colombia. Saitz and Cervenka, p. 134.

CHEEK, EYEBROW, HEAD, MOUTH

Admiration: Head forward, eyebrows raised, slight smile raising cheeks. Aubert, p. 124.

    Affection: Cf. s.v. Admiration, above.

Prosperity: Head thrown backwards, eyebrows raised,
mouth and cheeks expanded. Aubert, p. 127.

    Satisfaction: Cf. s.v. Prosperity, above.

CHEEK, FINGER

Admiration: Thumb and index touch the cheek and stroke down
to the chin, suggesting a smile of admiration. Anc. Gk. ?
Neapol. De Jorio, pp. 77-78; Wundt, I, p. 172, fig. 6; Spain.
Flachskampf, p. 229. Tip of right index run down the cheek
of a woman is a compliment. Lebanon, Syria. Semiotic.
Barakat, no. 127. Twisting tip of forefinger into cheek. Used
when speaking to a beautiful woman. Libya. Semiotic. Barakat, no. 126.

    Affection: Cheek of someone (usually a child) is taken be-
tween one's fingers. Anc. Rom. Sittl, p. 33. Pinching right
cheek of another person with tips of right index and thumb.
Egypt, Lebanon, Jordan, Syria, Saudi Arabia, Libya. Semiotic,
culturally determined. Barakat, no. 11.

    Approval: Tips of index and thumb united make a twisting
movement on the cheek, as if curling an imaginary moustache.
The origin is the Neapolitan gesture of approval of twirling the
tip of one's moustache. Ital. Efron, fig. 42.

    Boredom: Back of the fingers brush up and down over the
cheek. Allusion to the tediousness of shaving? French. Mitton, p. 150.

    Cunning: Index touches cheekbone; gesture accompanied by
slight nod. Sicily. Pitrè, p. 355; Flachskampf, p. 236.

    Disbelief: "Index finger of the right hand is applied to the
cheek in a circular motion, while the face is permitted to assume an expression suggesting the recent sucking of a lemon."
French. WW II. Alsop, p. 27. Fingers of right hand, loosely
cupped, scrub right cheek upwards and downwards; corners of
mouth drooping: "La barbe!" French. Brault, p. 378.

    Effeminacy: Raised index touches left cheek. Lat. Am.
Kany, p. 181.

    Embarrassment: Index placed tip against cheek. Ital.
Gherardini, pp. 110-111; Sittl, p. 273.

    Mockery: Tips of fingers and thumb joined and hitting on
distended cheek, exhaling as fingers strike cheek. Can also
signify that a given person is talking nonsense. Saudi Arabia.
Semiotic. Barakat, no. 232.

    Mourning: Scratching cheeks. Anc. Gk. Men. Sittl,
p. 25. Hellenistic oriental. Men. Sittl, p. 67. Widows.
Epirus, 19th cent. Sittl, p. 69.

    Plea: Stroking someone's cheek. Anc. Gk. Sittl, p. 33.
Medieval German. Kudrun, st. 386, 2.3.

    Shyness: Index placed with tip against cheek. Anc. Gk.
Sittl, p. 273.

    Sorrow: Cheek rested against tips of fingers. Refined.

Anc. Gk. Sittl, p. 24.
   Surprise: Index placed tip against cheek. Ital. Gherardini,
p. 110-111; Sittl, p. 273.
   Threat: Tips of fingers and thumb joined and hit against
cheek: admonition to a child to behave or that his mother will
deal with him later. Saudi Arabia. Semiotic. Barakat, no.
231.
   Warning: Index touches cheek just below eye, then arm is
extended to point in direction of danger. Colombia. Saitz and
Cervenka, p. 147.

CHEEK, FOREHEAD, MOUTH
   Admiration: Biting of lower lip, eyebrows raised, lips and
cheeks extended as in laugh. Aubert, p. 131.
   Disapproval: Cheeks raised, direct stare, brows frowning,
corners of mouth drawn down. Aubert, p. 109.
   Joy: Unexpected joy is expressed by biting of lower lip,
raising eyebrows, lips and cheeks extended as in laugh. Aubert,
p. 131. Lips extended in grin pushing up cheeks to form
wrinkles under eyes, brows raised, forming lines across forehead. Aubert, p. 132.
   Sensibility: Opposing movements of brows and wrinkles on
forehead. Contraction of the cheeks. Corners of mouth drawn
down. Aubert, p. 139.
   Sorrow: Cf. s.v. Sensibility, above.

CHEEK, HAND
   Affection: " 'You're a sweet pet, my love,' replied Mrs. Colonel
Wugsby, tapping her daughter's cheek with her fan..." Dickens,
Pickw., II, p. 123. Pinching cheek of another person. Can be
show of affection or a promise to do something. Jordan. Semi-
otic. Barakat, no. 237.
   Amazement: Placing the palm on either the cheek or be-
hind the ear. Ghetto Jews. Efron, p. 146.
   Anger: Hand rubs cheek: "and I rubbed my cheek for vex-
ation." Richardson, Clarissa, v, p. 225.
   Boredom: Hand rubbed against cheek. French. Life
(9/16/1946), pp. 12-15.
   Confirmation: Slap on the cheek. Early Christian. Sittl,
p. 146.
   Despair: Hands grasp cheeks. Albanian women. Hahn, II,
p. 153; Sittl, p. 23.
   Embarrassment: Hand scratches cheek under one ear.
Heliodorus; Sittl, p. 19. One hand placed against cheek. Anc.
Rom. Sittl, p. 273.
   Farewell: "Mr. Pickwick...patted the rosy cheeks of the
female servants in a most patriarchal manner..." Dickens,
Pickw., I, p. 165.
   Fatigue: Hands palm to palm, placed along cheek, head in-
clined to side, resting on back of hand. Eyes often closed sim-
ultaneously. Women. U.S., Colombia. Saitz and Cervenka,
p. 125. Cf. s.v. CHEEK, EYE, HAND, Fatigue and EYE,
HAND, HEAD, Fatigue.

Fear: Hands grasp cheeks. Albanian women. Hahn, II, p. 153; Sittl, p. 23.

Impatience: "he rubbed one side of his face impatiently" Richardson, Clarissa, iv, p. 154.

Insult: Slap on cheek. Anc. Rom. Sittl, p. 109.

Kindness: " 'I was wrong...' said I, patting her cheek as kindly as a rough old fellow like me could pat it" Dickens, Pickw., II, p. 437.

Magnitude: Cheeks filled with air as hands indicate girth of a fat person. Colombia, U.S. Saitz and Cervenka, p. 51.

Mockery: Cheeks puffed out, left hand clenched against abdomen, right hand grasps nose, upper part of body doubled over. Customarily a mute gesture. French. Brault, p. 379.

Mourning: Slapping one's cheeks. Women. Arab. Bauer, p. 218.

Oath: Hitting side of face with palm of right hand, then rubbing hand downward on cheek. Saudi Arabia. Semiotic. Barakat, no. 109.

Pain: Hands scratch cheeks. Women. Anc. Gk. and Rom. Sittl, p. 23. Holding flat palm against one's cheek. Dante, Purg., c. vii; De Jorio, p. 142.

Pensiveness: Cheek in hand. Celestina, 179. (Cf. also s.v. CHIN, HAND, Pensiveness.)

Punishment: Slap on cheek. Anc. Rom. Sittl, p. 105.

Regret: Cf. s.v. HAND, HEAD, Regret.

Shyness: Left hand placed on cheek. Baumeister, I, p. 589. Hand placed against cheek. Anc. Rom. Sittl, p. 273.

Sorrow: Cheek rested in palm of hand. Anc. Gk. and Rom.; Medieval Ital.: Dante, Purg., c. vii; Mod. Gk. Sittl, p. 24. Scratching cheeks. Anc. Gk. Men. Anc. Rom. Sittl, p. 25. Medieval. Haseloff, p. 305.

Surprise: One hand placed against cheek. Anc. Rom. Sittl, p. 273.

Thief: Hand, slightly cupped, scrapes cheek lightly. Colombia. Saitz and Cervenka, p. 138.

CHEEK, HAND, KNEE
Plea: Touching knees and cheek of a women. Performed kneeling. Anc. Gk. Sittl, p. 166.

CHEEK, HAND, LIP
Affection: While kissing, the person being kissed is grasped by the cheeks. Anc. Gk. Sittl, p. 40.

Greeting: When two men meet they kiss each other on the cheeks--first one cheek, then the other--while placing hands on each other's shoulders. Lebanon, Syria, Saudi Arabia. Semiotic. Barakat, no. 139.

CHEEK, HEAD, LIP
Complaint: Head bowed, brow furrowed, cheeks raised and wrinkled under the eyes, lips pouting. Aubert, p. 138.

Plea: Cf. s.v. Complaint, above.

Reproach: Head bowed, eyes raised, lips pursed, cheeks lowered. Krukenberg, p. 256.

CHEEK, HEAD, MOUTH
Humility: Head bowed, eyes raised, mouth smiling, cheeks raised. Krukenberg, p. 256.
Self-importance: Head thrown back, eyebrows raised, expansion of mouth and cheeks. Aubert, p. 127.

CHEEK, NOSE
Affection: Nose laid against the cheek of the beloved taking a deep breath, eyes closed, then lips make sound of a kiss without touching the cheek. Mongolian. Krukenberg, p. 111.
Approach: Man wrinkles his nose and one cheek simultaneously to a woman if he wants her to come to him. Saudi Arabia. Semiotic or culture-induced. Barakat, no. 166.

CHEEK, TONGUE
Concentration: Placing tongue in cheek. Krout, p. 24.
Contempt: "I signified my contempt of him by thrusting my tongue in my cheek." This after the other's assertion of his own valor, therefore the meaning may be disbelief. Smollett, Rod. Random, ch. liv.

CHIN
Fear: Chin falls. Anc. Rom. Sittl, p. 46.
Hesitation: Pulling, stroking, or kneading chin. French. Mitton, p. 146.
Interrogation: Chin raised in direction of someone and remaining raised. ("What do you want?" "What do you say?.") French. Mitton, p. 141.
Pleasure: " 'I am glad to have my judgment,' observed Gay, tilting up his chin with shining pleasure, 'confirmed by outside witnesses.' " Carr, To Wake the Dead, p. 113.
Pointing: Pointing with the chin in a direction or toward someone. Spain, Lat. Am. Green, p. 71. Gurkha. J. Masters, Atlantic Monthly (Dec. 1955), p. 38, cited by Hayes, p. 279.
Snobbishness: Chin lifted several inches; often eyes are partially closed. Colombia, U.S. Saitz and Cervenka, p. 128.
Submission: Knocking chin on ground. Anc. Persian. Sittl, p. 158.

CHIN, FINGER
Assistance: Grasping chin with tips of fingers of right hand indicates need for assistance. Saudi Arabia. Semiotic. Barakat, no. 13.
Boredom: Cf. s.v. FINGER, Boredom.
Challenge: Gently grazing another person's chin with tip of right index: threat or challenge. Lebanon, Saudi Arabia. Semiotic. Barakat, no. 81.
Contempt: Tips of fingers passed rapidly from back to front three or four times under the chin. French. Mitton, p. 151.
Disappointment: Thumb rests between chin and lower lip while fingers, extended, move from side to side. Colombia.

Saitz and Cervenka, p. 32.

Effeminacy: Extended index touches chin, smiling. Lat. Am. Kany, p. 182.

Indifference: Tips of fingers rub slowly under chin. Ital. Time (Apr. 9, 1965), p. 67. Fingers of one hand close together, palm towards gesticulator, fingertips under chin; then the hand is suddenly flipped outward. The gesture originated with flipping the beard. Southern Ital., French. Efron, p. 156.

Mockery: Back of hand, fingers extended, placed beneath chin, fingers wiggling at someone: person to whom gesture is made is regarded as old. Saudi Arabia. Semiotic. Barakat, no. 241.

Negation: Thumb rests between chin and lower lip while fingers, extended, move from side to side. Frequent in public markets. ("We don't have any.") Colombia. Saitz and Cervenka, p. 32. Cf. s.v. Disappointment above.

Pensiveness: Grasping chin with thumb side of right fist: sign of wisdom or maturity. Saudi Arabia. Semiotic. Barakat, no. 78. Thumb and index grasp chin. Colombia, U.S. Saitz and Cervenka, p. 140. Thumb under chin, index along cheek. Colombia, U.S. Saitz and Cervenka, ibid. Both gestures often accompanied by brow wrinkling and eye narrowing. Cf. s.v. FINGER, LIP, Pensiveness.

Respect: Stroking chin with fingers of right hand with downward motion. Saudi Arabia. Semiotic. Barakat, no. 108. Cf. s.v. Shame below.

Shame: Holding extended right thumb near chin with heel of hand out: "shame." Jordan, Syria. Semiotic. Barakat, no. 209. Stroking chin with fingers of right hand with downward motion. Saudi Arabia. Semiotic. Barakat, no. 108. Cf. s.v. Respect above.

Threat: Gently grazing another person's chin with the tip of the right forefinger. Lebanon, Saudi Arabia. Semiotic. Barakat, no. 81. Cf. s.v. Challenge above.

Wisdom: Grasping chin with thumb side of right fist: sign of wisdom or maturity. Saudi Arabia. Semiotic. Barakat, no. 78. Cf. s.v. Pensiveness above.

CHIN, FINGER, HEAD, NOSE

Admiration: Extended index of right hand laid alongside the nose, the other fingers clasping chin, head bowed. Arab. Bauer, p. 224.

Pensiveness: Cf. s.v. Admiration above. German. Bauer, p. 224.

CHIN, FOOT, HAND

Contempt: Roman contemplating death places foot on spear as sign of disdain of death. Simultaneously he places hand to chin. Sittl, p. 196.

CHIN, FOREHEAD, HAND, LEG

Pensiveness: Wrinkling the forehead, crossing the legs, palm of right hand under chin, elbow resting on left hand. Anc. Rom. Baden, p. 453. Cf. s.v. CHIN, HAND, Pensiveness.

CHIN, HAND
   Affection: Taking a person's chin between one's fingers (stopping friends on street). Anc. Rom., 19th cent. Ital. (Manzoni, c. xv), Sittl, p. 33. Anc. Gk. Children. Sittl, ibid.
Maternal affection. Odyss. xix. Chucking under chin. Erotical-
ly affectionate rather than avuncular. Psalter, Flemish, ca.
1300, Oxford, Bodl. Douce 6, fol. 80. Robertson, p. 113.
Flicking the underside of a woman's chin with the tip of right
index: conciliatory, "cheer up." Jordan, Syria, Lebanon.
Culture-induced. Barakat, no. 32.
   Boredom: Backs of fingers of one hand lightly travel up
and down over the chin. French. Mitton, p. 150.
   Concentration: Plucking of beard or stroking of chin.
Chetto Jews. Efron, p. 146. Cf. s.v. Pensiveness below.
   Fatigue: Hand holding chin. Baudoin de Sebourc, I, 72.
   Fear: Grasping one's beard. Arab. Sachau, p. 189;
Goldziher, Zeitschr., p. 382.
   Hesitation: Pulling, stroking, or kneading chin. French.
Mitton, p. 146.
   Indifference: Tips of fingers of one hand (except thumb)
touch under the chin and then are flipped forward. Southern
Ital. Efron, pp. 154, 156. Hand, palm inwards, fingers slight-
ly bent, nails touching underside of chin, is quickly whipped out
to the front. ("What do I care?") Ital. N.Y. Times (March 1,
1959).
   Insult: Pulling someone's chin or imaginary beard down-
ward. Lat. Am. Kany, p. 64. Holding right hand, back of
hand forward, under chin, then lightly brushing the tips of the
fingers beneath the chin several times with forward motion.
Saudi Arabia. Semiotic. Barakat, no. 137.
   Negation: Right hand is catapulted out from under the chin.
Southern Ital. Sittl, p. 86.
   Nothing: Fingertips flipped out from under the chin three
or four times. Childish. French. Mitton, p. 151.
   Oath: "Stroke your chins, and swear by your beards that
I am a knave." Shakesp., As you Like it, I, ii, 76.
   Pensiveness: "I had placed into my hand my chin and one
cheek." Medieval German. Walther v. d. Vogelweide 8, 5ff.,
and miniature in Heidelb. Ms. C. (Cf. s.v. CHEEK, HAND,
Pensiveness). Cf. Rodin, "The Thinker." Palace of the Legion
of Honor, San Francisco. "...tapping his chin with the cover
of the book, in a thoughtful manner." Dickens, Twist, p. 87.
Plucking of beard or stroking of chin demonstrate thoughtfulness,
deliberation, doubt. Ghetto Jews. Efron, p. 146. "Then rubbing his chin with his hand and looking up to the ceiling as if to
recall the circumstances to his memory..." Dickens, Pickw., I,
p. 347. One hand grasps elbow or rests in armpit of the other,
other hand against side of chin. Colombia, U.S. Saitz and
Cervenka, p. 139.
   Plea: Pleader touches chin of person he is flattering. Anc.
Gk. Ohm, p. 240; Sittl, p. 282. Medieval German. Kudrun,
st. 386, 2.3. Placing right hand on beard or chin. Polite request. Saudi Arabia. Semiotic or culture-induced. Barakat,

no. 190.

Prayer: Hand covered by toga and laid against chin. Anc.
Rom. Ohm, p. 290.

Promise: Open palm of right hand rubbed down one's face
to the chin, then grasping chin with tips of fingers and thumb.
Saudi Arabia. Semiotic. Barakat, no. 170.

Rejection: Thumb is moved forward, tip to underside of
chin, and the whole hand catapults forward; or the same movement is made by the back of the right hand. Sicily. Pitrè,
p. 350. Spain. Cervantes, Don Quijote, II, chap. liv.
Flachskampf, p. 234.

Silence: Gently grazing chin of another person with right
fist: admonition not to argue. Saudi Arabia, Syria. Semiotic.
Barakat, no. 80.

Sorrow: Chin rests on both hands. Anc. Gk. and Rom.;
one hand: Ital. Bresciani, Edmondo, chap. iv. Sittl, p. 24.

Threat: Hand, index extended, shaken near someone's chin,
back of hand outward. Aubert, p. 91, fig. 138.

CHIN, HAND, KNEE
Pensiveness: "Thereupon [the knee] I placed my elbow; I had
placed into my hand the chin and one of my cheeks." Medieval
German. Walther v. d. Vogelweide, 8, 5ff. Cf. also the miniature in the Heidelberg Ms. C. Universitätsbibl. cpg. 848 (see
illustration 3). Cf. s.v. CHIN, HAND, Pensiveness and CHIN,
FOREHEAD, HAND, LEG, Pensiveness.

Plea: One hand grasps knee of another person, the other
hand the chin or beard, sometimes repeatedly. Performed
kneeling. Anc. Gk. Sittl, p. 165.

CLOTH, HAND
Farewell: Waving handkerchief. Thomas Mann, Buddenbrooks,
ch. xii.

Invitation: Dropping a handkerchief invites courtship. DEP,
2nd ed., p. 274.

Marriage: During prayer at marriage ceremony the newly
wedded pair is covered by a precious cloth. Medieval German.
Partonopier 10807; Schultz, I, p. 629; Zeller, p. 26.

CLOTHING, HAND
Apology: Cf. s.v. FINGER, Apology.

Applause: Waving a corner of a piece of clothing. Anc.
Gk. and Rom. Sittl, p. 62.

Attention: Cf. s.v. HAND, Attention.

Despair: Cf. s.v. HAND, Despair.

Determination: Cf. s.v. HAND, Determination.

Disapproval: Cf. s.v. HAND, Disapproval.

Disbelief: Right hand fingers tie, eyes half closed, mouth
puckered in condescending smile: "Oui, bien sûr...mais,
enfin..." French. Brault, p. 379. Hand(s) pull(s) up trouser
leg(s) as if one were wading through manure. Usually humorous.
Men. U.S. Saitz and Cervenka, p. 42.

Greeting: Cf. s.v. HEAD, Greeting. Waving clothing in

3. Walther von der Vogelweide; Heidelberg, Universitäts-Bibl., cpg. 848 (the Manesse Manuscript) (see CHIN, HAND, KNEE-- Pensiveness).

greeting over a distance. Plutarch, <u>Pomp.</u> 73.

Joy: "...was so relieved that he could not restrain his joy, but took off his little straw-hat and threw it up into the air. Trollope, <u>Can you forgive her</u>?, II, p. 258.

Ignorance: Cf. s.v. HAND, <u>Ignorance.</u>

Judgment: Tearing of clothes as sign of excommunication. May have originated at the Synod of Paris (577) called by Chilperic. Schilling, p. 141. Cf. also Aimoin, I, iii, c. 26, and

Wesselski, pp. 140ff. Grasping the coattail as symbol of con-
veyance of land or execution of a judgment. Medieval Low German. Schiller-Lübben, IV, p. 243. Judge ties a man's hands
together with a head-cloth: sign that the man is a felon. Saudi
Arabia. Semiotic. Barakat, no. 243. Bedouin spreads out
garment before judge and holds one end with his left hand then
smoothes it out with the right, indicating that he can obtain sufficient witnesses to substantiate his claim in a dispute. Rwala
Bedouin. Kuwait, Iraq, Syria, Saudi Arabia. Semiotic. Barakat, no. 204.

Luck: Upon seeing three priests or three negroes, a girl
scratch, knot her headscarf, which is to bring her luck in finding a husband. Colombia. Saitz and Cervenka, p. 83.

Mockery: Women raise skirts. Anc. Persian, anc. Egypt.,
anc. Gk. and Rom. Sittl, 104.

Mourning: Cf. s.v. HAND, Mourning.

Oath: The Frisians swore lesser oaths by their clothing or
the coattails. Grimm, DRA II, p. 550.

Poverty: Insides of trouserpockets pulled out. Men. Colombia, more common in U.S. Saitz and Cervenka, p. 90.
"gave four distinct slaps on the pocket of his mulberry inde-
scribables with his right as if to intimate that his master might
have done the same without alarming anybody much by the clinking of coin." Dickens, Pickw., I, p. 262.

Praise: Cf. s.v. HAND, Praise.

Pregnancy: Cf. s.v. HAND, Pregnancy.

Sorrow: Cf. s.v. FACE, Sorrow.

DOCUMENT, HAND

Judgment: Tearing the document of proscription. Since the
15th cent. v. Künssberg, p. 30; Tudichum, ZDR xx (1861), 158;
v. Möller, p. 68, n. 1. Tearing the bull of excommunication.
Since beginning of the 19th cent. v. d. Recke, p. 95.

EAR, EYE, HAND, LIP

Affection: Greek girls kiss one another on the eyes while holding the other's ears. Guys, I, p. 31; Sittl, p. 40.

EAR, FINGER

Approval: "the ear-pinching Portuguese" signal passage of an
attractive woman by pinching the ear. Birdwhistell, Introd.,
p. 9.

Cuckoldry: Fourth fingers of both hands placed in ears with
the backs of the hands forward and other fingers spread out.
Syria, Saudi Arabia, Lebanon. Semiotic. Barakat, no. 1.

Enthusiasm: Cf. s.v. FINGER, Enthusiasm.

Influence: "describing small circles in the air with the index finger of one hand in the area of the speaker's ear" signifies
the exercise of influence by someone close to a high official.

Madrid. Green, p. 73.
    Insult: Index rubs earlobe. ("I have no confidence in your
masculinity.") Ital. Graham, p. 26. A thumb placed in each
ear, flat hands up. Amer. schoolchildren. Seton, p. xxiii.
Tips of thumbs placed into ears or on temples, fingers spread,
palms to the front, fingers may or may not be waggled back and
forth. Children. Perry, "Gasoline Alley," Los Angeles Times
(Dec. 15, 1957).
    Interrogation: Earlobe rubbed with tips of right forefinger
and thumb. ("Do you want me to answer the question for you?")
Saudi Arabia. Semiotic or culture-induced. Barakat, no. 212.
    Pleasure: Wiggling ear lobe with thumb and index of right
hand. Univ. of Calif. Berkeley. King, p. 264.
    Silence: To exclude extraneous noise while telephoning, the
Lat. Amer. places tip of finger into unencumbered ear, the
Spaniard places tip of finger slightly below outer ear and pushes
upward. Green, pp. 51-52. Hooking extended index over ear
from the back, then moving it slowly over the ear to the front
signifies to a person not to argue with the gesticulator. Saudi
Arabia. Semiotic. Barakat, no. 224.
    Teasing: Picking the top of the right ear with right thumb
and index. Lebanon. Semiotic, possibly culture-induced. Bar-
kat, no. 58.
    Threat: Making a circular motion around the ear with the
index: mother's threat to child to behave or that she will attend to him later. Saudi Arabia. Semiotic. Barakat, no. 230.
Mother grasps earlobe with index and thumb: indicates that she
will admonish the child later and probably punish it. Used in
the presence of others. Saudi Arabia. Semiotic or culture-
induced. Barakat, no. 169.

EAR, FINGER, MOUTH
    Debauchery: Yawning, scratching behind ears with little finger.
Anc. Rom. Baden, p. 455.
    Magical: Priest moistens finger with his saliva and places
it upon upper lip and ears of candidate. Early Christian.
Duchesne, pp. 304-305. Baptism. Roman liturgy. Ohm,
p. 227: "At the words 'Ephpheta, quod est Adaperire' the priest
puts saliva on the ears [of the neophyte] and at the words 'In
odorem suavitatis. Tu autem effugare, diabole, appropinquabit
enim judicium Dei' on the nose."

EAR, HAND
    Amazement: Palm placed behind ear. Ghetto Jews. Efron,
p. 146.
    Anger: Both hands, palms at right angles to each other,
laid against ear. Anc. Rom. Sittl, p. 84. Spain. Flachskampf, p. 239. Hand scratches ear. Anc. Rom. Sittl, p. 19.
    Concentration: "When Mr. Pickwick arrived at this point,
Joe Trotter, with facetious gravity, applied his hand to his ear,
as if desirous not to lose a syllable he uttered." Dickens,
Pickw., I, p. 433.
    Disbelief: Scratching ear. Martial d'Auvergne, p. 320.

"The legate scratched himself thoughtfully behind his ear, the single one which remained to him since yesterday." Weissel, p. 99.

Dislike: Flicking the ear while referring to someone. Russian. E. Bowers, p. 98.

Displeasure: Hands placed over ears, so as not to hear. Anc. Gk. and Rom. Sittl, p. 85.

Gossip: Left ear cocked in direction of gossip, right arm extended downward, holding garment out from body. Woodcut, Brant, p. 276.

Greeting: The Gond pull one another's ears in salutation. Dawson, p. 94.

Indecision: Half-open right hand makes a downward and upward movement at the back of the ear, suggesting a semicircle formed downward. Spain. Flachskampf, p. 215.

Insult: Slap on ear. Anc. Gk. Sittl, p. 109. Hands, palm forward, lifted to head, thumbs in ears. Anc. Rom., not class. Gk. Sittl, pp. 109-110. Right thumb placed in right ear, remaining fingers wave, suggesting donkey's ears. Ital. De Jorio, p. 304; Sittl, p. 109. Ears are twisted, or thumbs placed in ears and fingers fluttered. Engl. children. Opie, p. 319. Tugging at one's ear questions the virility of the person at whom the gesture is directed. Time (Apr. 9, 1965), p. 68. Cf. s.v. EAR, FINGER, Insult.

Louder: "the constable put his hand behind his ear, to catch the reply." Dickens, Twist, p. 270. Hand held cupped behind one ear. Ruesch and Kees, p. 77.

Memory: Those present in the Roman senate were reminded to give their opinions by being pulled by the earlobe. Seneca, Apocol., traceable to the 6th cent.: Lex Baiuvar., 15, 2 (16, 6). Sittl, p. 146. Frequent in Bavarian law between the 8th and 12th centuries as reminder to witnesses. Grimm, DRA I, p. 199. In general the pulling of the ear, or slapping of someone's ear, is ancient Germanic and still in the 18th century boys' ears were pulled or slapped on important occasions so that they might always remember what they witnessed. Grimm, DRA I, p. 198. Plaintiff grasps witness by the earlobe to refresh his memory. Also in use generally, since the earlobe was considered the seat of memory. Anc. Rom. Sittl, p. 146.

Mockery: Hands, palm forward, lifted to head, thumbs in ears. Anc. Rom., not class. Gk. Sittl, pp. 109-110. Hands placed to ears make waving movements, suggesting donkey's ears. HDV I, p. 323.

Pederasty: Fondling the back of one's ear alludes to the pederasty of the person at whom the gesture is directed. Ital. Time (Apr. 9, 1965), p. 68.

Pensiveness: Pulling one's ear. Krout, p. 24.

Poverty: Right thumb placed in right ear, remaining fingers wiggle. Indicates that one lacks money. Portug. Flachskampf, p. 231; Urtel, p. 18.

Punishment: Slap on ear. Anc. Gk. Sittl, p. 109. Pulling one's own ear (e.g. in anticipation of punishment). Colombia.

Saitz and Cervenka, p. 98.
  Refusal: Cf. s. v. HAND, Refusal.
  Telephone: Fist rotates at side of ear, as if turning a
handle. Colombia. Hand closed, as if holding French telephone
receiver, held near ear. Colombia, U.S. Saitz and Cervenka,
p. 136.
  Warning: Touching, pulling earlobe or pushing it forward
slightly as if eavesdropping, is a warning of the presence of
secret police. Lat. Am. Kany, p. 121.

EAR, HAND, LEG
Adoration: "he crosses the hands, lets them hang, puts them
flat against the ears, kneels, stands up, throws himself to the
ground several times, arises again..." Mohammedan. Bauer,
p. 13.

EAR, HAND, LIP
Affection: While kissing, each person grasps the ears of the
other. Anc. Gk. and Rom. Sittl, p. 40. "The worthy old
gentleman pulled Arabella's ear, kissed her without the smallest
scruple, kissed his daughter also with great affection..." Dickens, Pickw., II, p. 452.

ELBOW
Avarice: Touching table with the elbow, saying "es codo" or
"suda antes por el codo que gastar un peso." Lat. Am. Kany,
p. 70.

ELBOW, EYE
Sorrow: " 'And what's become of the others, sir?'... The old
gentleman applied his elbow to his eye as he replied, 'Gone,
Tom, gone...' " Dickens, Pickw., I, p. 230.

ELBOW, FINGER
Foolishness: Fingertips of one hand joined and held at elbow of
the other arm, fingertips of the other hand also joined, hand
waving back and forth. Southern Ital. Efron, p. 157.

ELBOW, HAND
Avarice: In many regions of Lat. Amer. the left forearm is
held up with fist clenched, the right palm strikes the left elbow,
or the left elbow strikes any surface, and the clenched fist
opens. Kany, p. 70. Mexican Indian. Key, p. 94. Cupped
hand, or fist, strikes elbow several times in succession. Colombia. Saitz and Cervenka, p. 129.
  Foolishness: Fingertips of one hand are held together at
the elbow of the other arm, fingertips of other hand are also
held together while hand is waved back and forth. Southern
Ital. Efron, p. 157.
  Threat: Elbow half bent, right forearm is moved diagonally,
so that the right hand arrives near the shoulder, the hand remains there for a moment and then falls again. ("Will you shut
up?" "You deserve a slap." "Aren't you ashamed of yourself?"

"If I didn't restrain myself....") French. Mitton, p. 145.

ELBOW, MOUTH (Cf. ARM, MOUTH)

ELBOW, RIB
Attention: Neighbor is nudged with elbow. Proper only with close friends. Colombia, U.S. Saitz and Cervenka, p. 23.
Emphasis: " 'She's a Miss, she is; and yet she ain't a Miss--eh, Sir--eh?' And the stout gentleman playfully inserted his elbow between the ribs of Mr. Pickwick, and laughed very heartily." Dickens, Pickw., I, p. 61.
Reminder: Poking someone in the ribs with the elbow. Spain, Lat. Am. Green, p. 44.

EYE
Apotropy: Bride must weep on the way to church, for someone who weeps is not envied and is therefore safe from the evil eye. Poznan. Seligmann, II, p. 207. For the same reason one bites a child in the finger in order to make it weep. Bengal. Seligmann, ibid. Whoever is involuntarily the center of interest must look at his nose (Syria), at his nails (South Slavic) before looking at his relatives and friends. Seligmann, II, p. 287-288.
Approval: Winking eye. Usually performed by men. U.S., Colombia. Saitz and Cervenka, p. 20.
Attention: Looking at a person while closing one eye. French. Mitton, p. 145.
Awaken: "The clerk repeated the question thrice, and receiving no answer, prepared to shut the door, when the boy suddenly opened his eyes, winked several times,..." Dickens, Pickw., II, p. 433.
Concentration: Gaze directed at the sun while praying. Amaterasu cult of Shinto. Gaze directed at the shrine in the ancestor cult of Shinto. Ohm, p. 183. Gaze directed at point of nose during prayer. Yogi. Ohm, p. 184. Gaze fixed on navel. Hindu, Hesychasts, Palamites. Ohm, pp. 184-185. Fixing one's eyes in the distance without perceiving any object. Buddhist, Christian during prayer. Ohm, pp. 180-181.
Contempt: Closing of eyes during prayer not only aids concentration, but signifies contempt of surroundings. Buddhist, Christian. Ohm, p. 187. In the monastery of Tulasīdas, Benares, the monks sit in a corner and turn their backs to the world in order to separate themselves from it. Schjelderup, p. 149.
Conviviality: A quick wink of one eye. U.S. Saitz and Cervenka, p. 55.
Direction: "The priest raises his eyes to heaven when he elevates the host to denote that the oblation is made to God." Mass, p. 35.
Disbelief: Winking. Lat. Am. Kany, p. 70. U.S. Saitz and Cervenka, p. 40.
Dislike: Eyes closed. Late Rom. Sittl, p. 84.
Embarrassment: Wandering of the eyes. Anc. Gk. Sittl, p. 48. " 'Mamma!'...Georgiana protested,...and dropped her

eyes." Huxley, ch. xix.

Emphasis: Winking an eye to hint at emphasis. Portug.
Basto, p. 56.

Enmity: Eyes fixed on ground. Neapol. De Jorio, p. 188.

Facetiousness: "Here Mr. Weller winked the eye...with
such exquisite facetiousness, that two boys went into spontaneous
convulsions..." Dickens, Pickw., I, p. 314.

Fatigue: Blinking eyelids. Krout, p. 22. Drooping eyes.
ibid. Rubbing eyes. Krout, p. 25. Eyes closed, head inclined
laterally, cheek reposes on the back of one hand which is joined
to the other palm to palm. French. Mitton, p. 148. Cf. s.v.
EYE, HAND, HEAD, Fatigue.

Flirting: "This involved the necessity of looking up at the
windows also; and as the young lady was still there, it was an
act of common politeness to wink again, and to drink to her good
health in dumb show." Dickens, Pickw., II, p. 279. "Mr.
Samuel Weller had been staring up at the old red brick houses;
...bestowing a wink upon some healthy-looking servant girl as
she drew up a blind..." Dickens, Pickw., I, p. 386. Rolling
eyes. Krout, p. 24. Winking eye. Colombia, U.S. Saitz and
Cervenka, pp. 20, 55.

Gratitude: "Mr. Bumble raised his eyes piously to the ceiling in thankfulness." Dickens, Twist, p. 241. Cf. also s.v.
Mourning below.

Greeting: "Good friends who pass close to each other may
wink in greeting." Univ. of Calif. Berkeley. McCord, p. 291.
Weeping for joy. Gen. 43, 30ff.; 45, 2, 14ff.; I Sam. 20, 41,
etc. Ainu women weep when they meet after parting. Batchelor, pp. 101-106. Men and women observe the same custom in
the Andaman Islands. Man, pp. 147-148, pl. ix, fig. 2; Dawson, p. 95.

Humility: "he [the priest] again lowers his eyes in token of
his own unworthiness." Mass, p. 35.

Joy: Weeping. Boggs, p. 320.

Magical: One gets the evil eye if one turns around during
communion. Lauenburg, Mecklenburg, similarly in the Langue-
doc, if one turns around three times while the priest reads the
gospel. Seligmann, I, p. 175.

Mockery: Crossing the eyes. Univ. of Calif. Berkeley.
McCord, p. 291.

Modesty: Lowering eyes during prayer. Mod. Christian.
Ohm, p. 180.

Mourning: "She had one eye declined for the loss of her
husband, another elevated that the oracle was fulfilled." Shakesp.,
Winter's Tale II, ii, 81.

Passion: "The poet's eye, in a fine frenzy rolling."
Shakesp., Mids. Night's Dream V, i, 12.

Plea: Raising one's eyes to heaven as if seeking support or
confirmation of what one is saying. Madrid. Green, p. 80.
"'I hope you are not angry with me, sir!' said Oliver, raising
his eyes beseechingly." Dickens, Twist, p. 102.

Poverty: Closing both eyes and holding them closed while
saying "estoy así" or "ando ciego" or "estoy seco" or "ando

pato. " Argentina. Kany, p. 89.

Prayer: Whoever calls upon the manes turns the glance toward the ground. Seneca, Oedip. Sittl, p. 193. In praying to the Olympians, one glances toward heaven. Anc. Gk. and Rom. Sittl, ibid. Achilles looks toward the sea while praying. Iliad. Sittl, ibid. Eyes directed toward the sky. Prim. Germanic, Gk., Mohammedan, early Christian. Ohm, pp. 163ff. Eyes directed toward East or rising sun. Anc. Egypt., Babylonian, Roman. Ohm, pp. 168ff. Tibetan monks pray lying down on their backs, contemplating the sky and sun. Ohm, p. 186. Weeping during prayer. Anc. Germanic. Ohm, p. 200. Anc. Gk. Chryses praying to Apollo. Iliad. Islamic. Wensinck, p. 110; Goldziher, Islam, p. 304f. ; Ohm, p. 201. Particularly among the Sūfī. Lammeus, p. 138; Smith, pp. 155-157. India. Worship of Krishna. Grønbech, p. 150ff., and Japan, Ohm, p. 201. Christian. Verba sen., prol. 163; Chrysostomos, col. 685. Biblical. Ohm, p. 202. Not modern Christian. Ohm, p. 208. Lowering of eyes. Particularly Old Testament, but also Christian. Ohm, pp. 177-178. Kikuyus worshipping Nja are not allowed to look up during thunderstorm. Kenyatta, p. 310; Ohm, p. 178.

Prohibition: Eyes closed. Late Rom. Sittl, p. 84.

Recognition: One eye, looking in direction of referent, closes slowly. ("Creo que lo conozco. ") Colombia. Saitz and Cervenka, p. 99.

Secrecy: Winking any eye to imply having some secret knowledge, unknown to others, or inferring the understanding of some particular action, puzzling to others. Dickens, Pickw., I, pp. 190, 143, 262, 372, etc. (Cf. s. v. Understanding below.)

Shame: Lowering of the eyes. Ezra 9, 5f.; Luke 18, 13. Also common later. Heiler, p. 327; Ohm, p. 179.

Sorrow: Eye directed at the ground. Ohm, p. 166.

Surprise: "Opening her eyes very wide, she then closed them slowly and held them closed for several words. " Birdwhistell, Introd., p. 30. "The meeting looked at each other with raised eye-lids, and a murmur of astonishment ran through the room. " Dickens, Pickw., II, p. 72. Surprise is indicated by raising the eyes or opening them wide. Boggs, p. 321.

Sympathy: "It is conjectured that his unwillingness to hurt a fellow-creature intentionally was the cause of his shutting his eyes. " Dickens, Pickw., I, p. 35.

Understanding: Winking one eye indicates complicity. Spain, Lat. Am. Green, p. 44. Amer. schoolchildren. Seton, p. xxi. Shakesp., Mids. Night's Dream, III, ii, 238. " 'You wouldn't think to find such a room as this in the Farringdon Hotel, would you?' said Mr. Roker, with a complacent smile. To this Mr. Weller replied with an easy and unstudied closing of one eye; which might be considered to mean, either that he would have thought it, or that he would not have thought it, or that he had never thought anything at all about it: as the observer's imagination suggested. " Dickens, Pickw., II, 214. Winking at another person suggests that there is a secret between them or that one is putting the other on. Arab. Culture-induced. Bara-

kat, no. 162. (Cf. s.v. Secrecy above.) "Fearing their conversation in Agnew's office--adjacent to the White House--would
be overheard or taped, Green said he referred to the payment
as a political contribution. He said he raised his eyes to the
high ceiling in the room so that Agnew would understand the
reference." L.A. Times (Oct. 11, 1973), p. 1.

EYE, EYEBROW
Mistake: Eyebrows raised, eyes looking upward. Colombia,
U.S. Saitz and Cervenka, p. 52.

EYE, EYEBROW, FIST
Anger: Fists clenched in front, eyes staring, eyebrows drawn
down. Aubert, p. 121.

EYE, EYEBROW, HEAD, JAW
Ecstasy: Eyebrows raised, eyes turned toward heaven, head
thrown back, lower jaw dropped. Aubert, p. 144.

EYE, EYEBROW, HEAD, LIP
Pain: Raising eyebrows, dilated eyes, grinning, open lips, contraction of all facial muscles. Aubert, p. 141.
    Suffering: Eyebrows drawn down, fixed look, facial muscles
relaxed, head bowed, line of lips drawn low. Aubert, p. 116,
fig. 162.

EYE, EYEBROW, JAW
Concentration: Cf. s.v. Deception below.
    Deception: Lowering of brows, gaze directly ahead, jaws
tightly closed. Aubert, p. 114, fig. 160.
    Determination: Cf. s.v. Deception above.

EYE, FINGER
Admiration: Index pulls down lower eyelid, while the other hand
indicates object of admiration. Ital. N.Y. Times (March 1,
1959). Cf. s.v. FINGER, Admiration.
    Anger: Right index extended from fist, pointing upwards,
eyes looking upwards: anger or swearing an oath. Saudi Arabia,
Syria. Semiotic or culture-induced. Barakat, no. 72.
    Apotropy: Tip of right index on right eyelid, rubbing lightly:
bad luck to person to whom the gesture is directed or as pre-
vention of the evil eye. Saudi Arabia. Semiotic. Barakat, no.
73.
    Approval: Index touches skin below eye. Used frequently
to refer to members of opposite sex. Colombia. Saitz and
Cervenka, p. 19.
    Attention: Index pointed to eye, then to object to which at-
tention is to be directed. If no such object, the index is merely
pointed at the eye. Colombia. Saitz and Cervenka, p. 21.
    Awareness: Awareness of a secret: Index touches lower
lid of the right eye, sometimes pulls it down a little. Accompanying an "ojo!" Spain. Flachskampf, p. 236. Neapol. De
Jorio, p. 174. Roman, French. Meschke, p. 337.

Censure: Cf. s.v. EYE, HAND, Censure.

Cleverness: Index draws down the outer corner of the eye.
Neap. Critchley, p. 89.

Disbelief: Index pulls down lower eyelid. French. Life
(Sept. 16, 1946), pp. 12-15. Brault, p. 377: " 'Et mon oeil?'
The American expression 'In a pig's eye!' is a rough equivalent, but no such gesture is ever used." Index pulls down lower
lid of left eye. Near East. Critchley, p. 91. Exposing white
of eye with finger. Amer. schoolchildren. Seton, p. xxi. One
eye sometimes half closed, fist clenched, thumb points to speaker. U.S. Saitz and Cervenka, p. 41.

Distrust: Finger pulls down lower eyelid. Southern Ital.
Röhrich, p. 28 and pl. 12; also German soldiers, WW II. Ibid.,
p. 28.

Embarrassment: Shutting eye with fingers drawn together
and one hand behind the back. Anc. Rom. Baden, p. 453.

Fatigue: Forefinger in vicinity of right eye. Brant, p. 114.

Greeting: Forefinger pointed, thumb raised, then brought
down in imitation of the hammer of a pistol. A wink often accompanies this gesture. Informal, slightly patronizing. Univ.
of Calif. King, p. 264.

Insult: Tip of right index placed on lower lid of right eye
implies that the person to whom the gesture is made is stupid.
Saudi Arabia. Semiotic. Barakat, no. 34.

Jealousy: Shutting eye with fingers drawn together. Teren-
tian masks. Anc. Rom. Baden, p. 452. Same, with one hand
behind back. Ibid.

Leniency: Looking with one eye through spread fingers of
one hand placed vertically upon the face. Röhrich, p. 34, pl.
37. Cf. s.v. FINGER, Understanding.

Magical: Finger pulls down lower eyelid = the evil eye.
Röhrich, pp. 27-28.

Nothing: Finger pulls down lower eyelid. Insolent, vulgar.
French. Mitton, p. 150.

Readiness: Index tugs loose skin below lower eyelid. Spain,
Lat. Am. Green, p. 77. Pointing to the eye with the index.
Spain. Green, p. 77.

Sorrow: With index at each eye, trace course of tears.
Mock sorrow. Amer. schoolchildren. Seton, pp. xxi, 54.

Surprise: Shutting eye with fingers drawn together, one
hand behind the back. Anc. Rom. Baden, p. 453.

Suspicion: Cf. s.v. Surprise above.

Warning: Index touches lower eyelid of right eye, sometimes pulls it down a little. Portugal, Spain, Morocco, France.
Flachskampf, p. 236.

EYE, FINGER, MOUTH, TONGUE

Mockery: Sticking out tongue and at same time pulling down
lower eyelids with indexes of both hands, while middle fingers
stretch corners of mouth. Hans Maler, "Christ bearing Cross,"
Chicago Art Inst.

EYE, FOREHEAD
Fear: Forehead furrowed in pain, eyes opened wide. Insane. Krukenberg, p. 132.

EYE, HAND
Affection: Hands of beloved pressed against one's eyes. Anc. Gk. and Rom. Sittl, p. 34.

Amazement: "signified his amazement on the whole, by lifting up his eyes and hands..." Smollett, Random, ch. xliv. "There was casting up of eyes, holding up of hands." Shakesp., Winter's Tale, V, ii, 51.

Anger: Lift hands and eyes, strike three times on stomach. Butler, I, ii; R. H. Bowers, p. 271.

Blessing: "The priest looking up to God, raises his hands, folds them reverently, and makes the Sign of the Cross over the oblation." Mass, p. 37.

Censure: Pulling down the skin of the lower eyelid. Partic. to children eyeing toys. Arab. Bauer, p. 222.

Concentration: "As Tom was gazing at a chair, it seemed to change and assume the features and expression of an old shrivelled human face, so he rubbed his eyes as though to wipe away the illusion." Dickens, Pickw., I, p. 226.

Confidence: Eyes steady and directly forward, one hand in pocket, the other forward and holding paper. Birdwhistell, Colliers (March 4, 1955), p. 57.

Disbelief: Rubbing eyes. Mod. Gk. and Ital. Bresciani, c. viii; Sittl, p. 47.

Displeasure: Hands and eyes raised. "Such aggravating looks; such lifting up of hands and eyes; such a furrowed forehead, in my sister!" Richardson, Clarissa, I, p. 148.

Distress: "Messrs. Dodson and Fogg intreated the plaintiff to compose herself. Sergeant Buzfuz rubbed his eyes very hard with a large white handkerchief..." Dickens, Pickw., II, p. 79.

Fatigue: Fist placed in each eye. Amer. schoolchildren. Seton, p. xxi. Hand, palm to face, moves slowly across brow or eyes. Colombia, U.S. Saitz and Cervenka, p. 144.

Helplessness: "He looks at him with a pitiful expression. Closes his eyes and wrings his hand in a gesture of helplessness." Weyland, p. 19.

Horror: Cf. s.v. HAND, Horror.

Magnitude (amount of money): Hitting or patting of the flat hand against the pocket, simultaneously looking alternatively at the person one is talking to and at one's pocket. Arab. Bauer, p. 221.

Mourning: Holding cloak before one's eyes. Odyss., Bk. iv.

Oath: Hand laid on eyes. Samoan. Röhrich, p. 12.

Prayer: Arms bent at elbow, forearms lifted skyward, fingers closed, palms pressed together, eyes skyward. Woodcut in Brant, p. 72.

Recognition: "he began to gaze in the same direction, at the same time shading his eyes with his hand, as if he partially recognized the object... and wished to make quite sure of its

identity. " Dickens, Pickw., I, p. 330.
    Refusal: Cf. s. v. HAND, Refusal.
    Rejection: "At this inquiry, Mrs. Weller raised her hands
and turned up her eyes, as if the subject were too painful to be
alluded to. " Dickens, Pickw., I, p. 449.
    Self-gratitude: "...and after such feasts, upon meeting
gruff Pnin, Serafima and Oleg (she raising her eyes to heaven,
he covering his with one hand) would murmur in awed self-
gratitude: 'Gospodi, skol'ko mi im dayom!' (My, what a lot we
give them!)--'them' being the benighted American people. "
Nabokov, p. 71.
    Sorrow: " 'Where,' said Mr. Tupman, with an effort--
where is--she, Sir?' and he turned away his head, and covered
his eyes with his hand. " Dickens, Pickw., I, p. 297. "At the
conclusion of this address,...Mr. Jingle applied to his eyes the
remnant of a handkerchief... " Dickens, Pickw., I, p. 128.
    Surprise: Cf. s. v. Amazement above.
    Time: Glance at wrist. Colombia, U.S. Saitz and Cer-
venka, p. 143.
    Understanding: Index of right hand pulls down the lower eye-
lid. Anc. Rom. Meschke, col. 337.
    Warning: Index pointed at the eye means "look out for that
fellow!" Southern Ital. Efron, p. 154.

EYE, HAND, HEAD
Curiosity: Blinking one eye, head turned slightly to side and
moved forward, hand moved forward and to the side, fingers
somewhat apart. Accompanied by "What's up?" Arab. Bauer,
p. 223.
    Fatigue: Putting head sideways with eyes closed, resting it
upon the right hand. Spain. Flachskampf, p. 230. Eyes closed,
head inclined to one side, cheek leaning against two hands placed
palm to palm. French. Mitton, p. 148. Cf. s. v. CHEEK,
HAND, Fatigue; EYE, Fatigue.

EYE, HAND, MOUTH
Disbelief: Eyes fixed and straight ahead, hands folded in front
of mouth. Birdwhistell, Colliers (March 4, 1955), p. 57.

EYE, HEAD
Attention: Head to one side, gaze directly forward, eyebrows
raised, smile. Aubert, p. 130. Head to one side, eyes turned
to the side. Listening. Aubert, p. 104.
    Concentration: Fixed look, head forward. Aubert, p. 98.
    Curiosity: Cf. Concentration above.
    Disapproval: Head raised, angry glance. Anc. Gk. and
Rom. Sittl, p. 93.
    Greeting: Head inclined forward, eyelids droop. Aubert,
p. 97, fig. 141.
    Interrogation: Look, nod, brows raised. Seton, p. xxiii.
    Mockery: Nodding head or winking at someone who is a
stranger. Plutarch, cf. Bresciani, Edmondo, ch. vii; Sittl,
p. 94.

Modesty: Bending head forward, drooping eyelids. Aubert, p. 97, fig. 141. Head bowed, glance downward. Krukenberg, p. 256.

Pointing: Nod of head and movement of eyes indicating location. Siriono Indians, Chama Indians (Bolivia). Key, p. 94.

Surprise: Head raised, astonished glance. Anc. Gk. Sittl, p. 93.

Uncertainty: Head to one side, eyes turned to the side. Aubert, p. 104.

Understanding: " 'That 'ere young lady, ' replied Sam. 'She knows wat's wot, she does. Ah, I see. ' Mr. Weller closed one eye and shook his head from side to side... " Dickens, Pickw., II, p. 140.

EYE, HEAD, LIP, TOOTH

Pleasure: Head back, eyes cast upward. Upper eyelids drooping. Eyebrows raised, line of lips stretched taut to disclose upper teeth. Aubert, p. 134.

EYE, HEAD, MOUTH, NOSE

Discouragement: Head drawn backwards, frown, eyes squinting, raised nose, corners of mouth drawn down. Aubert, pp. 111-112.

Disgust: Cf. s.v. Discouragement above.

Distrust: Cf. s.v. Discouragement above.

EYE, JAW

Depravity: Eyebrows raised, drooping of upper eyelids, jaw, and all the muscles of the lower part of the face. Aubert, p. 135.

Exclamation: Glance upward, dropping of jaw. Aubert, p. 110.

Horror: Frown, eyes wide open, dropping lower jaw. Aubert, p. 118.

EYE, LIP

Relief: "Peyrol did not take his eyes off Catherine's straight back till the door had closed after her. Only then he relieved himself by letting the air escape through his pursed lips and rolling his eyes freely about. " Conrad, p. 179.

EYE, LIP, NOSE

Disgust: Lips turned outward and pulled apart, upper lip raised, mouth assumes rectangular form, nostrils flare, eyes closed. Krukenberg, p. 257.

EYE, LIP, TOOTH

Frustration: "One turned up his eyes to heaven, and bit his nether lip. " Smollett, Peregr. Pickle, ch. lxix.

Silence: Biting lips, eyes lowered. Anc. Gk. Sittl, p. 54. Biting lips, winking. Arab. Bauer, p. 222.

EYE, MOUTH
Affection: Kiss on eyes. Among men. Anc. Rom. Sittl,
p. 40. In general. Anc. Gk. and Rom. Sittl, ibid.
    Anger: Eyes wide open, clenched teeth, lips pulled back so
that teeth are visible. Krukenberg, p. 257.
    Cunning: Lowered eyelids, raised eyebrows, face muscles
tense, lips tightly closed. Krukenberg, p. 254.
    Magnitude: Lips pursed, eye muscles contracted. Women,
speaking of something small. Krukenberg, p. 118. Mouth and
eyes are opened wide in relating something large or important.
Krukenberg, ibid.
    Sorrow: Deep and irregular breathing and raising of the
eyes. Boggs, p. 319.
    Warning: One eye closed, the other wide open, face drawn
down, lips pursed. Aubert, p. 106.

EYE, NAVEL
Prayer: Staring at one's navel. Hindu, Hesychasts. Ohm,
pp. 184-185.

EYE, NOSE
Prayer: Staring at tip of one's nose. Yoga. Ohm, p. 184.

EYE, TONGUE
Contempt: Alternately winking with left and right eye, lips
stretched laterally, tip of tongue protruded. Spain. Alas, p. 6.

EYEBROW (Cf. s.v. FOREHEAD)
Affirmation: Eyebrows pulled down. Anc. Gk. and Rom., mod.
Gk., Neapol. De Jorio, p. 40; Sittl, p. 92.
    Anger: "How eagerly I taught my brow to frown." Shakesp.,
Two Gent., I, ii, 62; Hamlet, I, ii, 231; etc.
    Anticipation: "and elevating his eyebrows in a rapture of
anticipation." Dickens, Twist, p. 170.
    Arrogance: Raised eyebrows. Anc. Gk. and Rom. Sittl,
p. 94. Spain, 18th cent. Cadalso, p. lxxxii.
    Concentration: "See how the ugly witch doth bend her brows,
as if, with Circe, she would change my shape!" Shakesp.,
Henry VI, V, iii, 34.
    Disapproval: "Why do you bend such solemn brows on me?
Think you I bear the shears of destiny?" Shakesp., King John,
IV, ii, 90. "...and I confess that my conduct in the City, as
the Wodehouse story puts it, would have caused raised eyebrows
in the fo'c's'le of a pirate sloop." Carr, To Wake the Dead,
p. 87.
    Disbelief: "slowly raised and lowered one eyebrow." Bird-
whistell, Introd., p. 33.
    Disdain: Forehead wrinkled, eyes together, moving from
side to side, head moves from side to side at irregular intervals, cheeks distend. Pretending to know more than one is saying. Feijóo, in del Rio, II, 6a.
    Displeasure: "...and many good young people considered it
a treat and an honor to see Pnin pull out a catalogue drawer

from the... card cabinet and take it... to a secluded corner and there make a quiet mental meal of it, now moving his lips in soundless comment, critical, satisfied, perplexed, and now lifting his rudimentary eyebrows and forgetting them there, left high upon his spacious brow where they remained long after all trace of displeasure or doubt had gone." Nabokov, p. 76.

Flirting: Eyebrows moving up and down rapidly. Lebanon, Saudi Arabia. Semiotic, possibly autistic. Barakat, no. 101.

Ignorance: "One curious, patient gesture which never entirely left Ishi was characteristic of him in those days--a raising high of his mobile, arched eyebrows. It was an expression of wonder, but also of ignorance, of incomprehension, like our shrugging of the shoulders." Kroeber, p. 124.

Impatience: Frowning. Protug. Basto, p. 45.

Interrogation: "Luke's glance turned to the man in the horn-rimmed spectacles and his brows rose enquiringly." Allingham, p. 78. " 'It's almost certain, isn't it, that in writing down that he did take out an insurance policy he'll make some reference to why he did it?' She paused, raising her eyebrows." Carr, Constant Suicides, p. 155.

Negation: Eyebrows raised. Anc. Gk. and Rom. Sittl, p. 93.

Prohibition: Eyebrows raised. Odyss. Sittl, p. 93.

Scepticism: Cf. Birdwhistell s.v. Surprise below.

Surprise: Eyebrows raised. Krout, p. 24. "...lawyer is often a master of the raised eyebrow." Birdwhistell, Colliers (March 4, 1955), p. 56.

Teasing: Eyebrows moved up and down rapidly. Saudi Arabia, Syria. Culture-induced or semiotic. Barakat, no. 194.

Threat: Frowning. Portug. Basto, p. 45.

EYEBROW, FINGER

Homosexuality: Wetting tip of right little finger, it is then rubbed along right eyebrow: indicates that person spoken to or about is homosexual. Lebanon. Semiotic. Barakat, no. 39.

Shame: Tip of right index finger placed between eyebrows. May also be an admission of inability to do something. Saudi Arabia. Semiotic. Barakat, no. 229.

EYEBROW, FINGER, NOSE

Disapproval: "...nostrils are pinched between the thumb and forefinger with fingers 3, 4, and 5 remaining lax and with the brows bi-laterally and minimally raised." Birdwhistell, Introd., p. 9.

EYEBROW, FOOT, HEAD, MOUTH

Confusion: Head bowed, crosswise and double movement of the eyebrows, lips taut, weight of body on backward foot. Aubert, p. 137.

EYEBROW, HAND, HEAD

Perplexity: Head is scratched, eyebrows raised, lips often pursed. Colombia, more frequent in U.S. Saitz and Cervenka,

p. 135.
Remorse: Cf. s.v. EYEBROW, FOOT, HEAD, MOUTH,
Confusion.

EYEBROW, HAND, MOUTH
Surprise: Eyebrows raised, mouth open, hands placed on cheeks.
U.S.   Saitz and Cervenka, p. 135.

EYEBROW, HEAD
Attention: Cf. s.v. EYE, HEAD, Attention.
Despair: Eyebrows drawn down, fixed look, facial muscles
relaxed, head bowed low.   Aubert, p. 117.
Dignity: Head raised, brows lowered.   Aubert, p. 113.
Interrogation: Cf. s.v. EYE, HEAD, Interrogation.
Surprise: Eyebrows raised, head tilted or turned.   Colom-
bia, U.S.   Saitz and Cervenka, p. 134.

EYEBROW, HEAD, JAW
Interest: Head forward, lower jaw relaxed, eyebrows raised.
Aubert, p. 123.

EYEBROW, HEAD, LIP
Appetite: Head advanced and tilted backward, eyebrows raised,
slightly contracted, lips pursed.   Aubert, p. 125.
Attention: Cf. s.v. EYE, HEAD, Attention.
Desire: Cf. s.v. Appetite above.
Discouragement: Eyebrows drawn down, fixed glance, facial
muscles relaxed, head bowed, lips drawn down.   Aubert, p. 116,
fig. 162.
Greeting: Eyebrows raised and lowered quickly, often with
nod or smile.   Casual, across distance.   Colombia, U.S.   Saitz
and Cervenka, p. 69.
Perplexity: Cf. s.v. Discouragement above.

EYEBROW, HEAD, SHOULDER
Agreement: Eyebrows raised, head nodding, shoulders raised.
Spain, 18th cent.   Cadalso, ch. lxxx.

EYEBROW, JAW
Boredom: Lowering and drawing together of the eyebrows, jaws
contracted, corners of mouth drawn down.   Aubert, p. 115, fig.
161.
Concentration: Cf. s.v. Boredom above.
Depravity: Eyebrows raised, drooping of upper eyelids, jaw,
and all the muscles of the lower part of the face.   Aubert,
p. 135.
Desperation: Cf. s.v. Boredom above.
Disappointment: Raised and frowning brows, jaw lowered,
corners of mouth drawn down.   Aubert, p. 136.
Sorrow: (esp. after being punished).   Cf. s.v. Disappointment above.
Weakmindedness: Eyebrows raised, drooping of eyelids, jaw,
and all muscles of lower part of face.   Aubert, p. 135.

EYEBROW, LIP
Disbelief: Cf. s.v. EYEBROW, MOUTH, Disbelief.
Sorrow: Eyebrows drawn down, corners of mouth pulled down, lower lip forward. Krukenberg, p. 132.

EYEBROW, LIP, HEAD
Flirting: Head leaning to side, eyebrows raised, lips smiling and slightly pursed. Aubert, p. 126.

EYEBROW, MOUTH
Disbelief: Eyebrows raised, corners of mouth drawn down. Can also indicate disparagement. U.S. Saitz and Cervenka, p. 41.
Sorrow: Cf. s.v. EYEBROW, LIP, Sorrow.
Surprise: Eyebrows raised, eyes fully open, mouth open. U.S. Saitz and Cervenka, p. 135.

EYEBROW, MOUTH, SHOULDER
Amazement: Eyebrows raised, mouth open, shoulder raised. Aubert, p. 143.
Ignorance: Shoulders hunched, eyebrows raised, corners of mouth drawn down. Aubert, p. 128.
Uncertainty: Cf. s.v. Ignorance above.

EYELID (Cf. s.v. EYE)
Command: At a meal, the order for wine is given by looking at the wine steward and lowering the left and right eyelids alternately. Anc. Rom. Sittl, p. 220.
Hypocrisy: Glancing through nearly closed eyelids. Aubert, p. 101.
Negation: Eyelids raised. Anc. Rom. Sittl, p. 93.
Prohibition: Cf. s.v. Negation above.

EYELID, FINGER (Cf. s.v. EYE, FINGER)
Oath: Right index placed on right upper eyelid. Saudi Arabia. Semiotic. Barakat, no. 157.
Proxy: Touching lower eyelid with right index indicates one's readiness to act as proxy. Moving the finger from right to left while on the eyelid is a variant. Saudi Arabia. Barakat, no. 192.

FACE (Cf. s.v. HEAD)
Affection: Blush. Medieval French. Lommatzsch, p. 73. Medieval German. Nibelungenlied, st. 285, 4; 292, 2.
Anger: Red face, contraction of cheek-, mouth-, chin-, or brow-muscles. Boggs, col. 321. Twisting one side of face. Syria. Autistic. Barakat, no. 193.
Apotropy: Contorting face against the evil eye. Bothnia, India. Seligmann, II, p. 287.
Contempt: "Turn away her face." Shakesp., Love's Lab. Lost, V, ii, 148.

Disapproval: "a dead-pan look." Birdwhistell, Colliers (March 4, 1955), p. 56.

Mockery: "laughing...grinning contemptuously." Boggs, col. 321.

Mourning: Face turned away from funeral pyre while lighting it. Vergil, Aen. Sittl, p. 73. Covering face. II Sam. 19, 4.

Rejection: "The Lord will not turn away his face from you." II Chr. 30, 9.

Shame: Blush. Ital. Ariosto, 20, 130-31. Med. French. Lommatzsch, p. 71. "Ah, now thou turnst away thy face for shame!" Shakesp., Titus Andr., II, iv, 28.

Sorrow: Cloak drawn over face. Anc. Gk. and Rom. Sittl, p. 275. "For when the noble Caesar saw him stab ingratitude...quite vanquish'd him. Then burst his mighty heart, and in his mantle, muffling up his face,..." Shakesp., Caesar, III, ii, 192.

Submission: "...fell before the throne on their faces." Luke 24, 5. Also I Sam. 5, 3 and 28, 14.

FACE, HAND (Cf. s.v. HAND, HEAD)

Anger: Beating the face. Anc. Gk. and Rom. Sittl, p. 20.

Apotropy: Crossing the face. Medieval Spain. Cid, 20, 411. Crossing oneself to ward off the devil or for luck, as when a field is sown or a new loaf of bread is cut. Early Christian. Meschke, col. 335.

Concentration: Supporting face with hands. Krout, p. 26.

Confusion: Hiding face in hands. Portug. Basto, p. 24.

Curse: Priests and priestesses turn towards the West and shake purple cloths. Anc. Gk. Sittl, p. 197.

Despair: "...and covering his face with his hands, threw himself upon the grass." Dickens, Pickw., I, p. 98. Beating the face. Anc. Gk. and Rom. Sittl, p. 20.

Disgust: Face hidden behind hands. Anc. Gk. and Rom. Sittl, p. 84.

Dislike: Cf. s.v. Disgust above.

Embarrassment: Rubbing face with hand. Anc. Gk. and Rom. Sittl, p. 47. " 'Well, young sir, what do you learn at school?' was a standing question with uncle Pullet; whereupon Tom always looked sheepish, rubbed his hand across his face, and answered, 'I don't know.' " Eliot, p. 460.

Fatigue: Supporting face with hands. Krout, p. 26.

Fear: Hiding the face. Exod. 3, 6.

Horror: Cf. s.v. HAND, Horror.

Ignorance (pretended): Hand held over face, fingers extended to permit vision. Woodcut, Brant, p. 89.

Insult: Cf. s.v. HAND, Insult.

Jail: Spread fingers cover face as one says "Qué pena!" Lat. Am. Kany, p. 117.

Mourning: "...men and women were beating their faces and uttering loud cries, as it is the custom to do in the East when someone is dead." Frazer, IV, p. 8. Scratching face. Women. Anc. Gk. and Rom. Sittl, p. 27. Hands beating face.

Men. Anc. Gk. and Rom. Sittl, p. 24.

Nervousness: Rubbing face with hand. Anc. Gk. and Rom. Sittl, p. 49.

Prayer: One or both hands held in front of face. African negroes, Egyptians, Hittites, anc. Crete, anc. Germanic tribes. Ohm, p. 289.

Shame: Motion of pulling blanket over face. Gt. Plains Indians. Kroeber, IJAL 24, 10. Cf. Odyssey, bk. viii. Hiding face in hands. Portug. Basto, p. 24. Amer. schoolchildren. Seton, p. xxi.

Shock: Face hidden behind hands when suddenly seeing corpse. Anc. Rom. Sittl, p. 84.

Sick: Grimace accompanied by limp dropping of hands. Amer. schoolchildren. Seton, p. xxii.

Sorrow: Scratching face. Women. (Cf. s.v. Mourning above.) Sittl, p. 27. Covering face. II Sam. 19, 4. Hands placed vertically over face. Anc. Gk. and Rom. Sittl, p. 275. Hands beating face. Men. Anc. Gk. and Rom. Sittl, p. 24. Hands over face. Medieval German. Haseloff, p. 306.

FACE, HAND, KNEE

Adoration: Right hand touches knees of adored, left hand reaches up to touch face. Performed kneeling. Permitted as form of adoration during later Roman empire. Sittl, p. 165.

Affection: Cf. s.v. Adoration above.

Sorrow: Face placed on knees of a friend. Women. Anc. Gk. and Rom. Sittl, p. 34.

FINGER

Acceptance: "During Islamic conquest, a raised forefinger of the right hand signified acceptance of Islam." Quoted from Encycl. Mensuelle d'Outre-Mer, p. 10 by Hayes, p. 247.

Admiration: Index and thumb of right hand are placed respectively above and below the eye as if to make the eye larger. Spain. Flachskampf, p. 98. Cf. s.v. EYE, FINGER, Admiration. Placing thumb and index together to form a circle. French. WW II. Alsop, p. 28. Mouth firm, somewhat drooped, thumb of right hand erect and pushed forward as if pushing thumbtack, signifying "first class": "Elle est comme ça!" French. Brault, p. 379. "I recently observed a French student using an amusing variant of this gesture to describe admiringly a pretty girl's figure: the thumb is moved downwards in a configuration approximating a large 'S,' delineating in profile a form which an American would outline frontally with both hands as a figure 8." Brault, ibid. Thumb extended from right fist but not moving it: item referred to is best. Libya. Semiotic. Barakat, no. 86.

Admonition: Wagging the index. Western culture. Austin, pp. 594-595. Extended index, usually of the right hand. Painting of Camillus and Brennus by Perino del Vaga (c.1525) in Elworthy, Horns, p. 40, fig. 20; cf. also n. 171 in Taylor, p. 53.

Affection: Touching finger of beloved. Anc. Gk. Sittl,

p. 34.

Affirmation: Thumb and '
circle = o. k. L. A. Times
thumb of left hand form righ'
curls around left thumb, mi'
are snapped. ("You guesse'
Holding up the thumb. Ru'
index lowered. Amer. In'
Agreement: The two '
rubbed together. Near E
pushing someone with a '
medieval German. Grir'
fingers of right hands a'
ly repeating a warning = ıı.
Opie, p. 130. Indexes of both hanu.
lightly closed. Tips of indexes touch and ʋ.
Southern Ital. Efron, p. 59. " 'We didn't come u.
Jesús, ' said Concha. Jesús grinned broadly and made an ..
pressive gesture of thumb and middle finger. 'Hokay, Señorita
Pelayo. ' " Boucher, p. 206.

Anger: Fingers of both hands are extended to threaten the
eyes of one who has extended the fingers of one hand to threaten
the eyes of the former. Mod. Gk. Sittl, p. 46. Fingers of
one hand are pushed toward the eyes of another. Bresciani,
Ebreo, ch. xxxxix. Index and little finger stretched out as
threat toward someone's eyes. Neapol. De Jorio, p. 94. Extended index or all fingers pointed to the eyes of another. Anc.
Gk. Sittl, p. 45. In saying "están de punta" or "están así" the
tips of the fingers are struck together. Lat. Am. Kany, p. 64.
In this gesture the fingers may be reinforced by the extended
small fingers. Variation: Nails and knuckles of the two thumbs
may be struck together. Kany, ibid. The little fingers are,
hooked together and then released. This is repeated two or
three times. Near East. Critchley, p. 91.

Apology: After someone has said something pejorative about
someone else, he asks God's forgiveness and simultaneously
grasps his coat at his chest with two fingers and shakes it, as
if he wanted to shake dust off. Arab. Bauer, p. 222.

Apotropy: Cf. s. v. HAND, Apotropy. Thumb of right hand
placed into left, thumb of left hand into right. Talmud. Seligmann, II, p. 183. Raising index, middle and ringfinger in protection against evil spirits and illnesses. Early Christian.
Sittl, p. 329. The "fig" (clenched fist, thumb protruded between
middle and ringfinger) in form of amulet against barrenness.
Southern Germany. Röhrich, p. 20. Amulet thumbs worn
around neck against the evil eye. Rio de Janeiro. Seligmann,
II, p. 183. The "fig" as talisman against witchcraft. Temple
of Isis in Pompey. Chevalier, p. 283. The "fig" is made to
raise the spell of an evil oath. Meschke, col. 334. The "fig"
is made to someone whom one praises, to protect him from evil.
Yugoslavia. Röhrich, p. 20. The "fig" is made by a child
while clothing which he is wearing is being repaired "so that his
sense is not sewn up. " German. Röhrich, p. 20. The Jews

sia, if their children are admired or caressed,
admired child to make the "fig" behind the back
er. Globus, LIII, p. 316. The "fig" can be made
Ferdinand I of Naples, when in public, often made
his pocket against the evil eye. Röhrich, p. 20. Cf.
schke, col. 334. The "horns" (index and little finger
ed, other fingers folded down): " 'Oh, sure. But give
the sign once in a while and you'll have no trouble. ' He
beside his wife and pointed at her with extended first and
ittle fingers. " MacDonald, p. 73. "Then [the mortician] de-
cided to expand his business and established a second funeral
parlor on the other side of [the butchershop]. And with that, the
signore and the housemaids suddenly began to avoid the butcher-
shop like the plague. 'The customers, ' said [the butcher],
'thought that the dead bodies were casting an evil eye on my
veal chops...' ...this left him no choice but to transform his
shop into one giant amulet 'to beat the whammy once and for
all. ' Since many Italians believe that horns can jab away the
evil spirits of death, the embattled butcher ordered an 'arena of
horns' from Rome's abattoir... " Newsweek (Feb. 28, 1966),
p. 42. If the "horns" are jabbed with index and little fingers
toward the ground, they are used apotropaically. If the fingers
point upward, the gesture implies cuckoldry. Ital. Time (Apr.
9, 1965), p. 68. Its apotropaic use is also implied in a mosaic
of St. Luke in the church of San Vitale, Ravenna. Additional
instances in Elworthy, pp. 149, 174-175. The "horns" were
used in antiquity to chase away evil spirits by virtue of the di-
vinity of bulls' horns. French. Mitton, p. 149. "Horns"
against the evil eye. Spain. Flachskampf, p. 249; Sittl, p. 124.
"We cannot even remark on our good health without touching
wood or crossing our fingers or otherwise averting the gods'
anger at mortal well-being... " Tey, p. 144. Crossing fingers
(middle and index) against demons. Anc. Rom. Ohm, p. 274.
U.S. (used while lying, to ward off evil that lying might cause).
Saitz and Cervenka, p. 82. Cracking one's fingers to frighten
off evil spirits. Meschke, col. 336. When someone yawns,
Indians snap their fingers (middle finger against thumb) in order
to prevent the soul from leaving the body. HDA, II, col. 1489.
Snapping the fingers (index or middle finger against thumb) in
front of one's ear as a defense against demons which make the
ears ring. German. HDA, I, col. 322. Fingers pressed together (tip of index to tip of thumb?) against evil encounters,
such as with pigs. Anc. Rom. Sittl, p. 125. German.
Grimm, DWb, II, col. 849. "Present [the "fig"] towards the
person of whom you are afraid, but do it unobserved, and you
are safe. " Martial, Ep. 28. NQ (Oct. 5, 1867), p. 261.
Waving index of left hand three times after a witch. East
Prussia. Meschke, col. 336. Snapping fingers against ghosts.
HDA II, col. 1489. Snapping fingers when someone yawns to
prevent soul from leaving body. India. Ibid. Folding thumb
under fingers against evil eye. Spain, Ireland, Bretagne,
Noirmoutier. Seligmann, II, p. 178. Fist clenched, middle
finger extended. ("Mönch stechen. ") Meschke, col. 331;

("digitus infamis") HDA II, col. 1492f. and Seligmann, II,
p. 183.   Cf. s.v. Mockery below for "einen Mönch stechen"
[i.e. to stick a monk].   Cf. s.v. FINGER, HAND, Oath.

Applause: Thumbnails tapping against one another, one hand
held above the other.   Colombia.   Ironic applause.   Panama.
Saitz and Cervenka, p. 111.

Approach: (Cf. s.v. HAND, Approach.)   The master snaps
his fingers as signal for servant to approach.   At table this
meant that the matella is necessary.   Anc. Rom.   Sittl, pp. 222-
223.   Snapping middle finger against thumb to call a servant.
Anc. Rom.   Baden, p. 450.   Calling animals, one snaps middle
finger against thumb, palm facing down.   Spain.   Flachskampf,
p. 226.   Snapping index and thumb: call for someone to approach.   Saudi Arabia.   Semiotic.   Barakat, no. 182.   Index
crooked, moving repeatedly toward gesturer.   Familiar.   French.
Mitton, p. 143.   Rhetor calls his students together by snapping
his fingers.   Early Christian.   Sittl, p. 223.   Palm down,
fingers closed, index repeatedly straightened and bent.   Southern
Ital., southern Balkans, Near East, North Africa.   Röhrich,
p. 13 and pl. 7.   Also palm down, all fingers repeatedly
straightened and bent.   Spain, Portug., Morocco, Turkey, Arab
countries, southern Italy, Greece.   Flachskampf, p. 225.   Palm
up, fingers repeatedly straightened and bent: northern and central Europe, the Po-plain and Toscana.   In Naples both forms
(palm up and palm down) are used.   Flachskampf, ibid.   "He
beckoned to him slightly" Dickens, Twist, p. 229.   "'Oliver,'
cried Fagin, beckoning to him..." ibid., p. 503.   "...beckon-
ing furiously to his confederate." ibid., p. 248.   "Holding up
one finger and shouting..." to summon a taxi.   Univ. of Calif.
Berkeley.   McCord, 291.   One finger is used to beckon to animals, four fingers to beckon to people.   Vietnam.   L.A. Times
(West Magazine) March 26, 1972, p. 7.

Approval: Thumb and index join to form a circle.   Univ.
of Calif. Berkeley.   King, p. 264.   Also, "Wahre Begebenh.
am Stuttgarter Marktbrunnen" (see illustration 4).   Thumb erect,
corners of mouth drooping.   French.   Life (Sept. 16, 1949),
p. 12.   Hand closed, thumb erect, pointing upward.   Univ. of
Calif. Berkeley.   King, p. 264; Engl., 17th cent.   Bulwer,
p. 161; L.A. Times (Nov. 20, 1969), pt. 1, p. 28.   Putting
three fingers together.   Syria, Egypt.   Goldziher, Ztschr.,
p. 386.

Assistance: Index of one hand raised upward in a series of
spirals alongside the body and head, together with references to
divine wisdom or intervention.   Spain, Lat. Am.   Green, pp. 79-
80.

Attention: Snapping thumb against middle finger or ring
finger.   Familiar.   French.   Mitton, p. 146.   Spain, Lat. Am.
Green, p. 96.   Cf. also Krout, p. 25.   At auctions, the anc.
Roman raised a finger to draw attention of the auctioneer.
Sittl, p. 218.   "'and now attend to this,' and he raised his
finger."   Dante, Inf., c. x.

Avarice: Tips of thumb and index of the right hand joined,
accompanied by the exclamation "Ni tanto asf!"   Spain.   Flachs-

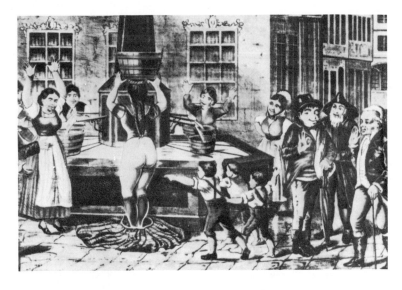

4. "Wahre Begebenheit am Stuttgarter Marktbrunnen, " Anon. , postcard, Zobel Verlag, Stuttgart (see FINGER--Approval).

kampf, p. 232. Rubbing the thumb over the tips of the first two fingers. Univ. of Calif. Berkeley. McCord, p. 291.

Begging: "Dearest, dearest Miss, concluded she, clasping her fingers, with the most condescending earnestness, let me beg of you... " Richardson, Clarissa, ii, 2.

Betting: If the other person does not lick his thumb or touch the other's, it signifies that a proposed bet is not accepted. Children. Opie, p. 129. Licking thumb and pressing it against the thumb of a disbeliever who has also licked his thumb signifies "you want to bet?" Children. Opie, ibid. Wetting thumb and holding it up, shouting "I bet you. " Children. Opie, ibid. Bettors link little fingers of one hand. Sometimes one strikes linked fingers with free hand. Colombia. Saitz and Cervenka, p. 24. (Cf. HAND, Agreement.)

Blessing: Cf. s.v. HAND, Blessing. Index and little finger extended, middle and ring finger bent (sometimes middle finger extended). Byzant. , partic. mosaics in Sicily. Haseloff, p. 301. Also medieval Serbian: Sta. Sophia, Ohrid; St. John the Baptist, Gračanica; Christ with angels at Lesnovo. Medieval Frescoes, pp. 6, 16, 23. Thumb and index extended, the other fingers separately bent so that third and fourth fingers cross index and little finger is curled toward thumb. Psalter of the landgrave Hermann of Thuringia. Stuttg. Bibl. fol. 24; Haseloff, p. 301. Third finger crosses index. Master of Vysebrod, "Ressurection, "

Prague, ca. 1350; Duby, p. 75. Thumb, index and little finger
extended, middle and ringfingers bent toward palm. Psalt. of
Herm. of Thur.; also Hamburg, Stadtbibl. In scrinio 85, fol.
11b; Haseloff, p. 301. Thumb, index, middle finger extended,
ring finger and little finger bent, ring finger touching thumb.
Donaueschingen, Bibl. 309; Kupferstichkab., Berlin, Hamilton-
Erw. 545; Haseloff, ibid. Also medieval Serbian: prophet Eze-
kiel at Resava. Medieval Frescoes, p. 25. Three first fingers
extended, ring and little finger bent. Wolfenbüttel, Cod. Helmst.
568 (521); Haseloff, ibid. Thumb and index extended, middle
finger bent, little finger extended. Hamburg, Stadtbibl. In
scrinio 85, fol. 12a; Haseloff, ibid. Thumb touches bent ring
and little finger, index straight, middle finger crosses over index. Greek. Hamburg, ibid., fol. 14b; Haseloff, p. 300; Otto,
I, p. 466. Thumb, index and middle fingers extended, ring and
little finger bent in toward palm. Haseloff, pp. 299-300. First
three fingers extended, last two bent against thumb or thumb
against the two bent fingers. Psalt. of Herm. of Thuringia,
fol. 3b; Breviary of St. Elizabeth, Cividale Museum, p. 17;
Cod. Helmst. 568 (521), fol. 29b; in scrinio, Hamburg, Stadt-
bibl., fol. 12a; Munich, cod. lat. 23094, fol. 91a; Haseloff,
p. 300. Christ makes the blessing gesture by making the
"horns," middle and ring finger not clasped by thumb, but loosely bent inward. Mural from church of Tosas, Rm. 14, Museo
de Arte de Cataluña, Barcelona. Three first fingers extended,
last two bent inward is the gesture of priestly blessing. HDA
II, col. 663. Making sign of the cross with finger or fingers
to oneself or another person. Ohm, p. 293. Index, middle
and little fingers extended, ringfinger bent in toward palm.
Byzant. 12th cent. Marciana lib., Ms lat. I, 100. Venice;
Formaggio and Basso, p. 13; cf. also Très Riches Heures, pl.
126. Thumb holding down bent ringfinger. Fresco at Mount
Athos; Didron, I, fig. 21. Index extended and crossing middle
finger, little finger extended, ring finger folded in, its tip
touching thumb. Fresco from Convent of Kaicariani, Mount
Hymettus; Didron, I, fig. 24; cf. also ibid., fig. 49. Index and
middle finger extended, thumb bent inward. Master Bertram
(ca. 1340-1414/15) "Creation of the Animals." See Johannes
Schermann, Graz; "Christus" (illustration 5).

    Boredom: Cf. s.v. HAND, Boredom. Backs of fingers of
one hand lightly travel up and down over the chin. French.
Mitton, p. 150. Fingers drum rhythmically on a surface, usually beginning with the little finger and moving to thumb. U.S.
Saitz and Cervenka, p. 74. "Father Pirrone had transformed
himself...into [a] Moslem sage and, with four fingers of his
right hand crossed in four fingers of his left, was rotating his
thumbs around each other, turning and changing their direction
with a great display of choreographic fantasy." di Lampedusa,
p. 130.

    Bravery: Touching together the thumbs and forming a W
with thumbs and indexes. Children. Opie, p. 231.

    Bribery: Thumb and index rubbed together. Mod. Gk.
Sittl, p. 115.

5.   "Christus," by Johannes Schermann, Graz, 1959 (see FINGER
--Blessing).

Censure: "and others thought he acted so in order to point
his third finger at the candidates for the doctorate and thereby
censure their folly." Mencken, p. 100.
Challenge: Little finger held up. Anc. Rom. Sittl, p. 97.
Bending the middle finger. Boys. Zürich. Schw. Idiotikon, I,
862. The "fig" (fingers form fist, thumb protruded between
middle and ring fingers). Shakesp., II Henry VI, V, iii, 123.
Christ: The ringfinger is the symbol of the soul, logos;
the thumb is the symbol of love. Tip of bent ringfinger touching tip of thumb is symbolic of Christ. Sittl, pp. 304-305;
Fischer, Antaios II, p. 323.
Clarification: Fingers of one hand stretched out and united
in one point. The hand in this position is lifted towards the
face of the gesticulator and is then moved several times towards

the other person and back. Neapol. De Jorio, p. 85. Thumb
and index united at the tip, the other fingers separately opened.
The hand is moved several times towards the other person and
back again towards the gesticulator's face. Anc. Rom. De
Jorio, pp. 85-86.

Cleansing: Priest rubs along each finger, repeating a dif-
ferent formula over each, symbolizing the driving out of impuri-
ties through the fingertips. India. Critchley, p. 71.

Command: Index raised. Breviary of St. Elizabeth, Cividale, Museum, fol. 173; medieval German: Haseloff, p. 302.
Index extended. Bulwer, pp. 162-166. Snap of fingers to command dogs to attack or to drive on the horses. Anc. Gk.
Metope of Seliunte; Sittl, p. 223. "The farmer snapped his fingers, as one might to recall a dog, and pointed toward the
path..." French. Simenon, p. 50.

Concentration: Putting together tips of five fingers to one
point. French. Life (Sept. 16, 1946), p. 12.

Confidence: Snapping index or middle finger. Walahfrid
Strabo. Sittl, p. 95.

Contempt: Cf. s. v. HAND, Contempt. Little finger held
up. Anc. Rom. Sittl, p. 97. Tips of fingers passed rapidly
from back to front three or four times under the chin. French.
Mitton, p. 151. Tips of fingers rubbed together. Ital. Sittl,
p. 97. Index, extended, is raised once or twice. Ital. Sittl,
p. 98. Thumb and index tip to tip, forming a circle. Neapol.
De Jorio, p. 134. "Miss Jenny, snapping her fingers, told him,
she did not value his resentment a louse." Smollett, Rod.
Random, ch. xi. "...said the beadle, snapping his fingers contemptuously." Dickens, Twist, p. 30. The "fig" (thumb protruded between clenched index and middle or middle and ring
fingers). HDA II, col. 1306. "thrusting out the middle finger."
Univ. of Calif. Berkeley. King, p. 263. Middle finger of either
hand extended, fist clenched, or at least the other fingers bent.
L. A. Times (Dec. 31, 1968), p. 3. The "fig": "A fico for the
phrase." Shakesp., Merry Wives, I, iii, 32. Also Portug.
Urtel, p. 35. Sittl, p. 103: brought by foreign mercenaries
from Italy to Germany and Slavic countries. Flachskampf,
p. 246: in Spain the "fig" is used only apotropaically. Francis
I of Naples, on the occasion of a popular demonstration, showed
the people his disdain by pressing the tips of his fingers together
and moving the hand repeatedly forward. Sittl, p. 97. Snapping
fingers toward person disdained. Amer. schoolchildren. Seton,
p. xxi. "Mr. Blandors snapped his finger and thumb again,
with one loud contemptuous snap." Dickens, Dorrit, II, p. 148.

Copulation: Bringing both indexes together or the index and
middle finger of one hand. Lat. Am. Kany, p. 166. Thumb
and index form circle, other fingers curl back slightly; circle
held parallel to ground, hand near waist. Colombia. Saitz and
Cervenka, p. 119. Right thumb extended from right fist and
moved in circular motion: obscenity or proposition of man to
woman. Saudi Arabia. Semiotic. Barakat, no. 85. Right
index placed in hole formed by joining tips of left thumb and index; right index is then moved in and out of the opening. Leba-

non, Libya. Semiotic. Barakat, no. 102.

Counting: Spaniards frequently use both hands in counting, beginning the count with the small finger and separating each finger from the others. Latin Americans often use only one hand and raise thumb and fingers of one hand as they simultaneously utter the numbers. Green, pp. 64-65. Thumb, index, middle finger of left hand are successively grasped by right. French. Mitton, p. 148. Thumb extended = "one." Aubert, p. 80. Right hand raised to the height of the face, clenched fist, thumb raised = "one." French. Mitton, ibid.; Brault, p. 379. Right hand raised to height of face, clenched fist, thumb and index extended = "two." French. Mitton, p. 148. Index of one hand points to the middle of the index of the other hand = "one half." Aubert, p. 80, fig. 118. Both hands raised to the height of the face, fingers extended, then both hands closed to fists and the right thumb extended = "eleven." French. Mitton, p. 148. Both hands raised to height of face, all fingers extended = "ten." French. Mitton, ibid. Right hand raised to the height of the face, fingers extended, left hand raised, thumb and index extended = "seven." French. Mitton, ibid. Right hand raised to height of face, fingers extended, left fist raised, thumb extended = "six." French. Mitton, p. 148. Right hand raised to height of face, thumb, index, and middle finger extended = "three." French. Mitton, ibid. Tip of index of left hand touches thumb of right hand = "first." ("Ticking off.") Schreiber and Heitz, pl. 1. Cf. pl. 2, 3, 5, 6 for process of "ticking off." (Cf. s.v. FINGER, HAND, Counting.)

Cuckoldry: Index and little finger raised ("the horns"). Old Lombard, anc. Gk. and Rom., Ital. Sittl, p. 103. 17th cent. French. Taylor, pp. 36-37. Colombia, U.S. Saitz and Cervenka, p. 121. Setting both thumbs against the temples and waving the fingers. 19th cent. English. Sittl regards this gesture as of modern origin. Taylor, p. 39. Index and little finger extended, the other fingers bent over, the hand in this position placed to the forehead. Neapol. De Jorio, p. 93. (Cf. s.v. FINGER, FOREHEAD, Cuckoldry.) Index and thumb extended. Arab. Semiotic. Barakat, no. 110.

Cunning: The "horns" (fist clenched, index and little finger extended) may be used in Mexico to indicate slyness, cunning, maliciousness, perverseness. In such a case the hand is not held near the forehead. Kany, p. 191.

Curse: Forking thumb and index. Ital. Hovorka and Kronfeld, I, p. 22.

Dance: Index pointed downwards, making a circle. Colombia. Saitz and Cervenka, p. 30.

Deafness: Finger placed in one ear. Mod. Gk. Sittl, p. 115.

Death: Placing thumb and index together at tip as if snuffing a candle. Lat. Am. Kany, p. 28. Index placed under chin. Critchley, p. 53.

Deception: Fingers placed between cravat and neck, rubbing the neck slowly with the back of the hand. Critchley, p. 89.

Decision: Man shuts eyes and holds out both hands with

fingers pointed towards each other slowly so that fingertips touch; if he succeeds, a trip may be taken, if not, it must be cancelled. Rwala Bedouin of Kuwait, Iraq, Syria, Saudi Arabia. Semiotic. Barakat, no. 133.

Defiance: Cf. s.v. HAND, Defiance. L.A. Times (Jan. 6, 1970), pt. 4, p. 14: "I raise my finger to you." The "fig" (clenched fist, thumb protruding between middle and ring finger) toward the heavens. Ital. Ulloa, Bk. iv, p. 65. Left index and middle finger form an inverted V, right index placed between the V and moved back and forth rapidly. Jordan, Lebanon. Semiotic. Barakat, no. 64.

Depart: Finger extended in direction of desired departure signifies a request to someone to depart. Colombia, U.S. Saitz and Cervenka, p. 80. Fingers held in pear-shaped configuration so that they point forward, then opened quickly: "go away!" Egypt. Semiotic. Barakat, no. 151.

Derangement: Tapping forehead with index, then describing a circle with it. Amer. schoolchildren. Seton, p. xxi. Cf. s.v. FINGER, FOREHEAD, Foolishness.

Desperation: Cf. s.v. HAND, Desperation.

Destruction: Cf. s.v. HAND, Destruction.

Direction: Index raised or extended. Breviary of St. Elisabeth, Cividale, Museum, fol. 206, 262, 313; Haseloff, p. 302. Index pointed, the other fingers in any other position, usually turned back. French. Mitton, p. 143. Cf. s.v. FINGER, HAND, Direction.

Disagreement: Hooking one's little finger into that of another person, then suddenly pulling them apart. Arab. Bauer, p. 220. Linking thumbs, shaking them up and down, accompanied by a verbal formula. Children. Opie, p. 324. Indexes pointed at each other and moved repeatedly apart and together. Colombia. Saitz and Cervenka, p. 36.

Disappearance: Snapping the fingers accompanied by verbal indication of disappearance or absence. Spain. Green, p. 87.

Disapproval: "Allied to the Digitus Impudicus in both form and meaning is the classical Latin gesture of the Pollex Infestus or extended thumb. Both an erect thumb and a thumb turned down were signs of disapprobation. Juvenal writes 'Et verso pollice vulgi Quemlibet occidunt populariter' (Sat. 3, 36-37), which Dryden (1693) translated 'Where... with Thumbs bent back they popularly kill.' Dryden understands that the thumb is erect and is bent backward, but the quotation need not necessarily be read in this way. A thumb turned down is now generally regarded as a gesture of condemnation. There is, however, evidence to show that raising a member of the body, and especially the thumb, was an unfavorable gesture. A thumb turned back, up, and away shows hostility to the suppliant." Taylor, p. 53. Cf. refusal to shake hands in greeting by extending right hand, then suddenly raising right thumb and jerking hand upward as if pointing to something behind one with the thumb. Life (Sept. 3, 1945), p. 25.

Disbelief: "this story seemed so outlandish that she asked the manager of the hotel about it. The manager crossed his fingers and confirmed the fat man's tale." I.e. he refused to commit himself to the truth which he asseverated. Randolph, p. 3. Index and little finger extended (the "horns"). Univ. of Calif. Berkeley. King, p. 263. Lightly hitting thumbnails of both hands together. Saudi Arabia. Semiotic. Barakat, no. 173.

Discord: Indexes of both hands placed tip to tip to one another in a straight line. Each is then alternately bent, while the other continues to touch its tip. French. Mitton, p. 147.

Dislike: Thumb extended and turned down. Grimm, DWb, II, col. 849.

Drink: Extended thumb (other fingers clenched) directed towards a glass or cup may mean "pour"--a gesture seen in coffeehouses when someone wishes the waiter to pour him a cup of coffee. Lat. Am. Kany, p. 82. Making a "C" or "T" with the index or indexes signifies a request for coffee or tea or an invitation to the taproom. Univ. of Calif. Berkeley. McCord, p. 290. Space between extended index and thumb indicates size of drink desired. Colombia, U.S. Saitz and Cervenka, p. 44. Space between extended index and little finger indicates size of drink desired. Colombia. Saitz and Cervenka, p. 45.

Dropping: Points of index and thumb are tightly joined and turned down, as if holding an imaginary object. Then the points are moved apart from one another, as if dropping the object held. French. Familiar, seldom used. Mitton, p. 150.

Embarrassment: Tip of index vertically placed to lips. Anc. Gk. and Rom. Sittl, pp. 272-273.

Emphasis: Hand raised, index and middle fingers extended, forming a "V." Austin Statesman (Texas) (Oct. 15, 1962), p. 13. Lowering the joined thumb and index of one hand, palm down, directly in front of the gesticulator's face to a position in which the fingers of the hand are spread apart widely. This movement is executed sharply and ends at the waist level of the speaker. Suggests an ultimatum. Essentially feminine movement. Spain, Lat. Am. Green, p. 39. " 'But we didn't.' Ashmore tapped his finger on the arm of his chair. 'Christopher succeeded.' " Robinson, p. 233. Thumb in contact with tip of middle or index finger, forming a ring. French. Mitton, p. 151. Bunched fingers of one hand pushed toward imaginary point in the air. Madrid, Lat. Am. Green, p. 29. Raising the slightly clenched fingers of one hand, palm up, to or above the speaker's chest. Occasionally both hands. When performed with one hand, the fingers may be rotated back and forth with the wrist serving as an axis. Accompanies expressions indicating a nucleus of an entity or survey or synopsis. Madrid, Lat. Am. Green, p. 31. "He leaned forward and jabbed at Denis with his finger. 'That's my secret.' " Huxley, ch. vi.

Encouragement: "Horns" (index and little fingers extended, other fingers folded over) as "Hook 'Em Horns" employed in the context of the Texas-TCU football game as "Hex TCU" sign and encouragement to the team of the Univ. of Texas. Austin Statesman (Nov. 15, 1963). Thumb extended and turned up signifies encouraging verification, i.e. "See, I told you so." India.

Simple encouragement. Univ. of Calif. Berkeley. King, p. 264.

Enmity: Tips of indexes of each hand moved repeatedly toward each other until they touch. Spain. Pérez Galdós, pt. IV, iii, vi. French. Mitton, p. 147. Indexes extended, one diametrically opposed to the other, the other fingers closed. Neapol. De Jorio, p. 188. (Cf. also s.v. Disagreement above.) Middle fingers horizontally extended, covering the extended index and then suddenly detaching itself from it. Covering the index with middle finger indicates friendship, separating them indicates broken friendship. Neapol. De Jorio, p. 186. Index and thumb, touching each other at the tips, are separated by the index of the other hand. Neapol. De Jorio, p. 184. Fists clenched, nails and knuckles of thumbs beaten together. Spain. Kaulfers, p. 257. Children join little fingers of right hands. Lebanon, Saudi Arabia. Semiotic. Cf. s.v. Friendship below. Barakat, nos. 37, 38. Little fingers of right hand moistened and linked, shaking them up and down. Children. Croydon, England. Opie, p. 324.

Enthusiasm: Wiggling lobe of ear with thumb and index of right hand. Extreme: right hand is passed behind head and lobe of left ear is wiggled. São Paulo. King, p. 264. Thumb(s) of one or both hands pointed up, fist clenched. Popular during WW II. England, U.S. Cited by Hayes, p. 308.

Equality: Indexes extended, outer side up, horizontally moved away from and towards gesticulator as if over an imaginary surface. Neapol. De Jorio, p. 88.

Etiquette: "her little finger, elegantly crooked, stood apart from the rest of her hand. " This while holding a drumstick of chicken. Huxley, ch. xix.

Exchange: Hooking little fingers and shaking them while chanting "Touch teeth, touch leather, no backsies for ever and ever. " Children. Swansea, Wales. Opie, p. 132.

Facility: Cf. s.v. HAND, Facility.

Farewell: Arm raised, all fingers except thumb flapped, palm facing gesticulator. Spain. Kaulfers, p. 260.

Fatigue: Thumb of one hand extended upwards, stroking the forehead slowly from side to side. Neapol. De Jorio, p. 151.

Fear: Hands folded, fingers pressed until joints crack. Anc. Rom. De Jorio, p. 265; Sittl, p. 23.

Finished: Extended index. Sittl, pp. 97-98; Spectator, (April 16, 1712), cited by Taylor, p. 17.

Flattery: Turning of the thumb. German. Meschke, p. 331.

Friendship: Linking little fingers of right hands, shaking them up and down. English schoolchildren. Opie, p. 324. Two indexes extended and placed parallel with each other. Morocco. Flachskampf, p. 230. Holding up two fingers close together. Univ. of Calif. Berkeley. McCord, p. 291. Middle finger crosses index of same hand. U.S. Saitz and Cervenka, p. 57. Index and middle finger together, other fingers pressed tightly into palm under the thumb. Saudi Arabia. Semiotic. Barakat, no. 77. Children join indexes of right hands. Lebanon. Semiotic. Barakat, no. 38. (Cf. s.v. Enmity above.) Children join little fingers of right hands. Lebanon. Semiotic. Barakat, no. 37. (Cf. also Enmity above.)

Frustration: Fist bangs slowly and repeatedly on table.
Lips usually tight. Colombia, U.S. Saitz and Cervenka, p. 58.

Gossip: Thumb and middle finger opening and closing while
moving the hand away from the body as if cutting with scissors.
Southern Ital. Efron, p. 66.

Greeting: Cf. s.v. HAND, Greeting. Squeezing nostrils
with index and thumb of left hand, and pointing to the navel with
the index of the right. Friendly greeting. Astrolabe Bay, New
Guinea. Comrie, p. 108. "Mr. Smauker dovetailed the top
joint of his right hand little finger into that of the gentleman
with the cocked hat, and said he was charmed to see him looking so well." Dickens, Pickw., II, p. 144. Index extended on
raised hand, as children signify their readiness to answer the
teacher and vassals report to their lord. Therefore the finger
is called salutaris. Martianus Capella 1, 90; Isid. Hisp. 11, 1,
70.

Gunshot: Right index is placed into the juncture of left
thumb and index. French. Mitton, p. 148.

Health: Little finger is symbolic of the body. Christ as
apothecary holds scales in hand and raises little finger. Ganzinger, p. 14; Fischer, Antaios II, fig. 9.

Homosexuality: Extended middle finger, Seligmann, II,
p. 183.

Hot: Middle finger wetted in mouth, extended forward and
jerked back. Amer. schoolchildren. Seton, p. xxiii.

Humility: "...and then, touching his fur cap in token of
humility..." Dickens, Twist, p. 19.

Idea: Thumb extended, other fingers loosely closed. Hand
swings down and up again, thumb forward, as if to dig out something with the thumb. Ghetto Jews. Efron, table 32.

Idealism: Raising index to the side of the head and describing small circles in the air. Spain, Lat. Am. Green, p. 48.

Identification: Snap of fingers used among conspirators as
signal of identification. Anc. Rom. Sittl, p. 223. Index points
at chest. ("I," "Me.") U.S. Saitz and Cervenka, p. 113. Cf.
also s.v. HAND, Identification.

Idleness: Four fingers of one hand interlaced with the four
fingers of the other, thumbs turn around each other. Twiddling
thumbs. French. Mitton, p. 151.

Ignorance: Jerking the fingers means "I don't know."
Europe, India. Rose, p. 312.

Impatience: Fingers drumming on an object. Krout, p. 23.
Fingers drum on a surface rhythmically, usually beginning with
little finger and moving to thumb. Also may signify boredom.
U.S. Saitz and Cervenka, p. 74. Snapping thumb against middle
or ring finger. Impatience while trying to think of something.
France. Mitton, p. 146.

Indecision: Putting finger against tongue and shaking it as
if it had been burnt. Arab. Bauer, p. 223.

Indifference: Middle finger snapped against thumb. Spain.
Kaulfers, p. 253. "Well, let him forfeit the estate, then! Do
you think any of us would care a snap of our fingers..." Carr,

Hag's Nook, p. 49. Extended fingers slowly rubbing the under-
chin. ("I couldn't care less.") Ital. Time (Apr. 9, 1965),
p. 67.
Infidel: Index raised, then bent to touch its lowest joint =
non-Moslem. Saudi Arabia. Semiotic. Barakat, no. 93.
Insult: The "pistola": the extended right index briskly
thrust between extended or circled left thumb and index. Lat.
Am. Kany, p. 175. The "fig": thumb thrust between index
and middle fingers of the same hand. Lat. Am. Kany, ibid.
Middle finger extended erect as phallic symbol, the other fingers
folded into palm. Lat. Am. Kany, ibid. Colombia, U.S.
Saitz and Cervenka, p. 114. Anc. Gk. and Rom. Sittl, pp. 101-
102. Extended right thumb. Lebanon, Syria, Saudi Arabia.
Semiotic. Barakat, nos. 44, 87. Little finger held up. Anc.
Rom. Sittl, p. 97. Tips of right middle finger and thumb
touch, forming a circle, other fingers extended. Lebanon,
Syria. Semiotic. Barakat, no. 47. Stiff middle finger extended, other fingers pressed into palm, back of hand forward.
Lebanon, Syria. Semiotic. Barakat, no. 43. The extended
middle finger, or digitus impudicus, "is an ancient opprobrious
gesture that often has obscene implications. Diogenes insulted
Demosthenes with it. Although the identification is not certain,
Caligula may have used this gesture when he aroused scandal
by his manner of holding out his hand to be kissed. Sittl believes that the hostile attitude of the Roman church explains the
disappearance of this gesture in the West, while it remained in
use in Byzantium and has survived in modern Greece. However,
the gesture has not disappeared as completely in the West as
Sittl seems to imply." Taylor, pp. 52-53. Tip of right thumb
on second joint of middle finger of right hand with other fingers
extended. Lebanon, Syria, Saudi Arabia. Semiotic. Variation:
thumb between index and middle finger of right fist, i.e. "fig."
Barakat, no. 45. "...with the thumb between the index finger
and second finger, though the thumb between the index and third
finger is not unknown. Often the wrist of the fist making the
fica is caught in the other hand, and the fist is then shaken. In
variations of this one grabs the inside of the elbow, the biceps
and even the shoulder with the other hand." Ital.-Amer. King,
p. 263. Left index extended, inverted "V"-configuration formed
with right index and thumb and placed over the lower part of
the left index near thumb. ("I'll ride you like a donkey.")
Saudi Arabia. Semiotic. Barakat, no. 227. "Horns": index
and little finger extended, other fingers folded into palm.
Röhrich, p. 23, pl. 18. The first and second fingers extended,
slightly parted, are jerked upwards, the back of the hand facing
outward. English schoolchildren. Opie, p. 319. Raised index
and middle finger, palm facing body, hand pumped up and down
several times. Lebanon, Syria, Saudi Arabia. Semiotic. Barakat, no. 130. A variation of this consists of placing the "V"-
configuration of index and middle finger beneath the nose and
pumping it up and down. Barakat, ibid. Tips of left fingers
and thumb placed together so that hand faces right, then the tip
of right index is placed on left fingertips. Insult directed at

one's birth or parentage: "You have five fathers." Saudi Arabia. Semiotic. Barakat, no. 234. Palm of right hand placed on back of left hand with fingers slightly interlocked, thumbs rotated several times. Lebanon, Saudi Arabia. Semiotic. Barakat, no. 60. Thumb and index rubbed together at tip. Lebanon, Syria. Semiotic. Barakat, no. 66. Right hand extended, palm down, index pointing down, other fingers extended stiffly. Lebanon, Syria, Saudi Arabia, Jordan. Semiotic. Barakat, no. 59. Thrusting four extended fingers into someone's face. ("Animal" to Koreans in Japan.) Osaka. L. A. Times (Sept. 5, 1973), pt. 1A, p. 6. "...made the hitchhiking gesture, thumb over his shoulder, which proclaimed to all the world 'What a rotter that one is!' " Ital. Graham, p. 26. Thumb jerked over left shoulder, implying illegitimate birth. London. Post-middle 18th cent. Thomas Burke, The Streets of London (London, 1949), p. 94, cited by Hayes, p. 233. Two fingers jerked upwards. London. 20th cent. Burke, ibid.

Invitation: The "fig" (thumb thrust between middle and ring fingers of fist) as invitation to sexual intercourse. Röhrich, p. 21. Pointing at another person may signify an invitation to join in going somewhere. Univ. of Calif. Berkeley, p. 291.

Jail: Crossing the index and middle finger of one hand over those of the other (May also indicate a "julia," i.e. a police wagon). Mexico. Kany, p. 118. Extending fingers of the right hand over the extended fingers of the left to form a grating suggestive of prison bars. Lat. Am. Kany, p. 117. Two fingers of one hand laid across two fingers of the other. Russian. F. Bowers, p. 98.

Judgment: In outlawing someone, judge and people raise a finger. Medieval German. Sachsenspiegel, II, 4, para. 1; Ermisch, xxi, para. 2. The Zwickauer Rechtsbuch prescribed the raising of two fingers. AGA IX, p. 128; His, I, p. 445. In Eastphalian territory the proscription was lifted by the pronouncement of a formula while raising the finger. Zwickauer Rechtsb. III, 2, 23, para. 2. "Point up or down, to signify good or bad." Edwin Booth's promptbook to Shakesp. Othello, I, iii, 328. The presiding judge of the collegium agrimensorum, in rendering judgment, placed the tip of the ringfinger (signifying the word) to the tip of the thumb (signifying love). Anc. Rom. Fischer, Antaios, II, p. 343.

Kill: Thumb down, right hand closed, thumb outside fist, pressed close as in grasping a knife, and jerked, thumb edge down, sharply. Austin, p. 596.

Life: Middle finger (symbolic of life) bent inward, all other fingers of left hand (signifying the past) extended. Viennese woodcut of Janus bifrons, early 16th cent. Fischer, Basler Nachr. (Oct. 30, 1960), pl. 2.

Limits: Describing one or more small circles in the air with the extended index of one hand pointing downward. Madrid, Lat. Am. Green, pp. 59-60.

Luck: Crossing fingers while looking at the person on behalf of whom the gesture is made. (Crossing index and middle finger.) Univ. of Calif. Berkeley. McCord, p. 291. Index

and little finger extended ("horns") pointing down, arm vertical.
Ital. N.Y. Times (March 1, 1959). Pressing the thumb with
the rest of the fingers means that the person for whom thumb
is pressed will have success. Anc. Rom., Ital., German.
Meschke, p. 331. Thumb erect, fist closed for luck. West
German. Sartori, I, p. 87; II, p. 187; Meschke, p. 331.
Thumb enclosed by fingers of same hand. Anc. Rom. Sittl,
p. 125. "The Spanish movement associated with spilled wine is
performed by dipping the finger or fingers into the spilled wine
and touching the forehead of those present or seated at the
table...The movement is no longer common, but...may be observed occasionally...Olga Bauer enjoins etiquette conscious
Spaniards from executing this gesture, and she holds a similar
view with respect to the act of throwing spilled salt over the
shoulder." Green, pp. 93-94. Middle finger of one or both
hands crossed over index. U.S. News and World Report (March
27, 1961), p. 117. Colombia, U.S. Saitz and Cervenka, p. 82.
    Magical: Crossing of fingers prevents births. Pliny.
Röhrich, p. 29. Hooking of little or middle fingers into one
another prevents an animal from giving birth. HDA, II, col.
1487. If two people pronounce the same word simultaneously,
they hook their little fingers of their right hand into one another,
in order to bring about whatever they are thinking at the time.
Silesia. HDA, II, col. 1491. Interlacing of fingers often serves
magical purposes. Ohm, p. 176. In looking through the three
fingers with which one makes the sign of the Cross, one can
recognize demons. Eisel, no. 207, cited in HDA, col. 1489.
    Magnanimity: Showing ring finger of left hand to emphasize
statement of willingness to give someone everything. Anc. Rom.
Sittl, p. 114.
    Magnitude: Smallness: Joining tips of index and thumb.
Palm facing either up or down. Or palm up, thumb on first
joint of the index of same hand. Or snapping fingernails of index and thumb of same hand. Spain. Green, pp. 33-34. Index
extended, thumb rests against first joint of index. Colombia.
Saitz and Cervenka, p. 126. Index of one hand points at tip of
index of the other. Aubert, p. 81, fig. 119. Index extended
from fist, tip of thumb placed on lower joint. Lebanon, Syria.
Semiotic, culture-induced. Barakat, no. 148. Nothing: Raising
bunched fingers of one hand to the level of the chest with palm
facing speaker. Spain, Lat. Am. Green, p. 30. With expressions suggesting a limited scope or range, small circles are
described in the air with the spread fingers of one hand, palm
down, at level of waist. Madrid. Green, p. 31. Many people:
indexes hooked one into the other. Arab. Bauer, p. 221. Expressions suggesting emergence or growth can be accompanied
by gestures of raising the bunched fingers of one hand, fingers
upward, from the waist to approx. the level of the chest (Spain,
Lat. Am.), or by drawing the bunched fingers of each hand,
waist high, palms facing inward, gradually apart. Madrid.
Green, pp. 65-66. Large crowd: rapid and repeated opening
and closing of the bunched fingers of one or both hands in front
of gesticulator. Spain, Lat. Am. Green, p. 69. Small: index

of right hand separated slightly from index of left hand. Spain.
Flachskampf, p. 233. Thinness: Raising extended little finger,
saying "Es asf." Lat. Am. Kany, p. 41.

Marriage: Bridal ring is put on the fourth finger, from
which the veins go to the heart. Pliny, Nat. hist., xxx, 34, I;
xxii, 59, I; HDA, II, col. 1494. Index finger taps ring finger.
Colombia (ring finger of right hand), U.S. (ring finger of left
hand). Saitz and Cervenka, p. 84. Indexes of both hands linked.
Colombia. Ibid.

Medico-magical: In order to still a nosebleed, the arm on
the bleeding side is raised with middle finger extended, the
other arm points downwards, also with middle finger extended.
Thuringia. Wuttke, p. 347, para. 518; HDA, II, col. 1493.
According to Sir Thomas Browne, ancient physicians mixed their
medicines with the third finger, the digitus medicinalis. HDA,
II, col. 1494. Dirt and spittle laid on with the middle finger
heals the effects of the evil eye. Petron., Sat. 131; Persius 2,
32; Sittl, p. 123. The medico-magical and apotropaic use of
the middle finger is widespread; hence the digitus impudicus becomes the digitus medicinalis. The ring finger is also sometimes regarded as digitus medicinalis. HDA, II, col. 1495. If
one's leg falls asleep, one should wet the middle finger with
spittle and make the sign of the Cross over it. Belgium.
Wolff, p. 225, no. 290; HDA, II, col. 1491. Ringfinger bent,
all others straight: stops hiccups and bleeding. Fischer,
Antaios, II, p. 323. Thumb and little finger touch at tip to
regulate sexual relations. Indian relief in Kamrisch, pl. 69
(ca. 740); Fischer, Antaios, II, fig. 10. Middle finger crosses
over index of same hand. Gesture made by kings in healing by
laying on of hand. Schroeder, p. 157; Fischer, Antaios, II,
fig. 1. (Cf. HAND, Authority.) Little fingers of both hands
hooked into one another prevents diarrhoea. Rural Europ.
Fischer, Antaios, II, p. 333. Thumb and little finger touch at
tip. Through the ring thus formed, he who would be cured of
impotence must urinate. Swabian, 19th cent. and before. Buck,
p. 25; Fischer, Antaios, II, p. 322. In medieval symbolism
the middle finger symbolized life. In being bled a woman extends the middle finger. Schultze, p. 186; Fischer, Antaios, II,
fig. 8 and p. 341.

Mercy: Raising a finger was a plea for mercy by a gladiator. Anc. Rom. Otto, p. 117. If the patron of a gladiatorial
combat wished a surrendering gladiator to be spared, he raised
his thumb; if not, he turned his hand over, thumb downwards.
Juvenal. The spectators as a whole expressed their wishes in
this respect in the same manner. Horace, Prudentius. Sittl,
pp. 218-219.

Minimization of difficulties: Snapping index or middle finger
against thumb. Walahfrid Strabo; Sittl, p. 95.

Mockery: Cf. s.v. FINGER, HAND, Mockery; FINGER,
NOSE, Mockery; HAND, Mockery. Thumb put to the lips and
fingers spread. Gulliveriana (1728); Taylor, p. 18. "We cannot safely identify the Shanghai Gesture [thumb tip to nose, fingers spread] with the classical Sign of the Stork (ciconiam fa-

cere, curvare), although both gestures involve use of the fingers
and have a derisive sense.   According to both a scholiast on
Persius and St. Jerome, this classical gesture consisted in interlacing the index and middle fingers to resemble a stork's
bill [Sittl, pp. 109-110].   Since the verb 'curvare' is ordinarily
used in describing the gesture, we can probably infer that the
interlaced fingers are bent [Urtel, p. 12, n. 2...].   The bending of the fingers... is not altogether appropriate to a stork,
which has a straight bill.   The reference to a stork seems,
moreover, to imply a horizontal position of the fingers.   This
opprobrious use of the stork is curious because the bird has no
characteristically unpleasant associations in either classical or
modern times.   In the modern German "Storch stechen' or
'Storchschnabel stechen' the fingers are said to be interlaced
and raised, although...'stechen' might suggest a thrusting forward [Meschke, col. 332, n. 61: "to raise the index like the
neck of a stork and to bend it. "].   Rudolf Kleinpaul regards
(p. 265) this gesture as obsolescent and only partially intelli-
gible.   The allied German gesture known in Carinthia as 'den
Guler stechen (zeigen)' that consists in thrusting forward the
the two index fingers laid over each other is used in mockery
[Meschke, col. 332, no. 51; Kleinpaul, pp. 265-266, 374;
Grimm, DWb, IV, 1a, col. 1121; Schweizer. Idiotikon, II,
cols. 57-59, 65].   In identifying this with the Swiss 'einem ein
Gäbeli machen,' i.e. to mock with the fingers thrust out like a
fork [DWb, IV, 1a, col. 1121], the editors of the DWb seem to
have introduced a confusion with another gesture of similar
meaning.   Since forks originally had only two tines, they were
very much like two fingers thrust out.   Leopold Schmidt dis-
cusses a gesture with interlaced fingers,... citing it from
children's games without mention of classical or other parallels
[pp. 243-244].   De Jorio suggests that the Sign of the Stork is
the Digitus Impudicus,...[pp. 136-137]. "   Taylor, p. 52.
"Some cried, some swore, and the tropes and figures of Billings-
gate were used without reserve in all their native zest and fla-
vour; nor were those flowers of rhetoric unattended with significant gesticulations.   Some snapped their fingers, some forked
them out, some clapped their hands, and some their backside;
at length they fairly proceeded to pulling caps, and everything
seemed to presage a general battle. "   Smollett, Clinker, letter
of Jerry Melford, April 30; Taylor, p. 18 and notes 32-35.
German "Eselbohren, " i.e. index and little finger or middle
finger extended in imitation of mule ears.   Meschke, col. 332.
The "fig" (thumb thrust through clenched fingers between middle
and ring or index and middle fingers).   Anc. Rom.   Meschke,
col. 331.   14th and 15th cent.   German songs.   Röhrich, p. 21.
Also used by Luther, Sachs, Grimmelshausen, Abraham a Santa
Clara.   HDA, II, 1309.   North Korean photograph of captured
crew of USS Pueblo.   L. A. Times (Dec. 31, 1968), p. 1.   Fool
points to other figures with left hand, index and middle finger
extended, fourth and fifth fingers folded into palm, thumb extended, tongue sticking out, right hand holding branch.   Woodcut,
Brant, p. 79.   The "fig": a young woman, riding a hen, makes

the "fig," mocking husband whose sexual performance is inadequate. Engraving from 1650. Bolte, p. 78-79. Cf. also the "fig" in Dürer's drawing of hands, Röhrich, p. 20 and pl. 14. Rubbing of one index on the other (Germ. "Rübenschaben). HDV, I, col. 324. (Ital. "far pepe.") HDA, II, col. 1487. Left index pointed at person, all other fingers closed, right index rubs on back of left from middle to tip and beyond. Seton, p. 180. "Rübenschaben" on altarpiece of Hans Holbein the Older. Röhrich, pl. 27; medieval depictions of Christ's Passion. Röhrich, pl. 28, and in Abraham a Santa Clara. Röhrich, pp. 28-29. Extended middle finger signifies homosexuality. Seligmann, II, p. 183. "Horns" (index and little finger extended, other fingers folded over). France. Childish. Mitton, p. 149. Snapping of fingers. Drunken faun of Herculaneum. Naples Museum. Sardanapaulus is said to have been represented on his tomb as snapping his fingers. Kleinpaul, p. 269. A Danish instance in Klitgaard, p. 89. "Then you'll cross over into Illinois and you can...snap your fingers under the nose of them that ordered you around..." Kroll, p. 194. "To snap one's fingers as a gesture signifying delight or contempt from 1742 to the present...The former use is rare, and the latter use is recent and frequent. Compare also the idiom 'Not to care (give) a snap of one's fingers for...,' which is also classical Greek and is known in Latin use of uncertain date... NED (Snap, 12b)," Taylor, pp. 65-66, n. 33. "When Frederick the Wise gave an audience to Dr. Luther, he received him most graciously...Only when the good man had left, he snapped his fingers at him ('schlug ihm ein Schnippchen') in his pocket or 'stach ihm einen Mönch,'" which, according to Adelung, means that he made the sign of the "fig" at him. Thümmel, II, p. 293. According to Meschke, col. 331, however, the meaning of the German phrase "einen Mönch stechen" (i.e. to "stab a monk") refers to the extension of the middle finger as apotropaic or mocking gesture. One finger of right hand extended and moved up and down as if playing a guitar. Children. Mexican. Lomas, p. 35. Index of right hand slides between angle of thumb and index of left hand, moving slowly as if playing a violin. Mexican. Lomas, p. 35.

Money: Accompanying expressions suggesting either possession or lack of money, thumb is rubbed over fingertips of same hand. Spain, Lat. Am. Green, p. 32. Movement of dropping money piece by piece between thumb and index. French. Familiar. Mitton, p. 147. An open circle made with thumb and index, the other fingers bent in on palm. Lat. Am. Kany, p. 182. Rubbing tips of thumb and index together. Neapol. De Jorio, p. 126. Indicates wealth. Ital. Graham, p. 26. Can also signify "to pay." U.S. Saitz and Cervenka, p. 90. Fist closed very loosely and the four fingertips then brush the palm inward several times. Lat. Am. Kany, p. 95. Rubbing back of the thumb against the ball of the index. Lat. Am. Kany, p. 94. Palm facing person addressed, fingers move back and forth either together or one after the other. Colombia. Saitz and Cervenka, p. 88.

Mourning: Women digging up the earth on grave mound with their fingers. Petronius. Sittl, p. 74. Fingers interlaced. Ammian. Sittl, p. 72.

Negation: Tip of middle finger placed under the thumb and catapulted forward. Benedictine monks. Critchley, p. 53. Right arm at full length, fingers closed, thumb extended and pointing downward. Roman. Seton, p. 211. Tip of thumb, hand open, placed against throat, then catapulted forward. Or the same with all fingers. Southern Ital. De Jorio, p. 224; Sittl, p. 95. Index extended, moving from side to side. Colombia. Saitz and Cervenka, p. 151. "...that peculiar backhanded shake of the right forefinger which is the most expressive negative in the Italian language. Dickens, Dorrit, I, p. 10. Show all fingers except the thumb. Trappist monks. Critchley, p. 53. "Now he stretches finger and thumb and turns his hand, to say, 'No money, nothing doing!'" Ital. Graham, p. 26.

Nervousness: Twiddling thumbs. Colombia, U.S. Saitz and Cervenka, p. 92.

Nothing: Point of index is catapulted off the underside of the thumbnail. Anc. Gk. Sittl, p. 95. Upper incisor scratched with thumbnail signifies "nothing" or "nothing for you." France. Familiar. Mitton, p. 149. "'The girls he went out with didn't even mean that to Mel.' He snapped his fingers." Kemelman, p. 113. "'you won't wonder I wouldn't vally a feller like that-- no, not that much!' and her ladyship snapped her little fingers." Thackeray, Virg., II, ch. xxv. Thumb placed under the upper incisor and rapidly flicked forwards. Southern France. Critchley, p. 91. Spain. Blasco Ibañez, p. 29. Lower eyelid is pulled down with the finger. ("My eye!") France. Insolent, vulgar. Mitton, p. 150. "and [he] marked the black of the fingernail of his little finger." Spain. Pereda, ch. xii. (Cf. FINGER, Contempt.)

Oath: "Wet my thumb, wipe it dry, cut my throat if I tell a lie." Children. Farnham, Surrey. Opie, p. 127. Raising of thumb or laying of thumb upon table of justice. Medieval German. Grimm, DRA, I, p. 196. Three fingers extended. "The first is the thumb, signifying God the Father, the next signifies God the Son, the third God the Holy Ghost." Handbook of Appenzell (Switzerland) (1585). HDA, II, col. 663. Crossed middle and index fingers make an oath invalid. Rural Balkans. Hellwig, p. 58. Link little fingers and spit, saying "spit your death." Children. Liverpool. Opie, p. 126. Linking little fingers of the right hand and shaking the hands up and down. Asia Minor. 19th cent. Opie, p. 131. Spit and cross the throat, or spit over wrist or little finger, saying "spit your mother's death." Children. Cumberland. Opie, p. 126. Crossing two forefingers, saying "Cross God's honor." Children. Opie, p. 122. One finger extended. Medieval German. Grimm, DRA, I, p. 195. Fingers raised. Anc. Persian. Niebuhr, II, tab. 33; Grimm, DRA, I, p. 196. Placing index and middle finger on object sworn by. Medieval German: perh. Wolfr. v. Eschenbach, Bk. I, 902-03; Hartmann v. Aue, 7923; Grimm, DRA, I, p. 195. "All of them repeated it with three fingers raised." Stage direction, Schiller, <u>Wilh. Tell</u>, II, ii. "He swore to me, interlacing his fingers, by the crosses thus formed." Spain. 19th cent. Pereda, <u>Peñas</u>, p. 397. "By the life of my father I swear,...and by this sign of the cross [making the cross with two fingers] which I kiss with my dirty mouth." Spain. Cervantes, <u>Novelas</u>, p. 136. Child making oath crosses fingers, and the other child puts his fingers through them, snapping them apart. "Breaking the cross." Hertfordshire. Opie, p. 125. Holding right index down with thumb and extending other fingers. Saudi Arabia. Semiotic. Barakat, no. 79.

Obedience: Index extended on raised hand, as children signify their readiness to answer the teacher and vassals report to their lord. Therefore the index is called "salutaris." Martianus Capella, Isiddor. Hisp.; Sittl, p. 162. Index, extended on raised hand, is held up by vassal before his lord. Prutz, I, pp. 487, 682.

Oppression: Describing a circle with right thumb and index around left index. "I wind him around my finger." Amer. schoolchildren. Seton, p. xxii. Pressing firmly down with tip of right thumb. "I have him under my thumb." Amer. schoolchildren. Seton, p. xxii.

Ordering (wine): The classic "horns" (index and little finger extended, other fingers folded into palm). When the hand is held vertically rather than horizontally in gesturing toward a glass, it may mean facetiously "dos dedos de vino." Lat. Am. Kany, p. 191. Cf. also s.v. FINGER, MOUTH, <u>Drink</u>.

Pain: Index taps on middle finger of same hand, thumb touches middle finger. Other fingers folded over into palm. Neapol. De Jorio, p. 141.

Past: Verbal expression suggesting the past accompanied by pushing the fingers of the cupped hand away from the side of the gesticulator's head. Madrid, Lat. Am. Green, p. 65. Snap index and thumb, then thrust out hand with index extended. Saudi Arabia. Semiotic. Barakat, no. 213.

Pay: Thumb and index of same hand rubbed together. German. Sittl, p. 115. French. Mitton, p. 147. Index rubbed against ball of thumb, hand clenched, forearm extended at right angles to body. Spain. Kaulfers, p. 256.

Peace: Tips of indexes pressed together, arms raised, accompanied by the formula "Friedouf bis ins Himmeli ouf." Swiss. SAV, XXI, p. 76; <u>HDA</u>, II, col. 1486. Middle finger crosses <u>index</u>. Truce, "King's X, " "King's Cross, " "Fins, " "Bar up, " "Pax. " Claim to exemption. Amer. schoolchildren. Seton, pp. xix, xxii: "This is a very ancient sign and seems to refer to the right of sanctuary. The name 'King's Cross,' used occasionally in England, means probably the sanctuary in the King's palace. "

Pensiveness: Drumming with fingers. Krout, p. 23.

Perfection: Thumb and index joined at tips, forming circle held at right angle to ground at eye level. Hand sometimes moves back and forth slightly. Colombia, U.S. Saitz and Cervenka, p. 95. Thumb and index or middle finger joined at tip, brought to the lips, then suddenly removed from lips, which are left pursed. The fingers remain some distance from the face for a moment, slightly parted. France. Mitton, p. 151. Cf. s.v. Praise below; FINGER, LIP, Admiration and Superlative.

Pleasure: Index and thumb joined at tip. L.A. Times (Nov. 20, 1969), pt. 1, p. 27.

Plenty: "Preguntóle a ella si tenía galanes o pretendientes. --Si tiene?, respondió la abuela; así, así. Y menaba los dedos levantando la mano." Spain. Foz, p. 192.

Pointing: Pointing at object of conversation. Anc. Gk. and Rom. Sittl, pp. 51-52. In speaking of someone, index is pointed at him. Anc. Rom. Sittl, p. 49. "And more than a thousand shades he showed me with his finger, and named them." Dante, Inf., c. v; Purg., c. vi. Pointing finger. Dürer, woodcut of Last Supper (1523). Prohibition against pointing with the finger to the heavens. Boehm, p. 29. "The good lady pointed, distractedly, to the cupboard." Dickens, Twist, p. 241. "He leaned forward, and with a raised forefinger marked his points as he made them. Huxley, ch. vi. Whoever points at a mourner with his finger will die or someone in his family will die. Erzgebirge. HDA, II, col. 1485. The ancient Greeks often pointed with all fingers of one hand, particularly with the palm upwards. Baumeister, 1293, 1985; Sittl, pp. 289-290. It is impolite to point at someone; if one points at someone one stabs an angel. Weise, Ertznarren (1683), p. 226. If one points toward heaven, one kills an angel or deprives him of his eyesight; whoever points at a thunderstorm will be struck by lightning; pointing at a witch will draw the evil eye to oneself. German. Röhrich, p. 30. Thumb protrudes from fist and points backward. U.S. (rude), Colombia (acceptable). Saitz and Cervenka, p. 34. Spaniards use thumb to identify or point out someone or something, since it is considered impolite to point with the finger. Also Lat. Am. Green, pp. 70-71.

Poverty: Index and middle finger of the right hand take nose between them and, closing, slide downward = "broke." Spain. Flachskampf, p. 232. Thumb is raised quickly while other fingers are extended, index first = "broke." Ital. Efron, p. 148. Drawing the index across the throat and snapping the relaxed index and middle fingers. Venezuela. Kany, p. 88.

Praise: Holding up both thumbs. Bulwer, pp. 161-162. Fingers pressed together (tip of index to tip of thumb?). Anc. Rom. Sittl, p. 125. Also German, cf. DWb, II, col. 849.

Prayer: Interlacing fingers of one hand with those of the other. Protestant. Ohm, p. 273. First mention in Christianity in the account of Santa Scholastica. Gregor. Magn., Dial., II, p. 33; Heiler, p. 103. Also Roman. Heiler, p. 103. Sarcophagus (5th cent.) from a catacomb at Syracuse: woman with fingers intertwined squats before Mary. Sittl, p. 176; Heiler, p. 103; Liell, p. 344.

Precision: Lowering and raising index and thumb joined at tip, palm down, directly in front of the speaker, or at the side of his head; or drawing joined thumb and index across the body from shoulder to shoulder. Madrid, Lat. Am. Green, p. 70.

Tips of fingers and thumb of right hand joined and agitated gently; eyes often squint: "Comment dit-on déjà?...voyons voir un
petit peu." France. Brault, p. 380.

"Probably": One finger raised. Ital. Time (April 9,
1965), p. 67.

Promise: Wet finger and make sign of the cross on one's
heart. Children. Yorkshire. Opie, p. 124. With right index
make little cross over the heart. Amer. schoolchildren. Seton,
p. 53.

Prostitute: Indexes and thumbs of both hands joined at tips
to form diamond shape. Colombia. Saitz and Cervenka, p. 118.

Quickly: Snapping fingers. U.S. Saitz and Cervenka,
p. 99.

Reconciliation: Linking little fingers of right hand and then
separating them, saying "We'll never break any more." Children.
South Molton. Opie, p. 325. Hooking indexes one into the
other. Palest. Bauer, p. 220.

Redemption: Thumb (symbolic of Love in the Middle Ages)
and middle finger (symbolic of Life) touch at tip (the so-called
"Mittelfingerbrücke"). The Virgin as portrayed by the Master
of the Garden of Paradise. Pl. iv in Fischer, Basler Nachr.
(Oct. 30, 1960).

Refusal: Holding up of the thumb is sign of contemptuous
refusal. India. Rose, p. 313.

Reminder: Index or middle finger snapped on thumb = forgot something. Arab. Autistic. Barakat, no. 112. Snapping
fingers in an effort to remember something. Colombia, U.S.
Same in the moment of remembering. Saitz and Cervenka,
p. 86. If one has overlooked or forgotten something, one should
put the index into one's mouth, say "fff! ai! ai!," and make
the sign of the cross. HDA, II, col. 1483.

Repetition: Circling motion with index pointed down on extended hand. Colombia. Saitz and Cervenka, p. 102.

Reproach: Middle finger placed tip to thumb, the other
fingers extended. Leonardo da Vinci, "Modesty and Vanity."
Baden, p. 454. Index of right hand is wagged vigorously to
left and right, hand at chest level or belt level: "Non, non:
pas de ça!" France. Brault, pp. 379-380.

Result: Snapping fingers in association with expressions
suggesting revelation or the solution of a problem. Spain, Lat.
Am. Green, p. 64.

Retreat: Snapping the thumb against the middle or index
finger with forearm usually raised upward and outward. Lat.
Am. Kany, p. 111.

Royalty: Middle finger crosses index of same hand. Symbolic of kingship, perhaps as symbolic of the power to heal by
touch. (Cf. above s.v. Medico-magical; Peace.) Seal of Waimar II of Salerno. Mabillon, Supp., p. 115. Also modern
woodcarving, "Christ," by Johannes Schermann (1959).

Sanctuary: Cf. s.v. Peace, above.

Seeking: Looking about and pointing finger in same directions as those in which one glances. Amer. schoolchildren.
Seton, p. xxii.

Separation: Fingers extended, moved from position of hands palm to palm with fingers touching lightly at tips, to a position in which the fingers are still extended but separated slightly and palms have separated and turned slightly toward gesticulator. Madrid, Lat. Am. Green, p. 69. Holding an imaginary object between thumb and index and making the gesture of letting it fall on the ground. France. Familiar, seldom used. Mitton, p. 150. Accompanying expressions of dissociation, the fingers of both hands are rapidly raised and lowered, chest-high, palm down. Madrid, Lat. Am. Green, p. 41.

Shame: Fingers closed into a fist, index and little finger raised and extended. ("Horns.") Childish. French. Mitton, p. 149. First mentioned in Germany by Heinrich of Erfurt (1178) as signum probrosum. Sittl, p. 103; HDA, II, col. 1308. Indexes extended from fists, one index crossing the other, rubbing it several times. Children. U. S. Saitz and Cervenka, p. 123. (Cf. s.v. Mockery above.)

Shyness: Tip of index, vertical, placed to lips. Anc. Gk. and Rom. Sittl, pp. 272-273.

Silence: (Cf. s.v. FINGER, LIP, Silence and FINGER, MOUTH, Silence.) Placing index over closed mouth. France. Mitton, p. 145. "Still your finger on your lips, I pray." Shakesp., Hamlet, I, v, 188; Troil., I, iii, 240. Ringfinger bent, all others straight. Gk. and Rom. antiquity. Fischer, Antaios, II, p. 323. Thumb and middle finger in an open and closed motion while moving the hand away from the body, "as if cutting with scissors... cutting off yards of gossip." Southern Ital. Efron, p. 157. Pointing vigorously at floor or ceiling ("Be quiet, the landlady is an ogre"). Univ. of Calif. Berkeley. McCord, p. 291.

Sorrow: Hands folded, fingers pressed until joints crack. Anc. Gk. and Rom., Neapol. De Jorio, p. 265; Sittl, p. 23. With index at each eye, trace course of tears = mock sorrow. Amer. schoolchildren. Seton, p. xxi, 54.

Stealing: Extending thumb and index, or index and middle finger, toward a vest pocket or an inner coat pocket, closing the fingers and withdrawing them. Lat. Amer. Kany, p. 106. Extending the fingers like claws and then bending first and second joints inward as if scratching something, or the hand thus formed is drawn down the cheek as if scratching it. Lat. Am. Kany, p. 107. Scratching empty space with fingers is an accusation of being a thief. Mexican. Lomas, p. 36.

Stop: Putting thumbs up, or licking them, signifies desire to drop out of a game. Children. Scotland. Opie, p. 143. Crossing fingers, sometimes index and middle finger of one hand; usually fingers of both hands must be crossed and raised. Children. England, Wales. Opie, p. 143. Crossing one's fingers and uttering a truce formula. Children. England. Opie, p. 142. (Cf. s.v. Peace above.)

Superiority: Hands raised to level of chest, palms facing one another, tips of fingers of one hand lightly touching tips of fingers of the other. Righteous superiority. Birdwhistell, Time (Jul. 15, 1957), p. 68. "Steepled fingers indicate a feel-

ing of superiority. " Birdwhistell, Colliers (March 4, 1955),
p. 56.

Superlative: (Cf. FINGER, LIP, Admiration.) Thumb and
index or middle finger touch, and are placed on the lips, from
where they are pulled abruptly. Simultaneously lips produce
sound of kiss. Hand remains for a moment, fingers half open,
palm towards face at some distance from it. French. Mitton,
p. 151. Snapping the fingers. Spain, Lat. Am. Green, p. 72.
Raising the bunched fingers of one hand to the level of the chest
and with the palm facing the speaker. Madrid, Lat. Am.
Green, p. 30. Raising the bunched fingers of one hand, palm
up, to approximately the level of the speaker's chest, then
spreading the bunched fingers abruptly. Madrid, Lat. Am.
Green, p. 71-72.

Surprise: Tip of index, vertical, placed to lips. Anc. Gk.
and Rom. Sittl, pp. 272-273.

Surrender: In Athenian fistfights the defeated signals surrender by raising his index. Anc. Gk. Sittl, p. 219. (Cf.
s.v. Mercy above.)

Taste: Laying finger on tongue. Amer. schoolchildren.
Seton, p. xxi.

Teasing: Hitting thumb nails of both hands together lightly.
Saudi Arabia. Semiotic. Barakat, no. 173. Touching tips of
index and thumb, then pointing them at someone. Saudi Arabia.
Semiotic. Barakat, no. 217. Placing tip of right thumb on
middle joint of extended index, other fingers pressed into palm,
then moving index in pecking motion several times. Saudi
Arabia. Semiotic. Barakat, no. 168. Rubbing both indexes
together several times while fingers are extended forward.
Saudi Arabia. Semiotic. Barakat, no. 77a. Rubbing tips of
thumb and index together. Saudi Arabia. Semiotic. Barakat,
no. 172.

Threat: (Cf. s.v. HAND, Threat.) Holding right index
down with thumb, other fingers extended; rapidly executed.
Saudi Arabia. Semiotic. Barakat, no. 79. Right index firmly
held down by the right thumb, other fingers extended like a fan,
hand is then moved several times. Lebanon, Syria, Saudi Arabia. Semiotic. Barakat, no. 46. Fingers of one hand pushed
toward the eyes of another. Ital. Bresciani, Ebreo, c. xxxxix;
Sittl, p. 45. Shaking clenched fist in the direction of offender.
Or index extended accompanies verbal threat. Or crossing one's
arms. Spain, Lat. Am. Green, p. 40. Index raised and extended stiffly, other fingers clenched. Boggs, col. 321. Holding up index. Bulwer, pp. 166-167. Right index extended from
fist, then shaken at someone. Jordan, Lebanon, Libya, Syria,
Saudi Arabia. Autistic or culture-induced. Barakat, no. 21.
Right index extended and pointed directly at someone without
moving it. Jordan, Lebanon, Syria, Saudi Arabia. Autistic
or culture-induced. Barakat, no. 22. Index and middle finger
extended from fist with back of hand up, then hand is moved
forward once or twice toward another person's eyes. Saudi
Arabia. Semiotic. Barakat, no. 201. Fingers of both hands
are extended to threaten the eyes of one who has extended the

fingers of one hand to threaten the eyes of the former. Anc.
Gk. Sittl, p. 46. Index and little finger ("horns") extended
toward someone's eyes. Neapol. De Jorio, p. 94; Sittl, p. 46.
Index pointed at someone and violently agitated up and down from
the wrist. France. Mitton, p. 144. Extended index or all
fingers as threat to the eyes of another. Melampus; Sittl,
p. 45. "but wag his finger at thee." Shakesp., Henry VIII, V,
iii, 130. Hitting table with index while making verbal threat.
Argentine. Wéyland, p. 36.

Tomorrow: Index extended, starting close to the chest,
describes half circle forward, curving up. Neapol. De Jorio,
p. 142. Semicircle drawn in the air with the index, from below upward. Neapol. Critchley, p. 89. Extended index held
about waist-level, then moved up in circular motion to its original position = "see you the day after tomorrow." Jordan, Lebanon, Saudi Arabia, Syria. Autistic, possibly semiotic. Barakat, no. 92.

Tortuousness: Little fingers of both hands are hooked together, both hands moved forwards in zigzag fashion. Neapol.
Critchley, p. 89.

Truth: Right index moved forward emphatically from cor-
ner of mouth. Amer. Indian. Austin, p. 594. Wagging index.
Austin, p. 595. Index pointing straight forward under the chin,
then moving forward with an upward curve. Seton, p. 210.
Middle finger (symbolic of Truth and Justice in the Middle Ages)
extended. Sculpture at cathedral of Freiburg; Hans Holbein,
"Dead Christ" (1521) in the Kunstmuseum, Basel; Fischer,
Basler Nachr. (Oct. 30, 1960), pl. 1.

Understanding: "using the forefinger as an imaginary chalk
to mark a board (the finger is occasionally dampened on the
tongue at the start)..." Univ. of Calif. Berkeley. McCord,
p. 290. Tip of index tapped against forehead. Ital. Manzoni,
c. xiv; Sittl, p. 115. Indexes on the table, zigzagging back
and forth (away and then together again). Southern Ital. Efron,
p. 154. Fingers held up in front of the eyes, squinting through
them. DWB, III, col. 1654, 10; Schwäb. Wb., II, col. 1506.
(Cf. EYE, FINGER, Leniency.)

Undetermined (future): Index draws as many semicircles
as one's arm's length will permit, starting at the chest. The
semicircles increase in shape and in the end the index is raised.
Neapol. De Jorio, p. 143. Thumb (symbolic of Love in the
Middle Ages) and index (symbolic of the Spirit) of right hand
(symbolic of that which is yet to be manifested, the future) form
circle by touching at the tip. Viennese woodcut of a Janus
bifrons (early 16th cent.) in Fischer, Basler Nachr. (Oct. 30,
1960), pl. 2.

Union: Intertwining rigidly held fingers of each hand in
front of gesticulator may accompany verbal expression of fusion.
Madrid, Lat. Am. Green, pp. 68-69. The two indexes united.
Aubert, p. 92. Interlacing fingers. Islam. Goldziher,
Zeitschr., p. 376.

Useless: Index is passed horizontally under the nose of
someone or under one's own nose. "No go!" "Nothing doing!"

Familiar, uncommon. France. Mitton, p. 149.

Vengeance: Thumbnails touch each other repeatedly, hands one above the other. ("I told you so.") Colombia. Saitz and Cervenka, p. 111.

Victory: Index and middle finger extended, forming a "V," other fingers folded toward palm, hand raised. In connection with politics: L. A. Times (May 30, 1963), p. 1; in connection with sports: Austin Statesman (Texas) (Nov. 8, 1962). Characteristic gesture of Winston Churchill during WW II. Ruesch and Kees, p. 76. Colombia, U. S. Saitz and Cervenka, p. 145. Thumb and index write 4. 0 in the air. Univ. of Calif. Berkeley. McCord, p. 290. Holding up index and middle finger, palm forward, other fingers pressed into palm. Lebanon, Syria. Semiotic. Barakat, no. 129.

Warning: "giving Oliver a sly pinch, to intimate that he had better not say he didn't." Dickens, Twist, p. 24. "And in conclusion, very slowly, Pnin showed how, in the international 'shaking the finger' gesture, a half turn, as delicate as the switch of the wrist in fencing, metamorphosed the Russian solemn symbol of pointing up, 'the Judge in Heaven sees you!' into a German air picture of the stick--'something is coming to you!' " Nabokov, pp. 41-42. Index and middle fingers extended, forming a "V." Among truckdrivers of the San Francisco area, perhaps the entire West Coast of the U. S., a warning to a truck going in the opposite direction, that there is a highway patrol car ahead. Oakland Trib. (Nov. 13, 1955), Suppl. Parade. Right index raised, other fingers closed, hand turned so as to have right eye, index and the whole person in line, simultaneously head is shaken a little. Seton, p. 221. Index raised. Amer. schoolchildren. Seton, p. xxi. Index shaken. U. S. Saitz and Cervenka, p. 149; cf. also Wéyland, p. 160. Index extended and moving from side to side. Colombia. Saitz and Cervenka, p. 148. Holding fingers in pear-shaped configuration with tips pointing up at about waist level, hand is moved slightly up and down ("Wait until later," "Enough," "Be careful"). Lebanon, Saudi Arabia. Semiotic. Barakat, no. 152.

Wish: Little fingers of right hand interlocked with those of another, then unlocked simultaneously. Children. Illinois. Opie, p. 312. Linking fingers and pressing thumbs together. Children. Glasgow. Opie, p. 311. Thumbs pressed together. Children. Iowa. Opie, p. 312.

Work: Rubbing the forehead with the thumb from side to side indicates hard work. Neapol. Critchley, p. 89.

FINGER, FOREHEAD

Cleverness: Pointing to the forehead with the index of one hand or tapping forehead with fingers of one hand. Spain, Lat. Am. Green, p. 75-76.

Cuckoldry: The "horns" (index and little finger extended, other fingers folded into palm), hand held near or over forehead. Lat. Am. Kany, p. 190. (Cf. s. v. FINGER, Cuckoldry.)

Decisiveness: Verbal suggestion of clarity of thought can

be accompanied by raising the fingertips of each hand, palms inward, to the forehead. Hands are withdrawn suddenly and held in front of speaker, palms inward. Madrid. Green, p. 79.

Enlightenment: Tip of index touching forehead, then quickly pointing outward, palm facing in. Aubert, p. 92.

Fatigue: Thumb of one hand extended upwards, stroking the forehead slowly from side to side. Anc. Rom., Neapol. De Jorio, p. 151.

Foolishness: Placing the index at the temple, making the movement of drilling it into the head. France. Mitton, p. 147. Tapping one's forehead with the index slightly curved. France. Mitton, ibid. Ital. N. Y. Times (March 1, 1959). Spain. Kaulfers, p. 258. Raising index and middle finger to forehead. Lat. Am. Kany, p. 59. " 'He must be a little touched here, ' my lord said, tapping his own tall placid forehead. " Thackeray, Virg., II, ch. xxiv. Finger pointing at forehead. Portug. Flachskampf, p. 231. Tips of all fingers of one hand together touch forehead. Palest. Bauer, p. 223. Raising index of one hand to temple and twisting it back and forth slowly or simply raising index to temple. Spain, Lat. Am. Green, pp. 53-54. Cf. s.v. FINGER, Derangement.

Gratitude: When someone is lighting one's cigarette, touch the back of his hand with the tips of one's fingers of the right hand, then place them on one's forehead, bowing the head slightly. Syria, Jordan, Saudi Arabia. Semiotic. Barakat, no. 6.

Luck: Cf. s.v. FINGER, Luck.

Mockery: "The gesture of the Ass's Ears consists in placing the thumbs of one or both hands at the temples and waving the fingers. [In] an example cited by Kleinpaul (p. 265)... the identification of the gesture as the Ass's Ears is probable but not certain. On the occasion of a shooting match at Coburg in 1614, a figure of a man was placed on the target. It waved a flag for a hit and made the sign of the Ass's Ears for a miss. Kleinpaul, who does not quote the exact words of his source, goes on to say that the master of ceremonies at other shooting matches presumably of the same period called up the marksman who had missed the target and, after mocking him in a short speech, asked the musicians to strike up a tune and suggested that if the audience wished to mock him with the "Eselsohren, " this might be decently done behind his back. Hermann Schrader calls "den Esel bohren" [to "drill the ass(es) ears)"] an unfamiliar idiom in northern Germany. Borchard-Wustmann cites the idiom from a glossary of 1735 with the definition "asininis auribus manu effictis illudere... " Taylor, p. 37. "The gesture... is, however, much older... For example, an allusion in verses ...that were published in 1537... shows the identification of ass's ears and frustration:... si truogen alle esel orn: ir gang und müeje heten s' verlorn. [They all wore asses' ears: their walk and labor was in vain.] ...At the end of the thirteenth century Meister Stolle... implies a similar idea:... Er welte ouch löuwen sprünge pflegen:/do erkos an im sin meister esels oren, /er strakte in (al)so mit slegen, /...[He (the ass) also wanted to leap like a lion: thereupon his master recognized that he wore ass's ears, he beat him so thoroughly...] Meister Stolle's mention of the ass's ears is altogether literal, but their significance appears in his comment. By an easy development gestures arise from such allusions. The gesture implies that the one who mocks observes that the persons mocked have ass's ears, that is, have been disappointed or have exhibited their folly, or he expresses his wish that they may have them. Somewhat later Der Teichner...puts ideas of this sort into the concrete form of a gesture: Als ir secht [seht] mā zaichent torn / Mit eim wunderleichñ snit, Das man sew [sie] Erkenn damit / Einem macht man esel orn. [As you see one designates fools in a curious manner, so that one can recognize them by it, one makes them ass's ears.]" Taylor, p. 39. "Nor mocked by a hand nimble at mimicking white donkey's ears." Persius, Sat., I, 59; Sittl, p. 109-110. "A modern Portuguese variation shows some difference in form and use. It consists in putting the thumbs between the neck and collar and waving the extended fingers up and down. It accompanies the colloquial phrase 'andar a voar' (to go flying, i.e., to have no money)." Taylor, p. 39. (Cf. s.v. FINGER, HAND, TONGUE, Mockery).

Perplexity: Raising fingertips of one hand, palm inward, to the forehead. Fingers are withdrawn immediately and hand dropped, palm down. Madrid, Lat. Am. Green, p. 78.

Plea: All fingers and the thumb of the right hand are joined together and the united points are pressed upon the forehead. Neapol. Critchley, p. 89.

Promise: Moisten index and make sign of the cross on the forehead or neck. Children. Liverpool. Opie, p. 124.

Reminder: Tip of index touching the forehead, then slowly pointed outward, palm facing in. Aubert, p. 92, fig. 140.

Sorrow: Raising cupped fingers of one hand to the forehead, palm facing outward. Predominantly women. Spain, Lat. Am. Green, p. 80.

Threat: Tip of index placed against forehead. Spain. Sittl, p. 115.

Understanding: Tip of index tapped against forehead. Ital. Manzoni, c. xiv; Sittl, p. 115.

Work: Cf. s.v. FINGER, Work.

FINGER, HAND

Anger: Middle finger held down with thumb, other fingers extended, then hand is shaken at someone. Saudi Arabia. Semiotic. Barakat, no. 71. Both fists clenched at waist level, thumbs extended in opposite directions. Lebanon, Syria. Semiotic, autistic. Barakat, no. 16.

Apotropy: (Cf. s.v. FINGER, Apotropy.) The "fig" (thumb protruded between clenched index and middle, or middle and ring fingers) is made in the vicinity of Lorient and Béarn accompanying the formula "my angel guards me." Seligmann, II, p. 186. In Andalusia, if a mother carrying an infant in her arms meets a person of suspicious aspect she will form the child's hand into a "fig." 19th cent. de Custine, I, p. 173. In Somerset and Yorkshire the "fig" serves as protection against witchcraft. A.

Cook, p. 135.   In Asia Minor the "fig" not only serves to protect from the evil eye, but also to bring misfortune on the person against whom it is directed.   NQ (Nov. 2, 1867), p. 365.
Basques use the "fig" against witches with the formula "witch,
retreat from me."   Seligmann, p. 186.   In Naples, plaster and
terracotta "figs" are placed on doorposts and shopwindows to
protect the building against misfortune.   Seligmann, II, p. 308.
In Brazil the loss of a "fig" amulet is feared, since it is believed that the wearer is now susceptible to all adversities of
life.   Cascudo, p. 311.   In Java the "fig" amulet is an object
of devout worship, esp. by childless women.   Elworthy, p. 177.
In 1859 a child had a severe "crick" in the neck.   The Italian
physician recommended that a coral "fica" be tied around its
neck and believed that the little girl had been "overlooked."
NQ (Aug. 9, 1879), p. 118.   For the use of the "fig" as amulet
against the evil eye, cf. Marques-Rivière, p. 78; Hastings,
Encycl., VI, p. 495; Hildburgh, p. 214.   When King Ferdinand
of Naples appeared in public, he made the "fig" from time to
time in his pocket, to avert the evil eye that someone on the
street may have cast on him.   NQ (Apr. 25, 1874), p. 325.
Seligmann, II, p. 186.   Neapolitans make a "fig" under their
coat or in their pocket in order to avoid obviously insulting a
person as a witch or, in general, at a social gathering.   Seligmann, II, p. 185-186.   "Everybody knows to double your thumb
in your right hand averts danger."   Elworthy, p. 256.   If one
sees someone who may entrance one, one should hold some gar-
lic and make the sign of the "fig" with the left hand to avert the
evil eye.   Portug.   Leite de Vasconcellos, p. 35.   Anc. Rom.
used the "fig" as protection against ghosts.   Seligmann, II,
p. 185.   The Talmud recommends the double "fig" (thumb of
one hand between index and middle finger of the other) against
the evil eye and the demonic influence of even numbers.   Bischoff, II, p. 181; HDA, II, col. 1307.   In the neighborhood of
Hennebont, France, ropemakers, coopers and tailors are considered uncanny.   To guard against their evil influence, the gesture of the "fig" is recommended together with the formula "Ar
garet."   Early 19th cent.   Michel, I, p. 171.   For the preser-
vation of their hair the women of Madrid are said to carry jet
figas on any part of the body, but the women of Toledo place
them in the hair itself, so that the desired effect may be more
immediate.   Kunz, p. 368.   The "fig" as protection against
ghosts.   Ovid, Fasti, 5, 433f.   The "fig" was used against
snakes, according to the hieroglyphics of Pyramid 672.   Marques-
Rivière, p. 78.   In Guarda, Portug., the "fig" is made when a
witch is in a whirlwind.   Leite de Vasconcellos, p. 37.   The
Portuguese also use the "fig" against sinister people, especially
the deformed and witches.   Leite de Vasconcellos, ibid.   King
Victor Emmanuel continually made the sign of the fig during the
battle of Solferino (1859) to protect his army.   Seligmann, II,
p. 186.   Index and little finger extended ("horns"), and rotates
from side to side several times while the gesturer says "lagarto"
(lizard) to counteract the possible effect of an utterance of the
taboo word "culebra" (snake).   Colombia.   Saitz and Cervenka,

p. 83. (Cf. s.v. Oath below.)

Approach: Hand raised, palm outwards, fingers moved downwards and toward palm. Beckoning. Mohammedan tribes of India. Rose, p. 313. Hand raised, palm inwards at level of face, arm half bent, tips of fingers moved inward. Aubert, p. 84. Greeks and romans, when beckoning, bend fingertips down. Sittl, p. 216. (Cf. s.v. FINGER, Approach.)

Approval: Hand raised, thumb and index forming a circle. Ruesch and Kees, p. 77. Tips of all fingers of the right hand joined at tip of thumb, tips directed upward, hand moved up and down a few times. Near East. Critchley, p. 91. Extended index is pointed at referent, then hand is placed on chest. Colombia. Saitz and Cervenka, p. 20.

Assurance: All fingers spread out, thumb curled up. Diagram of the "Abhaya mudra." Rose, p. 314.

Attention: Snapping fingers (either middle or ringfinger against thumb). France. Familiar. Mitton, p. 146. Hand extended with fingers together. U.S., Colombia. Saitz and Cervenka, p. 22 (U.S. student eager for attention waves raised hand from side to side, Colombian student thrusts it forward repeatedly). Hand raised, finger extended. Common in classrooms. Colombia. Saitz and Cervenka, p. 22.

Blessing: The "small cross" in form of a cross or "T" made with one or several fingers, is used for crossing oneself or other objects, and is used liturgically as well as privately. Appears to be the oldest of the forms of the sign of the cross and is mentioned by Tertullian. It was first made over the forehead and mouth, then it was applied to other parts of the body also, as well as to objects. An early development was the signing of mouth and breast or heart, or forehead, mouth, and heart. Gaudentius, col. 890. Double cross is still used in baptism: "accipe signum sanctae crucis tam in fronte quam in corde." Ohm, p. 292-293.

Bravery: "Fig" as amulet was worn as an ornate, vulgar part of the costume to show gallantry and display bravery. Portug. d'Abreu Brás, p. 626.

Calmness: Thumbs of both hands hooked over belt, hands at rest. 15th cent. Lacroix, p. 399.

Cheating: One hand crossed over the other, the little finger of one hooked into that of the other. Neapol. De Jorio, pl. 20, fig. 7; Fischer, Antaios, p. 333.

Cigarette: Index and middle fingers form "V" in front of lips. U.S. and Colombia. In Colombia it may also mean "Your car is smoking, burning." Saitz and Cervenka, p. 25.

Contempt: The "fig": "El fe le fiche a Dio 'l superto vermo." Frazzi, II, 19. Over the gates of the fortress of Comora there is a stone image of a maiden showing the "fig" to the enemy in contempt: an illusion to the impregnability of the virgin stronghold. NQ (Jul. 11, 1885), p. 32. In 1228 the Florentines defeated the inhabitants of Carmignano, the latter having erected an ivory statue of a "fig" on a cliff facing in the direction of Florence. Seligmann, II, p. 185. "Poi facea con le man le fiche al cielo." Trissino, c. xii. Cf. also Frezzi,

iii, 10; Dante, Inf., c. xxv. Caligula used the "fig" to greet
his guard tribune Cassius Chaerea, to show he thought he was
effeminate. Seligmann, II, p. 184. Hand extended, fingers in
shape of claws, moved back and forth several times. Saudi
Arabia. Semiotic. Barakat, no. 177. Francis I of Naples expressed his opinion of the populace at a riot by joining the fingertips of one hand and moving it forward repeatedly. Sittl,
p. 97, n. 4.

Copulation: Tip of right index placed into left palm and
twisted. Egypt. Semiotic. Barakat, no. 150. Tips of index
and thumb held together with other fingers pressed into palm,
hand moved rapidly up and down in pecking motion. Lebanon,
Libya. Semiotic. Barakat, no. 105. Right index tip ground
into left palm. Lebanon, Syria. Semiotic. Barakat, no. 118.
Palms together so that fingers are in contact, then all fingers
are moved back into palm except the two middle fingers which
remain extended: used by men to imply that they have slept
with the woman to whom the gesture is made. Saudi Arabia.
Semiotic. Barakat, no. 235. Scratching woman's palm with
index or middle finger when shaking hands. Colombia, U.S.
Adolescent. Saitz and Cervenka, p. 116. (Cf. s.v. HAND,
Copulate.)

Counting: Two hands at level of face, palms turned outward,
fingers curved. Extending the right thumb = 1, extending thumb
and index = 2, etc. Extending the fingers of the right hand and
the thumb of the left hand = 6. Both hands, fingers extended =
10. Extending the fingers of both hands, then making a fist with
both hands, then extending the right thumb = 11, etc. The gesture serves mostly to announce the hour of a rendez-vous. For
each ten the two fists are quickly opened and closed. France.
Mitton, p. 148. Clasping successively with the right hand the
thumb, the index, and the middle finger of the left hand. France.
Mitton, p. 148. Fingers bent, thumb extended upward = 30.
Islam. Goldziher, Zeitschr., p. 385. Hand raised, index extended = 1. Aubert, p. 80, fig. 114. (Cf. s.v. FINGER, Counting.)

Cuckoldry: The "fig" exhibited to someone intimates that he
is a cuckold. Potter, I, p. 452.

Deception: Cf. s.v. HAND, Deception.

Defiance: Both fists clenched at waist level, thumbs extended in opposite directions. Lebanon, Syria. Semiotic, autistic. Barakat, no. 16.

Depart: Hand, thumb extended, moves back and forth indicating direction of desired departure. Male. Impolite. U.S.
Saitz and Cervenka, p. 80.

Desperation: Cf. s.v. HAND, Desperation.

Direction: Jerking thumb over shoulder indicates a backward direction. Amer. schoolchildren. Seton, p. xx. Used
particularly by drivers to indicate that another vehicle is coming.
Colombia, U.S. Saitz and Cervenka, p. 55. Left hand held out
flat, palm down, right index run across it, signifies "across."
Amer. schoolchildren. Seton, p. xx. Pointing up indicates upward direction. Amer. schoolchildren. Seton, ibid. Index
swung forward and down in a curve, indicates "forward." Amer.

schoolchildren. Seton, ibid.

Emphasis: Inserting hand or finger into clenched fingers of other hand. Krout, p. 23. Poking with index on palm of other hand. Ghetto Jews. Efron, p. 146. Fingers of each hand joined at tips, tap chest. Men. Colombia. Saitz and Cervenka p. 47.

Encouragement: Spit on fingertips or palms and rub hands together. Children. Opie, p. 231.

Gossip: Cf. s.v. HAND, Gossip.

Greeting: While walking, if one has his hands at his side with the index finger extended, it is a sign of recognition and greeting to fellow hipsters, a cool way of shaking hands, if the thumb is extended, women in the know will realize one is seeking sexual intercourse. DAS, p. 470. Hand raised to level of head, index and middle finger extended, held together tightly, pointing upwards. Casual. Colombia. Saitz and Cervenka, p. 65.

Hitchhiking: Hand extended, thumb up and in direction the gesturer wishes to go. U.S. Saitz and Cervenka, p. 70.

Homage: Hand vertical, palm inward, held at the level of the face, arm half bent, moving of the fingertips from the heart. Aubert, p. 84.

Impossibility: Poking with the index on the open palm of the other hand. Implication: this will happen when grass grows on the palm. Can also signify the hammering in of an idea. Ghetto Jews. Efron, p. 146.

Insult: Index inserted in loose fist of other hand and moved back and forth several times. Colombia, U.S. Saitz and Cervenka, p. 116. Ragamuffins are known to make four "violins" (index and middle finger of one hand placed on either side of the nose and moved downward as if bow were being drawn over violin strings) at once with quadrupled force of the insult: the little finger is placed below the mouth, the tongue extruded, ring finger placed below nose, middle finger below eye, thumb behind ear. Mexico. Kany, p. 175. Hand outstretched for handshake, but just before contact with other person's hand, it is withdrawn--fingers closed as to a fist with thumb raised, the hand is jerked upward so that at terminus of movement the thumb points to the back of the gesticulator. Life (Sept. 3, 1945), 25. The "fig." Insult to prostitutes, used particularly in Southern France. Mitton, p. 151. Thumb extended from fist, which is jerked up and down several times. Vulgar. Men. U.S. Saitz and Cervenka, p. 78. The "fig." Colombia. Saitz and Cervenka, p. 115. Right index extended from fist, which is slapped into palm of left hand so that index goes between thumb and index of left hand. Colombia. Saitz and Cervenka, p. 115. Thumb is placed in mouth, rubbed down on tongue, hand is then dropped to waist level, heel of hand outward, and jerked forward once or twice. Lebanon. Semiotic. Barakat, no. 246. Hands placed back to back, interlocking fingers, then twisted in opposite directions until thumb protrudes from opening made by hands. Saudi Arabia, Syria. Semiotic. Barakat, no. 74.

Interrogation: Both hands held half cupped, palm up, finger-

tips pointing toward speaker, thumb pressed against index.
"What do you want?" Ital. Efron, p. 149. Fingertips of each
hand are united, pointing up, both hands held in front of body,
palms turned in, hands moved slightly up and down. Ital. Efron, p. 149, fig. 45.

Invitation: Right hand extended, palm down, fingers pointing
down. Spain, Portug., Morocco, Asia Minor, Arab. Flachskampf, p. 225. (Cf. s.v. FINGER, Approach.)

Magical: Left thumb held in right hand when hiccoughing.
African. Augustin. Doctr., 2, 20. If one dislikes someone,
one makes the sign of the "fig" with both hands, accompanied
by the formula "Vilôa, vilôa, danada, / Quando Deus veio ao
mundo, / tu não eras nada." As a result the person is dis-
oriented and is unable to move until after one has left. Portug.
Leite de Vasconcellos, p. 35.

Magnitude: To indicate height of a child: the fingers held
one above the other so that the little finger is nearest to the
ground. It is considered improper to indicate height of a child
by holding the hand so the palm is turned to the ground--a gesture used for animals and objects only. Medellín, Colombia.
Ades, p. 325. (Cf. s.v. HAND, Magnitude.)

Masculinity: Fist, thumb resting on index, moves up and
down sharply and repeatedly. Colombia. Saitz and Cervenka,
p. 85.

Medico-magical: In 1859 a child had a severe "crick" in
the neck. The Italian physician recommended that a coral "fica"
be tied around its neck and believed that the little girl had been
"overlooked." NQ (Aug. 9, 1879), p. 118. Hands crossed,
thumbs bent into closed fist, stops bleeding. Hovorka and Kronfeld, II, p. 563. (Cf. s.v. FINGER, Medico-magical.)

Mockery: (Cf. s.v. FINGER, Mockery; HAND, Mockery.) Fingers of one hand boring into the palm of the other. Switzerl.
Meschke, p. 337. One index pointed at the person mocked, the
other drawn along it several times in the same direction. Amer.
schoolchildren. Seton, p. xxi. (Cf. FINGER, Mockery "Rübenschaben.")

Money: Extended fingertips of the right hand (sometimes
only of the index) brush up into the open left palm. (May also
mean "pay.") Lat. Am. Kany, pp. 94-95; Colombia. Saitz
and Cervenka, p. 89. Rubbing tips of right index and thumb,
other fingers pressed into palm. Egypt, Lebanon, Jordan,
Syria, Saudi Arabia. Semiotic. Barakat, no. 7.

Mourning: Cf. s.v. HAND, Mourning.

Negation: Hand pointing upwards, palm out, or the first
three fingers, or the index is moved from the wrist as pivot
from side to side. Ital., 19th cent.; Amer. Indian. Sittl,
p. 86; Fischer, Transact. of the Ethn. Soc., I (1896), p. 283.
Semi-rotating hand with thumb and index up. ("No can do.")
Ital. Time (April 9, 1965), p. 67.

Negro: Moving extended right index once or twice across
the back of the left hand, a motion that indicates "color of skin:
negro." Lat. Am. Kany, p. 31.

Oath: Three fingers extended. Künssberg believes that this

gesture originated from the ancient apotropaic gesture of extending three fingers as protection against the evil eye and the demons. Ohm, p. 251. (Cf. s.v. FINGER, Oath.)

Obedience: Cf. s.v. FINGER, Obedience.

Overcoming obstacles: Fingers pointing to the front, palm
vertical to the side, hand undulating: (1) To thread oneself
through a maze of obstacles; (2) To overcome obstacles by going
around them. French. Mitton, p. 147.

Past: Cf. s.v. FINGER, Past.

Pay: Closed hand extended, palm up, rubbing thumb and
index tips together. Amer. schoolchildren. Seton, p. xxiii.
Patron simulates writing on palm in asking for the check in a
restaurant. U.S., Colombia. Saitz and Cervenka, p. 109.

Pensiveness: Hands out to sides, fingers and thumbs of
each hand rubbing together. Colombia. Saitz and Cervenka,
p. 139.

Plea: Hands clasped in front of body, fingers tightly interlocked, then hands moved several times from the wrists: plea
for mercy. Saudi Arabia, Lebanon. Culture-induced or autistic.
Barakat, no. 167.

Plenty: Both hands raised, fingertips pointing up, bending
fingers a few times quickly to the thumbs. Spain. Flachskampf,
p. 222.

Praise: Bending four fingers, thumb turned up and pointing
at person whom one applauds. Arab. Goldziher, Zeitschr.,
p. 385.

Prayer: Hands palm to palm, thumbs crossed, right over
left. "A Adoração dos Reis Magos, " Mestre do Retabulo de S.
Bento, early 16th cent. Lisbon.

Reconciliation: Hooking little fingers, touch thumbs and then
turn hands over and clap. Children. Radnorshire. Opie,
p. 325.

Regret: Cf. s.v. HAND, Regret.

Rejection: Thumb and index of the right hand joined at tips
and thus lengthening the pointed lips. Rejection of an importu-
nate gossip. Spain. Flachskampf, p. 230.

Request: Hand extended, palm up, fingers (except thumb)
rapidly moving back and forth. Colombia, U.S. Saitz and Cervenka, p. 104. Index pointing up or down is rotated to ask for
another round of drinks. U.S. Saitz and Cervenka, p. 110.

Resignation: Hand held out horizontally with palm upwards,
fingers in disarray. Rose, p. 314.

Result: Cupped hand pushed outward in an arc from the
chest, index extended. At conclusion of movement the palm
faces up. Madrid. Green, p. 65.

Rise: Fist clenched, thumb pointing upwards, fist suddenly
raised. Used only in addressing a group of people. France.
Mitton, p. 145.

Self-irony: Both hands placed one on top of the other, backs
of the hands upward, extended thumbs move like fins: "I was
as dumb as a fish; I didn't know a thing in the exam. " Spain.
Flachskampf, p. 232.

Sorrow: Wiping tears from eyes with back of hand, index

or thumb. Anc. Rom. Sittl, p. 275.

Stealing: Extending the open hand, palm down, then gradually folding the fingers, one after another, to the right downward and inward upon the palm, beginning with the little finger, with fanlike motion, imitating the seizure of some object and holding it in the fist. Lat. Am. Kany, p. 106.

Stop: Fist raised, thumb extended upwards. "Pax." France. Children. Mitton, p. 149.

Surrender: Gladiator who wants to surrender lowers his weapon and raises the hand which had carried the shield, index extended. Anc. Rom. Sittl, p. 218.

Teasing: Tip of right index placed into left palm and twisted. Egypt. Semiotic. Barakat, no. 150.

Threat: Hand raised vertically, index extended, pointing upward and turned repeatedly. Eastern frieze of the Parthenon; Sittl, p. 288-289. Middle finger held down with thumb, other fingers extended toward someone as hand is shaken. Saudi Arabia. Semiotic. Barakat, no. 71.

Time: Index taps wrist. Colombia. Saitz and Cervenka, p. 143.

Truth: Hand raised, index bent, accompanied by the formula "Hookey, Hookey Walter" or "With a hook," indicates that what is said is to be taken as a lie. British. (Cf. HAND, NOSE, Truth, ca. 1810.) WF XXIII (1964), p. 114.

Union: "He [the priest] takes the Host between the thumb and forefinger of his right hand, and makes the sign of the cross with it three times over the chalice..." Mass, p. 69.

Vengeance: Cf. s.v. HAND, Vengeance.

Wish: Scratching the palm of one hand with the fingers of the other indicates the desire to possess an object. Neapol. De Jorio, p. 172.

Withdraw: Holding up one hand, three fingers extended, indicates the desire to withdraw from a game. Children. Bradford-on-Avon. Opie, p. 143.

FINGER, HAND, MOUTH

Apotropy: "The Mass was long and solemn: the mayor... crossed himself by bringing the thumb of his right hand to his mouth according to the time-honored custom of the Isnello women at the approach of thunder to avert a storm." Carlo Levi, p. 46.

Drink: Thumb extended, pointing toward lips, fingers closed. French. WW II. Alsop, p. 29. Index and little finger extended from closed hand and brought to mouth while head is tilted back a little. Arab. Semiotic. Barakat, no. 198. Holding thumb side of right fist on mouth. Saudi Arabia. Semiotic. Barakat, no. 199.

Eating: Hand moved to mouth, all fingers united at tips. France. Vulgar. Mitton, p. 148. Tips of right index and thumb touching and brought to slightly open mouth, head tilted back a little. Arab. Semiotic. Barakat, no. 197.

Gratitude: Modest kiss of the hand, limited to kiss of the fingers. Anc. Gk. and Rom. Sittl, p. 168.

Greeting: Both hands stretched out, united at fingertips, touching other person's hand in same position, then leading them to lips. Moslem. Women. Goldziher, Zeitschr., p. 379.

Medico-magical: "Put thy hand upon me, sign me with thy thumb, / could I but kiss thy hand, / I would be healed of all this affliction." Berceo, 340-342.

Pensiveness: "Biting the thumb, thumbnail, fingers, or hands may be a selfregarding act that indicates doubt, hesitation, or annoyance and is, in such uses, not a gesture directed toward another person. It is allied to the gesture of putting the thumb into the mouth to signify that one is giving thought to a matter. An early instance of this is... the figure of a young Egyptian god with his left thumb in his mouth as represented on a wooden coffin of the twenty-first dynasty. Sittl regards (pp. 17-18) the act of biting the thumb in this sense as characteristically Roman in origin. Persius mentions it as a symbol of vexation... Horace knew it when he wrote 'in versu faciendo saepe caput scaberet vivos et roderet ungues' (Sat. 1, 10, 70). In this use the act becomes a topos with a long history. Persius imitated Horace, when he wrote 'nec emorsos sapit ungues' (Sat. 1, 106)..." Taylor, p. 56.

Plea: Kiss of the fingers. Anc. Gk. and Rom. Sittl, p. 168.

Silence: Index or hand laid vertically across lips. Anc. Gk. and Rom. Sittl, p. 54. Pressing mouth with fingers and right hand. Anc. Rom. Sittl, p. 215, n. 4.

FINGER, HAND, NOSE
Mockery: "Silently he placed both outstretched hands before his nose and wiggled the fingers. Even this derisive action drew no comment." Boucher, p. 115. (Cf. s. v. FINGER, NOSE, Mockery.)

FINGER, HAND, TONGUE
Insult: Thumbs to ears, fingers of both hands extended and moving backwards and forwards, tongue stuck out. Children. Colombia, U. S. Saitz and Cervenka, p. 76. (Cf. s. v. FINGER, FOREHEAD, Mockery.)

FINGER, HEAD
Apotropy: Extended indexes placed on top of head against evil eye, and against cats. Southern Ital. In Germany against dogs. Meschke, col. 332.

Concentration: "Then lays his finger on his temple..." Shakesp., Henry VIII, III, ii, 112. Tip of right or left index scratches back of one's head: concentration or possibly indicating veracity of someone's statement. Egypt, Jordan, Lebanon, Kuwait, Saudi Arabia, Syria. Autistic. Barakat, no. 3.

Cuckoldry: The "horns." Anc. Gk. and Rom. Sittl, p. 103; who interprets the two fingers as referring to the two men. Spain. Flachskampf, p. 248. The gesture already appears on Etruscan tombs of the 6th cent. B.C. Meschke, col. 31; Sittl, p. 103. Colombia. Saitz and Cervenka, p. 121.

Tips of thumbs placed on both temples, palms facing forward, fingers spread widely and moved back and forth. Syria. Semiotic. Barakat, no. 19.

Disbelief: Indexes of both hands extended and placed along temples, pointing upward. Univ. of Calif. Berkeley. King, p. 263.

Embarrassment: Scratching the head. Anc. Rom. Sittl, p. 48.

Foolishness: Thumb against temple, hand open. Neapol. Critchley, p. 89. Suggestion in Booth's Prompt-Book in connection with Othello, I, iii, 308 "If thou do'st, I shall never love thee after. Why thou silly gentleman" is "Tapping him playfully on the forehead." Tapping center of forehead. ("Do you think I'm stupid?") Ital. Time (Apr. 9, 1965), p. 67. Index points to temple and makes circular motion. U.S., Colombia. Saitz and Cervenka, p. 75. Index taps temple. U.S., Colombia. Ibid. Right index makes circular motion near right temple, head tilted slightly. Arab. Culture-induced or semiotic. Barakat, no. 61. Right index taps right temple, then is thrown out to side of head as head is tilted slightly to one side and brows are wrinkled. Arab. Culture-induced or semiotic. Barakat, no. 62.

Greeting: Cf. s.v. Respect below.

Hesitation: Head is scratched with one or more fingers of one hand. France. Mitton, p. 146.

Idealism: Raising index to the side of the head and describing small circles in the air. Spain, Lat. Am. Green, p. 48.

Insult: Ragamuffins are known to make four "violins" (index and middle finger of one hand placed on either side of the nose and moved downward as if a bow were being drawn over violin strings) at once with quadrupled force of the insult: the little finger is placed below the mouth, the tongue extruded, ring finger placed below nose, middle finger below eye, thumb behind ear. Mexico. Kany, p. 175.

Intelligence: Index taps lightly against temple or forehead; or it is simply placed against temple. Colombia, U.S. Saitz and Cervenka, p. 78.

Meditation: "J'ai beau frotter mon front, j'ai beau mordre mes doigts." Boileau, Sat. 7.

Mistake: Index extended, tip at temple, thumb extended or bent. Colombia, U.S. Saitz and Cervenka, p. 52.

Negro: Touching the head with the curled index to indicate kinky hair. Lat. Am. Kany, p. 31.

Oath: Finger moistened, shown, wiped--usually in the armpit--head tilted back, finger drawn across throat. Children. Opie, p. 126.

Respect: Right fingertips touched to forehead while bowing head slightly. Saudi Arabia, Jordan, Kuwait. Semiotic and culture-induced. Barakat, no. 54.

Warning: Right index raised, other fingers closed, hand turned so as to have right eye, index, and the whole person in line, simultaneously shaking the head a little. Seton, p. 221.

FINGER, HEAD, MOUTH

Pointing: "jerked his thumb, cocked his head, and gestured with the corner of his mouth toward him." Birdwhistell, Introd., p. 33.

FINGER, HEAD, NOSE

Disbelief: Holding one's nose with index and thumb, ducking head as if to say "me hundo para que pase." Lat. Am. Kany, p. 70.

FINGER, KNEE

Oath: The swearer of an oath laid down arms, helmet or hat before kneeling and raising two fingers. Medieval Wendic-Rugian. Grimm, DRA, II, p. 556.

FINGER, LIP

Admiration: Tips of right index, middle finger and thumb held in pear-shaped configuration and kissed while bowing slightly forward, whereupon the head is flicked up. Jordan, Lebanon, Syria. Semiotic. Barakat, no. 89.

Affection: Fingertips of right hand kissed and thrown forward. Amer. schoolchildren. Seton, p. xxii. Palm toward body, tips of fingers against lips, then hand extended toward someone. France. Mitton, p. 147; Aubert, p. 84. U. S., Columbia. Saitz and Cervenka, p. 79.

Approval: Fingers of one hand joined at tips and pressed against lips, then opened quickly and spread. Used more frequently by men. Can refer to a person or an object. Colombia. Saitz and Cervenka, p. 19.

Attention: "I in order that the leader should attend, put my finger upward from my chin to my nose. Dante, Inf., c. 25.

Drink: Touching lips with the tip of the extended thumb. Other fingers closed. French. Vulgar. Mitton, p. 147. Extended thumb (from clenched fist) jerked toward mouth. Eyebrows raised: "On va voire un coup?" Brault, p. 378. Bending finger and putting it to the lips. Benedictine monks. Critchley, p. 53.

Drunkenness: Cf. s. v. HAND, Drunkenness.

Embarrassment: Tip of index placed vertically to lips. Anc. Gk. and Rom. Sittl, pp. 272-273.

Exquisiteness: Cf. s. v. HAND, Exquisiteness.

Farewell: Fingertips to lips, then thrown forward. Intimate and casual. Colombia, U. S. Saitz and Cervenka, p. 63.

Foolishness: Extending lower lip, or pulling the lower lip downward with the index. Lat. Am. Kany, p. 49.

Mockery: Cf. s. v. FINGER, Mockery.

Mysterious: "He laid his finger on his lips mysteriously, walked in, and closed the door." Dickens, Pickw., I, p. 127.

Oath: Thumb and index form a cross and are led to the lips. Spain. Flachskampf, p. 242; Green, pp. 91-92. Variant: forming a cross with the indexes of both hands and kissing the point at which the fingers bisect. Spain. Green, ibid.

Pensiveness: Index or index and middle finger touch lower

lip. Sometimes all fingers rest against lower lip. U.S. Saitz
and Cervenka, p. 141. Tips of fingers touch in front of or at
lips or chin. Colombia, U.S. Saitz and Cervenka, p. 142.

Perfection: (Cf. s.v. Admiration.) Thumb and index or
middle finger joined at tip, brought to the lips, then suddenly
removed from the lips, which are left pursed. The fingers remain some distance from the face for a moment, fingers slightly
parted. France. Mitton, p. 151.

Regret: One or more fingers inserted between lips and
teeth. Colombia, U.S. Saitz and Cervenka, p. 102.

Respect: Touching tips of right index, second finger and
thumb to mouth, bowing slightly. Variation: touching mouth,
then forehead as body is bowed. Jordan, Lebanon, Syria, Saudi
Arabia. Semiotic, or culture-induced. Barakat, no. 24.

Silence: Pressing lips together with index and thumb of one
hand. Mexico. Jiménez, p. 34; Spain. Nieto, p. 32; Flachskampf, p. 226; Ital. De Jorio, p. 293; Sittl, p. 54. Index
of one hand brought to the lips. Cervantes, Quijote, II, xxxiii.
Shakesp., Troilus, I, iii, 240. Cf. also Green, p. 43. Shutting lips with finger. Krout, p. 25. Head advanced, index
laid on pursed lips, eyebrows raised. Aubert, p. 148. "laying
his finger on his lip, drew his companions back again, with the
greatest caution and circumspection." Dickens, Twist, p. 81.
Touching lower lip of a child with tip of right index. Jordan,
Lebanon, Libya, Syria, Saudi Arabia, Kuwait. Culture-induced
or semiotic. Barakat, no. 27. Laying finger on lip. Colombia,
U.S. Saitz and Cervenka, p. 123. Thumb extended moves from
one corner of closed lips to the other. May also mean "keep it
secret." Colombia, U.S. Ibid.

Superlative: Fingers of one hand bunched, hand is brought
to the lips and fingertips are kissed before the fingers are opened.
Spain, Lat. Am. Green, p. 72. France. Brault, p. 377:
reserved "for expressing the more subtle and refined emotions
(e.g. describing a fine wine) and for this reason usually execute[d]...very gently. In its ultimate form, only the thumb and
forefinger are pressed together, placed parallel to the face and
...softly brushed with the corner of the lips."

Surprise: Tip of index vertically placed to lips. Anc. Gk.
and Rom. Sittl, pp. 272-273. Expressions of feigned shock
may be accompanied by bringing the fingertips of one hand, palm
inward, to the lips. Spain, Lat. Am. Green, pp. 80-81.

Teasing: Tip of index placed below lower lip, then flipped
up so that it barely grazes the underside of the tip. Saudi
Arabia. Semiotic. Barakat, no. 223.

FINGER, MOUTH

Admiration: Taking tips of bunched fingers to the mouth. Pérez
Galdós, pt. 2, iv, vi.

Affection: Index put in mouth, then joined to middle finger
and placed between breasts. 1001 Nights, II, p. 302-303.

Deception: Holding the right index and middle finger a little
in front and to the right of the mouth, pointing to the left, moving the hand to the left, past the mouth and downward. Seton,

p. 119.

Disappointment: Thumb at corner of mouth, fingers extended, palm facing away from the body. Colombia. Saitz and Cervenka, p. 37.

Disbelief: Brushing fingers outward from the mouth, meaning "de dientes para afuera" or "de labios afuera," that is, what has been said is "idle talk." Lat. Am. Kany, p. 70.

Drink: (Cf. s.v. FINGER, Ordering [wine].) Putting thumb into mouth. Palest. Bauer, p. 223. Spain. Pardo Bazán, p. 27. Thumb jabbed at the mouth ("Waiter, bring some wine"). Ital. Time (April 9, 1965), p. 67. Thumb extended, pointing to mouth, little finger raised; hand rocks back and forth. Colombia. Saitz and Cervenka, p. 44. Can also indicate intoxication. Ibid., p. 45. (Cf. s.v. HAND, Drunkenness.)

Eating: Thumb is repeatedly waved vertically before mouth. Southern Europe. Sittl, p. 115. Tips of thumb and index applied around the mouth with rapid alternations in a vertical and horizontal direction. Neapol. Critchley, p. 89. Cupped fingers of one hand move back and forth in front of open mouth. Women often move one finger after another. Colombia. Saitz and Cervenka, p. 56. Mouth wide open, fingers of one hand bunched at tips and brought to the mouth. France. Life (Sept. 16, 1946), p. 12. Chin raised, fingers and thumb of the right hand pinched together, curved and jerked two or three times toward the open mouth; eyebrows raised: "On va bouffer?" France. Brault, pp. 378-379.

Embarrassment: Raising hand to mouth and covering mouth with fingers. Spain, Lat. Am. Green, p. 81.

Encouragement: Spitting on fingertips or palms and rubbing hands together. Children. Opie, p. 231.

Insult: Fingers in mouth. Dürer, "Christ at Pillar." Tip of right middle finger placed in mouth, lips pursed around it, then it is removed and held out with back of hand forward, other fingers pressed into palm: obscenity directed at female members of family of person to whom gesture is made. Saudi Arabia. Semiotic. Barakat, no. 165.

Mockery: Indexes of each hand pull corners of mouth apart. Brueghel, "Pride," in Gowing, p. 12. Cf. also Röhrich, figs. 20, 23, 26. Index and middle finger of both hands pull mouth apart at the corners, thumbs at temples. Variant: same with one hand. Lucas Cranach the Elder, "The Mocking of Christ," (1538), L.A. County Museum of Art.

Negation: Clicking of tongue, index of right hand raised and moved from right to left at level of chest, head slightly raised. Neapol. De Jorio, p. 224. Spain. Flachskampf, p. 237.

Oath: Link little fingers and spit, saying "spit your death." Children. Liverpool. Opie, p. 126. Spit and cross the throat, or spit over wrist or little finger, saying "spit your mother's death." Children. Cumberland. Opie, p. 126.

Pensiveness: Index of left hand raised to mouth, lips pursed. Woodcut, Brant, p. 3. Placing finger in mouth and sucking or gnawing it. Bulwer, pp. 158-160.

Poverty: Putting index into mouth as if sucking it. Palest.

Bauer, p. 221.
   Reminder: If one has overlooked or forgotten something,
one should put the index into one's mouth, say "fff! ai! ai!,"
and make the sign of the cross. HDA, II, col. 1483.
   Silence: (Cf. s.v. FINGER, Silence; FINGER, LIP, Silence.) Tip of finger placed over closed mouth, index vertical.
France. Mitton, p. 145. Also Pliny, Juvenal, Apuleius, Martianus Capella, Jerome. Sittl, p. 213. Bulwer, pp. 168-170.
Palest. Bauer, p. 223. Placing extended right index in front
of mouth and blowing on it. Saudi Arabia. Semiotic. Barakat,
no. 75.
   Speaking: Finger curved and put to the mouth. Trappist
monks. Critchley, p. 53. Expressions suggestive of loquacity
may be accompanied by raising the bunched fingers of one hand
to the mouth. Spain. Green, p. 81.
   Surrender: Thumbs of both hands placed in mouth, other
fingers pointing directly at someone. Rwala Bedouin of Kuwait,
Iraq, Syria, Saudi Arabia. Semiotic. Barakat, no. 131.

FINGER, MOUTH, TONGUE
   Mockery: Two fingers spread mouth at corners, tongue stuck
out. Rabelais, Bk. I, ch. xviii. Numerous gargoyles on European buildings, occurrences in German masques of the 15th and
16th centuries, the Schembartlauf of Nürnberg of 1539 and depictions of the mocking of Christ. Röhrich, p. 26 and pl. 20,
23, 24, 26.

FINGER, NECK
   Death: Drawing the index, or index and middle fingers, representing a knife, quickly across the throat. Lat. Am. Kany,
p. 27. "He looked at the sentry...and, pointing with one finger,
drew the other across his throat." Hemingway, pp. 36-37.
   Drink: Tip of thumb touching tip of middle finger and one
of these snapped against throat. Palest. Bauer, p. 223.
   Hanging: Moving index across throat. Lat. Am. Kany,
p. 107.
   Insult: Moving the fingers between collar and neck as if
brushing back hair behind the ear, with annoyed facial expression, or moving index and thumb back and forth on the neck.
Lat. Am. Women. Kany, p. 176.
   Mistake: Index horizontally extended and moved across
throat. Colombia, U.S. Saitz and Cervenka, p. 51.
   Mockery: Cf. s.v. FINGER, FOREHEAD, Mockery.
   Mourning: Scratching neck. Women. Anc. Gk. Sittl,
p. 27.
   Negation: Tip of thumb, hand open, placed against throat,
then catapulted forward. Or the same with all fingers.
Southern Ital. De Jorio, p. 224; Sittl, p. 95.
   Oath: Licking tip of index and making sign of the cross on
the throat. Children. Opie, p. 122. (Cf. also s.v. HAND,
Neck.)
   Poverty: Drawing index across throat and snapping relaxed
index and middle finger. Venezuela. Kany, p. 88. Thumb on

throat, fingers up. Cervantes, Quijote, II, liv. Putting thumbs
between the neck and collar and waving the extended fingers up
and down, accompanied by the colloquial phrase "andar a voar"
= "to go flying, " i. e. to have no money. Portug. Taylor,
p. 39.

FINGER, NOSE

Amazement: "To express amused amazement, it is only necessary to place the index finger along the nose and assume an expression of amazed amusement. " French. WW II. Alsop,
p. 27. Index of right hand placed alongside of nose, mouth
slightly open, eyes wide open: "Pas possible" or "Non, sans
blague!" French. Brault, p. 376.

Attention: "I in order that the leader should attend, put my
finger upward from my chin to my nose. " Dante, Inf., c. xxv.

Cleverness: " 'Why, one need be sharp in this town, my
dear, ' replied the Jew, sinking his voice to a confidential whisper; 'and that's the truth. ' Fagin followed up this remark by
striking the side of his nose with his right forefinger... " Dickens, Twist, ch. xlii. " 'Pay attention to the reply, constable,
will you?' said the doctor, shaking his forefinger with great
solemnity of manner, and tapping the bridge of his nose with it,
to bespeak the exercise of that worthy's utmost acuteness. "
Dickens, Twist, ch. xxx. Thumb and bent index placed to nose
(as if blowing the nose). Neapol. De Jorio, pp. 55-56; Sittl,
p. 111.

Copulation: Rubbing side of index over bridge of nose:
proposition to a woman. Jordan. Semiotic. Barakat, no. 239.

Cunning: " 'By the way, Baron, suppose he should be a
guet à pens, that young Creole? Suppose our excellent friend
has invented him up in London, and brings him down with his
character for wealth to prey upon the innocent folks here?'
'J'y ai souvent pensé, Milor, ' says the little Baron, placing his
finger to his nose very knowingly, 'that Baroness is capable of
anything. ' " Thackeray, Virg., I, chap. xxv. "If Gastone
moved his forefinger and thumb up and down each side of the
bridge of his nose, his verdict on my new landlord was 'A
smart one!' But if, instead, he tapped one side of his nose,
he was telling me, 'Watch out! He's a fishy chap, he stinks. ' "
Ital. Graham, p. 26.

Defiance: Right index hooked over tip of nose. "I'll do it
in spite of you. " Saudi Arabia. Semiotic. Barakat, no. 153.

Disappointment: Left thumb placed against nose. Ital.
Manzoni, ch. xvi, 198; Sittl, p. 116.

Disbelief: "The Shanghai Gesture is in current use in
Greece... Persons born in the Peloponnesus have informed A. R.
Nykl that it is ordinarily accompanied by the expletive 'Na!' and
implies 'If you believe this story, you are a d--- fool. ' " Taylor, p. 49. "So the burgess of Preston who has charged a
married woman with unchastity must proclaim himself a liar
holding his nose with his fingers. " Pollock and Maitland, II,
xv. "He wears his forefinger perpetually upon the side of his
nose. He is not to be amused with fancies and chimeras. "

Simms, p. 31. "I could see the critter [the seacaptain] had
heard on him afore, by the way he twisted his mouth around the
long nine [cigar]; but when I told him about the carriage and the
rooster and so on, he jest took and give the long nine a fling,
clapped his thumb again the side of his nose, and winking one
eye, made his finger twinkle up and down for as much as a min-
it without saying a word." Slick, I, p. 144; Taylor, p. 22.

Dissatisfaction: Holding nose with thumb and index. Univ.
of Calif. Berkeley. McCord, p. 291.

Drink: Touching nose with tip of index. Trappist monks.
Critchley, p. 53.

Emphasis: " 'What do you think them women does t'other
day, ' continued Mr. Weller, after a short pause, during which
he had significantly struck the side of his nose with his forefinger, some half-dozen times... 'Goes and gets up a grand te
drinkin' for feller they calls their shepheard, '... " Dickens,
Pickw., I, p. 363.

Etiquette: Index extended and placed below the nose, exert-
ing mild pressure inward and upward to stifle a sneeze. Spanish and Lat. Am. Regarded as mildly offensive in Lat. Am.
Green, p. 94.

Fecetiousness: "Mr. Jackson's fingers wandered playfully
round his nose at this portion of his discourse, to warn his
hearers that he was speaking ironically... " Dickens, Pickw.,
II, p. 310.

Familiarity: "...as he remarked afterward to Pen, winking
knowingly, and laying a finger on his nose. Thackeray, Pendennis, ch. v.

Greeting: Squeezing nostrils with index and thumb of left
hand, and pointing to the navel with the index of the right.
Friendly greeting. Astrolabe Bay, New Guinea. Comrie,
p. 108.

Humiliation: Thumb to nose, fingers extended: "tanto di
naso." Neapol., late 16th cent. Taylor, p. 45.

Ignorance: "Mr. Jackson struck his forefinger several
times against the left side of his nose, to intimate that he was
not there to disclose the secrets of the prison-house, and playfully rejoined: 'Not knowin,' can't say.' " Dickens, Pickw., II,
p. 28. (Cf. s.v. Secrecy below.)

Insult: The so-called "violín" (Mex.) in which index and
middle fingers of one hand are placed on either side of the nose
and moved downward as if a bow were being drawn over violin
strings. Lat. Am. Kany, p. 175. Index and middle finger
form a "V, " the other two fingers are held down by the thumb.
Hand is then raised to nose, so that the "V" formed by the
fingers surrounds nose. Mex. Jiménez, p. 37. Index taps
one side of the nose ("I have no confidence in your masculinity.")
Ital. Graham, p. 26. Thumb to nose, fingers extended, moving from side to side. Children, U.S.; Adults, Colombia.
Saitz and Cervenka, p. 77. Thumb of one hand to tip of nose,
thumb of other hand to little finger of the first hand, fingers
extended and moving from side to side. Colombia. Saitz and
Cervenka, p. 77. Picking nostrils with right index and thumb

6.   "The Mocking of Christ," M. 917, f. 53 (cat. 19), the Pierpont
Morgan Library, New York; publ. in The Hours of Catherine of
Cleves (pl. 19) by George Braziller, Inc., New York (see FINGER,
NOSE--Mockery).   Reproduced by permission of the library
and the publisher.

("Go to hell").   Syria.   Barakat, no. 33.   Pushing tip of nose
in with right index (implies that the person to whom the gesture
is made is a Negro).   Saudi Arabia.   Semiotic.   Barakat, no.
103.   Flicking tip of nose with tip of right index (implies that
the person to whom the gesture is made is a homosexual).
Lebanon, Syria.   Semiotic.   Barakat, no. 18.   Picking nostrils
with tips of right index and thumb, then thrusting out middle
finger stiffly.   Libya, Syria.   Semiotic.   Barakat, no. 12.   Cf.
s.v. Mockery below.
      Joke: Index rubs side of nose.   Amer. schoolchildren.
Seton, p. xxi.
      Mockery: Index and thumb of one hand pull down lower lip,
index and thumb of the other pull up tip of nose.   "Mocking of

Christ, " Hours of Catherine of Cleves, Guennol Coll., N.Y.,
f. 53.   Cf. The Hours of C. of C., N.Y., n.d., pl. 19 (see
illustration 6).   Thumb or index presses tip of nose upwards.
Spain.   Flachskampf, p. 231; Portug.   Urtel, p. 29.   Fingers
of both hands spread wide open, one thumb applied to tip of nose,
the other to the tip of the little finger of the other hand.   British.
WF 23, p. 114.   (Cf. s.v. HAND, NOSE, Truth.)   Thumb to
tip of nose, fingers extended ("The long nose").   HDV, I, p. 323.
(Cf. s.v. FINGER, Mockery.)   Placing the thumb of the left hand
on the tip of the nose, joining the thumb of the right hand to the
little finger of the left and spreading the fingers to the fullest
extent.   Hone, Jan. 1831; Opie, p. 318.   "The seventeenth-
century satirist Scarron is an altogether appropriate person to
show knowledge of the [Shanghai] gesture (tip of thumb to nose,
other fingers extended).   In Book III of Le Virgile travesti (1651)
Célaeno, one of the harpies, complains that Aeneas and his companions are trespassers.   The narrator of the scene concludes
'Elle nous fit un pied de nez; / Et nous laissant bien étonnez,
/ La mal-plaisante prophétesse / S'envola de grande vitesse.'
And in Book IX the gesture is used again in the same sense..."
Taylor, pp. 15-16.   "The earliest illustration of the Shanghai
Gesture that has come to my knowledge is a print of 1560 en-
titled "La Fête des fous" by Peter Brueghel.   Here a fool
makes the tandem (thumb of one hand to nose, fingers extended,
thumb of other hand to little finger of first hand) gesture with
the thumb of his left hand placed just beneath his nose and not,
as is usually the case, at the tip of the nose.   This minor variation in form does not appear to be significant."   Taylor, pp. 11-
12.   " 'Panurge suddenly lifted up in the air his right hand, and
put the thumb thereof to the nostril of the same side, holding
his four fingers straight out closed and orderly in a parallel
line to the point of his nose, shutting the left eye wholly and
making the other wink with a profound depression of the eyebrow
and eyelids.   Then he lifted up his left hand, with hard wringing and stretching forth his four fingers and elevating his thumb,
which he held in a line directly correspondent to the situation
of his right hand, with the distance of a cubit and a half between them.   This done, in the same form he abased toward
the ground both the one and the other hand.   Lastly, he held
them in the midst, as aiming right at the Englishman's nose.'
...The Englishman responded to Panurge suitably enough with a
modification of the tandem gesture: 'Then made the Englishman
this sign: his left hand all open he lifted up into the air, then
instantly shut into his fist the four fingers thereof, and his
thumb extended at length he placed upon the gristle of his nose.
Presently after, he lifted up his right hand all open, and abased
and bent it downwards, putting the thumb thereof in the very
place where the little finger of the left had been and did close
in the fist, and the four right-hand fingers he softly moved in
the air.   Then contrarily he did with the right hand what he had
done with the left, and with the left what he had done with the
right.' "   Taylor, pp. 9-10.   "Like Rabelais' use of the gesture,
the association with a fool in both [Brueghel's] example and the

following sketch by Bernardo Passeri that was made in Rome and engraved in Antwerp seems important. It will be noted that this association is characteristic of the earliest uses of the gesture and occurs in widely separated places." Taylor, pp. 11-12. "A superb example of the tandem gesture occurs in 'a design illustrating a passage in the parable of the Prodigal Son' as found in 'Wierix's Bible, 1594.'...'Wierix's Bible, 1594' that Hone cites in the Year Book...never existed. What Hone means is a series of engravings of scenes in the New Testament planned by Hieronymus Natalis (Jerome Nadal, 1507-1580) at the suggestion of Ignatius Loyola." Taylor, p. 12. "'Truth stripping a fine lady of her false decorations, with one hand removes a painted mask, and with the other pulls away her 'borrowed' hair and headdress, showing an ugly face, and a head as round and smooth as a bullet. Below there are four little satyrs, one of whom is taking a single sight, or making a 'nose' at the lady; whilst a second is taking a double sight, or 'long nose,' towards the spectator.' " Quoted by Taylor, p. 17, from a description (1875) of a depiction of 1702. William Hone refers to it as "a ludicrous practice..., which suddenly arose as a novelty within the last twenty years [after 1812] among the boys of the metropolis." Hone, col. 65. "In 1845 Benjamin Disraeli refers to 'putting his thumb to his nose.' " Taylor, pp. 21-22. "But the varmint didn't wink, but stood still as a post, with the thumb of his right paw on the end of his smeller, an wigglin' his t'other finger thus (and Mike went through with the gyration)..." Burke, quoted by Taylor, p. 24. Ezra Pound alludes to the gesture in 1917 in his Lustra. Taylor, pp. 25-26. " 'I've been naughty, have I?' 'You know best about that, old boy. No, I don't feel you quite get my drift. I happen to think Bill Evans is rather a good chap, you see. And if you don't mind my saying so, I'm not very much of the same opinion about you. Quite the contrary, in fact. Sorry to have to mention it.' Barking excitedly, I gave him the English snooks (left hand to nose with fingers extended, right hand subjoined with fingers extended), then the German snooks as Jean had demonstrated them (left hand as before, but right hand curled up and rotated as if cranking a movie camera), then the donkey's-ears treatment with raspberry or Bronx cheer obbligato. This completed, I moved off once more, feeling a little toned up for the moment." Amis, p. 232, quoted from the Engl. ed. by Taylor, p. 27. "...the definition in Maller's dictionary of 1561, which equates 'einem eine Nase machen' and 'uncis naribus indulgere,' concerns a phrase which often means the Shanghai Gesture in later use and is apparently accepted in that sense by the editors of the Deutsches Wörterbuch...However, the Latin definition has been obviously suggested by Persius, Sat. 1. 40-41: 'Rides,' ait, 'et nimis uncis naribus indulges' ('You are scoffing,' he says, 'and use your turned-up nose too freely'), and this does not mean the Shanghai Gesture." Taylor, p. 35. "Especially curious are the figures of a devil cocking a snook that Elworthy describes and illustrates [pp. 111-112]. Crouching forward with his bovine tail flying up over his back, and with horns on his

head, he cocks a double snook with his left hand at his nose.
Elworthy found figures of this sort on the back of a cab horse
in Naples, in oxidized silver in Rome, and also in silver in
Florence, and yet again...in shops in Paris and London around
1900.   Presumably such figures had originally an apotropaic use
and became articles of commerce.   Elworthy comments, 'This
is the attitude of vulgar mockery among all people.   Neapolitans
call this Beseggiare....   Hence it may be assumed that the
devil is looked upon generally as a contemptuous mocking personage, with a dash of vulgar humour.'   His word 'Beseggiare'
is an error...for 'fefeggiare,' i.e. to mock, and has no exclu-
sive reference to the Shanghai Gesture."   Taylor, p. 46.   "References to the use of the Shanghai Gesture in Spain, Portugal,
and Latin America are rare, but friends assure me of its current use in all these lands.   The Spanish idiom 'hacer un pito
catalán' (to make a Catalan fife [horn, whistle])' is significant
for the use of the same metaphor...in Servian and French
names for the gesture."   Taylor, p. 46.   "Urtel [p. 17] reports
a Portuguese idiom 'achetar o beque' (to buy the prow of a
ship).' "   Taylor, p. 47.   Extended fingers with thumb to nose.
Palest.   Bauer, p. 224.   "Here Mr. Jackson smiled once more
upon the company, and, applying his left thumb to the tip of his
nose, worked a visionary coffee-mill with his right hand: thereby performing a very graceful piece of pantomime (then [1828]
much in vogue, but now, unhappily, almost obsolete) which was
familiarly denominated 'taking a grinder.' "   Dickens, Pickw.,
II, pp. 28-29.   "Mr. Jackson's fingers wandered playfully
round his nose, at this portion of his discourse, to warn his
hearers that he was speaking ironically."   Dickens, Pickw., II,
p. 280.   "Hacer un pito catalán"--extended and waving fingers
resembling those of a fife player.   Lat. Am.   Kany, p. 145.
Cf. s.v. Insult above.

    Poverty: Placing right index and middle finger on either
side of one's nose and (optional) drawing fingers downward.
Spain.   Flachskampf, p. 232; Kany, p. 89.   Placing slightly
curved index on the nose.   Guatemala.   Kany, ibid.

    Prayer: The Phrygian sect of the Kataphryges put finger to
nose (sign of submission to God's will, as an animal submits to
being led by its driver).   Sittl, p. 186.

    Promise: Touching tip of nose with tip of right index, ac-
companied by the formula "on my nose," indicates promise to
do something.   Libya, Saudi Arabia, Syria.   Semiotic, or culture-induced.   Barakat, no. 96.

    Refusal: Passing the index horizontally under the nose of
another person, or one's own nose.   France.   Familiar, seldom
used.   Mitton, p. 149.

    Retraction: The person guilty of slander, in retracting his
statements, had to pull himself by the nose.   Norman.   Grimm,
DRA, I, p. 198.

    Revulsion: Nostrils held shut briefly by thumb and index.
(Unpleasant smell.)   Colombia, U.S.   Index, extended horizontally, moves up and down between upper lip and nose.   Men
sometimes spit in presence of unpleasant smell.   Colombia.

Saitz and Cervenka, p. 127.

Secrecy: "Mr. Jackson struck his fore-finger several times against the left side of his nose, to intimate that he was not there to disclose the secrets of the prison-house,..." Dickens, Pickw., II, p. 19. " 'Ah,' said the coot profoundly, that's telling.' He looked out of the corners of his eyes at Fabian, leered, and with a ridiculously Victorian gesture laid his finger alongside his nose." Marsh, p. 157. "[he] clapped his finger on the side of his nose, thereby recommending secrecy and discretion." Smollett, Peregr. Pickle, I, ch. xix. (Cf. s.v. Understanding below.)

Silence: Putting index to nose. Portug. Flachskampf, p. 226.

Solemnity: "shaking his finger with great solemnity of manner, and tapping the bridge of his nose with it..." Dickens, Twist, p. 270.

Suspicion: Index placed alongside nose. Neapol. Critchley, p. 89. Index laid tip to side of nose. Ital. N.Y. Times (March 1, 1959).

Threat: Pushing tip of nose in with index. Saudi Arabia. Semiotic. Barakat, no. 95.

Understanding: "...laying a finger beside the nose to indicate full awareness of a situation...occurs in J. J. Hooper's description, written in 1845, of a man who 'chuckled longer than before, at the wit of calling corn-whisky 'spring water,' and put his fingers by the side of his old cut-water of a nose!' " [Simon Suggs' Adventures, p. 120.] Taylor, p. 23. "In an aquatint of 1818 dealing with counterfeit claims to public benefits, 'The lame sailor approaches the begging-can with a finger to his nose, but holding a coin in his left hand; his face is twisted to show that he is not deceived.' In an engraving that has reference to a scandal connected with the Derby of 1826, 'A man stands beside [the wife of a man accused of trickery] with a pair of top-boots under his arm; he puts a finger to his nose, grinning, and says: 'I'll bet my Awl! I'm up to snuff, Mum.' In a lithograph of the same year, 'A John Bullish fellow grins knowingly at Heath, his finger pressed against his nose' and thus indicating his full understanding of the situation.' A vignette, also of the same year, is much to the same effect.... Heath himself, who published the last two scenes in his Northern Looking Glass, meant the reader to consider him to be a knowing spectator. Such examples as these suggest that J. J. Hooper, and Mrs. Stephens [Jonathan Slick] have consciously or unconsciously mingled two gestures." Taylor, p. 23. "Upon which Mr. Weller struck three distinct blows upon his nose in token of intelligence, smiled, winked, and proceeded to put the steps [of a coach] up, with a countenance expressive of lively satisfaction." Dickens, Pickw., II, p. 177.

Useless: Index is pressed horizontally under the nose of someone or one's own nose. ("No go!" "Nothing doing!") French. Familiar, uncommon. Mitton, p. 149.

FINGER, NOSE, TONGUE
Hurry: Tip of right index placed on tongue, then on tip of nose:
sign for person to hurry. Saudi Arabia. Semiotic. Barakat,
no. 228.
Mockery: Nose pressed upwards with thumb, tongue extruded. Children. Opie, p. 319. "A child holds his hands
with the palms together and both thumbs against the nose. Another child that does not know the trick is asked to pull the
little finger of one hand. Thus, one hand slips over the other,
the fingers spread, and the Shanghai Gesture is made. The
tongue is often stuck out as an accompaniment to it. [Wehrhan,
p. 17.]" Taylor, p. 7.
Teasing: Extended index placed sideways over nose, then
moved across nose several times with tongue extended. Egypt.
Semiotic. Barakat, no. 216.

FINGER, SHOULDER
Insult: Cf. s.v. FINGER, HAND, Insult.
Mockery: "At this inquiry Mr. Martin looked, with a
countenance of excessive surprise, at his two friends, and then
each gentleman pointed with his right thumb over his left
shoulder. This action, imperfectly described in words by the
very feeble term of 'over the left,' when performed by any number of ladies or gentlemen who are accustomed to act in uni-
son, has a very graceful and airy effect; its expression is one
of light and playful sarcasm." Dickens, Pickw., II, p. 214.
Pointing: Right thumb held out from fist and moved back
and forth over right shoulder: indicates where someone has
gone. Jordan, Lebanon, Saudi Arabia, Syria. Semiotic or
culture-induced. Barakat, no. 88. (Cf. s.v. FINGER, Direction; FINGER, Pointing.)

FINGER, TEMPLE (Cf. s.v. FINGER, FOREHEAD, and FINGER,
HEAD)
Cuckoldry: Cf. s.v. FINGER, Cuckoldry.
Derangement: (Cf. s.v. FINGER, FOREHEAD, Foolishness.)
Index placed with tip against temple and given the motion of a
drill. France. Familiar. Mitton, p. 147. Spain. Flachs-
kampf, p. 231.
Disbelief: Pointing the indexes of both hands, placing them
along the temples, pointing upward. Univ. of Calif. Berkeley.
King, p. 263.
Understanding: Tip of index placed against temple. Anc.
Gk. Sittl, p. 115.

FINGER, THROAT
Poverty: "Putting a thumb to his throat and extending his hand
upward he gave them to understand that he had not a coin of
any kind on him." Cervantes, Quijote, II, liv.

FINGER, TONGUE
Betting: Cf. s.v. FINGER, Betting.
Gossip: Index touches tip of tongue. Spain. Flachskampf,

p. 230.   Colombia.   Saitz and Cervenka, p. 64.

Greeting: Customary Tibetan greeting to a fellow traveller: thrusting up thumb of right hand and thrusting out tongue.   Asia, xxvi (1926), p. 320, cited by Hayes, p. 223.

Indecision: Placing finger against the tongue and shaking it as if it had been burnt.   Palest.   Bauer, p. 223.

Medico-magical: Cf. s.v. FINGER, Medico-magical.

Success: Tip of index touches tongue and then makes an imaginary figure "1" in the air.   Indicates that speaker has said something particularly effective, clever, witty.   Colombia, U.S. Saitz and Cervenka, p. 134.

Taste: Laying finger on tongue.   Amer. schoolchildren. Seton, p. xxi.

FINGER, TOOTH

Anger: Biting one's thumb.   DEP, p. 46.   Biting fingers. Dante, Inf., c. xxxiii, lviii;   Neapol.   De Jorio, p. 265.   Ital. Bresciani, c. li.   Spain.   Sittl, p. 18, n. 10.   (Cf. s.v. Chagrin below).

Apology: Biting middle joint of right index with heel of hand pointing forward, hand closed.   Saudi Arabia.   Semiotic. Barakat, no. 155.

Chagrin: Moving the index laterally between the upper and lower rows of teeth while biting it lightly.   Palest.   Bauer, p. 219.

Contempt: "First, you place the nail of the right thumb inside the upper front teeth,...   You then bring the thumb and enclosed fist forward in a sharp, throwing motion.   While making this gesture it is permissible...to make a hissing noise, which can be roughly transliterated as 'Pssssst.' "   French. Alsop, p. 27.   Right thumbnail placed under tip of upper front teeth, then withdrawn rapidly, creating a noise.   Arab.   Goldziher, Zeitschr., p. 370.   Fist of right hand is clenched, thumbnail inserted under upper front teeth, then snapped forward, face scornful: "Celui-là, je ne lui donnerais seulement pas ça!"   French.   Brault, p. 381, who quotes Randle Cotgrave (1611):   "Nique, faire la: To mocke by nodding or lifting the chinne;   or more properly, to threaten or defie, by putting the thumb naile into the mouth, and with a ierke (from th'upper teeth) make it to knacke."   Always vulgar.   (Cf. s.v. FINGER, Nothing.)   Also Anc. Gk., Sittl, p. 96, who draws attention to the German "nicht was schwarz unterm Nagel ist."

Embarrassment: Biting the bent index.   Palest.   Bauer, p. 219.

Flirting: Thumb placed in mouth sideways and bitten, then removed and shaken.   Syria.   Semiotic.   Barakat, no. 206.

Frustration: "But don't fret your pretty self, Mrs. Jones-- for dinner passed and tea-time came, but no Jones.   Mrs. Jones began to get snappish, and by ten o'clock she had bitten all the ends from her taper finger, besides dreadfully scolding the servants, all round."   Kelly, p. 189;   Taylor, p. 57.

Insult: Biting one's thumbs.   DEP, p. 46.   "The very offensive gesture of biting the thumb has a meaning somewhat related to that of the Shanghai Gesture, but appears never to be understood whimsically. It also differs from the Shanghai Gesture because the fingers are very rarely said to be spread. ...In a Danish gesture described as "pege Fingre" [to point the fingers], one thrusts the thumb into the mouth and spreads the fingers in the direction of the person to whom the gesture is addressed. Klitgaard cites this along with gestures excerpted from sixteenth- and seventeenth-century legal records, but seems to imply that "pege Fingre" is more recent than these. However this may be, biting the thumb is an old and very famous insult, best known perhaps from the quarrel of Mercutio and Tybalt in Romeo and Juliet, I, i: 'Do you bite your thumb at us, sir?' 'I do bite my thumb, sir.' Sittl traces the gesture back to classical times.... The form of the gesture varies. It may consist in merely biting the thumb, in putting the thumb in the mouth or against the front teeth and withdrawing it with an emphatic motion, or, as in the Danish example, in biting the thumb with the accompaniment of spread fingers. Urtel cites (pp. 13-14) two forms, one in which the thumb with an open perpendicular hand is drawn emphatically forward from under the chin and another in which a finger with the palm of the hand upward is similarly drawn forward. This means that the person to whom the gesture is addressed is ruined or done for. This variation of the gesture is current in Portugal, Spain, and with some modification in Italy. According to Urtel (p. 16), a gesture in which the thumb is placed against the upper teeth is widely known. He cites it from Portugal, Spain (the thumb is placed against the upper lip rather than the teeth), France, Italy, Greece and the North American Indians. ...Biting the thumb may degenerate into meaning 'Nothing!' [cf. below], which may, according to the situation, be more or less insulting or may be merely a comment on a situation." Taylor, pp. 54-55. Serious insult. Italy. Graham, p. 25.

Luck: Placing index sideways in mouth and biting it, then removing it, shaking it vigorously: reference to luck of another person. Lebanon, Syria, Saudi Arabia. Semiotic. Barakat, no. 67.

Medico-magical: Letting the ringfinger glide over the teeth at the daily ablutions protects against toothache. HDA, II, col. 1495.

Mourning: Putting the index of one hand between the rows of teeth and letting the head sink into the palm of the other. Palest. Bauer, p. 219.

Negation: Thumbnail against front teeth, then catapulted forward. Gk. and Ital.; Sittl, p. 95.

Nothing: Thumbnail placed against front teeth, then catapulted forward. Gk. and Ital., Sittl, p. 95. Fist raised, thumb extended, pointing with the tip to the upper teeth. Aubert, p. 81. Scraping upper incisor with the thumbnail. French. Familiar. Mitton, p. 149. Thumb snaps from teeth, meaning "absolutely nothing doing." French. Life (Sept. 16, 1946), p. 12. Thumb placed under the upper incisor, then rapidly flicked forwards. Southern France. Critchley, p. 91. Spain. Blasco Ibáñez,

p. 29. Putting tip of nail of the right thumb to the upper teeth
and pulling it back. Arab. Goldziher, Zeitschr., p. 370.
  Oath: "And they [the Saracens] put their fingers to their
teeth--cut them to pieces after that and they would not lie."
Chevalerie Vivien, Ms. B, 1. 215-216.
  Pain: Biting fingers. Dante, Inf., c. xxxiii; Neapol. De
Jorio, p. 265; also Bresciani, c. li. Spain. Sittl, p. 18, n. 10.
  Poverty: Putting thumbnail against one of the upper teeth
and catapulting the hand forward. Palest. Bauer, p. 221.
  Regret: Cf. s.v. FINGER, LIP, Regret.
  Reminder: If one has forgotten or overlooked something,
one should bite one's finger three times, so that one sees the
traces on it. Bohemia. HDA, II, col. 1485.
  Secrecy: Biting the index. Russian. F. Bowers, p. 98.
  Threat: Biting the thumb. Meschke, col. 331-332; Klein-
paul, p. 176. Biting right index placed sideways into mouth.
Egypt, Saudi Arabia. Semiotic. Barakat, no. 125. (Cf. s.v.
Insult above.)
  Warning: To indicate to another driver that a traffic police-
man is following, one may bite the ends of the three middle
fingers. Mexico. Kany, p. 121.

FINGER, WRIST
  Greeting: "The salutation between Mr. Weller and his friends
was strictly confined to the freemasonry of the craft [coachmen],
consisting of a jerking round of the right wrist, and a tossing
of the little finger into the air at the same time." Dickens,
Pickw., II, p. 247.

FINGERNAIL
  Desperation: "She, desperate, with her nails her flesh doth
tear." Shakesp., Lucr., 739.
  Disbelief: Cf. s.v. FINGER, Disbelief.
  Insult: Rubbing or pressing thumbnails together. Spain.
Flachskampf, p. 234.
  Nothing: Cf. s.v. FINGER, Nothing.
  Self-satisfaction: "The fingernails are first breathed upon
and then rubbed against the right coat lapel--I congratulate my-
self." Ital. Graham, p. 26.
  Vengeance: Cf. s.v. FINGER, Vengeance.

FINGERNAIL, TOOTH
  Anger: Biting nails. Anc. Rom., 19th cent. Ital. Sittl,
pp. 17-18.
  Chagrin: "...another gnawed his fingers, as he stalked
across the room." Smollett, Peregr. Pickle, ch. lxix.
  Concentration (nervous): Biting nails. Anc. Rom. Sittl,
p. 18.
  Contempt: Cf. FINGER, TOOTH, Contempt.
  Desire: Biting nails. Anc. Rom. Sittl, p. 18.
  Embarrassment: Biting nails. Anc. Rom. Sittl, p. 18.
  Forgetfulness: Cf. s.v. Embarrassment above.
  Frustration: Cf. FINGER, TOOTH, Frustration.

Insult: Cf. FINGER, TOOTH, Insult.
Jealousy: Biting nails. Anc. Rom. Sittl, p. 18.
Negation: Biting nail of right thumb, then quickly protrud-
ing the hand. Aleppo. Women. Goldziher, Zeitschr., p. 379.
Cf. also FINGER, TOOTH, Negation.
Nothing: (Cf. s.v. FINGER, TOOTH, Nothing.) Nail of
right thumb catapulted off the upper incisor. Spain. Flachs-
kampf, p. 233. Ital. De Jorio, p. 231. Arab. Goldziher,
Zeitschr., p. 370. Portug. Urtel, p. 15. Anc. Gk. and Rom.
Sittl, pp. 95ff. Cf. also s.v. FINGER, TOOTH, Nothing.
Oath: Saracens swore by tapping fingernail against teeth.
Grimm, DRA, II, p. 550.
Poverty: Flick right thumbnail on front teeth: "I have no
money" or "I have only a little." Jordan, Lebanon, Syria,
Saudi Arabia. Semiotic. Barakat, no. 97. Cf. also s.v.
FINGER, TOOTH, Poverty.
Sorrow: Biting nails. Anc. Rom. Sittl, p. 18.

FOOT
Adoration: Taking off shoes in entering sacred place. Palest.
Bauer, p. 192.
Anger: "The girl stamped her foot violently on the floor as
she vented this threat." Dickens, Twist, p. 142. Stamping the
feet. Anc. Rom. Sittl, pp. 14-16. "Let go my hand!--stamp-
ing with her pretty foot: How dare you, Sir!" Richardson,
Clarissa, iv. "Stamp, rave, and fret." Shakesp., III Henry VI,
I, iv, 91. "'Damn you,' Gombauld repeated, and stamped his
foot again." Huxley, ch. xxi. "Mr. Weller--quite transfixed
at his presumption, led him by the collar to the corner and dis-
missed him with a harmless but ceremonious kick." Dickens,
Pickw., II, p. 483. Kicking. Krout, p. 23. Trample. Isa.,
63, 3. Tapping floor with the foot. Lat. Am. Kany, p. 64.
Standing up. Portug. ("cresce" = "he grows" i.e. to attack).
Basto, p. 6.
Apotropy: In some villages of Brandenburg, the newly married couple must step over an axe or a horseshoe on the way
home. Beitl, p. 163.
Approval: Stamping feet at basketball game. Univ. of
Calif. Berkeley. McCord, p. 292.
Attention: "I sat down before [the bench] and knock'd with
my foot, a boy came presently, and I bad him fetch me a pint
of warm ale." Defoe, II, p. 13.
Blessing: Gods as well as priests bless with the lotus-
anointed foot. Ohm, p. 321.
Contempt: Stroking the ground with one's foot several times
as if to trample something that one has thrown away. Neapol.
De Jorio, p. 131. Moving the foot as if administering kicks.
Used particularly in speaking of someone absent. Neapol. De
Jorio, ibid. Treading on an imperial coin was prohibited in
ancient Rome. Vita Beati Stephani; Sittl, pp. 107-108. Treading on sacred ground. The Greeks complained that the Turks
trod on the ground of Sta. Sophia at the conquest of Constanti-
nople. Sittl, p. 108. Treading the cross. It was prohibited

to portray a cross among decorations on the floor. Cod. Iustin. I, 8; Sittl, p. 108. The Huguenots trod upon crosses and sacred images. Holzwarth, p. 167. In Prud., Peristephanon 3, 74 Eulalia threatens: "Idola protero sub pedibus." Sittl, p. 108. Treading on someone or something by jumping, e.g. a grave. Eurip., El. 327f.; Sittl, p. 108. Treading on recumbent person, living or dead. Anc. Rom. Sittl, p. 107. Spain. Cervantes, Quijote, I, ch. xvi. Ital. Bresciani, ch. xi.

Depart: Kicking as if kicking a ball is a command to someone to leave. Men. Rude, often comic. U.S., Colombia. Saitz and Cervenka, p. 81.

Determination: "...and beating his foot upon the ground, as a man who is determined to deny everything." Dickens, Twist, p. 460.

Embarrassment: Shuffling the feet. Birdwhistell, Introd., pp. 30, 34. Also Anc. Gk. and Rom. Sittl, p. 48.

Emphasis: In classical antiquity it was common to patter with the feet during religious song. Paulus Energeticos. Ohm, p. 321.

Etiquette: Men rising from a sitting position in the presence of a lady. Medieval German. Kudrun, st. 342, 1. Messengers rise when delivering a message. Kudrun, st. 768, 1-2.

Fatigue: Dragging the feet. Krout, p. 22.

Fear: Stepping back. Krout, p. 22. Jumping up from sitting position. Anc. Gk. and Rom. Sittl, p. 14.

Finished: Termination of affair: kick (not made in presence of former partner). Colombia. Saitz and Cervenka, p. 137.

Greeting: The Japanese remove a slipper when they salute ceremoniously. Eichler, p. 159. Islanders in the Philippine archipelago take a person's hand or foot and rub it over their face as greeting. Eichler, p. 162. "In the straits of the Sound [Philippines] it is customary to raise the left foot of the person greeted, pass it gently over the right leg, and then over the face." Eichler, ibid. Natives of the Philippines bend very low, raising one foot in the air with the knee bent. (They also place their hands on their cheeks in saluting a friend.) Eichler, ibid. Among the people of Arakan it is still the custom to remove the sandals in the street and the stockings in the house as sign of greeting. Eichler, p. 159.

Impatience: "I even stamped with impatience!" Richardson, Clarissa, II, p. 277. "'Do you hear me?' cried Nancy, stamping her foot on the ground." Dickens, Twist, p. 417. "'Come in!' he cried impatiently, stamping his foot upon the ground." Dickens, Twist, p. 344. Tapping foot several times on ground. Arms may be akimbo or folded across chest. Colombia, U.S. Saitz and Cervenka, p. 73.

Insult: "To keep on one's shoes on entering a friend's home or the temple was bad manners." Cited by Hayes, p. 247 from A. C. Bouquet, Everyday Life in New Testament Times, p. 144. Showing the sole of one's foot is an insult, therefore one should not cross one's legs. Japan. L.A. Times (West Magazine) March 26, 1972, p. 7.

Investiture: In some ecclesiastical courts-leet the lord, on

the occasion of an investiture, stepped with his right foot upon
that of the vassal. Grimm, DRA, I, p. 196. Cf. s.v. Submission below and FOOT, HAND, Submission.

Joy: Stamping with the feet. Ezek., 25, 6.

Magical: On St. Andrews' night one is to turn around barefoot upon the threshold, thereafter one will see one's future
beloved. Thuringia. ZfVk, V (1895), p. 97. Stepping on one's
foot, looking over the shoulder to see spirits. Bolte and Polivka, II, p. 320, n. 1 and p. 518, n. 1. The temporary king
must stand on one foot during a ceremony in order to win a victory over evil spirits. Siam. Frazer, IV, p. 150. The
Pontificale Romanum prescribes that the candidate for confirmation is to place his foot upon the right foot of the sponsor.
HDA, III, col. 246. The custom of stepping upon someone's
foot in order to obtain his supernatural powers such as seeing
spirits, flying, hearing over great distances, also occurs in
Denmark, France, Corsica, mod. Greece, among the southern
Slavs, and in Celtic belief. HDA, III, col. 244-245. The
oldest mention of this gesture occurs in a poem of the Stricker
(13th cent.) HDA, III, col. 243.

Medico-magical: A strong man should place his bare foot
upon a person suffering a stroke and remain in this position for
some time. HDA, III, col. 850. In a charm of the 11th to
12th century it is advised that one step on the right foot of a
horse suffering from stiffness of the limbs. HDA, III, col. 245.
"Dextro pede" was used by Juvenal (10, 5) almost in the sense
of "feliciter." Boehm, p. 27f. King Sancho of Castile set his
foot on the throat of a patient. Bloch, pp. 151-152, 155. Pyrr-
hus "could cure the spleen by sacrificing a white cock and gently
pressing with his right foot on the spleen of the persons as they
lay down on their backs." Plutarch, Pyrrh. 468-469.

Mourning: Go barefooted and bareheaded. Ezek., 24, 16.17;
Mic. 3, 7. Bare feet were part of the Roman mourning ritual.
HDA, II, col. 850.

Oath: In taking an oath, the ancient Greeks stepped upon
the cut up sacrificial animal. Sittl, p. 143. A cross made
with the foot on the ground is an oath not to return to a certain
place. Neapol. De Jorio, p. 170. The Saxons of Siebenbürgen
swore in cases of boundary disputes with bare feet, loosened
belt, and a lump of earth upon their heads. 14th cent. ZV,
XVIII (1908), p. 116.

Pain: Stamping foot on ground. Ital. Bresciani, c. xlviii.

Possession: In claiming a plot of land, the right foot must
be placed upon it. Medieval German. Grimm, DRA, I, p. 197.

Prayer: Standing in prayer. Ethiopian Hosannah liturgy.
Löfgren, p. 81. In general standing is the prayer posture in
oriental Christian liturgy. Ohm, p. 326. The Romans ascended
to the temple by starting with the right foot; a remnant of this
is probably the custom that the priest in the Roman liturgy as-
cends to the altar with the right foot first. Ohm, p. 304.
Stepping up to pray. Awesta. Bartholmae, p. 102; Ex. 24, 1f.;
3 Cor. 19, 11; Ohm, p. 304. Kneeling as symbolic of original
sin is inappropriate during Easter in the Roman liturgy, there-

fore one stands; similarly during the reading of the Gospel at
Mass. Ohm, pp. 326-327. Mohammedans take off shoes before
praying or entering a mosque. Wächter, pp. 23f. Greek temple
inscriptions require the taking off of shoes. Aurich, pp. 200f.
At the offering of sacrifice Greeks and Romans went unshod; Roman women prayed "nudis pedibus" for rain. Wächter, p. 23f.;
Petron., Sat. 44. Taking off shoes while praying to the sun.
Peru. Heiler, p. 104. Standing as prayer posture was common
among the Sumerians, Brahmins, anc. Jews. Ohm, p. 324.

Rejection: In baptism of a former heathen, after the formula for rejection of heathen deities has been pronounced, the neophyte places his foot upon that of his godfather (cf. s.v. Magical above). Medieval German. Grimm, DRA, I, p. 197.

Respect: In Persia, everyone who approaches the royal
presence bares his feet. Eichler, p. 159. Among the Damaras
of South Africa it was considered courteous to take the sandals
off before entering the house of a stranger. Anderson, p. 231.
Similarly in Morocco. Dawson, p. 97.

Submission: Falling before a person's feet. Shakesp.,
Love's Lab. Lost, IV, i, 92; Richard II, I, i, 165; King John,
V, iv, 13. In Morocco a bride mounts a ram representing the
husband over whom she thus asserts superiority. She hangs on
it a necklace to make him weak, and when the ram has been
killed she puts her right foot on its stomach. James, pp. 60-
61. "I had read in a Hebrew book of an approved plan by which
one spouse might secure lordship over the other for life. One
was to tread on the other's foot at the marriage ceremony; and
if both hit on the stratagem, the first to succeed would retain
the upper hand. Polish Jewish. Maimon, ch. x. Also 13th
cent. Germany: Bastow, pp. 318-19. Cf. FOOT, HAND, Submission.

Vanity: Looking at one's feet. Medieval French. Li Chev.,
2726, Medieval German. Thom. v. Circl., 433.

Victory: Setting foot upon the vanquished. (Cf. s.v. Magical, Rejection, Submission above.) Grimm, DRA, I, p. 196.
Shakesp., Cor., I, iii, 49; Cymb., III, ii, 92.

FOOT, HAND

Blessing: Girl standing on one foot, with cakes in lap and a
cup of brandy in her right hand for blessing the flax crop.
Prussia. Frazer, IV, p. 156.

Joy: "...then there was a great clapping of hands, and
stamping of feet, and flourishing of handkerchiefs; to all of which
manifestations of delight..." Dickens, Pickw., II, p. 71.

Medico-magical: "A gesture which is restricted to women
and which is probably distinctively Spanish is performed when
one or both legs have become numb as a result of lack of activity or simply from having been crossed for long periods.
The movement consists of wetting the thumb of one hand with
saliva and drawing a sign of the cross on the instep of the
foot.... In urban Spain, the gesture is performed in the pri-
vacy of one's home; in rural areas, the movement is doubtless
more publicly observable. Men tend to rub the affected area

vigorously or to strike the area with the open hand to restore
normal circulation..." Green, p. 93.

<u>Submission:</u> If the bride is to be the ruler of the house-
hold, when her hands are joined to those of the groom, hers
must lie on top, her left foot must be on top of that of his, and
she must rise first after kneeling at the altar. Beitl, p. 163.
(Cf. s.v. FOOT, <u>Submission.</u>) Hands of the vassal are folded
before his standing lord, vassal kneels before his sitting lord.
In the latter case the vassal laid his hands upon the feet of his
lord. Medieval German. Grimm, <u>DRA,</u> I, p. 193.

FOOT, HAND, HEAD

<u>Greeting:</u> Bowing, touching feet and raising hand to head. Hin-
du. Son to parents, pupils to teachers, laymen to religious
heads. Thomas, p. 80.

FOOT, LEG

<u>Determination:</u> Kicking oneself on the shins. Boys. Opie,
p. 230.

<u>Flirting:</u> "When a woman sits with legs crossed, one foot
curled, it often indicates she's interested in a nearby man."
Birdwhistell, <u>Colliers</u> (March 4, 1955), p. 56.

<u>Joy:</u> Stamping on the ground with joy. Anc. Gk. and Rom.
Sittl, p. 12.

<u>Nervousness:</u> "young girl changes stance and exhibits rest-
less behavior when a breeze ruffles a lock of her hair." Birdwhistell, <u>Introd.</u>, p. 8.

<u>Prayer:</u> Legs folded under the body with the right foot on
the left thigh, the left on the right thigh. "Lotus position."
Buddhist. Critchley, p. 68.

FOOT, LIP

<u>Adoration:</u> As modest request Phaedra wishes to kiss the foot
of Hippolyte. Vincentius Anthol., Sittl, p. 166.

<u>Gratitude:</u> Kissing the foot of a person. Achill. Tat.;
Sittl, p. 170, n. 1. Kissing the foot of the Ethiopian king.
Heliodor.; Sittl, ibid.

<u>Greeting:</u> (Cf. s.v. LIP, <u>Greeting.</u>) Diocletian seems to
have required senators and other dignitaries to kiss his foot at
their reception and their departure. Sittl, p. 170. Relatives
of Roman emperors had to kiss the imperial foot. Sittl, p. 170,
n. 1. At the end of the Empire, arrivals were heartily greeted
by kissing their feet. Sittl, p. 170.

<u>Homage:</u> The younger Maximinus had his feet kissed. Sittl,
p. 169. Emperor Tiberius II kissed the foot of Pope Constanti-
nus. Sittl, p. 170. Since the Germanic invasions of the Roman
empire, the kissing of the foot obtains only if a cross sanctifies
the shoe. Sittl, p. 170. Kissing the foot: Persian since Cyrus:
Xenoph.; Punic: Polyb.; Hebrew: <u>Isaiah</u> 49, 23; <u>Luke</u> 7, 38;
Sittl, p. 169. Caligula and Domitian had their feet kissed (cf.
s.v. <u>Greeting</u> above). Sittl, ibid.

<u>Plea:</u> Slaves and clients kiss the feet of their masters.
Anc. Rom. Sittl, p. 169. Lover kisses foot of beloved. Anc.

Rom. Sittl, ibid.
Respect: Kissing feet and hands of dead emperors and
bishops. Sueton.; Vita S. Hucberti; Sittl, p. 170. Kissing feet
of a dignitary. Saudi Arabia. Semiotic. Barakat, no. 121.
(Cf. s.v. LIP, Humility.)
Submission: (Cf. s.v. LIP, Submission.) "I will kiss thy
foot." Shakesp., Tempest, II, ii, 153; Love's Lab. Lost, IV,
i, 86.

FOOT, HAND, LIP
Homage: Kissing feet and hands of dead emperors and bishops.
Suet.; Vita S. Hucberti; Sittl, p. 170. Soldiers and common
people voluntarily kiss Otho's hand at his election as well as
after his death. Sittl, p. 167.

FOREHEAD (Cf. s.v. EYEBROW.)
Concentration: "Contract and purse thy brow together, as if
thou then hadst shut up in thy brain some horrible conceit."
Shakesp., Othello, III, iii, 13. Scratching forehead. Krout,
p. 25.
Disapproval: Frown. I Sam., 3, 13. OED, p. 572.
Homage: Falling to the earth and striking forehead to the
ground. Lower Nile. Eichler, p. 95.
Submission: Greek orthodox secular clergy touch forehead
to the ground three times before the metropolitan. Sittl, p. 160,
n. 4.

FOREHEAD, HAND
Affection: Stroking someone's forehead. Japan. Sittl, p. 33,
n. 11.
Anger: "I recollect, as I passed by one of the pierglasses,
that I saw in it his clenched hand offered in wrath to his fore-
head..." Richardson, Clarissa, IV, p. 173.
Awareness: Palm of hand struck against forehead. ("Oh!
I forgot!") France. Mitton, p. 146. Fingers of both hands
on both sides of forehead. France. Life (Sept. 16, 1946),
p. 12.
Concentration: (Cf. s.v. HAND, Concentration.) Thumb
edge of hand placed to eyebrows or forehead. Anc. Rom.
Baumeister, I, p. 589. Hand rubs forehead. Ital. Bresciani,
Edm., c. v. Sittl, p. 47.
Confusion: "[Miriam] seemed bewildered, and pressed her
hand upon her brow." Hawthorne, ch. xii.
Despair: Beating the forehead. Anc. Gk. and Rom., Ital.
Bresciani, Ebreo, ch. xlix; Sittl, p. 21.
Dismay: "She gave herself a great slap on the forehead,
like one who hears a dreadful piece of news" Celestina, vi.
Emphasis: Fingers extended, heel of palm strikes forehead.
"El es / esta el más..." Colombia. Saitz and Cervenka, p. 46.
Greeting: A careless salute is used as a greeting. Univ.
of Calif. Berkeley. McCord, p. 290.
Hot: Hand, fingers extended, palm to forehead, moves
across forehead, then is shaken out once. Hot weather or dis-

comfort. U.S. Saitz and Cervenka, p. 72.

Intelligence: "If he placed his forefinger to his forehead, he was saying 'That's a bright girl, quite intelligent.' But if he struck his forehead with the side of his outstretched hand, the message changed to 'She's pazza! Crazy!'" Ital. Graham, p. 26.

Pain: Hand (palm) placed on forehead. Baumeister, I, p. 588.

Plea: A supplicant for protection, sitting, puts his forehead down on his hands, which are on his knees. Anc. Gk. Sittl, p. 173.

Reconciliation: "At 5 in the afternoon on Jan. 30, 1948, Mohandas K. Gandhi,...drew the folds of his dhoti about his wizened 78-year-old body and started across the lawn of Birla House in New Delhi.... On the garden path a khaki-shirted man suddenly stepped forward and fired three pistol shots into Gandhi's chest and abdomen. "Ram! Ram!" ("God! God!") the Mahatma whispered, touching his palm to his forehead in a gesture of forgiveness to his assassin. Then he crumpled to the ground." Newsweek (March 19, 1962), p. 121.

Relief: Mopping the brow. ("The exam was difficult.") Univ. of Calif. Berkeley. McCord, p. 291.

Reminder: "'Ah' said the invalid, passing his hand across his forehead; 'Hutley--Hutley--let me see.' He seemed endeavoring to collect his thoughts..." Dickens, Pickw., I, p. 44. Slapping forehead with extended fingers of right hand. Argentina. Kaulfers, p. 253. Placing extended fingers of one hand on forehead in effort to remember. Colombia, U.S. Saitz and Cervenka, p. 87. Slapping the forehead with the fingers of one hand or with the base of the palm of the open hand. Spain, Lat. Am. Green, pp. 63-64; U.S. Saitz and Cervenka, p. 46. "Snapping the fingers--the standard American gesture associated with recall--is rarely observed in this social context in Spain." Green, ibid. Sudden intuition or recall is expressed by fingertips of both hands slapping forehead sharply. French. The corresponding American gesture is snapping one's fingers. Brault, p. 380.

Stupidity: Cf. s.v. Intelligence above, Surprise below.

Surprise: Striking the forehead. Nonn. Dion.; Cicero; Dracont.; Sittl, p. 21. Spain. Celestina, vi; Cervantes, Quijote, I, prol. Striking forehead with palm of right hand, head moving back as hand makes contact: expression of surprise or one's own stupidity. Saudi Arabia, Syria, Jordan, Lebanon. Autistic. Barakat, no. 29.

FOREHEAD, HAND, NECK, NOSE

Insult: "When low city rascals meet a superior on the road and wish to insult him with a pretence of respect they do not salam in the ordinary way but bring the hand up to the nose, then to the forehead and then to the neck, rubbing these parts of the body as if they felt itchy." Chauvé, p. 125; Taylor, p. 33.

FOREHEAD, HEAD
Assurance: Head raised, brows lowered, firm glance.   Aubert, p. 113.

FOREHEAD, KNEE
Prayer: In Asia, pure proskynesis with forehead touched to the ground. Sittl, p. 179.

FOREHEAD, LIP
Affection: Kiss on forehead. Anc. Gk. and Rom.   Sittl, p. 40.

Anger: "His mouth was drawn down and his upper face was pulled into a tight frown. Birdwhistell, Backgr., p. 14.

Greeting: Man kisses woman on forehead; son kisses mother on lips or forehead, girls kiss older woman on forehead. Saudi Arabia. Semiotic or culture-induced. Barakat, no. 141.

Respect: Kissing a person's forehead, nose, feet or right hand. Saudi Arabia. Semiotic. Barakat, no. 115.

GENITALS
Apotropy: Touching one's genitals through the holes in one's pockets. HDA, II, col. 334. Touching one's genitals against the evil eye. Italy, Greece, Russia. HDA, III, col. 731. Phallus gestures do not seem to appear in Germany. Meschke, col. 330. Baring the cunnus of a menstruating woman against hail and storm. Pliny 28, 7, 23. Baring the phallus against the evil eye, transferred to phallic amulets. Anc. Rom. Jahn, pp. 66ff., 72ff.; Sittl, p. 122. A phallus was suspended under the chariot of a triumphant Roman general. Pliny, Nat. hist. 28, 7.

Contempt: "They must not be sent away without a cup of good Christmas ale, for fear they should p-ss behind the door." Swift's Polite Conversation, p. 148.

Insult: Showing phallus to women. Anc. Gk. Sittl, p. 100.

Medico-magical: Pressing the left testicle against stomach ache. South Slavic. HDA, III, col. 731.

Mockery: Persian and Spartan women bared their cunnus to fleeing warriors, asking them if they wanted to take refuge in their bodies. Sittl, p. 104. Women travelling on the Nile mocked those on the shore similarly. Anc. Egypt. Sittl, ibid. "When the crowd hooted at a bullfighter in Mexico because of unsatisfactory performance, he insulted them by touching his trousers at the crotch." Hayes, p. 309.

Threat: Showing of phallus. Priapus' threat to thieves. Anc. Gk. and Rom. Sittl, pp. 100-101.

GLOVE (GAUNTLET)
Calmness: Playing with gloves in hand. Pel. de Vie hum., 1893.

Challenge: Throwing a glove (gauntlet). Medieval Europ. Gottfr. v. Strassburg, 6458; Rein. vos., 4, 5; Ms. Harl. 4380,

fol. 141 in Coulton, p. 94; Du Cange, III, p. 977; Grimm, DRA,
I, p. 212; DWb, IV, 2, col. 417.
  Laziness: Leisurely playing with gloves. Medieval French.
Rec. gén., I, 307.
  Permission: "And the king should justly send his glove
along, to show that it is his will." Medieval German.
Sachsensp. 2, 26, 4.
  Pledge: As part of a pledge to marry, a Swabian freeman
must give his intended seven gloves. Müllenh. and Scherer,
p. 239; DWb, IV, col. 417.
  Possession: Transference of land was accompanied by a
glove handed over or thrown down. Medieval German. Grimm,
DRA, I, p. 209.
  Proscription: The king or judge threw down the glove as
sign of proscription about to be pronounced. Medieval German.
Grimm, DRA, I, p. 211.

HAIR, HAND
  Affection: Stroking someone's hair. To animals: Aristoph.;
Philostr.; Livy; Sittl, p. 33. To children, slaves, and to the
grown man by his mother: Herodot.; Michael Psellus; Terence;
Iliad; Sittl, p. 33. Cf. also Petron.; Claudian; Sittl, p. 34.
Teachers to pupils: Plato; Plutarch; Lucil.; Sittl, p. 33.
  Age: "Expressions suggesting aging may be accompanied
by... running the fingers of one hand through the hair, as if to
draw attention to the gray hairs on the head." Spain, Lat. Am.
Green, p. 64.
  Approval: Patting the hair. Birdwhistell, Colliers (March
4, 1955), p. 56.
  Bargain: Pulling a hair from the head, blowing on it and
saying "Pelillos a la mar," seals a bargain. Children. Spain.
Hayes, p. 300.
  Despair: Tearing hair. Ohm, p. 230. Ital. Bresciani,
Ebreo, c. xxxxix. Men: Martial; Augustin; Soph.; Aristoph.;
Callim.; Hippocr.; Xenoph.; Symeon Metaphr.; Theod. Prodr.;
Ovid; Seneca; Sittl, p. 22. Women: Philodem.; Lucian; Helio-
dor.; Synes.; Charito; Syntipas; Virgil; Ovid; Claudian; Curtius;
Apuleius; Plutarch; Sittl, p. 22. Jerome. Sittl, p. 19. Me-
dieval German: Orendel, 680. Shakesp., Troil., IV, ii, 113.
18th cent. Germany: Wieland, p. 232. Amer. schoolchildren.
Seton, p. xxi.
  Emphasis: "adding force to his declamation by striding to
and fro, pulling his hair..." Dickens, Pickw., I, p. 400.
  Frustration: "the expression 'Estoy hasta la punta del pelo'
(student, Univ. of Madrid) is a female movement and expression.
The mover raises a single hair in the rear of the head." Spain,
Lat. Am. Green, p. 89.
  Gratitude: "...pulling at the forelock of his shock head of
hair in honour of the steward's clemency, and giving it another
double pull at it in honour of the farmer's kindness." Trollope,
Barchester Towers, II, p. 138.

Mourning: Women cut off bits of their hair. Palest.
Bauer, p. 211. Tearing hair. Bresciani, Giudeo, c. xxxxix;
Sittl, p. 22. Men: Hellenistic Orient; Sittl, p. 67. Tearing
hair out and strewing it over the corpse, perhaps as proof of
sorrow. 19th cent. Greek, also anc. Gk. and Rom. Sittl,
p. 71. Only men in the heroic age: Sittl, p. 25. Among
Arabs it was customary, esp. for women, to scratch face and
shave off hair; similarly among Israelites, despite Deuteronomic
prohibitions. Hastings, Dict. III, p. 454.

Oath: Frisian men swore by touching their hair. Grimm,
DRA, II, p. 549. Touching chest and the hair hanging over the
shoulder. Medieval Bavaria, Swabia. Grimm, DRA, II, p. 548.
Grasping another man's moustache with fingers of right hand.
Saudi Arabia. Semiotic. Barakat, no. 183.

Prayer: Shaking and pulling hair. Cybele cult. Ohm, p.
230. Women loosen hair. Brissonius, I, c. lxiv; Sittl, p. 185.

Respect: "the rather broad-set but active figure, perhaps
two years older than himself, that looked at him with a pair of
blue eyes set in a disc of freckles, and pulled some curly red
locks with a strong intention of respect. Eliot, p. 571.

Shame: Cut off a man's plait of hair. Variations: cutting
off a man's right hand or cutting off a man's beard. Rwala
Bedouin of Kuwait, Iraq, Saudi Arabia, Syria. Semiotic or
culture-induced. Barakat, no. 161.

Sorrow: Pulling beard. Biblical. Ohm, p. 230. Gk. and
Roman antiquity. Sittl, p. 274; Röhrich, pl. 36. Early 16th
cent. Europe. Röhrich, pl. 35; cf. also Röhrich, p. 34.
Malory, II, ch. vii. Shakesp., Much Ado, II, iii, 153; Romeo,
III, iii, 68. (Cf. also s.v. Mourning above.) "if they [women]
are pressed by sorrow, they are to tear their veils, browbands,
caps or whatever else they may have, off their heads and tear
their hair and wring their hands." Amira, ABA, XXIII, gloss.
to the Sächs. Landrecht, II, 64.

Surrender: Hair is drawn through dust. Anc. Rom. Sittl,
p. 161. At capitulations Gallic women showed their disordered
hair. Sittl, ibid.

HAIR, HAND, MOUTH
Sorrow: Biting the thumb and tearing the hair. Boggs, p. 319.

HAIR, LIP
Affection: Kissing the hair. Anc. Rom. Sittl, p. 41.

HAND
Absence: Right hand held in front of face, back of hand facing
forward, then flipped so that palm is up: person asked for is
not present. Saudi Arabia. Semiotic. Barakat, no. 200.

Acceptance: The newly born child lies on the floor until
the father declares whether he wants it to live or not. If he
accepts it he lifts it up or has it lifted up. Then it is sprinkled
with water and given a name. Medieval Scandin. Grimm, DRA,
I, pp. 627-628.

Accolade: After the sword belt has been put on, there

follows the blow with the sword, the alapa militaris. This blow, administered by the knight accepting the squire into knighthood, is directed against the neck and accompanied by formal admonitions. Schultz, II, p. 185.

Accompaniment: Man takes woman by the hand or the wrist in walking. Anc. Gk. Sittl, p. 81.

Acknowledgement: "She still had the curious trick--shared by two or three other small-town young women within Pnin's limited ken--of giving you a delayed little tap on the sleeve in acknowledgment of, rather than in retaliation for, any remark reminding her of some minor lapse:..." Nabokov, p. 152. "...stuck out his hand as though to shake hands" in acknowledgment of an introduction. Birdwhistell, Introd., p. 34.

Address (passionate): Both hands extended toward someone. Anc. Gk. and Rom. Sittl, p. 50.

Admiration: Hand shaken as if burnt. Particularly signifies admiration of feminine beauty. N.Y. Times (March 1, 1959). With palms facing each other, hands move downward from ca. shoulder-level to hip-level, exaggerating an attractive female figure. Colombia, U.S. Saitz and Cervenka, p. 54. (Cf. s.v. FINGER, Admiration.) Clapping hands. DWb, IV/2, col. 414. "...advancing with extended hand, 'I honour your gallantry. Permit me to say, Sir, that I highly admire your conduct...'" Dickens, Pickw., I, p. 37.

Admonition: Right hand oscillates obliquely or semi-vertically in front of nose. Spain. Kaulfers, p. 252. "...slapped him across the anterior portion of his upper leg." Birdwhistell, Backgr., p. 14.

Adoption: Slavs raised the adopted child up in their hands. Grimm, DRA, I, p. 640. (Cf. s.v. Acceptance above.)

Adoration: Raising the hand. Oriental. Ebert, V, p. 93. Holding or carrying an object in a cloth or on a cloak signifies respect for that object. Haseloff, pp. 304-305. "...holding the Host over the Chalice with his right hand, and holding the Chalice with his left [the priest] elevates it a little together with the Host, saying the words 'omnis honor et gloria.'" Mass, p. 69. "St. Thomas tells us that after the Consecration the priest does not make the Sign of the Cross for the purpose of blessing or consecrating, but to commemorate the virtue and power of the Cross and the manner of Christ's death." Mass, p. 63. "The priest makes the Sign of the Cross three times-- once over the Host, once over the Chalice and once on himself; by which is represented that the torments which Christ endured in His Flesh and which He suffered in the effusion of His Blood, profit and always will benefit both priest and people to eternal salvation..." Mass, p. 66. Both hands raised, palms toward the object of adoration. Anc. Egypt. Heiler, p. 101. Clapping hands in adoration of spirits. Ohm, p. 285.

Affection: Pressing a person's hand. Amaranthes (1710), cited in DWb, IV/2, col. 367. Woman pressing a man's hand. Happel, cited in DWb, ibid. Man pressing woman's hand. Grobianus (1552), cited in DWb, IV/2, col. 331. Paternal pressing of someone's hand. Rabener (1757) cited in DWb, ibid.

Man and woman pressing each other's hand. Nibelungenlied, st. 294. "The sick man drew a hand of his old fellow prisoner towards him, and pressing it affectionately between both his own, retained it in his grasp." Dickens, Pickw., II, p. 277. Hand(s) of one person grasped by hand(s) of another. Stephani, pp. 69-113. "... and pressing her son's hand, affectionately..." Dickens, Twist, p. 310. Taking someone's hand. Shakesp., Tempest, I, ii, 377; Mids. Night's Dr., IV, i, 90. Touching or tapping someone lightly for whom affection is felt. Siriono Indians (Bolivia). Key, p. 97. Handshake while conversing. Gk. and Rom. antiquity. Sittl, pp. 28-29. Not a matter of mere etiquette with the anc. Romans, but an expression of emotion; if, therefore, the context of the handshake is insignificant, the performer of the handshake is regarded as a flatterer. Sittl, p. 28. Love to animals manifests itself in stroking them. Palest. Bauer, p. 321. "Slaps of affection can be observed striking the back of the head, the back of the neck, the stomach, and the chest of the listener." Spain, Lat. Am. Green, pp. 36-37. Stroking someone's cheek. Shakesp., Troil., V, ii, 51. "'You're such a good man, Mr. Farragan!' the old one shrieked. She had taken both his hands fiercely into her own and immediately knocked over his glass of beer." McHale, p. 160.

Affirmation: Palm upward, hand is moved in a slight curve upward and to the side. Assim. Eastern Jews. Efron, p. 117. Hands raised to level of head and clasped vigorously. Colombia. Saitz and Cervenka, p. 15.

Agreement: Palm of right hand is touched to the palm of the right hand of the partner, then the right hand is presented to be touched by the palm of the partner's right hand. Mutual agreement concerning a transaction. France. Mitton, p. 142. Handslap, i.e. German "Handschlag." Regarded as purely Germanic by Sittl, p. 136. Handshake. Colombia, U.S. Saitz and Cervenka, p. 24. Right hand of one person grasps right hand of another so that thumbs touch. German, possibly anc. Gk. Sittl, pp. 136-137. Raising the hand. Early New High German. DWb, IV/2, col. 331; Schiller, Tell, II, ii. "A man striketh hands and becometh surety." Prov., 17, 18. Sealing agreement with handshake. II Kings 10, 15. The handclasp was common in early medieval northern England and Scotland accompanying marriage in church, not between bride and groom, but between father of the bride and the groom. Vinogradoff, p. 246; Ebert, V, 95. Right hand of one person clasps that of another in confirmation of a treaty. Insufficient in actuality, used as poetic license. Anc. Rom. Sittl, p. 137. "Take hands, a bargain!" Shakesp., Winter's Tale, IV, iv, 394. At a sale of animals the right hands of seller and buyer grasp thrice. Palest. Bauer, p. 167. One party strikes the palm of the other. Butler, II, 1, 540. "'I have said so my dear friend. I have said so already,' replied Mr. Wardle, shaking the right hand of his friend,..." Dickens, Pickw., I, p. 276. Joining hands, grasp broken by a blow from the hand of a third party. South Molton. Children. Opie, p. 130. Handclasp, a

bystander separates the hands by bringing the edge of his right
hand down upon the clasped hands, signifying the conclusion of
a bargain. German. Röhrich, p. 31. In reaching an agreement, Estonians shake hands, covering the handshake with a
coattail and whinnying. Hupel, II, pp. 149-150. "Bouvard was
tired out. He let everything go for a sum so contemptible that
Gouy at first opened his eyes wide, and exclaiming 'Agreed!'
slapped his palm." Flaubert, ch. ii, cited by Hayes, p. 221.

Alarm: "all shall clap the hands over thee." Nahum 3, 19.

Amazement: "The ring was answered by a very smart and
prettyfaced servant-girl, who, after holding up her hands in astonishment at the rebellious appearance of the prisoners..."
Dickens, Pickw., I, p. 413. Palm on cheek or behind ear.
Ghetto Jews. Efron, p. 146. Shaking loosely held fingers of
slightly cupped hand in front of the speaker or at the side at
waist-level. Spain, Lat. Am. Green, p. 56.

Anger: Fist moved from left to right several times at ca.
chin level. Colombia. Saitz and Cervenka, p. 54. Striking
the open palm of one hand with the closed fist of the other hand.
Spain, Lat. Am., but particularly frequent in Spain. Green,
pp. 74-75. Twitching hands. Schiller, Tell, III, iii. Hands
beaten together. IV Moses 24, 10; Abraham a Sancta Clara,
p. 139. Anc. Gk. and Rom. Sittl, p. 19. Quivering hands.
Ziegler und Kliphausen, p. 98; Immermann, II, p. 13. Knuckles of both hands rubbed together. Lat. Am. Kany, p. 64.
"clenched his fist and shook it expressively at the object of his
indignation." Dickens, Pickw., I, p. 142. "shook his fist in
the countenance of the Honourable Samuel Slumkey." Dickens,
Pickw., I, p. 213; also Bulwer, pp. 57-59. Clenching fists.
Krout, p. 22. " 'They had better not!' said Mr. Bumble, clenching his fist." Dickens, Twist, p. 244. Also Colombia, U.S.
Saitz and Cervenka, p. 16. Striking left hand with right, or fist
into palm. Bulwer, pp. 32-34. " 'She would assure me, if
ever again'--And there she stopped, with a twirl of her hand.
When we meet, I will, in her presence, tipping thee a wink,
show thee the motion, for it was a very pretty one. Quite
new." Richardson, Clarissa, IV, p. 45. Right fist rubbed on
the extended left palm. Lat. Am. Kany, p. 64. Fists held
together and twisted as if wringing cloth. Colombia, U.S.
Saitz and Cervenka, p. 17. Hands hanging at side and clenched.
Aubert, p. 83. " 'I tell you,' said the man, clenching his
hands, and stamping furiously on the floor." Dickens, Twist,
p. 43. Clenched hands crossed behind back. Wieland cited in
DWb, IV/2, col. 334. Hands vertically extended, palms facing
out, fingers separated and hooked. Aubert, p. 87. Clenched
fists held so that knuckles face downward, forearms extended in
front parallel to ground; fists make short, sharp downward and
upward motion. Colombia, U.S. Saitz and Cervenka, p. 16.
When the angry person feels superior to the other, he will approach, staring, grab the other by the lapel or an arm, or
touch his face and fingers. Equal adversaries grab each other.
Portug. Basto, p. 7.

Anticipation: Right palm rubbed rapidly over horizontally

extended left palm; the face is joyful; shoulders sometimes
hunched. France. Brault, p. 377. Colombia, U. S. Saitz
and Cervenka, p. 17. Hands palm to palm or clasped in front
of body. Women. U. S. Saitz and Cervenka, p. 18.

Antipathy: Hands extended, palms facing outward. Ohm,
p. 44. Same, palms facing down. Yuki Indians (Calif. Coast).
Ohm, ibid.

Apology: One hand, palm outward, raised to the side of the
speaker's face, suggesting the warding off of anticipated criti-
cism. Spain, Lat. Am. Green, p. 83.

Apotropy: (Cf. s. v. FINGER, Apotropy.) Passing the hand
over one's mouth to ward off the evil eye. Germany. Meschke,
col. 336. Touching the wall of one's house to pass on the evil
influence of a witch that one has just met, or touching the
witch's right hand. England. Meschke, ibid. Meeting of a
witch calls for touching of the shoulder of the witch. Tirol,
Messina, Cambrésis. Meschke, ibid. Making sign of the cross
with oil over animals at a time of epidemic protects the animal.
Gregory of Tours cited by Sittl, p. 127. Making sign of the
cross over one's open mouth while yawning. Early Christian.
Sittl, p. 127. German. Meschke, col. 335. Tirol. Zingerle,
Tirol, p. 58. Extending index and small finger (pref. of the
left hand), middle fingers bent inward on palm and thumb holding them in place ("horns"). Lat. Am. Kany, p. 190. One
thumb crossed by the other against the evil eye. Island of
Noirmoutier, also Poitou. Seligmann, II, p. 183. The fig as
protection against an evil spell. Neapol. De Jorio, p. 155.
Making the sign of the cross. Spain. Flachskampf, p. 243.
Colombia. Saitz and Cervenka, p. 29. Image of a hand on
walls, or amulet in metal or glass against evil eye. Mohammedan. Seligmann, II, p. 168. Crossing oneself against devils.
Kaufringer, no. 2, 187-195. Upon entering a house where but-
ter is being made, one must lay one's hand on the butterkeg as
proof that one is without evil intentions and that one is willing
to drive off influences of the evil eye. Northeastern Scotland.
Seligmann, II, pp. 185-186. The "fig" against the evil eye,
made under one's cloak in order to avoid insulting the person
with whom one is speaking. Neapol. Seligmann, II, ibid.
Making the sign of the cross when entering public baths, for
these were sometimes considered as evil. Early Christian.
Sittl, pp. 127-128. Making sign of the cross when lights were
lit, since that is the hour when demons start wandering about.
Joh. Chrysost.; Sittl, p. 128. Washing hands by wedding guests
prevents dangerous contacts. South Slavic. Ebert, V, col. 94.
Washing hands before beginning work in the garden or field, in
order to prevent infection of plants by touch of hand which may
have been cursed by touching certain trees, leaves, etc. Ewe
(West-Africa). Ebert, V, col. 93. To protect someone from
the evil influence of a spell, the sign of the horns is directed
against several parts of a person's body, as if to sprinkle him
with a liquid. Neapol. De Jorio, p. 99. The sign of the
"horns" is made in the direction of the eyes of the person
against whose spell one wants to protect oneself, for the eyes

7. "Noli me tangere," late 11th-century Spanish ivory panel, leaf of diptych; the Metropolitan Museum of Art, New York; gift of J. Pierpont Morgan, 1917 (see HAND--Apotropy). Reproduced by permission.

are regarded as the source of the spell. Neapol. De Jorio, p. 98. In protecting oneself against evil spirits, the hand, making the sign of the "horns," is moved around in the air aimlessly, since it is presumed that evil spirits roam in the air. Neapol. De Jorio, p. 97. One hand extended, making a blessing-gesture with thumb, index and middle finger extended toward another figure, the other hand makes the "horns" in the same direction. "Noli me tangere." Ivory panel, late 11th cent. Spanish. Metrop. Museum, N.Y., in de Palol and Hirmer, pl. 79 (see illustration 7). Thumb bent under the other fingers of one hand against the evil eye. Spain, Ireland, Bretagne, Noirmoutier. Seligmann, II, p. 178. Index extended and bent three times while silently stepping behind old women protects against their evil eye. East Prussia. Seligmann, II, p. 183; Meschke, col. 336. Amulet of a hand of which the tip of the thumb touches

the tip of the index, or a hand with extended index against the
evil eye. Seligmann, II, p. 182. Extending thumb, index and
middle finger simultaneously to ward off evil spirits. Early
Christian. Meschke, col. 335. Tip of index placed to tip of
little finger against the "Häcker." HDA, II, col. 1496. Middle
finger laid across index against the "Letzten." Ratzeburg.
Ibid. Old women make the sign of the cross over the open
mouth of yawning children and say "Heiligs Kreuz" simultaneously. Bavarian. Sittl, p. 127. Clapping hands when someone
sneezes, to frighten demons away. Turkey. Sittl, p. 117.
The hand extended, fingers spread. "Hand of Fatima." North
Africa, Sicily, Spain. Taylor, pp. 53-54 and n. 74. Cf. also
Insult below.

Appeasement: Hands horizontal, arms straight, palms down,
arms folded slowly, moving from above downwards. Aubert,
p. 89.

Applause: Clapping hands. DWb, IV/2, col. 368. Ob-
jectionable to anc. Romans as expression of joy. Sittl, p. 10.
Limited to barbarians, sailors, children, and characters in
Petronius. Similarly among the anc. Gks. Sittl, p. 11. Wo-
men did not clap in the theater. Portug. Urtel, pp. 12-13.
Similarly Germany, early 19th cent. (1839). Sittl, p. 56.
Clapping of hands in applause in the theater was common in anc.
Greece and Rome, likewise to speeches of the emperor, both
Rom. and Byzant., whence it is taken over by the Franks.
High officials were received with applause. Anc. Rom. The
Emperor Julian was applauded in visiting the temples. Sittl,
pp. 55-59. No applause in the theater in 18th cent. France
when the king was present. Rousseau, Conf., Bk. viii.

Appreciation: Two hands curved in the air to suggest an
attractive female shape may express appreciation or sensuous-
ness. Ruesch and Kees, p. 82. (Cf. s.v. Admiration above.)

Approach: (Cf. s.v. FINGER, Approach.) "Writing in the
air with an imaginary pen or pencil--intended to simulate the
act of computing the check--is a movement observed frequently
in Spanish restaurants. The movement often replaces verbal
behavior of any kind, but it may accompany expressions such
as 'La cuenta, por favor!'... This movement is socially acceptable in any environment. Voiced gestures, such as 'Chist!,'
simply raising the hand, or snapping the fingers are all movements which can be observed in Spanish restaurants. [Snapping
fingers. Colombia. Superiors to inferiors, or equals informal-
ly. Saitz and Cervenka, p. 28.] Clapping the hands...is acceptable only in mesones or tascas.... As a general rule,
American movers consciously avoid movements and gestures
which tend to attract attention...." Green, p. 57. Arm and
hand extended in front of chest, palm down, fingers lowered
and raised repeatedly. Spain. Rare in urban social contexts
and "probably largely confined to rural areas.... The movement can be observed...performed by recent arrivals to more
densely populated areas and by somewhat older madrileños.
Young children in the care of middle-aged nannies can also be
observed performing this movement. The gesture most fre-

quently observed today in association with expressions of beckoning is performed exactly as it is in many parts of the United
States, that is, by bending the index finger of one hand toward
the gesticulator.... The movement can also be performed using
all of the fingers of one hand...When beckoning toward...taxi
drivers, Spanish movers tend to extend one arm directly to their
front and lower and raise the rigid arm repeatedly and brusque-
ly." Green, pp. 37-38.   Index finger bent repeatedly toward
gesticulator, palm up. Colombia, U.S.   Saitz and Cervenka,
p. 28.   Same, palm down, other fingers folded in and held by
the thumb. Colombia. Saitz and Cervenka, ibid.   Clap hands
once or twice: signal for waiter to come. Saudi Arabia, Lebanon. Semiotic. Barakat, no. 219.   "He beckons with his hand
and smiles on me." Shakesp., I Henry VI, I, iv, 92.   "He
beckoned to him that he should come to shore." Dante, Inf. c.
xvii.   "...produce from the breast-pocket of his coat, a short
truncheon surmounted by a brazen crown, with which he beckoned
to Mr. Pickwick with a grave and ghost-like air." Dickens,
Pickw., I, p. 406.   Peter beckoning to them with the hand.
Acts, 12, 17.   In beckoning with the hand, the palm is held
vertically. Anc. Gk., Etruscan. Sittl, p. 216.   "The officer
evinced his consciousness of their presence by slightly beckoning with his hand; and the two friends followed him at a little
distance..." Dickens, Pickw., I, p. 34.   Drawing in flat of
hand, palm toward gesturer. Amer. schoolchildren.   Seton,
p. xx.   Hand flapped, palm down. Southern Ital.   Efron,
p. 156.   Palm down, fingers repeatedly straightened and bent.
Southern Italy, southern Balkans, Near East, North Africa.
Röhrich, p. 13 and pl. 7; Colombia. · Saitz and Cervenka, p. 27
(fingers together or moving separately, usually beginning with
the smallest; the latter primarily by women).   Fingers repeatedly straightened and bent, palm up. Eastern Mediterranean.
Ohm, p. 45.   Colombia, U.S.   Saitz and Cervenka, p. 27 (often
used in Colombia to call people at short distances).   Clapping
hands. Oriental, Spanish. Röhrich, p. 13. Mongolian.   Ohm,
p. 285.   Japanese. Ohm, p. 286.   Also Sittl, p. 222:   Anc.
Gk. (common people). Waving hand, palm inwards in direction
of gesturer. Anc. Gk. Sittl, pp. 215-216.   Also a signal to
the enemy to approach for a conference. Polybius.   Sittl,
p. 216.   Signal to attack. Anc. Rom. Sittl, p. 216.   Right
hand held up, palm down, then moved several times in slightly
clawing motion. Jordan, Lebanon, Bahrein, Saudi Arabia, Syria.
Semiotic or culture-induced. Barakat, no. 189.

  Approval: Shaking hands. Dickens, Pickw., I, p. 456; II,
pp. 155, 168.   "Your conduct is most noble, Sir"--as he
grasped hand. Dickens, Pickw., I, p. 199.   Stroking the chest
downwards with the right hand two or three times, accompanied
by the ironical exclamation "och! och!" Near East.   Critchley,
p. 91.   All five fingers of one hand joined at the tips, held to
mouth, then suddenly spread out. French. Life (Sept. 16,
1946).   The Israelites clapped their hands when Joash was
anointed king. II Kings 11, 12.   "The ladies waved a choice
collection of pocket-handkerchiefs at this proposition." Dickens,

Pickw., II, p. 67. Pretending to curl the tip of an imaginary moustache. Southern Ital. Efron, p. 148. Slapping another man's palm with open palm: sign that that person has done something good. Jordan. Semiotic. Barakat, no. 240.

Arrogance (of another): Indicate a swelled head. Amer. schoolchildren. Seton, p. xxi. The sign of the "horns" (cf. s.v. FINGER, Mockery). Neapol. De Jorio, p. 95.

Assistance: The Assyrian king, before ascending the throne, stopped before the statue of Bel and took his hands. Winkler, p. 20. The king of Babylon, at the New Year's feast, took the hands of the Marduk idol. Frazer, IX, p. 356.

Assurance: Person giving assurance of something to another, gives him the right hand. Anc. Gk. and Rom. Sittl, p. 135. " 'I assure you, Ma'am,' said Mr. Pickwick, grasping the old lady's hand..." Dickens, Pickw., I, p. 82.

Astonishment: " 'for to the best of my knowledge, I was never here before.' 'Never in Ba--th, Mr. Pickwick!' exclaimed the Grand Master, letting his hand fall in astonishment." Dickens, Pickw., II, p. 114. Crossing oneself. Celestina, v, ix.

Attention: "He gave the child a shake to make him obedient." Dickens, Pickw., II, p. 43. "He raised himself in bed, and extended his hand, as if he were about to say something more." Dickens, Pickw., I, p. 382. Clapping hands to call attention of spirits, awaken and call souls of ancestors during worship. Japan. Ohm, p. 286. Hand cupped behind ear, indicating that one is giving attention. Amer. schoolchildren. Seton, p. xxi. Gently pulling the skirts of someone's coat to get his attention. Dickens, Pickw., I, p. 462; II, p. 231. Hand extended forward, palm down, fingers together. Hand is lowered several times. Used only when addressing a group of people. France. Mitton, p. 145. Clapping hands. Common in anc. Rome, has spread in France during the 18th cent. and is used only when a great number of people are to be brought to attention. France. Mitton, p. 146. Clapping to call waiter. Colombia. Saitz and Cervenka, p. 106. (Cf. s.v. Approach above.) "It was at the end of the chorus to the first verse, that Mr. Pickwick held up his hand in a listening attitude..." Dickens, Pickw., II, p. 50. "...leaned toward his mother and pulled at her sleeve." Birdwhistell, Backgr., p. 14. "...grasped her upper arm tightly." Ibid. Raising hand to get waiter's attention. U.S. Saitz and Cervenka, p. 107. (Cf. s.v. FINGER, HAND, Attention.)

Authority: The hand as symbol of power. Anc. Egypt, Babylon. Ebert, V, col. 95. Roman, Phoenician, Libyan, Babylonian, Carthaginian, Irish, Celtic, pre-Columb. Central Americ. Seligmann, II, p. 165. Medieval Europ. "dextera dei." Ibid. Hand on hip, chest out, head high. Typical in portrayals of generals and heroes. De Jorio, p. 199. Hand raised, or image of right hand, middle finger crossed over index, seal of Waimar of Salerno 11th cent. (see illustration 8).

Avarice: Clenched fist. Persian. Rose, p. 312. Lat. Am. Kany, p. 70. Spain. Pérez Galdós, II, vi, p. 246. Hands extended horizontally, fingers separated and hooked.

8.   Seal of Waimar of Salerno (1040); in: J. Mabillon, De re diplomatica II (supplementum), Paris, 1709, p. 115 (see HAND--Au-
thority).

Aubert, p. 86, fig. 129.   Left fist raised, right hits under left
elbow, simultaneously the fingers of the left fist open.   Spain.
Flachskampf, p. 231.
     Begging: Holding out the cupped hand, palm up.   Bulwer,
pp. 59-61.   Polish beggars throw dust on themselves while
standing.   Sittl, p. 158.
     Betting: Handclasp.   DWb, IV /2, col. 414.
     Blessing: (Cf. s.v. FINGER, Blessing; FINGER, HAND,
Blessing.)   Raising hand toward those to be blessed.   Lev. 9,
22; Luke 24, 50.   Placing hand on the head of person to be
blessed.   Gen. 48, 14.   Laying on of hands also served to trans-
fer sins to sacrificial animals.   Lev. 4, 4, 24, etc.   Ohm,
p. 290.   Sacred Judaic blessing gesture, according to Hayes,
p. 229, citing Aharon Amramy as source, consists of holding
'palms down, thumb nails touching, index and middle fingers
touching but held separated from the ring and little fingers which
touch each other.   Gesture is covered by a cloth.   If an ordinary person sees the gesture he will go blind.   It may only be
given by high priests, descendants of Aaron.   Sophocles has
Oedipus put his hands upon his children to bless them before
his death.   Frequent non- and pre-Christian form of blessing.
Ohm, p. 290.   Also Christian.   Mark 10, 16; Immermann,
p. 40.   "And Israel stretched out his right hand and laid it on
Ephraim's head, who was the younger, and his left hand on
Manasseh's head, crossing his hands--for Manasseh was the
first-born."   Gen. 48, 14.   "Hold up thy hand."   Shakesp., II
Henry VI, III, iii, 28.   "And hold your hand in benediction o'er
me."   Shakesp., Lear, IV, vii, 57.   Making the sign of the
cross with or without accompanying formula.   Since the 2nd

century. Ohm, p. 296. After exorcism the bishop makes the
sign of the cross over the neophyte's forehead, ears and nose
according to the Aegyptian liturgy. Ohm, p. 298. Cross is to
be made over the neophyte before baptism according to St. Augustine. Ohm, p. 298. Luther advised use of the sign of the
cross upon arising in the morning, but rejected its use in the
liturgy. Ohm, pp. 299-301. Making the sign of the cross over
saddles of horses before mounting to enter judicial combat.
Medieval Spain. Cid, c. iii. For variations of the sign of the
cross, see Ohm, pp. 292-293 and particularly Bäumer, cols.
1135-1141. The right hand is regarded as the blessing hand.
Ohm, p. 249. The sign of the cross is made either with the
hand or with a sacred object. A distinction is made between
the "Roman" and the "Greek" cross: in making the latter, the
hand is moved from forehead to the breast vertically and then
from the right to the left shoulder, the former is made by moving the hand from forehead to breast and then from the left to
the right shoulder. The first positive evidence for this "Roman"
major cross dates from the 11th century. Endres and Ebner,
p. 302. As late as the 13th century the form of the major
cross was still not settled in the Roman liturgy. Ohm, pp. 293-
295. In Greek liturgy the gesture of blessing is the raised index, middle, and little finger (symbolic of the Trinity); the
thumb and ringfinger (symbolic of the two natures of Christ) are
folded toward the palm. Seligmann, II, p. 179. Roman blessing gesture is the extended thumb, index, and middle finger,
with the ring and little finger folded toward the palm. Seligmann, ibid. The priest sprinkles holy water in four directions.
Beitl, p. 260.

Boredom: (Cf. s.v. FINGER, Boredom.) Fingers of one
hand are interlaced with those of the other, and the two thumbs
continuously turn around each other. France. Mitton, p. 151.

Bribery: Hollow hand, palm up, held behind back of gesticu-
ulator. Amer. schoolchildren. Seton, p. xxiii.

Calmness: Outstretched hands, palms down, pushed toward
the floor, indicate request for calmness. Spain, Lat. Am.
Green, p. 43. Folding of hands indicates calmness. Ohm,
p. 269.

Carelessness: Twisting the open hand back and forth, fingers together, palm may face down. Madrid. Green, p. 90.

Challenge: Offering one's gauntlet to the enemy. Gottfr.
v. Strassburg, 6453-4. Throwing down the gauntlet to one's
enemy. (The challenge is accepted if it is picked up.) Shakesp.,
Richard II, IV, i, 46; also I, i, 146; I, i, 69. (Cf. s.v.
GLOVE [GAUNTLET], Challenge.) "that unaccountable person
flung the money on the pavement, and requested in figurative
terms to be allowed the pleasure of fighting him (Mr. Pickwick)
for the amount!" Dickens, Pickw., I, p. 8. "'Come on,' said
the cab-driver, sparring away like clockwork. 'Come on--all
four of you.'" Dickens, Pickw., I, p. 9. The inner side of the
right fist beats against the top of the outer side of the left fist,
accompanied by a formula of challenge. Turkish children.
Critchley, p. 91.

Change: "Verbal behavior suggestive of a change...may be accompanied by a movement performed by rotating both hands-- one after the other and with the palms facing the speaker--in a circular motion at the level of the mover's chest." Madrid, Lat. Am. Green, p. 68.

Claim: Seizure of a goblet and inverting a torch (as though to set fire to a field) represent seizure of territory. Wolfr. v. Eschenbach, III, 146.

Cleansing: Brushing hands. Krout, p. 22.

Cold: Rubbing hands together vigorously. Spain. Green, pp. 90-91. Colombia, U.S. Saitz and Cervenka, p. 26. Fists placed near shoulder and shaking. Amer. schoolchildren. Seton, p. xxiii.

Collect: "The priest joins his hands as if to collect the hearts of all those present,..." Mass, p. 42.

Commendation: The bride emerges from the house of her parents holding a bare sword vertically before her face; in the house of the groom she surrenders the sword. Palest. Bauer, p. 94. Vassals extend hands toward the lord at enfeoffment. Medieval German. Kudrun, st. 190, 1.2. Cf. s.v. Investiture below.

Complication: Fingers loose, hands rotate over each other. Colombia. Saitz and Cervenka, p. 29.

Concentration: (Cf. FOREHEAD, HAND, Concentration.) "Then goes he to the length of all his arm and with his other hand thus o'er his brow." Shakesp., Hamlet, II, i, 88. Index laid on brow, head lowered. Amer. schoolchildren. Seton, p. xxii.

Confidence: Arms raised to level of head, hands clasped. Berkeley Daily Gazette (June 2, 1964), p. 1.

Confirmation: Laying on of hands as sign of transmission of spirit or official duties. Anc. Gk., anc. Jewish, Christian. Ohm, p. 291. In one of the sanctuaries of the Ziggurat stood the image of Bel-Merodach, the annual touching of which by the kings of Babylon at the New Year's festival confirmed their title. Hastings, Dict., I, p. 213.

Congratulation: Handshake. Anc. Gk. and Rom. Sittl, p. 30. Clapping of hands. Claudian (repeated three times on a birthday, Propertius). Sittl, p. 54. Clapping raised hands. Bulwer, pp. 30-32. Grasping someone by the hand. Dickens, Pickw., I, p. 310. Hand extended to someone. Anc. Gk. and Rom., early Christian. Sittl, p. 50. Clinking glasses or milk cartons in drinking a toast. Students, Univ. of Calif. Berkeley. McCord, p. 291. (Cf. HAND, OBJECT, Toast.)

Consecration: (Cf. HAND, HEAD, Consecration.) Laying on of hands. Num. 27, 18; Acts 8, 18. Bishop elect is presented by two bishops to the archbishop of the province. The litany is said...after which, while two bishops hold the Gospels over the neck of the elect, all the other bishops touching his head, the consecrator begins "veni creator." Hand and hands of the elect are consecrated with chrism and oil. Swete, p. 207. At ordination of a bishop, a consecrator, chosen from the bishops, lays his hand on the head of the elect. Canons of Hippoly-

tus. 3rd cent. Swete, p. 200. At ordination in the English
church of the 8th cent., the imposition of hands followed the
Gallic rule: deacons received it from bishops, the priests from
the bishops and priests present, the bishop from the bishops
present while the open gospels were held over his neck. Swete,
p. 203. Ordination and consecration with visible laying on of
hands. Num. 8, 10; Acts 6, 6; 13, 3; I Tim., 4, 14.

Consolation: Placing the hand on someone's shoulder may
signify moral support or comfort. Ruesch and Kees, p. 85.
Deity clasps hand of mortal. Anc. Gk. Sittl, p. 276.

Contempt: (Cf. s.v. FINGER, Contempt; FINGER, HAND,
Contempt.) The "fig" (clenched fist, thumb protruding between
index and middle, or middle and ring fingers). A. Cook, p. 134.
Middle finger extended, rest of hand clenched into a fist. Bulwer, pp. 173-176. Clapping of hands. Ariosto, xvii, 91. An
imaginary pinch of sand thrown at person. Amer. schoolchildren. Seton, p. xxi. Open palm, fingers radiating from it
and bent slightly back. So. India. Rose, p. 314. Fingers of
one hand united at their extremities, taking the spittle from
under the tongue and making the gesture of throwing it towards
a person. Neapol. De Jorio, p. 131. Both hands form a
circle, 10-30 cm in diameter, indicating the size of the anus of
the person despised. Jiménez, p. 37. Slight wave of right
hand by moving it from the wrist outward in a rapid movement.
Anc. Gk. and Rom. Sittl, p. 98. Thrusting out the closed
hand and opening it, palm down. Aubert, p. 83. "...thrust
his hands beneath his coat tails." Dickens, Pickw., II; p. 429.
Holding out left hand, palm forward, in front of face, then hitting the back of it lightly with palm of right hand. Saudi Arabia.
Semiotic. Barakat, no. 176. Cf. s.v. ARM, WRIST, Contempt.

Copulation: Extended left fist is jerked downward or to the
side from a loose wrist two or three times, either in the air
or against a surface. Lat. Am. Kany, p. 187. The open
right palm is slapped down two or three times on the extended
left fist held upright or in oblique position, as if pushing a cork
into a bottle. Lat. Am. Kany, p. 187. Tickling the palm of
a woman when shaking hands, usually with the forefinger: proposition. Lebanon, Syria. Semiotic. Barakat, no. 82. Hitting
tightly closed right fist into left palm: proposition. Lebanon,
Syria. Semiotic, autistic. Barakat, no. 8. When shaking hands
with a woman, a man places his right thumb on the back of her
right hand and rubs the back slightly with the thumb: proposition. Lebanon, Syria. Semiotic. Barakat, no. 15. Hitting
right fist into left palm: obscenity. Saudi Arabia. Semiotic.
Barakat, no. 106. Placing palms together and bending two
middle fingers while other fingers are still extended in contact,
then moving hands in opposite directions so that middle fingers
are extended up and down, respectively: obscenity. Egypt.
Semiotic. Barakat, no. 142. (Cf. s.v. ARM, HAND, Copulate.)
Fist, front of hand outward, moved from right to left like a
pendulum. Mexico. Lomas, p. 36.

Creation: "...describing small circles in the air--in the
...vicinity of the mover's chest--with the slightly cupped hand...

The thumb moves minimally and seems to serve as an axis for
the movement of the hand... The movement observed in connection with expressions suggestive of setting in motion is performed similarly, but the circles described by the hand tend to
be larger and the hand less cupped. Madrid, Lat. Am. Green,
p. 67.

Cuckoldry: (Cf. s.v. FINGER, FOREHEAD; FINGER,
HEAD; HAND, HEAD, Cuckoldry.) Holding both indexes above
the temples ("horns"). Lat. Am. Kany, p. 190. The index
and little fingers extended upwards, other fingers closed
("horns"). Southern Ital. Efron, no. 59a.

Curse: Beating the ground with the flat hand. Mod. Gk.,
Neapol. Heiler, p. 103; Sittl, p. 191. Cursing the gods of
the underworld and the dead by beating on the ground with the
flat hand. Anc. Rom. Heiler, p. 103. Raising or extending
the open hand while swearing an oath is a curse upon oneself.
Oriental. Ebert, V, p. 93. Making the sign of the "horns"
toward someone. Neapol. De Jorio, p. 94. Holding up open
hands in front of shoulders, then moving them forward a few
times, palms facing forward. Jordan, Syria. Semiotic. Barakat, no. 40.

Death: Sign of the cross made in the air. Neapol. Critchley,
p. 89. Oldest son or nearest relative present closes the
eyes of the dead. Hastings, Dict., I, col. 332.

Deception: Swinging the clenched hand forward, palm down
and index extended, away from the chest in a half circle may
accompany expressions suggesting "undermining." Madrid.
Green, p. 40.

Dedication: Raising hands holding an object. Anc. Gk.
Sittl, p. 197 and n. 4. In dedicating a sacred building the
pontifex held a pillar with his hand, thus, according to Roman
law, transferring the building from the manus of man into that
of the deity. Sittl, p. 196.

Defiance: (Cf. s.v. FINGER, Defiance.) "the thief raised
his hands with both the figs." Dante, Inf., c. xxv. Right fist,
held vertically, rubbed on the flat palm of the left in a circular
motion. Palest. Bauer, p. 222. "...crimson silk pocket-
handkerchief attached to a walking stick, which was occasionally
waved in the air with various gestures indicative of supremacy
and defiance." Dickens, Pickw., II, p. 368. Throw a cap at
someone. DEP, 77. "deliberately depositing his hat on the
floor." Dickens, Pickw., II, p. 18. Demonstrate: Open hand
in front, palm upwards, finger tips down. Aubert, p. 91.

Denial: Hand raised, palm forward, or sometimes simply
the index extended, shakes rapidly sideways. Equivalent to
shaking the head. France. Mitton, p. 141.

Depart: To an inferior: hand moved downward a few times.
St. Jerome, Vita Pauli Erem.; Sittl, p. 221. Palm pushed
vertically forward. Amer. schoolchildren. Seton, p. xx. Wagging hands signify "let's get out of here." French. Life (Sept.
16, 1946). One hand horizontal at middle of body, palm up,
the other hand rapidly moves over it from wrist to beyond fingertips, palm inward, signifies "Let's beat it." Ital. N.Y.

Times (March 1, 1959). Edge of left hand makes chopping motion against the right wrist--"Go away!" Ital. Graham, p. 26.
Palm facing body, hand moves back and forth. Colombia.
Saitz and Cervenka, p. 81. Right arm extended, elbow close to
body, hand vertical, thumb up; "the palm of the left hand is
then moved over the wrist of the right hand with a quick jerk;
the face shows grave concern; the head is sometimes lowered,
as if taking cover; the hands may waggle, indicating trepidation:
Tout à coup, voilà le flic qui arrive...on se calte!... I recently observed a French-speaking Belgian woman using a very
discreet variant of this gesture. Her hands were held close to
the right side of the body, waist high; the left hand was vertical
and stationary, crossing the right hand at about the wrist of the
latter which was held palm up and which was flipped upward and
toward the speaker. General rout...: ...left hand bears down
on the crook of the right elbow, while the right forearm is
raised smartly to the height of the head;...There is an American
gesture which is analogous...: to indicate hasty departure...,
a person will sometimes make a rapid, sweeping, and slightly
rising motion to the right with the right hand, the fingers and
thumb being held together tightly. This gesture is sometimes
accompanied by a whistle and...the point of departure is frequently the left hand which...is held horizontally, palm down, in
front of the body, and chest high. French. Brault, pp. 377-
378. "He waved his hand in signal for Godfrey to be gone."
Smollett, Peregr. Pickle, ch. ci. Opening the hand and blowing into it. ("He has disappeared.") Near East. Critchley,
p. 91.

Despair: Holding up hands. Odyss., bk. ix. "And one
who had both hands lopped off, lifting the stumps..." Dante,
Inf., c. xxviii. Tearing clothing at the breast. Anc. Gk.
and Rom. Sittl, p. 22. Tearing one's clothes. Early
Christian. Sittl, p. 19. Wringing hands. Shakesp., Two
Gentlemen, II, iii, 9; Romeo, III, ii, 36; Hamlet, III, iv,
34. Wringing hands, beating breast. Shakesp., Richard III,
II, ii, 3. Elbows against body, hands clasped at the height
of the shoulders; from a position touching the chest they
are lowered. Feminine and clerical. France. Mitton,
p. 144. Wringing hands above one's head. Gessner, p.
36.

Desperation: While speaking, trying to be understood, emphasis is added by slightly cupping the hand so that tip of thumb
touches index, and moving hand rapidly up and down, palm up.
Ital. N.Y. Times (March 1, 1959). "...and beat his hands in
perfect desperation." Dickens, Twist, p. 140.

Destruction: Hands chest high, palms down, fingers pushed
back and forth vigorously. Verbal context is disintegration.
Madrid. Hands successively describe small circles. Verbal
context is dissolution. Madrid. Green, p. 42.

Determination: Fists clenched. English boys. Opie, p. 230.
"Giving the trousers a hitch shows that a man wants to feel equal
to an approaching task." Birdwhistell, Colliers (March 4, 1955),
p. 56.

Dignity: The hand as symbol appears on weapons, insignia of Roman legions, and as symbol of power and dignity. Seligmann, II, p. 166. (Cf. s.v. Authority above.)

Direction: Point up very high and look up (heaven). Amer. schoolchildren. Seton, p. xx. Hold out flat left, palm down, and above it hold right in the same way (over or above). Amer. schoolchildren. Seton, p. xx. Hold out flat left, palm down, and under it the right in the same way (under). Amer. schoolchildren. Seton, ibid. Index extended, pointing down (down). Amer. schoolchildren. Seton, ibid. Pointing down, hand swung in small circle (here). Amer. schoolchildren. Seton, ibid. Hand pointed toward seat or room in requesting someone to sit or enter. Anc. Rom. Sittl, p. 52. Hand zig-zags. (Pushing someone around.) Assim. Eastern Europ. Jews. Efron, p. 117. Hand points down (right here). Assim. Eastern Europ. Jews. Efron, pp. 49, 75. Hand moves forward, then turns and is moved toward the back (facing the back). Assim. Eastern Europ. Jews. Efron, p. 116. One hand flat, palm up, the other flat, palm down, glides forward over the former (in between). Trad. Eastern Europ. Jews. Efron, p. 72. Brushing movement of one palm against the other (sideswiping). Assim. Eastern Europ. Jews. Efron, p. 117.

Disagreement: Tightly bunched fingers of each hand, palms down, are brought toward each other ("collision," "conflict"). May be repeated. Madrid, Lat. Am. When accompanying verbal expressions suggest confrontation, fingers do not touch, but stop a few inches from one another. Green, p. 47. Twisting cupped hands away from the speaker at chest level, concluding with palms facing the listener. Madrid, Lat. Am. Expressions of contrast may be accompanied by bent arms at shoulder level or higher, palms facing each other. Madrid. Green, pp. 46-47. Hands moved up from ca. waist level with palms up. Lebanon, Saudi Arabia. Autistic or semiotic, possibly culture-induced. Barakat, no. 100.

Disappointment: Hand scratches back of head. Neapol. De Jorio, p. 121. Palm hits forehead. Intensity of blow determined by intensity of one's displeasure. Neapol. De Jorio, p. 123.

Disapproval: Shaking the collar or coat lapel with the right hand. Near East. Critchley, p. 91.

Disbelief: " 'I couldn't have believed it, sir!' said Mrs. Mann, holding up her hands." Dickens, Twist, p. 151. Cf. s.v. Doubt below.

Discouragement: Fingers close together, palms pressed together, thumbs depressed, hands rhythmically moved up and down. Neapol. Critchley, p. 89.

Disgust: Rubbing the hands together may accompany verbal expression of repugnance. Spain, Lat. Am. Green, p. 75. "Pnin waved a hand at the raconteur in a Russian disgusted 'ohgo-on-with-you' gesture..." Nabokov, Pnin, p. 160. One hand upright near the face, palm out, or both hands extended forward. Aubert, p. 86.

Dismay: "The gesture known as wringing the hands is one

that is seldom seen in real life." Wodehouse, pp. 18, 66.
"...he held up his hands, assured me he could do me no service,..." Smollett, Random, ch. xxxiv.

Dismissal: "But with an angry wafture of your hand gave
sign for me to leave you." Shakesp., Caesar, II, i, 246-7.
Edge of left hand is brought smartly down on wrist of extended
right hand ("Let's get the hell out of here"). French. WW II.
Alsop, p. 29. (Cf. s.v. Depart above.) Repeated rapid gesture
of discarding something with the flat hand. French. Mitton,
p. 143.

Distress: "The respectable old gentleman wrung his hand
fervently, and seemed disposed to address some observations to
his son,..." Dickens, Pickw., I, p. 455. " 'Oh!' said the
unhappy Bladud, clasping his hands, and mournfully raising his
eyes towards the sky." Dickens, Pickw., II, p. 133. " 'Oh no,
no, Mr. Weller,' said Arabella, clasping her hands." Dickens,
Pickw., II, p. 183. "Mr. Snodgrass and Mr. Winkle grasped
each other by the hand..." Dickens, Pickw., II, p. 12. "...the
two-hand dramatic splash of amazed distress;..." Nabokov, p.
51.

Doubt: Moving the open extended hand, palm out, back and
forth several times and with a wrist movement describing a semicircle. Lat. Am. Kany, p. 107. Cf. s.v. Disbelief above,
Hesitation below.

Down: Rapid downward movement of the palm. Assim.
Eastern Europ. Jews. Efron, p. 117. Hands horizontal, arms
straight, palms down, hands parting horizontally. Aubert, p. 89.
(Cf. s.v. Direction above.)

Drink: Closed fist, thumb extended and moved toward
mouth until tip of thumb touches lips. France. Vulgar. Mitton, p. 147. Hand moves as though strumming a guitar. Kany,
p. 78. "...he turned his glass upside down, by way of reminding his companion that he had nothing left wherewith to slake his
thirst." Dickens, Pickw., I, p. 262. Thumb extended, fist
clenched and moved toward mouth. Ital. Efron, p. 46.
" 'Drink?' he asked, making a motion with his hand decanting
his thumb downward." Hemingway, p. 141.

Drunkenness: Closed fist, thumb extended, and moved
toward mouth until tip of thumb touches lips. France. Mitton,
p. 147.

Duality: Raising bunched fingers of both hands, palms facing the speaker, to approx. shoulder level (groups of two, two
of a kind). Madrid, Lat. Am. Green, p. 50. "When discuss-
ing an issue...which has two facets or aspects, each view or
side of the issue may be accompanied by a sweep of the slightly
cupped hand, palm inward, beginning at the level of the chest
and terminating waist-high at the side of the gesticulator."
Madrid, Lat. Am. Green, p. 50.

Eating: Beating the ribs with the flat of the hand. Neapol.
Critchley, p. 89. Hand lifted to mouth, imaginary food trickled
in as in eating spaghetti by hand, as it was originally done.
Ital. Efron, p. 148. Uniting tips of all fingers of one hand,
move them repeatedly to the mouth and away again. Ital. Efron,

p. 148, fig. 43.

Effeminacy: Elbows close to the body, extended open hands
are waved to and fro from the wrist as if they were wings.
Lat. Am.   Kany, p. 182.

Emphasis: Striking chest with fist or open palm, or striking table with fist.   Dickens, Pickw., I, pp. 218, 276; II,
pp. 290, 315, 396.   "As the little man concluded, he took an
emphatic pinch of snuff, as a tribute to the smartness of Messrs.
Dodson and Fogg."   Dickens, Pickw., II, p. 25.   "'Leave the
house,' said Mr. Nupkins, waving his hand emphatically."
Dickens, Pickw., I, p. 433.   "'Pay it all--stick to business--
cash up--every farthing.'--Here Mr. Jingle paused and striking
the crown of his hat with great violence,..."   Dickens, Pickw.,
II, p. 423.   "Mr. Snodgrass dropped the hand which he had, in
the spirit of poesy, raised towards the clouds, as he made the
above appeal..."   Dickens, Pickw., I, p. 31.   "...and then he
struck the ground emphatically with his stick."   Dickens, Pickw.,
I, pp. 315-316.   Accompanying a word by hitting on the table
with one's fist.   French.   Mitton, p. 145.   Presenting the hand
vertically, palm forward, under the eyes of the other person.
Allusion to a written document supporting one's argument.
French.   Familiar.   Mitton, pp. 147-149.   "The performance
of the gesture [accompanying emphatic verbal behavior] com-
mences at the level of the neck or chest, palm facing the speaker, and consists of a rapid and sweeping motion of one hand.
Midway through the downward sweep of the lower arm, the hand
rotates at the wrist so that the palm faces away from the speaker at the conclusion of the movement.   ...Whereas men tend to
return the arm and hand to a neutral position of rest at the conclusion of the movement, women are often observed maintaining
the terminal position of the upraised hand."   Spain.   Green,
pp. 54-55.   Hand sweeps upward and outward, palm facing away
from body.   Colombia.   Saitz and Cervenka, p. 47.   Hammering motion of one fist on the other.   Assimilated Eastern Europ.
Jews.   Efron, p. 118.   Open hand in front, palm turned out,
hand raised, fingertips up.   Aubert, p. 91.   "Both hands are
held in front of the chest, all fingertips touching, and shaken up
and down--I beg you to explain yourself!"   Ital.   Graham, p. 26.
Fist strikes palm (or a surface as of a table) once or several
times.   Colombia, U.S.   Saitz and Cervenka, p. 46.

Encouragement: Clapping of hands.   Anc. Rom.   Sittl,
p. 56.   Spain, Lat. Am.   Green, p. 50.   Deity clasps hand of
mortal.   Anc. Gk. and Rom.   Sittl, p. 276.   Handshake.   Anc.
Gk. and Rom.   Sittl, p. 30.   "Cracket intimated, by a motion
of his hand as he left the room, that there was nothing to
fear..."   Dickens, Twist, p. 473.   "Matt stroked her hand in
encouraging silence."   Boucher, p. 207.   "A gesture observed
in the theater in association with expressions suggestive of
boosting morale or raising spirits is performed by raising both
spread hands, palms up, as if actually raising an object with
the open hands."   Spain.   Green, pp. 49-50.   "Mr. Barbecue-
Smith patted his arm several times and went on."   Huxley, ch.
vi.

Engagement: Handshake as sign of formal engagement. Röhrich, p. 32 and plate 30. Joining hands of bride and groom. Shakesp., Twelfth Night, V, i, 159; Winter's Tale, I, ii, 102.

Enmity: Edge of extended hand crosses the chest from left shoulder to the right. Neapol. De Jorio, p. 188. Drawing back the hand rather than reaching it out to grasp the hand of another. Bulwer, pp. 120-122. Drawing back the hand with thumb raised. Life (Sept. 3, 1945), p. 25.

Enthusiasm: Hands clasped in front of chest. Commonly female. Colombia, U.S. Saitz and Cervenka, p. 49.

Equality: Right and left hands raised and lowered alternately, as if balancing something. France. Mitton, p. 144. Hands horizontal, back of hands upwards, moved gradually away from and towards gesturer as if over an imaginary surface. Neapol. De Jorio, p. 88.

Etiquette: Consul took the hand of the person whom he brought into the senate. Anc. Rom. Sittl, p. 81. After greeting, one led guests to their appointed places by the hand. Medieval German. Gottfried v. Strassburg, 5747-49. Cf. also Bergemann, p. 50. Invitation to take a seat is accompanied by a lightly smoothing gesture of the right hand. Palest. Bauer, p. 224. Both hands are used to receive gifts. Africa. Ohm, p. 45. "...and the gentleman drew his chair aside to afford the newcomer a sight of the fire." Dickens, Pickw., II, pp. 167-168. Coffee, tea or food is always proferred from right hand to right hand of guest. Saudi Arabia and other Moslem countries. Culture-induced. Barakat, no. 159.

Excitement: Hand placed over heart. Helbig, 1242. Hands in front of body, palms facing about 12 inches apart; hands are then clasped. Colombia, U.S. Much more common in Colombia. Female. Saitz and Cervenka, p. 50.

Expectancy: (of gift or object): Hand extended, palm up and slightly cupped. Anc. Gk. and Rom. Sittl, p. 110.

Exquisiteness: Kissing joined fingertips of one hand, then throwing kiss into air. France, Spain. Kaulfers, p. 256.

Extreme: Shaking loosely hanging hand from the wrist. Palest. Bauer, p. 223. Both hands suddenly raised simultaneously upward and to the sides. Eastern Europ. Jews. Efron, p. 72. Gesticulating with hands high in the air. Late Roman. Sittl, p. 49.

Facility: Snapping thumb and middle finger ("just like that!"). Assim. Eastern Europ. Jews. Efron, p. 119.

Faithfulness: Clap hands on sword. Elizabethan England. R. H. Bowers, p. 271. Handclasp. Mainzer Landrecht. DWb, IV/2, col. 420; Arndt, p. 244; Haltaus, p. 814 (1609). In ancient Germanic law the hand symbolized the commitment of the entire person. Thus the hand symbolized the pledge of the person. Ebert, V, col. 94. One either clasps the hand of the partner or one's own hand. Spain. Flachskampf, p. 224.

Farewell: "I hold it fit that we shake hands and part." Shakesp., Hamlet, I, v, 127. "He wrung Bassanio's hand, and so they parted." Shakesp., Merchant, II, viii, 47. "...departed for the garrison, after having shook hands with every in-

dividual in the house." Smollett, Peregr. Pickle, I, ch. ix.
"lifting the pinched hat a few inches from his head, and care-
lessly replacing it very much on one side..." Dickens, Pickw.,
I, p. 16. German. DWb, IV/2, col. 332. Flat hand held
high, palm down and forward, fingers quickly waved up and
down. Amer. schoolchildren. Seton, p. xx. Hand moves up
and down at approx. face level, palm down. U.S. Saitz and
Cervenka, p. 62. Hand moves more slowly, fingers closer together than in the U.S. goodby wave. Colombia. Saitz and
Cervenka, p. 61. Or fingers spread apart, sometimes whole
arm waves vigorously. Ibid., p. 62. Arm extended in the direction of someone, hand relaxed but agitated in a lively manner
up and down, palm facing down. Familiar. French. Mitton,
p. 143. Waving at someone already out of hearing distance.
Apollon. Rhod., Ovid. Sittl, p. 216. Arm bent, hand approx.
shoulder level, fingers cupped, hand and arm moved repeatedly
and slightly up and down. Ital. N.Y. Times (March 1, 1959).
Hand waving, palm toward face of gesticulator at arm's length.
Southern Ital. Efron, p. 156 and fig. 62. "With palm upward
and fingers alternately clenched and outstretched, I bade Gastone
farewell." Ital. Graham, p. 26. Hand extended short distance,
palm faces gesticulator, tips of fingers repeatedly lowered and
raised rapidly, often tapping base of palm. Spain. Becoming
progressively less common. Principally older madrileños and
young children entrusted to the care of middle-aged nannies.
More common: open hand, palm out, held at side of head and
waved back and forth. Green, pp. 34-36. The handshake is
the customary ritual for closing a prayer meeting of the Quakers. Hayes, p. 258. Holding up right hand with palm facing
backward and moving fingers and hand back. Lebanon, Saudi
Arabia, Jordan, Syria. Semiotic. Barakat, no. 113.

Fear: Holding up both hands, palm forward. Amer.
schoolchildren. Seton, p. xxii. Hands beaten together. Ital.
Manzoni, ch. xiii. Hand(s) upright near the face, palm(s) out.
Aubert, p. 86.

Fervor: " 'Indeed, indeed, it was two other boys,' said
Oliver, clasping his hands passionately." Dickens, Twist,
p. 85.

Fight: The fists menace one another. Amer. schoolchildren. Seton, p. xxiv.

Finished: Turn up hand, palm up. ("It is finished.")
French. Life (Sept. 16, 1946), p. 12. Palm of one hand
brushes the other. Near East. Critchley, p. 91. Palms
placed together so that fingers are pointing forward, then twist
hands in opposite directions but keep them in contact. Saudi
Arabia. Semiotic. Barakat, no. 225. Rubbing hands lightly
in front of body. Arab. Autistic, possibly culture-induced.
Barakat, no. 147.

Flattery: Passionate handshake without sufficient familiarity
or reason. Anc. Rom. Sittl, p. 28.

Foolishness: "If thou hast done foolishly in lifting thyself
up, or if thou hast thought evil, lay thy hand on thy mouth."
Prov., 30, 32. Raising and lowering the cupped hand as if

trying the weight of an object. Lat. Am. Kany, p. 57. Hand held below the chin, palm up, and moved outward--or something similar. Lat. Am. Kany, p. 57. Fingertips of one hand joined and held at elbow of the other arm, fingertips of the other hand also joined, hand waving back and forth. Southern Ital. Efron, p. 157.

Forgiveness: Priest raises his absolving hand and pronounces words of forgiveness. Mass, p. 14.

Forwardness: Passionate handshake without sufficient familiarity or reason. Anc. Rom. Sittl, p. 28.

Friendship: "Give me thy hand..." II Kings, 10, 15. "I have called, and ye have refused; I have stretched out my hand, and no man regarded." Prov. 1, 24. The law of hospitality required that host and guest give each other the right hand. Anc. Gk. and Rom. Sittl, p. 135. Right hand of one person grasped by hand(s) of the other. Anc. Gk. and Rom. Stephani, pp. 69-113. Handshake sealing friendship. Anc. Gk. and Rom. Sittl, p. 30. Right hand of one deity clasps right hand of another as symbol of the unity of the cities symbolized by the respective deities. Anc. Gk. and Rom. Sittl, p. 137, n. 5. Handshake while conversing. Anc. Gk. and Rom. Sittl, pp. 28-29. Hand of one person holding hand of another, walking side by side. Anc. Gk. and Rom. Sittl, p. 31. Men walking hand in hand. William of Newburgh, 12th cent. Engl. Kelly, ch. xvi. Hand given as pledge of faith and friendship. Shakesp., Two Gentlemen, II, ii, 8; V, iv, 116; Merry Wives, II, i, 225; Troil., IV, v, 270; Hamlet, II, ii, 388; etc. Bulwer, pp. 109-120. " 'I do assure you, sir,' (says he, taking the gentleman by the hand), 'I am heartily glad to meet with a man of your kidney;...' " Fielding, Bk. II, ch. viii. "shaking him by the hand, called him his best friend." Smollett, Peregr. Pickle, I, ch. lvii. Holding up branches of trees, canoe paddles, sticks, poles decorated with feathers, white flags, pieces of cloth in token of friendship. Polynesian. Dawson, pp. 96-97. Handclasp in token of friendship not limited to Indoeuropean peoples, but also found among the Papuans of the central mountains of New Guinea and Australian aborigines. Ebert, V, col. 94. Handclasp in token of friendship. DWb, IV /2, col. 367-8. " 'I want your assistance.' 'You shall have it,' ...clasping his friend's hand." Dickens, Pickw., I, p. 31. "When the supper-table was cleared...Eckbert took Walter's hand and said: 'My friend, you should have my wife tell you the story of her youth sometime...' " Tieck, Der blonde Eckbert, p. 1. Passionate handshake is not given to chance acquaintances--only to loved or very much liked people, esp. before or after a long absence. Ital. Mantegazza, p. 229. Handshake is an offer of one's friendship and devotion. Became popular in France under the Second Empire. Mitton, p. 142. One's right hand shakes one's left hand while one looks in the direction of the other person. In China this takes the place of the Europ. handshake between two persons. Mitton, p. 142.

Frustration: Elbows against the body, hands at the height of the shoulders, right palm clasps left, both hands remain

joined. From a position touching the chest they are lowered.
("This is lamentable!" "Scandalous!") Feminine and clerical.
France. Mitton, p. 144. "Sir Benjamin, jarred thoroughly,
shook his fist in the air." Carr, Hag's Nook, p. 114. "Mr.
Scogan raised his hand and let it limply fall again in a gesture
which implied that words failed him." Huxley, ch. xiv.

"Gently": Flat hand held low, palm down, gently waved up
and down. Amer. schoolchildren. Seton, p. xx.

Gossip: Thumb and middle finger opening and closing while
moving the hand away from the body as if cutting with scissors.
Southern Ital. Efron, p. 66.

Graft: One hand, fingers extended, makes sawing motion
on edge of other hand. Colombia. Saitz and Cervenka, p. 64.

Gratitude: Handshake. Anc. Gk. and Rom. Sittl, p. 30.
Lowering the hand as sign of gratitude was part of Roman court
etiquette. Sittl, p. 149. Lowering the right hand as generally
polite expression of gratitude. Nonn., Dion.; Stat., Achill.;
Sittl, p. 149. Folding one's hands. Gottfr. v. Strassburg,
8215-16. "Mr. Winkle had fast hold of his friend's hand...
'My friend, my benefactor, my honored companion...' " Dickens,
Pickw., II, p. 274.

Greed: Rubbing palms together. Bulwer, pp. 40-41.

Greeting: Shaking hands of people or gods. Assyr., Babyl.
Ohm, p. 243. Hand extended to someone in greeting. Anc. Gk.
and Rom. Sittl, pp. 49-50. Hand extended toward someone by
someone reporting good news. Demosthenes. Sittl, p. 50.
Grasping the hand of statues standing along the way. Lucretius.
Sittl, p. 181. Raising right hand, so that palm remains posi-
tioned toward face, hand returned to mouth, kissing fingertips
and then throwing kiss toward divine image. Anc. Gk. and Rom.
Baumeister, I, p. 592. Junior official lowered or had the
fasces lowered by his lictors in the presence of a senior or superior official. Anc. Rom. Sittl, p. 154. Handshake (without
kiss) by the emperor succeeded kiss after Diocletian. Sittl,
p. 80. Lowering fasces. Anc. Rom. Sittl, p. 155. In the
circus the charioteer lowered his whip before the patrons. Sittl,
pp. 155-156. Handshake was custom of candidates for political
office. Anc. Rom. Sittl, p. 29. "I give you welcome with a
powerless hand,..." Shakesp., King John, II, i, 15. "Hatch-
way...thrust out his hand by way of salutation." Smollett,
Peregr. Pickle, I, ch. xviii. "He shook him heartily by the
hand." Ibid., I, ch. xiii. Handshake. DWb, IV/2, cols. 331-
332, 368, 385, 414. Dickens, Pickw., I, pp. 37, 61, 109, 297,
451, etc. "...but in the college one shook hands at the most
once a year, on one's first appearance each Michaelmas term."
Cambridge. C. P. Snow, p. 206. According to Moslem custom
the thumbs are brought into contact. In modern Egypt, at the
ceremony of joining hands between the bride's proxy and the
bridegroom, the parties sit on the ground face to face, grasp
one another's right hands, raising the thumbs and pressing them
one against the other. Lane, I, p. 219. "He [the chief] first
grasped my hand and pressed his thumb against mine as is the
custom." Krapf, p. 138. Cutting oneself with shark's teeth

and wailing as a form of receiving a friend or showing joy at
his arrival. Tahiti. Ellis, II, p. 337. Gashing face, breast,
and weeping in welcoming a friend. New Zealand. Ling Roth,
p. 179. Sprinkling water over one's head. New Hebrides.
Mallery, p. 5. Sprinkling sand or mud over one's body. South
Africa. Livingstone, pp. 276, 286, 296. Spitting (now [1904]
falling into disuse). Uganda. Johnston, II, p. 833. Among
the Uvinza, after an elaborate exchange of courtesies, the
parties slap their sides and pat their stomachs. Tanganyika.
Cameron, I, p. 226. The Gond pull one another's ears in salutation. Dawson, p. 94. In the Marianas they stroke the abdomen. Mallery, p. 4. Spear was thrust into the ground, the
free right hand was raised, the shield was held with the left
against an unexpected thrust. Primitive Germanic. HDV, I,
p. 317. Priest before ancestor's shrine clapped his hands while
bending knees, as greeting. Inamwanga, Tanganyika. Ohm,
p. 283. Handshake is common in Africa, and is recorded
among men of the Karague, Masai, Wagare, Niamniani, Mon-
butto, etc. Often accompanied by cracking or snapping of the
fingers. Speke, p. 203; Ling Roth, p. 168. Hand raised above
level of the head, turned toward someone, fingers extended and
slightly separated, hand agitated slightly in the direction from
thumb to little finger, palm inward. Friendly, informal. France.
Mitton, p. 142. Handshake performed by one person, his right hand
shaking his left while he is looking at someone who is generally at
too great a distance for the former to shake hands with him. Informal. French. Mitton, p. 142. Right hand grasps left wrist.
Mohammedan. Ohm, p. 276. Right hand of one grasps right hand
of another briefly. Intensity varies with the importance of the act
and its emotional content. Modern continental western Europe.
Révész, p. 143ff. Handshake in greeting more frequent in Colombia than in the U.S. Omission may be a discourtesy. In the U.S.
the handshake is formal, a mark of initial encounter and special
occasions. The Colombian handshake is likely to last longer than
the handshake as practiced in the U.S. Saitz and Cervenka, pp. 61,
65. "She greeted Pnin with a clapping of hands,..." Nabokov,
p. 121. Hand, palm up, extended to side, at waist-level or
slightly above. Used over distance or with "Que hubo." Men.
Colombia. Saitz and Cervenka, p. 66.

    Guilt: " 'What is it she does now? Look, how she rubs
her hands.' 'It is an accustomed action with her, to seem thus
washing her hands.' " Shakespeare, Macbeth, V, i, 30.

    Hard times: Fist makes firm belt-tightening gesture.
French. Life (Sept. 16, 1946).

    Harmony: Clasped hands. Etruscan, Roman. The Etrus-
can Concordia is characterized by clasped hands. Pauly-Wis-
sowa, IV, col. 834; Babelon, II, p. 42.

    Hatred: Shaking clenched fist at level of face, fingers in-
ward toward the gesturer. French. Mitton, p. 141. Fingers
extended and slightly apart, palm inward, at eye level, in direction of someone. French. Mitton, p. 142.

    Helplessness: " 'I thought at the time the people we picked
out went to a convalescent camp at Birkenau,' Neubert said,

turning up his palms in a helpless gesture as a twitter sounded
from the spectator gallery.   Birkenau housed Auschwitz's gas
chambers and ovens. " L.A. Times (Feb. 4, 1964), p. 2.
"...and the 'disjunctive' motion--hands traveling apart to signify
helpless passivity. " Nabokov, p. 41.   "He looks at him with a
pitiful expression.   Closes his eyes and wrings his hand in a
gesture of helplessness. " Weyland, p. 19.

Hesitation: Slow scratching of the head or the nose or playing with the lips or the chin.   French.   Mitton, p. 146.   Cf.
s.v. Doubt above.

Homage: Palms of hands forward, as if to ward off a blow
--submission of a defeated people.   Anc. Egypt.   Meyer, pl. to
pp. 242, 266.   Folded hands of vassal before his lord or lower
cleric before his bishop.   Tomb of Hincmar of Rheims.   Prutz,
I, p. 117.   The one receiving homage spreads his hand out and
the one rendering it strokes it softly or gives his hand.   Arab.
Goldziher, Zeitschr., p. 380.   Kneeling, kissing lord's hand.
Stoebe, p. 188.   Hands folded, the lord took them between his
own.   HDV, I, p. 319; Grimm, DRA, I, pp. 191-192.

Homosexuality: "Homosexuality has certainly not diminished
of late, nor grown more bashful.   Two M.P.'s, according to
the reported comment of a policeman stationed in the House of
Commons, might occasionally be seen going hand-in-hand through
the division lobby. " Muggeridge, p. 97.   One hand rests on top
of the other, palm to palm, as thumbs flap like wings.   ("Pa-
jaro. ") Colombia.   Saitz and Cervenka, p. 120.   Hand, palm
down, tipped to one side, then to the other, Colombia.   Saitz
and Cervenka, p. 120.   Flat palms rubbed together lightly.
Lesbian.   Colombia.   Saitz and Cervenka, p. 121.   When shaking hands with another person of same sex it is done loosely
rather than firmly.   Usually two men.   Sexual or homosexual
inference.   Lebanon.   Semiotic.   Barakat, no. 57.   Letting hand
fall, palm up and open.   Executed with delicacy and elegance.
Mexico.   Lomas, p. 36.   Fist, front outward, moved from right
to left like a pendulum.   If used by a man to a man it is an
accusation of homosexuality.   Mexico.   Lomas, p. 36.

Horror: Clasping hands together.   Goldziher, Zeitschr.,
p. 382.   One hand in one instance and in another both hands
covering eyes or face.   Giovanni di Paolo (1403?-1482), "Salome
presents the Head. " Chicago Art Inst.   "she put forth her hands
with an involuntary repellent gesture. " Hawthorne, ch. xxiii.

Humility: "Priest extends his hands and then folds them as
a mark of humility... " Mass, p. 23.

Hunger: Gesture of tightening the belt.   Vulgar.   French.
Mitton, p. 150.   Hand moves to mouth, fingers joined at tips.
Vulgar.   French.   Mitton, p. 148.   "The right hand is out-
stretched, palm down, and the hand is moved back and forth
horizontally at waist level--I am extremely hungry. " Ital.
Graham, p. 26.

Hurry: The palm of one hand gives a sharp blow to the
palm of the other, which rises at the same time as if to cata-
pult an object resting on it into the air.   French.   Mitton,
p. 149.   The flat of the hand is swung backward and forward

repeatedly. ("Pass rapidly." "Leave.") French. Mitton, p. 143. Drawing in flat hand, palm toward gesturer, vigorously and repeatedly several times. Amer. schoolchildren. Seton, p. xx.

Identification: Pointing to oneself. Amer. schoolchildren. Seton, p. xx. Tapping one's chest. Ibid. Placing one's hand on one's chest. French. Mitton, p. 143. Placing tips of index, middle finger and thumb on table, separated from each other, identifies one as a freemason. Mitton, p. 150.

Idleness: Hands folded. Bulwer, pp. 35-38.

Ignorance: Holding coat flaps open, one in each hand. Amer. schoolchildren. Seton, p. xxii. Hand, palms facing out, held up in front of body, then moved slightly to the sides. Slight pursing of lips usually accompanies the gesture. Colombia. Saitz and Cervenka, p. 92. One hand raised in front or to side of body, palm out; often mouth tightened, head tilted. Colombia. Saitz and Cervenka, p. 92.

Impatience: "Thus to be driven (and I wrung my hands through impatience) by the instigations of a designing, an ambitious brother..." Richardson, Clarissa, I, pp. 145-146. Rubbing the hand over the wrist or wristwatch. Univ. of Calif. Berkeley. McCord, p. 290. Hand makes gesture of sweeping something behind one. ("Spare us this.") French. Mitton, p. 147.

Impulsiveness: Seizing someone's hand. Dickens, Pickw., I, p. 312; II, pp. 269, 336, 441.

Indifference: Fingers of one hand close together, palm towards gesticulator, fingertips under chin, then the hand is suddenly flipped outward. This gesture had its origin in flipping the beard. French, Southern Ital. Efron, p. 156. Twisting the open hand back and forth, thumb and fingers spread apart and palm facing away from the speaker. Spain. Green, p. 90. Palm facing down, fingers extended, rocking from side to side. ("Más o menos," "more or less.") Colombia, U.S. Saitz and Cervenka, p. 91.

Influence: Describing small circles in the air with slightly cupped hand, gradually increasing the height until the hand is above the head of the gesticulator. Spain, Lat. Am. Green, p. 74.

Innocence: Washing one's hands. Deut. 21, 6; Matth. 27, 24; Otto, p. 210. Simulating the washing of hands. Bulwer, p. 40. Hands flat, palms outward and separated. French. Mitton, p. 143.

Insult: Open hand is put against another person's face or held up before him, accompanied by the formula "On your eyes." Near East. Critchley, p. 91. Open palm held up. India. Rose, p. 313. Hand extended, fingers spread. "Hand of Fatima." North Africa, Spain, Sicily. Taylor, p. 53-54 and n. 174. (Cf. s.v. Apotropy above.) Often accompanied by the formula "Five in your eyes." The "fig" (thumb protruded between index and middle or middle and ring fingers). Used by Caligula to insult the tribune Cassius Chaerea, whom he thought of as effeminate. Seligmann, II, p. 184. During the Middle

Ages the sign of the "fig" was outlawed by several statutes, which decreed penalties for its exhibition toward religious images. 1522 Johannes Pauli calls the exhibition of the "fig" a custom of the Italians. Seligmann, II, p. 184. Cf. also De Jorio, p. 156. Fingers of one hand from a tube. De Jorio, p. 134. Cupped hand moved up and down approx. 6 in. in front of the chest. Colombia. Saitz and Cervenka, p. 116. Thumb placed in each ear, flat hands up. Amer. schoolchildren. Seton, p. xxiii. Right hand, fingers together and extended, palm down, thumb extended, is placed on top of the left hand similarly formed. The two thumbs, one on each side of the stacked hands, are wiggled, representing the movement of a swimming turtle. Chinese (San Francisco). Univ. of Calif. Berkeley. King, pp. 263-264. The "fig" and the "horns" (index and little finger of one hand extended). Univ. of Calif. Berkeley. King, ibid. The flat of one hand placed on the inside of the bend of the other arm, while that forearm is raised with clenched fist. France. Very vulgar. Mitton, p. 151. Jerking clenched fist downward below the waist as one says "acá." Lat. Am. Kany, p. 147. The "araño": open hand extended with tips of fingers curved inward as in the act of scratching. Women. Lat. Am. Kany, p. 176. Tips of thumbs are placed into ears or on the temple, fingers spread, palms to the front, fingers may or may not be waggled back or forth. Childish. Perry, L. A. Times (Dec. 15, 1957). Holding out left hand, palm up, fingers slightly spread, then quickly and forcefully hitting the right wrist into it with clenched fist. Obscenity. Saudi Arabia. Semiotic. Barakat, no. 164. Holding out right fist, then grasping right wrist with left hand and moving the right hand up and down rapidly; wrist may be grasped from beneath or on top. Obscenity. Lebanon, Saudi Arabia, Syria. Semiotic. Barakat, no. 94. Holding right fist horizontally at left side, heel of hand facing forward, and pumping it vigorously and stiffly on that plane. Obscenity. Saudi Arabia. Semiotic. Barakat, no. 171. Holding out hand with fingers extended, then bending index. Obscenity. Egypt. Semiotic. Barakat, no. 143. Pressing tips of right index and thumb together with other fingers folded into palm, then moving the hand up and down with a pecking motion from the wrist. Obscenity. Saudi Arabia. Semiotic. Barakat, no. 50. Holding out left hand, palm up, fingers slightly curled, then moving right fist through left hand, grasp right forearm. Obscenity. Lebanon, Syria. Semiotic. Barakat, no. 42. Holding out right hand, turn it slowly, thumb and fingers loosely extended. Obscenity. Lebanon, Syria. Semiotic. Barakat, no. 41. Grasp left wrist or forearm with right hand, then move left fist up and down rapidly while right hand still grasps wrist or forearm. Obscenity. Lebanon, Saudi Arabia, Syria. Semiotic. Barakat, no. 17. Placing heel of right fist into left open palm and grinding it into palm. Obscenity. Lebanon. Semiotic. Barakat, no. 65. Hitting tightly closed right fist into left palm, extended middle finger just as right hand hits palm. Phallic obscenity. Lebanon, Syria. Semiotic. Barakat, no. 68. Turn right hand over quickly at waist level. Lebanon, Syria. Semiotic. Barakat, no. 35. Knocking off another man's agal. Syria. Semiotic. Barakat, no. 207.

Interrogation: Hand cupped behind ear. ("What?") Colombia, U.S. Saitz and Cervenka, p. 149. Hands, palm up, held out to side. Sometimes shoulders hunch and lips purse. U.S., more common in Colombia. Saitz and Cervenka, p. 150. Hand extended in front, palm up, chin and eyebrows may be raised. Colombia. Saitz and Cervenka, ibid.

Introduction: Right hand of one grasps right hand of another briefly. Intensity with which this is performed varies with the importance of the act and its emotional content. Modern continental western Europe. Révész, Univ., p. 143. "...it was towards him that Mr. Pickwick extended his hand, when he said, 'A friend of our friend's here.'" Dickens, Pickw., I, p. 39.

Investiture: The vassal extended his folded hands toward his lord, who enclosed these in his own; thereupon the oath of fealty was sworn. Medieval German: Kudrun, st. 190, 1612. Alphart, 10; Otto v. Freising, Gesta Frederici, II, 5. Medieval French: Elie de St. Gille, 1202.

Invitation: Grasping someone's hand in offering him a seat. Anc. Gk. Sittl, p. 81. Host takes hand of guest to lead him into the house or to the table. Anc. Gk. Sittl, ibid. Host puts hand on the coach of arriving guest. Anc. Gk. Sittl, ibid. Hand, palm up, moves toward seat in invitation. Colombia, U.S. Saitz and Cervenka, p. 124. A girl clapping hands is giving an erotic invitation in Alemetejo, Portugal. Urtel, pp. 12-13. The "fig" (thumb protruded between index and middle and ring fingers). Anc. Rom., Neapol. Erotic invitation. De Jorio, p. 157.

Jail: One hand grasps wrist of other hand. Colombia. Saitz and Cervenka, p. 74.

Jealousy: Woman rubs palms together several times: jealousy [and pleasure?] that her man cannot get another woman. Syria. Semiotic. Barakat, no. 218.

Joy: (Cf. s.v. Applause above.) Clapping of hands over discomfiture of someone else. Anc. Jews. Ohm, p. 284. Clapping hands with joy. Anc. Egypt. Ohm, ibid. In general. Ohm, p. 285; Boggs, col. 320; Sittl, p. 11. Clapping of hands in gratitude and in prayer of thanks. Ps. 47, 2; Ohm, pp. 284-285. Clapping of hands during a sermon of Gregorius Nazianzenus. PG, XXXVI, col. 313. The Church opposed clapping during prayer. Ohm, p. 286. Rapid, vigorous clapping of hands, always hitting the left with the right hand. Palest. Bauer, p. 224. "He was glad, he said, to find himself alive; and his two friends, clapping and rubbing their hands twenty times in an hour, declared, that now, once more, he was all himself--" Richardson, Clarissa, ix, p. 211. Clapping of hands. Children. France. Mitton, p. 146. "He sobbed, and wept, and clapped his hands, and hallooed, and finally ran down the street." Smollett, Clinker (Letter of Melford, Sept. 21). "...the children crowded round her, and clapped their hands for joy." Dickens, Pickw., I, p. 492. "Clinker skipped about, rubbing his hands for joy of this reconciliation." Smollett, Clinker (Letter of Melford, May 24). Rubbing of hands. DWb, IV/2, col. 331. "...and Job, rubbing his hands with delight..." Dickens, Pickw., I, p. 433. "The old man rubbed his hands gleefully together." Dickens, Twist, p. 164. Imaginary delight: "'I wish them horses had been three months and better in the Fleet, Sir.' 'Why, Sam?' enquired Mr. Pickwick. 'Vy, Sir,' exclaimed Mr. Weller, rubbing his hands, 'how they would go if they had been!'" Dickens, Pickw., II, p. 327. "Her joy with heaved-up hand she doth express." Shakesp., Lucrece, 111. "A tailor pounded the table in joy..." Boggs, col. 300. Out of merriment and enthusiasm "the company commenced a...thumping of tables." Dickens, Pickw., I, p. 115. "...was so relieved that he could not restrain his joy, but took off his little straw-hat and threw it up into the air." Trollope, Forgive, II, p. 258. After departure of an enemy or when one hears of the misfortune of an enemy, one breaks a pitcher or a pot in joy. Palest. Bauer, p. 221. Hand(s) rapidly agitated up and down. France. Children. Mitton, p. 146. Hands clasped over right shoulder and vigorously shaken: support or joy. Arab. Autistic, possibly semiotic. Barakat, no. 98.

Judgment: Oldest recension of Herzog Ernst (orig. ca. 1180) describes the proscription of the duke, at which the nobility had to swear enmity with raised hands. Ernst, 1182-83. Judges and participants in the "Thing" raise hand, palm inwards, and extend one finger in connection with proscription. v. Amira, p. 217. In depictions of the Last Judgment the palm of Christ's hand is turned towards the saved, the back of the other hand toward the damned. Haseloff, p. 307. Hands horizontal, backs turned up, on same level but apart from one another. Neapol. (Imitation of scale.) De Jorio, p. 171. Both arms extended forward horizontally, both hands in same position. Tips of index and thumb turned down and forming a cone. (Imitation of scale.) Neapol. De Jorio, p. 171.

"Kill": Right hand closed, thumb out, pressed closed as in grasping a knife, jerked thumb edge down. Indian, Sicilian. Austin, p. 596.

Laziness: Scratching limbs. Medieval French. Mathéolus, I, 1462. Putting hands into one's bosom, into one's lap, or into one's pocket. DWb, IV/2, col. 335. Palms turned upward, fingers slightly bent as though holding ostrich eggs. The hands move together up and down as if one were determining their weight. Gesturer is metaphorically weighing testicles of individual upon whose laziness he comments. Mexico. Jiménez, p. 35. Palm of one hand up as though to catch a drop of water, fingers bent, hand moving slightly up and down as though weighing something. Mexico. Lomas, p. 33.

Liberty: Hand open and fingers spread. Anc. India. Rose, p. 312.

Look: Flat hand, palm down, placed above eyes. Amer. schoolchildren. Seton, p. xxi. Pointing and looking in same direction. Amer. schoolchildren. Seton, p. xxi.

Luck: Knocking on wood. Spain, Lat. Am. Green, p. 95.

Magical: Extending hand starts plague. Ex. 8, 5; 8, 17; 9, 22; etc. When Moses held up his hand in the battle with the Amalekites, the Israelites won. When he let his hand fall, the enemy was victorious. Ex. 17, 11. Moses stretched out his hand, and the Red Sea parted. Ex. 14, 16. Folded hands of evil women hinder birth and recovery after childbirth. Anc. Rom. Sittl, p. 126. Hands folded around knees or legs hinder childbirth of another woman. Anc. Rom. Sittl, ibid. Folding of hands, due to its evil effect, was prohibited at official gatherings, ceremonies, etc. Anc. Rom. Sittl, ibid. Upon ascending the throne publicly, the emperor makes sign of the cross, thus commending himself to God's protection. Late Rom. Sittl, p. 128. Old women make sign of cross over open mouth of yawning children, saying "Heiligs Kreuz!" simultaneously. Bavarian. Sittl, p. 127. Rubbing the face of a god as an act of ceremonial greeting appears in funerary inscriptions of pyramid chambers of the fifth and sixth dynasties. In thus rubbing a god's face, the supplicant acquired the beneficent influence of the god. Dawson, p. 81. As part of New Year's wish, hiding the thumbs (folding them under the fingers of a clenched fist) to hold fast the incubus so that it won't interfere with anything. DWb, II, cols. 848-849; Meschke, col. 331. Touching one's genitals through holes in one's pockets, magically nullifies an oath. Meschke, col. 334.

Magnitude: Child raises both hands, palms forward, fingers spread, in answer to the question "How much do you love your mother?" Gesture means "this much." Saudi Arabia. Semiotic. Barakat, no. 76. Raising number of fingers to indicate price one will pay for an item. Arab. Autistic. Barakat, no. 123. Fingers hanging down loosely, hand is moved up and down, swaying. Plenitude of harvest. Palest. Bauer, p. 223. Thumb and index of one hand holding index of other hand in such a way as to indicate a small measurement. Southern Ital. Efron, p. 97. Flat hand, palm down, held up at arm's length. "So high." Amer. schoolchildren. Seton, p. xx. Hands horizontally extended and apart, arms straight, palms down, indicate a wide expanse. Auber, p. 89. Arm extended, fingers cupped, hand is brought to rest on a desk or table top, indicates a figurative limit. Madrid, Lat. Am. Green, p. 63. Hands, palms down, fingers extended, are pushed away from each other at the level of the gesticulator's waist. Gesture may accompany verbal behavior on the topic of mass thought or activity. Spain, Lat. Am. Green, p. 69. Fingers of both hands, held vertically a few inches from the chest, are pushed away from the body and then returned to the original position. Or: raising cupped hand to the side of the head and twisting the wrist and hand outward, so that palm faces listener. Gesture indicates distance. Spain. Green, pp. 61-62. Both hands raised to level of chest, fingers extended, palms facing one another: simultaneity. Madrid. Green, pp. 69-70. In indicating the height of an animal the palm is turned down; in indicating that of a child, the palm is vertical and the thumb thrust up. Mexico, Guatemala. Hayes, p. 259. Hand, fingers extended, held at a certain height with edge of hand down to indicate height of a human being. Colombia. Saitz and Cervenka, p. 70. Hand, fingers extended, held at certain height with palm down to indicate height of human being or animal. U.S. In Colombia, except for parts of north coast, this is used only to indicate height of animals. Saitz and Cervenka, ibid.

Manumission: Servant is taken by the hand, then released. Cid, 1043. Germanic: Grimm, DRA, I, p. 459. Slave freed by a blow. Butler, II, i, 235. If a master wanted to free one of his slaves, he led him to the praetor, who gave the slave a blow on the head as sign of his freedom. Siuts, p. 109. On freeing a slave, the owner places his hand on the slave's head, right hand or other part of the body, and then removes it with the words "Hunc hominem liberum esse volo." Anc. Rom., Lombard. Sittl, p. 132. On freeing a slave, the owner inflicts a last stroke with the cane on him. Anc. Rom. Sittl, pp. 132-133. On freeing a slave, the owner turns him around, to signify the slave's entirely new position in life. Anc. Rom. Sittl, ibid. On freeing a slave, the owner strikes him with his hand for the last time. Anc. Rom. Sittl, p. 133.

Marriage: In the Jātakas the great Being asks Amarā by gesture whether she is married or not. He clenches fist. She answered affirmatively by spreading out her hand. Rose, p. 312. Moslem religious leader places hands of bride and groom together so that their thumbs touch, and holds hands in this position while saying a prayer. Semiotic. Barakat, no. 222.

Masturbation: Loosely clenched fist moved up and down in front of body. Colombia, U.S. Saitz and Cervenka, p. 122.

Medico-magical: Christ healed by touch. Matth. 8, 3. The sick recuperated by touching him. Matth. 9, 20; Mark 3, 10; Luke 6, 19. St. Paul healed by laying on of hands. Acts 28, 8. Slap on the ear of a demon. Palladius, 31, col. 1089a. King of France touches forehead of scrofulous or epileptic subject by placing index and middle finger side by side. Window of the Eglise abbatiale in the former chapel of Saint-Michel de Circuit of Mont Saint Michel au Péril de la Mer (1488). Bloch, p. 145. The ritual laying on of the hand was last carried out by European royalty by Charles X of France in 1825. Wolff-Hürden, Basler Nachr. (Dec. 22, 1957). Hand of King Olaf II of Norway touches chest of patient. Fischer, Antaios II, p. 338. Charles II of England gave regular public notice of receptions in which he would heal by touch. Baker, p. 54. The touch of a dead hand (not criminal) was used for goiter and other afflictions, the stroke being applied nine times from east to west, and nine times from west to east. West Sussex. Baker, p. 51. In Northamptonshire crowds of sufferers congregated about the gallows on days of public executions to receive the "dead stroke" of the body's hand. Ibid. In Staffordshire it is held that a dead hand rubbed on warts causes them to disappear. Ibid. Hand of healer laid on head of patient. Fischer, Antaios II, p. 338; cf. Palest. Bauer, p. 11. "Maud A. Snow, music teacher, testified that as a result of laying on of hands [of evangelist Chas. S. Price], she had been cured of tumors,

Bright's disease, and other ailments." Cited by Hayes, p. 272,
from Manitoba Free Press as quoted in H. L. Mencken, Americana (1926), p. 240. For a cure of a sick cow by a similar
process, cf. Americana (1925), p. 20; Hayes, ibid.

Mediocre: Hand, palm down, index and little finger extended, turns repeatedly back and forth so that alternately one
of the two fingers is up, the other down. Neapol. De Jorio,
p. 127. Hand, palm down, fingers together and extended, moves
from side to side. Assim. Eastern Europ. Jews. Efron,
p. 117.

Minimization of difficulties: "Actress Russell, humped up
and hipped out till she resembles a superannuated ostrich, encompasses quite without caricature the standard repertory of
Jewish gesture--...the vigorous extension of the hands, chest
high and palms up, that means: you got problems? I got problems." Time (Jan. 19, 1962), p. 55.

Mockery: (Cf. s.v. FINGER, Mockery; FINGER, HAND,
Mockery.) Wagging the hand. Zeph. 2, 15. Striking someone
in the face. Luke 22, 64. Anc. Rom. Sittl, p. 108. The
"horns" (clenched fist, index and little finger extended). Pompeian mural, Roman amulets. Röhrich, p. 23 and pl. 17, 19.
The "fig" (thumb protruded between index and middle or middle
and ring finger). Medieval usage in Du Cange: "ficus facere."
Also Ital. Basile, I, p. 103; De Jorio, p. 155. Sticking out
the tongue and making the sign of the "fig." Hans Maler (ca.
1488-ca.1529), "Christ bearing the Cross." The "fig" is common in France, esp. southern France, England, Germany,
Spain, Lat. Am., Portugal, Italy, esp. Naples. If ridicule is
not seriously meant, gesture is executed under the cloak. Liebrecht, p. 186. "Horns" made by a cuckold riding a cock.
Bolte, ZV, XIX, pp. 78-79. Clapping hands. Palest. Bauer,
p. 224. "Mr. Jingle fluttering in derision a white handkerchief
from the coach window." Dickens, Pickw., I, p. 143. Shanghai Gesture. Cf. s.v. FINGER, Mockery. Raising index, then
flexing it. Meschke, col. 332. Crossed extended indexes.
Carinthia. Meschke, ibid. Right fist rubbed around on flat
left hand. Spain, Portugal. Urtel, p. 28. Hand put over
mouth, accompanied by mocking glances. France. Little girls.
Mitton, p. 145. Tips of thumbs placed into ears or on temples,
fingers spread, palms to the front, fingers may or may not be
wagged back and forth. ("Nuts to you!") Childish. Perry,
"Gasoline Alley" L.A. Times (Dec. 15, 1957). Flat hands
waved near shoulders, palms up. ("Jew!") Amer. schoolchildren. Seton, p. xxiii. "Men shall clap their hands at him."
Job 27, 23. "The which John Bacon was whistled and clapped
out of Rome." Ca.1555. OED, s.v. "clap." Right hand moved
up and down as if playing a guitar. Children. Mexico. Lomas,
p. 35.

Money: Putting hand on the pocket and tapping on it.
Neapol. De Jorio, p. 126. Hand extended, palm up. Request
for money or "give it to me." U.S. Saitz and Cervenka,
p. 89.

Moot: Hands raised, each in an outward arc, until both

are approx. shoulder high, palms up. Assim. Eastern Jews.
Efron, p. 117. Hand, palm down, is swung in a semicircle so
that the palm is up. (Two sides to a question.) Assim.
Eastern Jews. Efron, p. 150.

Mourning: Putting ashes on one's head. II Samuel 13, 19;
Rev. 18, 19. Laying one's hand upon one's head. II Sam. 13,
19. Tearing one's hair and beard. Ezra 9, 3. Rending
clothes and putting on sackcloth. II Sam. 3, 31. Hand extended toward grave in apostrophe of the dead. Anc. Gk. and
Rom. Sittl, p. 74, n. 2. Wife takes head of departed husband
between both hands. Anc. Gk. Sittl, p. 66. Wife places hand
on chest of departed husband. Anc. Gk. Sittl, ibid. Hand extended toward corpse and moving up and down in reproach.
Anc. Gk., Corsican. Sittl, ibid. Tearing of clothes. Anc.
Gk. and Rom. Sittl, p. 25. Hellenist. orient. Sittl, p. 68.
Weapons beaten together four times at burning of the body on a
funeral pyre with military honors. Anc. Rom. Sittl, p. 73.
Knight carrying his shield upside-down signifies his mourning
for the death of his lord. Wolfr. v. Eschenbach, Bk. II, 641-
43. Right hand clasps wrist of left. Abraham mourning death
of Sarah in Wocel, 26 pl. 13b. Slow beating of hands and rubbing of fingers. Palest. Bauer, p. 224. Light, slow beating
of one palm upon the other, in which sometimes one and sometimes the other palm is uppermost. Palest. Bauer, p. 219.
Women tear their clothes. Palest. Bauer, p. 211. Wringing
hands. Boggs, p. 319. Casting dust on oneself. Boggs, ibid.

Negation: Right hand raised, palm forward, fingers extended. Spain. Flachskampf, p. 237. Hand raised, palm outward, or simply the index raised, and shaken rapidly from side
to side. France. Mitton, p. 141. Moving extended index of
raised right hand from side to side. Lat. Am. Kany, p. 88.
Palm open. ("Probably not.") Ital. Time (April 9, 1965),
p. 67. Hand in front of body, palm forward, hand shaken vigorously from side to side. Saudi Arabia, Lebanon, Jordan,
Syria. Autistic or culture-induced. Barakat, no. 163.

Nervousness: "rubbing the palms of his hands nervously
together." Dickens, Twist, p. 232. Hands hanging down, opening and closing several times. Aubert, p. 82. Cracking
knuckles. Krout, p. 22. Jerking hands. Krout, p. 23.

"Never": Right hand, palm down and fingers stiff, is
moved from left to right across the body. Saudi Arabia, Jordan, Syria, Lebanon. Autistic. Barakat, no. 90.

Nothing: Hand held out, palm upwards, flat. Anc. Gk.
Sittl, p. 111. "Robert Jordan looked up at Primitivo's post and
saw him signal, 'Nothing,' crossing his two hands, palms down."
Hemingway, p. 283.

Oath: "I lift up my hand to heaven, and say, I live for
ever." Deut. 32, 40. Also Gen. 14, 22; Rev. 10, 5, 6.
"And he shall put his hand on the head of the burnt offering."
Lev. 1, 4. Soldiers, in taking an oath, dip their hands or
swords into the blood of the sacrificial animal, which was contained in a shield. Anc. Gk. Sittl, p. 143. In giving an oath,

both arms are raised (as if to call gods to witness). Anc. Gk.
and Rom. Sittl, p. 141. In giving an oath, the earth or
water is touched (as concrete representation of the deities
of earth and water). Anc. Gk. and Rom. Sittl, p. 142.
In swearing an oath in a court of law, the altar is touched.
Anc. Gk. and Rom., Carthaginian. Sittl, pp. 142-143.
Someone whose most valuable property consists in animals
will touch these in swearing. Anc. Gk. Sittl, p. 140.
In calling the Gods to witness an oath, the swearer raises
his hand to point at the sky. Anc. Gk. and Rom. Sittl,
p. 141 and n. 1, Fig. 11. In taking an oath, a ruler touches
his scepter, symbol of his dominion, as his most prized possession. Anc. Gk. and Rom. Sittl, p. 139. In making a cove-
nant, the Romans let a pebble he brought from the temple of
Jupiter Feretrius; the swearer held the pebble in his hand and,
in speaking the words "Si sciens fallo, tum me Diespiter salva
urbe arceque bonis liciat uti ego hunc lapidem," let it fall to
the ground. Sittl, p. 144. In swearing an oath, one touched
the bow of Artemis. Anc. Rom. Sittl, p. 142. If the Olympian gods were witness to an oath, the deity's statue or altar is
touched. Anc. Gk. Sittl, p. 142. The touching of a statue
was not common unless it stood on an altar, so that it and the
foot of the statue could be touched simultaneously. Anc. Rom.
Sittl, p. 142. In a court of law, oaths are given by a deity
and the hand is put upon some insignia representing that deity,
e.g. the scepter of Jupiter Feretrius. Anc. Rom. Sittl, ibid.
In taking an oath, a weapon is touched to signify that this
weapon is to take the life of one who breaks the oath. Anc.
Gk., Rom., pagan Frankish. Sittl, p. 134; Grimm, DRA, II,
pp. 546-547. Soldiers, in taking oath, hold sacrificial pig by
the neck and tail, and with the right hand point the sword to
heaven. Atella. Sittl, p. 144. In taking an oath, two soldiers
clasp hands as in a handshake, with the other hand grasping
their swords. Oscan. Sittl, ibid. Soldiers, in taking oath,
touch sacrificial pig with their hands. Capua, Atella. Sittl,
ibid. Soldiers touch sacrificial pig with the points of their
swords (Anc. Rom. Sittl, pp. 143-144) while servant holds pig.
Oscan. Sittl, p. 144. In taking an oath, the (right) hand is
placed over the heart, as the most valuable part of the body.
Liutprant, Legat. 33 and mod. Europe. Sittl, p. 139. In taking an oath, when a sacrifice is made to a deity, the hand is
pointed toward the sacrificial animal, or laid on it, so as to
identify the fate of the breaker of the oath or the perjurer with
that of the animal. Anc. Rom. and Byzant. Sittl, p. 143.
Hand is pointed toward the sun, since the sun-god is conceived
to be omniscient. Anc. Gk., Germanic, Byzant. Sittl, p. 141;
Grimm, DRA, II, p. 545; Simrock, p. 384. In taking an oath,
Christians lay hand on, or took hold of Book of Gospels. Ritual
legalized by Justinian. Cod. Iustin., 4, 1, 12, 5; Sittl, p. 145.
Jews touch Torah. Sittl, ibid. Anc. Rom. touched altar;
after Christianization of the empire the Christian altar served
the same purpose. Sittl, ibid. Handshake. Medieval German.
Grimm, DRA, I, pp. 191-192. Swiss. DWb, IV/2, col. 403.

The swearer of an oath touches the person whom he promises
something. DuCange, III, 1618: "Jurare manu posita super
caput ejus, com quo eis est. " Defendant holds hand of plaintiff
while swearing with the other. Medieval German. Grimm,
DRA, II, p. 551. Raising hand. Schiller, Wallenst. Tod, V.
xi. Hand on heart. DWb, IV /2, col. 331. Women: Grimm,
DRA, II, p. 548. Handclasp separated by a blow with the hand
of a third person. (Cf. s.v. Agreement above.) DWb IV /2,
col. 331. Each of two parties swearing to an agreement raises
one hand and places it, raised, palm to palm against that of the
other. Medieval German. v. Amira, Sachsensp., p. 239.
Hand raised, first three fingers extended. Prechristian. Cyrenaica, North Africa, anc. Gk., Ital., Switzerl., France, Belgium, England, Danubian states, Rhineland. Seligmann, II,
p. 180. Open hand extended. Jews, Orient. Seligmann, II,
p. 165. Whenever the word "ego" occurs in an oath, the swearer touches his breast. Rom. Macrob., Sat. 3, 9, 12; Heiler,
p. 102. Among the Saxons it was common for the swearer to
extend the index, later the index and middle fingers of the
raised right hand. Among the Franks it was customary in addi-
tion to offer a staff. v. Amira, Sachsensp., p. 239. Right
hand raised, index and middle finger extended. Medieval German. Grimm, DRA, I, p. 195. While the right hand is raised
in an oath, the left points down with extended index and middle
fingers in order to invalidate the oath. HDA, II, col. 667.
Left hand in pocket or behind swearer's back while the right is
raised in an oath, in order to invalidate oath. Touching one's
genitals through hole in pocket in order to invalidate an oath.
Meschke, col. 334. Handshake as treaty of peace. Medieval
German. Kudrun, st. 833, 4. Laying hand on judge's staff of
office. Medieval German. Wofr. v. Eschenb., iii, 151. "Sir
Gawain, swear to me here between my hands..." Wolfr. v.
Eschenb., viii, 418. "Taking his hand, Arthur pledged him..."
Ibid., vi, 331. Swearing by one's hand. Shakesp., Tempest,
III, ii, 56, 78; Measure, II, i, 172; Much Ado, IV, i, 327, 337;
etc. "And here, to pledge my vow, I give my hand." III
Henry VI, III, iii, 250. Also Neapol. De Jorio, p. 170.
Right hand pressed to the heart. Neapol. De Jorio, p. 168.
Sign of the cross made with the index or the whole hand on a
wall or on the floor or in the air indicates a resolution not to
do a certain thing any more. Neapol. De Jorio, p. 169.
Drawing a cross over one's heart with the fingers or crossing
the hands over one's breast. Amer. schoolchildren. Seton,
p. xxii. Raising hands with palm toward swearer, making a
cross with the arms, putting up right hand while saying "Here's
my Bible, Here's my cross, Here's my right hand up to God."
Schoolchildren. Scotland. Opie, p. 123. Pulling away the hand
raised to swear of one suspected of swearing a false oath.
Fischer, Antaios, II, p. 342. If the hand is held with the palm
toward the judge, the oath is invalid. Röhrich, p. 31. Right
hand of one grasps right hand of another briefly. Intensity with
which this is performed varies with the importance of the act
and its emotional content. Modern continental western Europe.

Révész, p. 143. " 'I swear,' said Pnin, raising his hand."
Nabokov, p. 168. "But, hand upon your heart, who, even
among germanists, has read the epic...in its entirety?"
Bücherschiff, XIV (March/April, 1964), p. 21. Holding right
hand before right shoulder, palm facing forward. Libya, Lebanon, Saudi Arabia, Syria. Semiotic. Barakat, no. 10.

Obedience: Right hand clasps the closed left. Sumerian,
Babylon., anc. Jewish, Mohammedan (at beginning of Salāt and
the first Sūre of the Koran), Benedictines clasp hands under the
cuculla. Ohm, p. 276. Right hand laid into left. Ibid.

Oppression: Wrist of one hand touching wrist of other hand.
Hands slightly bent back and either clenched or extended. Head
bent, facial expression of sorrow. Frisian slaves were represented thus in antiquity. Neapol. De Jorio, p. 272. Fist
raised and turned, as if turning a handle. Little used, vulgar.
("Put on the screws.") France. Mitton, p. 150.

Order (arranging in): Pushing both hands, perpendicular,
palms facing one another, down and away from the gesticulator.
Accompanies expressions suggestive of channeling or directing.
Madrid. Green, p. 73. Raising both hands, one in front of
the other, palms facing inward, directly in front of the gesticulator, then moving them back and forth horizontally, accompanying expressions of precedence or order. Madrid. Green,
p. 60.

Overburdened: Right hand held horizontally at the forehead,
left horizontally at the chin. French. Life (Sept. 16, 1946),
p. 12.

Pacification: "Matt stroked her hand in encouraging silence."
Boucher, p. 207.

Pain: Hands beaten together. Anc. Gk. and Roman. Sittl,
p. 19. Hands interlocked. Medea Ercolanese. De Jorio,
p. 141. Thumb touches extended middle finger, ring and little
fingers are closed, index extended. The hand is loosely shaken
up and down in this position, so that the index hits the middle
finger and produces a smacking sound. Neapol. De Jorio,
p. 139.

Pardon: Hands extended forward, lowered from above,
palms down. Aubert, p. 89. Joining hands in front, palms
touching, fingertips pointing to person addressed. Aubert, p. 89.

Pay: Beckon, then write on air. ("Give me my bill.")
Amer. schoolchildren. Seton, p. xxiii. (Cf. s.v. Approach
above.)

Peace: Laying down of weapons. HDA, I, col. 316. Handclasp. Wolfram v. Eschenbach, 691, 3; Kudrun, st. 833, 4;
v. Amira, Sachsensp., p. 198; Waissel. chron. (1559), 87a.
"and they could see a shield lifted up...with the point of the
shield upward in token of peace." Medieval Welsh. "Branwen"
in Mabinog., p. 25. After separating his hands during the beginning of the "Memento etiam...," the priest "joins them at
the words 'in somno pacis,' an indication of peace and rest."
Mass, p. 66. Accompanying expressions indicating peace or
truce, the bunched fingers of each hand may be brought together.
Madrid. Green, p. 47.

Pederasty: (Cf. s.v. Insult above.) The heel of the right hand is tapped on the left, which is cupped. Obscene. French. Mitton, p. 151.

Pensiveness: Picking one's teeth. French. Latter half of 16th cent. Lommatzsch, p. 58. Stroking the beard. Rhein. Wb., I, col. 478. Palms rubbed together repeatedly as hands are firmly clasped. Fingers may be interlocked. Extreme concern. U.S. Saitz and Cervenka, p. 141.

Piety: Upper arms low, arms bent at elbow, forearms raised, palms pressed together. Woodcut, Brant, p. 79. Colombia, U.S. Saitz and Cervenka, p. 112.

Pity: "She stretches out her hand to the poor." Prov. 31, 20. "with...folded, sympathetically wringing hands." DWb, IV/2, col. 385. " 'I am afraid, Sir,' said Mr. Pickwick, laying his hand gently and compassionately on his arm;..." Dickens, Pickw., II, p. 235. Cutting some part of the body is a symbol of pity and mourning for the dead among many primitive tribes. Frazer, IV, pp. 92-93.

Placation: "Some also, on seeing a little wine left in a glass throw it on the ground or ashes of the fire, crying 'Cottabus,' KOTT+Bus; this is a superstition, but not to be despised. It is said to placate the gods." Belloc, p. 12. "An amusement of young men in ancient Greece, much in vogue at drinking parties, consisting in throwing a portion of wine into some vessel, so as to strike it in a particular manner. 'The simplest mode was when each threw the wine left in his cup so as to strike smartly in a metal basin, at the same time invoking his mistress' name; if the whole fell with a distinct sound into the basin, it was a sign he stood well with her.' Liddell and Scott." OED, s.v. Cottabus.

Plea: Raised hands in supplication to God. Ps. 28, 2; 88, 9. Right hand raised while kneeling. Anc. Gk. and Rom. Sittl, p. 157, fig. 13, and p. 158. Kneeling, both hands grasped by suppliant. Anc. Rom. Sittl, p. 166. Hands sweep dust together while kneeling. Anc. Gk. Sittl, p. 158. Hands rub the earth while kneeling, indicating readiness to pick up dust and throw it on oneself. Sittl, ibid., n. 6. Both hands extended toward someone. Anc. Gk. and Rom. Sittl, p. 50. Right hand of someone held or shaken. Anc. Gk. and Rom. Sittl, p. 29. Hands extended toward the judge, women pleaded their case, since they were not permitted to grasp the hand of the judge. Anc. Rom. Sittl, p. 51. Handshake. Anc. Gk. and Rom. Sittl, p. 29. Clasping knees. "But he, clasping my knees with both hands..." Odyss., Bk. x; Grajew, pp. 25ff. Raising of the hands or of the right hand does not yet signify a submissive attitude during the Roman republic. Sittl, p. 148. Folding hands, palm to palm. Anc. India. Boggs, col. 322 (Pantschatantra III, ii.) Putting one's hand to someone's chin. Medieval German. Kudrun, st. 386, 2.3. Extending both hands. Dante, Inf., c. viii. Raising hand to heaven. Shakesp., Titus Andr., III, i, 207. "to thee my heaved-up hands appeal" Shakesp., Lucr., 638; Measure, I, ii, 179; etc. Folded hands placed on someone's feet. Medieval German. Ulr. v. Lichten-

stein, cited in DWb, IV /2, col. 331. Kneeling at someone's
feet and raising hands. Medieval German. Wigalois, 110, 37.
Extending hand to emperor. DWb, IV /2, col. 331. "and clasping his hands together, prayed that they would order him back
to the dark room." Dickens, Twist, p. 25. 'He [the priest]
extends [his arms] in an attitude of appeal in memory of our
Savior who, with arms extended upon the Cross, interceded with
His Heavenly Father for the whole human race." Mass, p. 23.
Polish beggars throw dust on themselves while standing. Sittl,
p. 158. Placing of hands together may be used in pleading or
begging; it can also mean "Please, I pray you to shut up, I
want to talk." Southern Ital. Efron, p. 157. Hands out,
palms up and inclined toward protagonist. Jewish. Austin,
p. 595. Hands palm to palm, fingers of one hand interlaced
with those of the other, the fingers of both hands then bent
down toward the knuckles. France. Mitton, p. 145. Flat
hands, palm to palm, pointing toward a person. Amer. schoolchildren. Seton, p. xxii. Joining palms of hands in front of
the chest. Spain. Green, p. 82.

Pleasure: Handshake signifies pleasure in the performance
of the person whose hand is being shaken. Anc. Rom. Sittl,
p. 30. "If the tag-rag people did not clap him...according as
he pleas'd...them" Shakesp., Jul. Caes., I, ii, 258. Hands
are rubbed together over good news or the view of a pretty girl.
France. Life (Sept. 16, 1946). 'he smiled to himself and
rubbed his large white hands together." Huxley, ch. vi. One
hand rubbing against the other, palm to palm, with a slight turning movement of one hand around the other. Regarded as
"typically French" by the English. French. Mitton, p. 146.
" 'Ohhhhhh, ' breathed Orson Jones, clasping his hands in ecstasy, 'exhibitionists, lots and lots and lots.' " Robinson,
p. 227. " 'Excellent,' murmured Ericson, literally rubbing his
hands together." Lathen, p. 114.

Pointing: In speaking of someone, the hand is pointed
toward him. Anc. Rom. Sittl, p. 49. Fist clenched, thumb
pointing horizontally towards the rear. Indication of a person
or object in the rear. France. Mitton, p. 143. The index extended in the direction of an object or person, other fingers in
any other position. France. Mitton, ibid. (Cf. s.v. FINGER,
Pointing.) Hand(s), all fingers together, extended in direction
indicated. Colombia. Saitz and Cervenka, p. 35.

Possession: In dedicating a sacred building, the pontifex
holds a pillar with his hand, thus, according to Roman law,
transferring the building from the manus of man into that of the
deity. Anc. Rom. Sittl, p. 196. Adopted adult is taken by
the hand by the adoptive parent. Anc. Rom. Sittl, p. 130.
Laying one's hand on someone. Putting one's hand on a slave
is followed by the slave being led away. Sittl, p. 130. Accuser lays hand on accused and thus brings him to court. Anc.
Rom. Sittl, p. 133. Criminal is captured by laying hand on
him. Sittl, ibid. At marriage ceremony the husband takes the
hand of the wife which is given to him out of the hand of her
father. Anc. Rom., Vedic Indian. Sittl, p. 131. An object of

which the possession is disputed is grasped by the hands of both
claimants before the judge. Anc. Rom. Sittl, p. 133. Father
lifts up new-born child. Anc. Rom. Sittl, p. 130. (Cf. s. v.
Acceptance and Adoption above.) Confiscation of an object is indicated by the confiscator placing his hand on the object. Anc.
Rom. Sittl, p. 133. At marriage ceremony husband takes hand
of wife, which is given to him out of the hand of her mother.
Anc. Gk. Sittl, p. 131. (Hellenistic Gks. adopted the Roman
form, cf. above.) In taking re-possession of stolen cattle, the
owner had to grasp the right ear of the animal with his left
hand while treading on the animal's front leg with his right foot.
Early medieval German. Ebert, V, col. 94. Grasping a
claimed object. Fischer, Antaios, II, p. 342. Fist, thumb
covered by the fingers, laid against chest denotes jealous possession. Neapol. Sittl, p. 111. Slapping pocket with flat hand.
Amer. schoolchildren. Seton, p. xxiii.

Possibility: " 'For instance...you ask him whether he can
get you a pair of opera tickets. And he answers, 'Forse,'--
'Perhaps.' But...there are two kinds of perhaps. There is
perhaps with the hands spread outward, palms up, which means:
'What you ask is almost impossible; I see no way of helping you,
even if I were willing to do so.' And then there is the other
perhaps, spoken leaning forward with the forefinger raised in a
vertical position...And this perhaps means: 'My cousin knows
a man whose brother is a scene shifter, and the opera tickets
will be yours if I have to go to my grave to get them.' " Ital.
Graham, pp. 25-26.

Poverty: Turning one's pockets inside out. Lat. Am.
Kany, p. 88. Tapping empty pockets. Lat. Am. Kany, ibid.
Fist clenched and belttightening pantomimed, face expresses
suffering. "On se la serre!" French. Brault, p. 380.

Praise: Shaking corner of one's clothing (before handkerchiefs became common) while waving with the other hand. Anc.
Rom. Sittl, p. 62. Waving handkerchiefs. Anc. Rom. Sittl,
p. 63. Clapping of hands at a wedding. Mod. Gk., Sardinian.
Bresciani, Costumi, II, p. 153; Sittl, p. 59. Right fist beating
into palm of left hand. Philostr. Sittl, p. 57. Clapping of
hands, standing. Anc. Rom. Sittl, p. 61. Germany, 1839:
only men clapped hands, women merely smiled. Sittl, p. 56.
Clapping of hands. Byzant., Egypt., Macedon., Frankish.
Sittl, p. 58. "matrons flung gloves, Ladies and maids their
scarfs and handkerchers, Upon him as he pass'd..." Shakesp.,
Coriol., II, ii, 252-255. Clapping hands. Shakesp., II Henry
VI, I, i, 160; Troil., II, ii, 87; etc.; Nettesheim, p. 236.
"Having said the last 'Kyrie,' the priest standing in the same
place extends his hands, raises them, and intones the 'Gloria
in excelsis Deo.' " Mass, p. 21. "There was a busy little man
beside him, though, who took off his hat at intervals and mo-
tioned to the people to cheer..." Dickens, Pickw., I, p. 195.
At the last lecture in a course, students clap loud and long if
they enjoyed the course, and softly and politely if they didn't.
Univ. of Calif. Berkeley. McCord, p. 291. "She is excited
now, and draws her thin hands together and separates them

again in a gesture of applause, in complete approval of her
father's performance." Howard, p. 99. (Cf. s.v. Applause
above.)

Prayer: Hands held palm to palm, fingers interlocked.
Sumerian, Turkish, Roman, Protestant. Ohm, pp. 273ff. But
also Fernando Gallego (1466-1507), "Calvary." Madrid. Cf.
Lassaigne, p. 71. Right hand extended, palm turned inward.
Babylon., Buddhist. Ohm, p. 246. In a series of Babylonian
hymns the request to raise the hand at the recitation recurs at
regular intervals. Heiler, p. 101. The Sumerians extended
their left hand towards the deity and held the right hand horizontally. Jean, p. 220. The Babylonians extended their right
hand and held their palm inwards. Ohm, p. 246. The Assyri-
ans pointed the right hand with outstretched index toward the
deity. Jeremias, p. 409. The anc. Gks. extended the right
hand, palm towards the deity. Ohm, p. 246. Folded hands.
Sumerian. Heiler, p. 103. Hands laid one into the other, the
palm of one supporting the back of the other hand. Sumerian.
Heiler, p. 103. Grasping the feet of the deity. Assyrian.
Heiler, ibid. Casting oneself down and grasping the hands of
the deity. Assyrian ritual. Heiler, ibid. "Assurpanipal opened
his hands and stepped before Nebo his lord." Inscr. Assyrian.
Heiler, p. 101. "I raised my hands and prayed to N.N." occurs
frequently in Assyrian inscriptions. Heiler, ibid. On some anc.
Egypt. depictions, the worshipper raises one hand, and lets the
other hang limply. Heiler, p. 102. Hands crossed in front of
chest. Anc. Egypt., anc. Rom., Buddhist, Russian, Dominican
friars. Ohm, p. 277. (Cf. s.v. ARM, Prayer.) Raising of
hands to level of head, palms turned outwards. Prayer before
Amon-Re. Brit. Mus. Stelae V. 43, in Brunet, p. 205. Beating one's breast with the fist while rejoicing ecstatically. Anc.
Egypt. Heiler, p. 102. "And standing at a distance, the tax-
collector would not even lift up his eyes to Heaven. But he beat
on his breast, saying O God, be merciful to me, a sinner!"
Luke 18, 13. Clapping of hands. Ps. 47, 2. Raising hands
toward heaven. I Tim. 2, 8. Jews laid hand on sacrificial
animal. Sittl, p. 192. "but he then called to the lord Poseidon
in prayer, reaching both arms up toward the starry heaven."
Odyss., Bk. ix. Anc. Gks. often merely raised the right hand
with fingers extended and apart. Heiler, p. 102. Callimachus
relates that the merchants landing on Delos who prayed for success, ran around the altar and then, with their hands on their
backs, went to a nearby olivetree in order to bite off pieces of its
bark. Callim. Hymn. Del. 321; Heiler, p. 103. The Delians, according to Callimachus (Hymn. 4, 321), beat each other. Sittl, p.
185. Raising hands holding an object. Anc. Gk. Sittl, p. 197, n.
4. Touching the altar. Anc. Gk. Sittl, p. 192. In raising or extending the hands, the Greeks kept the fingers extended and apart.
Heiler, p. 101. In praying to the chthonic powers, anc. Gks. and
Romans kept their hands directed downwards. "We pray to the gods
of the nether world with hands to the ground." Servius, Aen. 4, 205;
Macrob., Sat. 3, 9, 12. In making sacrifice, the right hand is
raised. Callimachus. Sittl, p. 189, n. 3. In making a sacri-

fice, the sacrifice is extended with the right hand, while the
left hand is raised. Anc. Rom., anc. Indian. Sittl, p. 189.
When a supplicatio was proclaimed in Rome, the women tore
their hair, scratched their cheeks and beat their shoulders.
Heiler, p. 102. Touching the altar. Anc. Rom. from earliest
times to the Augustan period. The manner in which the altar
was touched appears to have been regulated. Sittl, p. 192.
Touching the object to which prayer is directed. Neoptolemos
touches sacrifice with his left hand, right hand touches grave
mound of his father, upon whom he is calling. Anc. Rom.
Quint., 14, 306f.; Sittl, p. 193. In calling upon Gaia, hand was
extended to touch the earth. Sittl, p. 191. Raising the right
hand in prayer, left hand holds the worshipper's weapons. Anc.
Rom., Oriental. Christian soldiers must free both hands.
Lactant., De Mort. Persecut., 42, 11; Sittl, pp. 188-189.
"Templa deorum immortalium, quae foro imminent, Capitoli-
umque intuentem et manus nunc in caelum nunc in patentes ter-
rae hiatus ad deos manes porrigentem se devovisse." Liv. 7,
6, 4. The Kataphryges (or Quintiliani) put the right index to
the nose while praying. Heiler, p. 102. Embracing the knees
of the deity. Anc. Rom. Heiler, p. 103. Hands behind the
back. Tacitus, Germ. xxxix, remarks that the Germans do not
enter a sacred meadow unless it is with hands bound. Primitive Germ. Heiler, p. 103. Hands folded. Franconian, 7th
cent. Heiler, p. 103. In the catacombs, worshippers are portrayed with arms outstretched to the sides in imitation of the
crucifixion. Heiler, p. 102. Extending the hand during prayer.
Early Christian. This gesture was used in worship in contrast
to the spreading of the hands--the "orans"-gesture--which was
more common in prayer of supplication. Today the priest holds
out his hand in the prayers before the blessing and in the abso-
lution. Ohm, p. 247. Extension of hand is also Jewish. Ohm,
p. 246. Hands palm to palm, fingers intertwined. The origin
of this gesture is obscure. The anc. Rom. used it apotropaically against demons. According to Pliny it served to invalidate
an oath and was therefore prohibited in the Roman cult (Hist.
nat. 28, 6). According to Achelis the early Christians borrowed
the gesture from the Romans as protection against pagan demons.
Ohm, p. 274. Folding hands. In the first centuries A.D. the
gesture appears to have been unknown or was not used. An
abbot of Monte Cassino still disapproved of it in the 9th cent.
as a deviation from custom. In the latter part of the Middle
Ages it became more common and gradually took the place of
the old "orans"-gesture of raising and spreading the hands. The
folding of the hands by putting the flat palms together, fingers
pointing upwards is favored by catholicism, but is not common
among protestants. Ohm, pp. 269-270. (Cf. above for principally Protestant interlocking of fingers.) The folding of hands
and interlacing of fingers was common among the Sumerians,
Parthians, Turks, Romans and in East Asia. The first Christian evidence of it is on a sarcophagus of the 5th cent. from a
Syracusan catacomb on which a praying woman is depicted with
interlaced fingers. It, rather than the preceding gesture of

facing flat palms, is the common Protestant prayer gesture.
Ohm, p. 273. Hands folded so that fingers are interlocked and
palms together, hands in front of chest. Ritter, p. 375. Pope
Gregory I, Dial. II, 33, speaking of Sta. Scolastica: "insertas
digitis manus super mensam posuit, et caput in manibus omni-
potentem dominum rogatura declinavit." Cf. also De Jorio,
p. 203. Folding hands, palm to palm, not before eleventh
century, according to Sittl, p. 176, who cites the saint's image
of 1011 (Rome) depicted in Agincourt, Peintures, pl. 94, the
statue of King Robert (d. 1031) in Melun (Montfaucon, Monum.,
I, pl. 33), and the figure on St. Peter's at Calw (Mone, pl. 2).
Early medieval works of art frequently exhibit an "orans"-like
gesture of prayer in which the hands are held close to and in
front of the breast and not raised as high as in the "orans"-
gesture proper. Ladner, p. 247. An early panel with the image
of St. Francis (Pescia, 1235) by Bonaventura Berlinghieri shows
the transition from extended to joined hands: hands raised,
cupped, to receive stigmata. Another is the panel of S. Croce
in Florence (middle 13th cent.), depicting hands almost but not
quite joined. Ladner, p. 273. The second Vita of St. Francis
by Thomas of Celano states: "When a servant of God at prayer
is visited by the Lord with some new consolation, he ought, before coming forth from prayer, to raise his eyes to heaven and,
with joined hands [iunctis manibus] to say to the Lord..." Vita
2, 2, cap. 75, 99 cited by Ladner, pp. 269-270. The two
Franciscan Mass orders of the first half of the 13th century,
Paratus and Indutus planeta, speak of joined hands in connection
with pre-consecrational, not post-consecrational elevation of the
host. Ladner, p. 267. The Ordo Paratus, the first version of
which dates from ca. 1230, states, in a slightly later version,
that the priest is to elevate the host with joined hands [iunctis
manibus]. This, assumes Ladner, is probably the oldest occurrence of the gesture in liturgical manuscripts. Ladner, p. 265.
In the Indutus planeta, published at the Franciscan General Chap-
ter at Bologna, probably in 1243, the gesture of the joined hands
is for the first time mentioned in several of the places in which
it is still prescribed in the Missale Romanum. Ladner, pp. 265-
266. The newer gesture of joining the hands before the breast
and kneeling was probably introduced during the pontificate of
Gregory IX (1227-1241) and certainly not much later than the
death of Innocent IV (1254). Ladner, p. 247. In this respect,
the gesture referred to by Ladner is that of the laying together
of the palms with extended fingers, not folding or clasping of
hands with interlocking fingers--a gesture which Ladner does not
consider to have been common in the Middle Ages before the very
end. Ladner, p. 248. "The earliest instance of the feudal gesture [hands palm to palm] as prayer gesture occurs between 1120
and 1130 on the second pillar of the north aisle of Vézelay. The
first literary evidence is probably... Chanson de Roland 2392."
Bertau, I, p. 250. In the parallel passage of the Middle High
German Rolandslied the old "orans"-gesture of the raised hands
(cf. s.v. ARM, HAND, Prayer) is substituted. One hand raised,
palm outward. Munich, Cod. lat. 23094, fol. 93b; Stuttg. Bibl.

fol. 24, fol. 124b, etc. cited by Haseloff, p. 303. Hands,
palms outward or toward one another, before or at side of chest.
Stuttg. Bibl. fol. 24, fol. 109b; Breviary of St. Elizabeth, Cividale, 25, 313, 318, etc. cited by Haseloff, pp. 302-303. Hands
raised above head. Medieval German. Orendel, 457-8, 571-2,
1392, 3446; 17th cent. German: Abraham a Santa Clara, p. 119;
Islamic. Goldziher, Or. Stud., p. 322; Kikuyu. Heiler, p. 101;
Cinghalese. Heiler, p. 102. Hands raised and spread out toward
heaven. Bulwer, pp. 14-28. Hands palm to palm, not touching,
but slightly cupped; fingertips and thumbtips of one hand touching
those of the other. Master Bertram, "Agony," (after 1383);
also Perugia, Bibl. augusta Ms. 1238 (15th cent.) in Volpe,
p. 14. The priest "turns to the faithful, extends and rejoins
his hands, while he greets them with the words 'Orate, fra-
tres'..." Mass, p. 39; cf. also pp. 18, 47. In invoking
Adraseia-nemesis, the Greek Christian crosses himself. Sittl,
p. 181. "The priest makes the Sign of the Cross on the book
at the beginning of the Gospel, then on his forehead, lips, and
breast. This is a prayer that the holy Gospel may be, first,
on our mind,... secondly, on our lips,... thirdly, in our heart."
Mass, p. 29. With the flat right hand, fingers extended, touch
forehead, then the breast, first the left side, then the right.
Roman Catholic sign of the cross. Ohm, p. 294. Same gesture, but from right to left side of breast. Greek Orthodox.
Ohm, ibid. Stroking an idol. Pre-islamic Arab. Heiler,
p. 103. When you call upon God, show him the inside of your
hands and not the outside; when you are finished, put both hands
upon your face." Islamic. Cited from a commentary on the
Koran by Seligmann, II, p. 168. In the Moslem free prayer the
old Arabic gesture of raising and extending the hands has remained customary. Goldziher, Or. Stud., p. 321. In the Me-
dina Sura 8 it is said of the infidels: "And their prayer at the
house of God is nothing but whistling and clapping of hands."
Cited by Ohm, p. 283, n. 4. Indians extended their hands forwards palm to palm even before Buddhistic schism. Sittl,
p. 175. On Hindu reliefs and statues worshippers extend hands
palm to palm. Heiler, p. 103. Raising hands. Anc. Persian.
Heiler, p. 102. Folding hands. Buddhist, Tibetan. Heiler,
p. 103. Of Indo-European origin: cf. Vierordt. Bhil, Hindu,
Sikh, Yao, Chinese, Japanese, Korean. Ohm, pp. 268-269.
Raising hands and weapons in prayer. Yuiu (Australia). Heiler,
p. 101. Hand laid to head in passing woods, rivers or fields
inhabited by spirits of the dead. Tehuep (Patagonia). Heiler,
p. 102. Right index laid to nose. Taskodrugites (Galatia).
Heiler, p. 102. Clapping hands. Negroes, Egypt., Chinese,
Japanese. Ohm, p. 283. Clapping and rubbing of hands. Peru.
Heiler, p. 102. The new moon is greeted by clapping of hands.
Congo. Heiler, p. 102. Raised hands, clapping in prayer to
the spirits of the sun and the ocean. Kiziba. Heiler, ibid.
Clapping in prayer of thanks. Anc. Jews, Ewe. Heiler, ibid.
Clapping in morning prayer. Bantu. Heiler, ibid. Clapping
upon completing sacrificial prayer. Camerun. Heiler, ibid.
Hands raised, holding bundles of grass. Massai. Heiler, p. 101.

In times of distress, when the tribal chief or a boy in the public cult prayed, the oldest man clapped his hands, continually shouting "Pray, sir, pray!" and those present clapped in answer and as a gesture of thanks. Safwa. Ohm, p. 283. The Samaritans clap their hands at their Paschal feast on the Garizim during the sacrifice of animals. Ohm, p. 284. Among the Nyarunda (East Africa), a relative of the initiated kneels down in front of the demi-god Ryangombe, claps three times with his hands and prays for the initiated. Ohm, p. 283. Most frequent is the clapping of hands at Shinto shrines, where it is used before and after prayer. Ohm, p. 284. Japanese Buddhists also clap hands: "One does not look at Buddha, one worships him," whereupon the speaker clapped his hands several times and bowed. Ohm, p. 284. Among the Mulgoi-Kanuri (Africa), during a consecration ceremony after harvest, the master of the holy tree has to perform his prayer with his hands tied behind his back. Ohm, p. 279. The Sioux raise their arms, palms turned toward the object being worshipped or addressed, thereupon the hands are lowered toward the earth, without touching the object or person. Heiler, p. 101. Kneeling, turned toward the sun, folded hands with fingers extended and apart are raised from the ground to the forehead. China, Korea. Ohm, p. 282. In the 9th cent. Walahfrid Strabo criticizes those who beat their breast with fists in prayer. Heiler, p. 102.

Pregnancy: Lifting skirt over abdomen. Men execute same gesture, lifting the skirt of their clothing. Neapol. De Jorio, p. 173.

Preparedness: Both hands are slowly swept downward, palms rotating to face away from the gesticulator. Madrid. Green, p. 77.

Pride: Hand pressed to the side, elbow a little forward, head thrown back, the other hand at the upper chest and underneath the coat. Neapol. De Jorio, p. 201. Hands held aloft and clasped. Davidson, p. 4. "Expressions suggestive of pride of craftsmanship may be accompanied by a movement performed by rapping the finished product with the knuckles of one hand." Spain, Lat. Am. Green, p. 92.

Prohibition: "'Something to do with business,' said Mr. Deane, waving his hands, as if to repel intrusion into that mystery." Eliot, p. 707.

Promise: The person giving assurance of something gives the other his right hand. Anc. Gk. and Rom. Sittl, p. 135. After a promise is fulfilled, the person who promised again holds out his right hand, which is grasped by the receiver of his promise as a sign that the promiser has acquitted himself. Anc. Gk. and Rom., mod. Gk., Japanese. Sittl, p. 136. The emperor's right hand as assurance of life and freedom to one who is punishable. Anc. Rom., anc. Persian (Persian emperors sent picture of the right hand to assure one of forgiveness.) Sittl, p. 138. Emperor's right hand as assurance of goodwill. Anc. Rom. Sittl, p. 138. Handshake of right hand testifies to a promise to marry. In fiction (Eurip., Apollon., Vergil, Ovid) groom and bride shake hands, in reality groom and father of the

bride shake hands. Sittl, pp. 135-136. The "Handschlag"
(handclasp, manu complosa) is, according to Sittl, purely Germanic in this sense. Monum. Boica, XXIV, p. 348; Sittl,
p. 136. Also Hartmann v. Aue, 7894; HDV, I, col. 319. DWb
IV/2, col. 389 lists citations of handshake as promise in legal
context: Urfehde of Eckardt Kleinschmidt (1577), Archive of
Büdingen; Urfehde of Jost Pfieler (1580), Büdingen; and handshake "instead of a properly sworn oath" (1468) in Aschbach,
Gesch. d. Grafen v. Wertheim, II, p. 283. "Ere I could make
thee open thy white hand and clap thyself my love; then didst
thou utter 'I am yours for ever.' " Shakesp., Winter's Tale, I,
ii, 102-4. "and so clap hands and a bargain." Shakesp.,
Henry V, V, ii, 129. " 'I shall be sure to be with you,' said
Mr. Trotter, and wringing Sam's hand with the utmost fervor,
he walked away." Dickens, Pickw., I, p. 392. " 'Here's my
own right hand upon it.' " Dickens, Dorrit, I, p. 328. Right
hand of one grasps right hand of another briefly. Intensity with
which this is performed varies with the importance of the act
and its emotional content. Révész, p. 143-144.

Proof: Hand, vertical, palm outward, is held up to the
eyes of someone. France. Familiar. Mitton, p. 147.

Prostitute: One hand, flat, palm down, moves back and
forth in front of body. Colombia. Saitz and Cervenka, p. 118.

Protection: Roman generals extend hand to surrendering
people. Anc. Rom. Sittl, p. 368. Hands horizontal, arms extended straight, palms down. Aubert, p. 88.

Punishment: A Herr von Ruxleben recants (1576) a lie by
declaring that "with this slap he punishes his lying trap publicly"; cited by DWb, IV/2, 419.

Quickly: Palm of one hand strokes quickly over the top of
the other. Portug. Flachskampf, p. 222. Palms of both
hands face each other; one is rubbed quickly against the other
in an upward and downward movement. Spain. Flachskampf,
ibid.

Readiness: "As Sam Weller said this, he tucked up his
wristbands,--to intimate his readiness to set to work immediately." Dickens, Pickw., II, p. 184.

Reconciliation: "I have spread out my hands...to a rebellious people..." Isaiah, 65, 2. Handshake. Anc. Gk. and Rom.
Sittl, p. 30. Ecclesiastical forgiveness of sins after penitence
is symbolized by taking the penitent sinner by his right hand.
Jungmann, pp. 51ff., 93ff; Schmitz, I, 70ff.; Wohlhaupter,
p. 165. Henricus Ostiensis, middle 13th cent., reports that the
sinner, in being absolved, knelt before the church portal, reciting the Psalm "Miserere." With each verse he received a blow
on the head or shoulder, whose violence accorded with his sin.
Summa, V, de sent. excomm. n. 14. "Let the handclasp heal
the wound, which my tongue rashly caused." Schiller, Jungfr.,
II, ii. "he...extended the hand of reconciliation to that most
indignant gentleman." Dickens, Pickw., II, p. 429. "Mr.
Noddy...proffered his hand to Mr. Gunter. Mr. Gunter grasped
it with affecting fervor." Dickens, Pickw., II, 49. Grasping
the culprit by the hand. Palest. Bauer, p. 6. Putting head-

dress back on the head of the culprit. Palest. Bauer, ibid. The handshake is the sign of formal reconciliation among duellists. German. Sittl, p. 38. Handshake between Israeli and Egyptian generals on occasion of truce negotiations. L. A. Times (Nov. 15, 1973), p. 1.

Refusal: Forearm slightly raised, hand turned upward, palm out. Anc. Rom. Sittl, p. 85, fig. 6; p. 86, n. 5; assim. Eastern Europ. Jews. Efron, p. 118. In answer to a request and to indicate that one does not want to give more than the minimum, one makes the sign of the "horns" (fist clenched, index and little finger extended). Neapol. De Jorio, p. 94. Right hand seizes upper tip of coat and shakes it. Goldziher, Zeitschr., p. 370. Right hand, edge down, moves vertically downward, then, at right angle, horizontally from left to right. Spain. Flachskampf, p. 238. Extended right hand moves energetically from left top to right bottom. Flachskampf, p. 238. Flat hand moved horizontally. (Gesture for cutting.) French. Mitton, 143. One or both hands extended, palm facing forward. ("Stop!" "I don't want it!") French. Mitton, p. 143. Flat hand, palm facing the person addressed, describes an arc by moving rapidly in front of the chest from left to right or right to left. ("I refuse absolutely." "Don't insist upon it.") French. Mitton, p. 143. Shaking one hand, fingers slightly closed and palm outward at level of chest. Spain, Lat. Am. Green, pp. 44-45. Shaking index of one hand at or below the speaker's face. (Denial.) Spain, Lat. Am. Green, pp. 44-45. Holding flat hands to ears. ("I will not listen.") Amer. schoolchildren. Seton, p. xxii. Eyes covered by hands. (Refusal to look.) Amer. schoolchildren. Seton, ibid. Hands moved up and down, palms brushing each other. ("I wash my hands of it.") Colombia, U.S. Saitz and Cervenka, p. 32.

Regret: Rub slightly closed palms together in front of body. Saudi Arabia. Semiotic or culture-induced. Barakat, no. 114. Palm held in front of body, facing it; fingers held loosely and shaken up and down violently; or thumb and middle finger pressed together and arm snapped violently, so that index snaps against middle finger. Colombia. Saitz and Cervenka, p. 100.

Rejection: (Cf. s.v. Refusal above.) Transverse brushing movement with edge of one hand on palm of the other held supine. ("I don't want to hear about it.") Southern Ital. Efron, p. 100. Right palm brushing edge of left palm held vertically. ("I'm through with him.") Assim. Eastern Europ. Jews. Efron, p. 117. Hands simultaneously moved from middle of body to sides, palms down. ("I'm through with it.") Ital. N.Y. Times (March 1, 1959). "With an averted supercilious eye and a rejecting hand, half flourishing--I have no need of help, Sir!-- you are in my way." Richardson, Clarissa, II, p. 142. Palms horizontal at chest level, fingertips pointing upwards, right arm, nearest to body, left arm crossed in front of it; both hands are then uncrossed smartly, stopping while still in front of body. ("Rien à faire!") French. Brault, p. 379.

Relinquishment: "the one-hand downward loose shake of weary relinquishment;..." Nabokov, p. 41.

Reminder: Witness in court of law is pulled by the ear to aid his memory. Anc. Gk. and Rom. Margrave Luitpold of Babenberg. Röhrich, pp. 32-33.

Reproach: "Well then, rising (Bella silently with uplifted hands, reproaching my supposed perverseness), I see nothing can prevail with you to oblige us." Richardson, Clarissa, II, p. 3. "...he was often observed peeping through the bars of a gate and making minatory gestures with his small forefinger while he scolded the sheep with an inarticulate burr..." Eliot, p. 461.

Request: Flat hand opened and directed at someone. To lend emphasis to the gesture, it can be performed with both hands. Neapol. De Jorio, p. 85. Amer. schoolchildren. Seton, p. xxiv. Also Aubert, p. 82.

Resignation: "When she folded [her hands and arms] over her bosom in resignation;..." Thackeray, Pendennis, I, ch. iv.

Respect: In the circus the charioteer lowers his whip before the patrons. Anc. Rom. Sittl, pp. 155-156. Lowering the fasces before the lictors. Anc. Rom. Sittl, p. 155. Junior official lowered or caused the fasces to be lowered by his lictors in the presence of a senior or superior official. Anc. Rom. Sittl, p. 154. "Her hand, which he gently squeezed...in token of regard." Smollett, Peregr. Pickle, I, p. 19. "He took off his hat as Mr. Pickwick saluted him,..." Dickens, Pickw., II, p. 292. " 'Don't they, Sam?' 'Not they, Sir,' replied Mr. Weller, touching his hat." Dickens, Pickw., I, p. 311. "...with the touch of the hat which always preceded his entering into conversation with his master." Dickens, Pickw., I, p. 368. "They made way for Henry Wimbush, touching their caps as he passed." Huxley, ch. xviii.

Retreat: Extending one or both hands and moving them alternately and rapidly up and down, palms facing each other, imitating rapid motion of running feet. Lat. Am. Kany, p. 111. This is sometimes preceded by a clap of the hands. Kany, p. 112. Placing open right hand on the open, slightly curved left, palm to palm, then drawing the right forcibly backward. Lat. Am. Kany, p. 112. Dropping the slightly cupped hand, palm inward, from chest of speaker, twisting lower arm and wrist with extended index, concluding with palm down. Madrid. Green, p. 41.

Reverence: Extending hand down to the knee, then raising it. Anc. Egypt. Ohm, p. 282. "Lo! The angel of God; fold thy hands." Dante, Purg., c. ii.

Review: Fingers of one hand brush palm of the other repeatedly. (Review of written material.) Colombia. Saitz and Cervenka, p. 112.

Rise: Closed fist, thumb extended upward. Fist is raised with brusque movement. (Used in addressing a group, not a single individual.) France. Mitton, p. 145. Raising flat right hand, palm up, from level of hip. Amer. schoolchildren. Seton, p. xxiv. Also Aubert, p. 88.

Royalty: Raised right hand is symbol of kingship. H. P. L'Orange, cited by Wolff-Hurden. (Cf. s.v. Authority above.)

Sacrifice: Jews as well as pagans laid hand on the sacrificial animal. Sittl, p. 192. In making the sacrifice, it is extended with the right hand, while the left hand is raised. Altaic, anc. Rom. Sittl, p. 189. In making sacrifice, right hand is raised. Rare. Callimach.; Liban.; Sittl, p. 189, n. 3.

Salvation: In depictions of the Last Judgment the palm of Christ's hand is turned towards the saved, the back of the other hand toward the damned. Medieval German. Haseloff, p. 307.

Satisfaction: "thus one often breaks off with a gesture toward the walls, with which one can also say: here are the walls, 1, 2, 3, 4." ("Be satisfied.") Palest. Bauer, p. 223. "'Ah!' observed Mr. Pickwick, rubbing his hands,..." Dickens, Pickw., II, 2. "'Ah!' said Fagin, rubbing his hands with great satisfaction." Dickens, Twist, p. 358. Rubbing palms against each other, either up and down or in a rotating movement. France. Mitton, p. 146. One hand rubbing against the other, palm to palm, with a slight turning movement of one hand around the other. (Called "typically French" by the English.) France. Mitton, ibid. Rubbing hands together, often quite vigorously. Spain, Lat. Am. Green, p. 49.

Secrecy: Open hand closes the mouth. Usually used in a hostile manner. When one has said something insulting about another person one closes one's mouth suddenly in this manner, so that no more will escape. Neapol. De Jorio, p. 192. Hands lifted up half way to the head. ("It's strictly between us.") French. Life (Sept. 16, 1946), p. 12. Lowering and raising extended fingers of one hand, at level of waist and with palm down, may accompany discussion of clandestine activity. Spain, Lat. Am. Green, p. 43.

Seize: Open hand, fingers extended, palm down, is thrust forward at the level of the waist and is suddenly closed forcefully. Aubert, p. 83. "Expressions suggestive of seizing...are accompanied by...clutching an imaginary object in the air and bringing the object to the chest. Madrid. Green, p. 60.

Self-acknowledgment: Hand placed upon one's chest. ("It is I.") French. Mitton, p. 143.

Self-satisfaction: "like a rich merchant, who strolls around happily among the crates...rubbing his hands..." DWb IV /2, col. 386. Also Austin, p. 595. Hand moved to sleeve (cuff). Birdwhistell, Collier's (March 4, 1955), p. 57.

Separation: Moving the two hands apart. Efron, p. 150, fig. 49.

Series: "a succession of stop-and-go movements made with the semi-clenched fingers of one hand, moved progressively further and further away from the speaker.... The social context...: 'fueron dando una serie de batallas.'" "Another gesture performed under similar circumstances is executed by raising and lowering the fingertips of one hand on the surface of a desk or table top. The fingers are clenched somewhat and the palm of the hand faces the floor..." Madrid, Lat. Am. Green, p. 61.

Shame: Lowering eyes and covering face with hands. Amer. schoolchildren. Seton, p. xxi.

Shock: Raising of hands above head. Illustr. of public re-
actions to a maid's sudden loss of her skirt. "Wahre Begebenheit am Stuttgarter Markt-Brunnen," 19th cent. German.
Zobel Verlag, No. 13.

Shyness: Hands folded in lap. Medieval French. Lommatzsch, p. 34; also Larivey, p. 62.

Silence: Hand extended in front (waving up and down?).
Anc. Rom., late Rom., mod. Ital. Sittl, p. 215; Manzoni, ch.
xiii. Hand raised. Anc. Gk. Sittl, p. 215, n. 1. " 'My
friends,' said Mr. Humm, holding up his hand in a deprecatory
manner, to bespeak the silence of...the...ladies." Dickens,
Pickw., II, p. 70. Right hand, fingers extended and apart,
palm up, moves gently up and down. Spain, Portug. Flachskampf, p. 238. "Haggish's hand is high in the air, praying for
'silence.' " Surtees, 151. "Tom was going to speak, but Mr.
Deane put up his hand, and said--'Stop! hear what I've got to
say...' " Eliot, p. 566. Hand extended forward, palm down,
fingers together. Hand is lowered several times. (Used only
when addressing a group of people.) France. Mitton, p. 145.
One or both outstretched hands, palm(s) down, pushed toward
the floor. Spain, Lat. Am. Green, p. 43. One or both hands
held before body with palms down, then moved slightly up and
down several times. Egypt, Lebanon, Jordan, Saudi Arabia,
Syria, Libya. Semiotic. Barakat, no. 14. Hand is formed
like a jaw. ("Shut up.") Very vulgar. France. Mitton,
p. 150. Open right palm is slapped down two or three times
on the extended left fist held upright or obliquely, as if pushing
a cork into a bottle. Accompanies expression such as "lo calla-
ron," "lo metieron en tapón," etc. Lat. Am. Kany, p. 187.
"Johnny put both hands out in front of him, fingers spread wide,
to signal silence." Schulberg, p. 257. "...reached her right
hand in under her left arm and squeezed the boy's arm." Birdwhistell, Backgr., p. 14. "...placed her right hand firmly
across his thighs." Ibid.

Sincerity: Hands extended to the sides after touching breast.
Austin, p. 595. Hand placed on heart. Seiler, p. 246.

"Sit down": Drop flat hand, palm down. Amer. schoolchildren. Seton, p. xxiv.

Smell: Holding palm to nose. Amer. schoolchildren. Seton, p. xxi.

Sorrow: Placing hands over face while weeping. Odyss.,
Bk. xix. "and the black cloud of sorrow closed on Laertes. In
both hands he caught up the grimy dust and poured it over his
face and grizzled head, groaning incessantly." Odyss., Bk.
xxiv. Hands folded with extended fingers. Anc. Gk. Gazette
arch., pl. 17. Rubbing of hands. Anc. Gk., Sittl, p. 47.
Tearing of clothes. Anc. Gk. and Rom. Sittl, p. 26. "Silvia
prima soror, palmis percussa lacertos, auxilium vocat..."
Vergil, 503. Clapping of hands. Anc. Gk. and Rom., Irish.
Neckel, pp. 64-65. Beating breast. Old Saxon. Heliant, 3498-
99. Clapping hands. Old Saxon. Heliant, 2183-84. Also Old
Norse: Poetic Edda, first and second song of Gudrun and the
shorter song of Sigurd. Hands raised. Anc. Rom., Medieval

German: <u>Orendel</u>, 491. Seligmann, II, p. 166. "began to
wring his hands so they cracked like dry twigs." Medieval German: Wolfram v. Eschenb., IV, 219. Right hand grasps wrist
of left. Portal of Baptistry at Parma, murals of Sant' Angelo
in Formis. Haseloff, p. 306. Wringing hands in grief while
uttering curse. Johann v. Tepl, ch. i, ii. Wringing hands:
Bulwer, pp. 28-29; Cervantes, <u>Galatea</u>, I, 59; <u>Kudrun</u>, st. 919,
4. "The governor wrung his hands in the utmost grief and con-
sternation. Smollett, <u>Peregr. Pickle</u>, I, ch. xxxxvi. "Never,
never, wringing her hands, should she meet with a mistress she
loved so well." Richardson, <u>Clarissa</u>, I, p. 160; cf. also DWb,
IV /2, col. 385. Beating breast or head. Agrippa v. Nettesheim,
p. 236. "and he stood momentarily arrested, one long hand outstretched, warding off realization... To see him was like glimpsing a flame, an epitome of grief's impact." Allingham, p. 81.

 <u>Speed</u>: Hand rapidly describes vertical circle. Eastern
Europ. Jews. Efron, p. 72. Swift dorso-ventral motion, palm
vertical. Assim. Eastern Jews. Efron, p. 117.

 <u>Stand</u>: Fingers together and extended, hand extended and
moved up and down several times. Colombia, U.S. Saitz and
Cervenka, p. 129.

 <u>Stealing</u>: Hand extended, palm to side, little finger down,
fingers spread. As forearm remains in the same position,
hand is twisted, palm down, back and up again while fingers
close. Southern Ital. Efron, p. 154. Right wrist strikes open
left palm representing a diving board, then the right hand is
raised over and swung downward like someone diving. Lat. Am.
Kany, p. 106. Hand extended open, the fingers closed one by
one. Aubert, 84. Hand at thigh-level, palm facing backwards
moved as if throwing something backwards. Mitton, p. 148.
Hand at hip level palm to rear, then turned in circular motion
toward hip. Ibid., also Critchley, p. 91.

 <u>Stop</u>: Right hand raised, palm outward, canted toward protagonist or vibrated once or twice in that direction. Am. Indian. Austin, p. 595. Forearm slightly raised, hand pointed
upwards, palm out. Anc. Rom. Sittl, p. 86. " 'Stop, Mrs.
Mann, stop! saith the beadle, raising his hand with a show of
authority." Dickens, <u>Twist</u>, p. 150. "but as the Jew, looking
back, waved his hand to intimate that he preferred being alone..."
Dickens, <u>Twist</u>, p. 227. " 'Now then!' said a voice, as my
uncle felt a hand on his shoulder, 'You're booked for one inside.
You'd better get in.' " Dickens, <u>Pickw</u>., II, p. 351. " 'Let it
be,' said Sikes, thrusting his hand before her." Dickens,
<u>Twist</u>, p. 443. Extending hand, palm forward, toward someone.
France. Mitton, p. 143. Also Am. schoolchildren. Seton,
p. xx. Hand extended, palm forward, fingers spread, moving
quickly from side to side, rotating from wrist. U.S. Palm
down, fingers, hand or arm may be moved up or down. Colombia. Saitz and Cervenka, p. 130.

 <u>Strike</u>: Moving the open hand, palm up, with several lateral
strokes from the wrist from right to left, slightly downward and
inward, usually at chin level. Lat. Am. Kany, p. 126. Raising and extending clenched fist. Lat. Am. Kany, ibid. Striking

down with fist. Amer. schoolchildren. Seton, p. xxiv.

Submission: "She kissed his feet and anointed them. Luke 7, 38. "I gave my back to the strikers and my cheeks to those who plucked off the hair." Isaiah 50, 6. Palms of hands forward, as if to ward off a blow: submission of a defeated people. Anc. Egypt. Meyer, pl. to 242, p. 266. Putting one's own right hand on the shoulder of another. Anc. Egypt. Ohm, p. 277. Lowering the hands. Persian. Sittl, p. 146. Kissing the knee of someone. Persian proskynesis. Sittl, p. 169 and n. 6. "...but she screamed aloud and ran under my guard, and clasping both knees in loud lamentation spoke to me..." Odyss., Bk. x. In peacetime, folded hands belong to the eranic proskynesis. Sittl, p. 150. Hands rub the earth while kneeling, indicating readiness to pick up dust and throw it on oneself. Anc. Gk. Sittl, p. 158, n. 6. Hands folded in the manner of the captive awaiting binding and arms extended. Assyrian, anc. Gk. Sittl, p. 149. Emperor is received by the people with lowered hands. Anc. Rom., Byzant. Sittl, p. 149. Right hand raised while kneeling. Anc. Persian. Sittl, p. 157, fig. 13, and p. 158. Hands sweep together dust while kneeling. Hellenistic. Sittl, p. 158. Folded hands as sign of submission was part of the ancient Germanic formal homage. In commendation, the vassal extended his folded hands to his lord, who then took them between his own hands. v. Amira, pp. 242f., and du Cange, s.v. Hominium. Folded hands symbolized tied hands (v. Amira, ibid.), as well as the services which the vassal owes his lord (Herwegen, p. 328), as well as his need for protection. The current Christian prayer gesture appears to be an adaptation of this legal gesture. (Cf. s.v. Prayer above.) The commendation ritual has survived in the Catholic church: the newly consecrated priest lays his folded hands into those of the bishop, while giving his oath. Ohm, p. 271, n. 3; Ebert, V, p. 93; Prutz, I, p. 117. Holding someone's stirrup while he is mounting. Medieval German: Orendel, 2143. Among the Fellahim, the groom smites his bride on the head so that he shall not be ruled by her. Egypt. Bauer, p. 97. Hands raised to level of head, palms slanted up. ("I submit to your judgment.") Jewish. Austin, p. 595. Standing with hands behind back, right grasping left hand. 1001 Nights (tr. Burton), III, p. 218.

Suffering: Hands extended above head. Ohm, p. 263.

Superciliousness: "Māschálla 'āde [oh, habit!]" one says and makes a deprecating gesture, hand moving in and outwards from the wrist. Palest. Bauer, p. 224.

Superiority: Groom presses bride's hand at wedding to establish his superiority. South Slavic. Krauss, pp. 391, 396, 406, 417. (Cf. s.v. FOOT, Submission; FOOT, HAND, Submission.)

Surprise: Hands open, raised high above the head, or arms bent, raised to an equal height with the face. Fingers separated, palms toward person causing surprise. Can be indifferent, comic, pained, joyful, admiring and overdone by hypocrisy or abandon. Anc. Gk. and Rom. Sittl, p. 13. Clapping hands. Neapol. De Jorio, p. 299. Making sign of the cross. Mod.

Gk. and Rom. Sittl, p. 128, and n. 4. Clapping hands, edge
of the right against back of the left. Islam. women. Ohm,
p. 284. "Mrs. Mann raised her hand in astonishment." Dickens, Twist, p. 99. "...he flung up both his hands and performed other gestures indicating surprise and agitation."
Thackeray, Virginians, ch. xxxiv. Right hand moving up and
down violently, palm turned inward, thumb usually touching the
index and middle finger, the rest of the fingers loose, hitting
each other in the movement." Spain, Lat. Am. Flachskampf,
p. 220. Flat hand placed on open mouth. Amer. schoolchildren.
Seton, p. xxii.

Surrender: In anc. Gk. boxing the defeated indicates his
willingness to surrender by raising both hands. Sittl, p. 219.
Defeated wrestler signals surrender by hitting winner with his
hand. Anc. Gk. Sittl, p. 219, n. 4. Giving the victor one's
hand. Anc. Roman. Otto, p. 211. Defeated army lowers insignia as sign of surrender. Anc. Rom. Sittl, p. 156. Warriors surrendering or peaceably approaching the enemy camp do
so with right hand raised. Anc. Gk. and Rom. Sittl, p. 148.

Sustain: Hand at waist level, palm up, flat and jerked
slightly upward. Aubert, p. 88.

"Teach me": Hand at level of waist close to the body with
palm turned up flat. Aubert, p. 88.

Teasing: Hands placed together palm to palm, then separated so that the palms are facing forward and hands are next
to each other. Saudi Arabia. Semiotic. Barakat, no. 214.

Telephone: Describing series of small circles in the air in
the immediate vicinity of the ear. Performed with one hand
limp and cupped slightly. Spain. Green, pp. 56-57. Right
hand circles around right ear. Ital. Graham, p. 26.

Threat: Fists held up to someone's face. Anc. Rom.
Sittl, p. 43. Hands raised against someone. Anc. Rom. Ibid.
Hand turned over indicates total destruction. Anc. Rom. Sittl,
p. 113. Raised arm, clenched fist. Woodcut, Brant, p. 70.
Index and little finger extended as in "horns," held horizontally
towards someone's face. Neapol. De Jorio, p. 94. Hand
pressed to the side of body. Ital. Manzoni, I, p. 158; De
Jorio, p. 200. Fingers of right hand extended and together,
then moving the hand a few times in a chopping movement.
Palest. Bauer, p. 219. Fingertips of the first three fingers
together, hand shaken toward someone. Palest. Bauer, p. 219.
Extended arms and hands of mourners on Roman graves of
children. Ebert, V, p. 95. Death threatens with the raised
fist. Boggs, p. 321. Elbow half bent, right forearm moves
from right towards the left shoulder. The hand remains there
for a moment, then falls back to its original position. Vulgar,
familiar. French. Mitton, p. 145. Hand raised to face level
and clenched; fingers toward the gesturer. French. Mitton,
p. 141. Fingers extended and slightly apart, hand turned, palm
inwards, at eye level, in the direction of someone. French.
Mitton, p. 142. Fist raised. Amer. schoolchildren. Seton,
p. xxi.

Treaty: (Cf. s.v. Agreement above.) Handclasp. Ossetes,

anc. India. Ebert, V, p. 94. Cf. also DWb, IV/2, col. 331.

Trivia: Hand rapidly agitated, fingers pointing upward, from wrist outward with slack motion. ("It's nothing.") French. Mitton, p. 149.

Trust: Handshake, saying "Straight!" Children. Opie, p. 122. "She took his hand and held it in a clasp warm even through her glove; but there was nothing amorous about the gesture." Boucher, p. 207.

Truth: Hands flat, stretched out toward someone, palms up. ("This is clear, self-evident.") French. Mitton, p. 143. Open hand in front, palm turned out, finger tips down. Aubert, p. 90. Fist clenched, thumb extended vertically. Assim. Jews. Efron, p. 118. Chief of tribe places right hand under man's belt so that it barely touches sexual organ: man on whom hand is laid must tell the truth. Saudi Arabia. Semiotic. Barakat, no. 202.

Uncertainty: Right and left hands rising and falling alternately as if balancing two points of view. France. Mitton, p. 144.

Understanding: Hand forward, palm supine. Assim. Eastern Jews. Efron, p. 119.

Union: In marriage ceremony the priest unites the hands of bride and groom and ties them together with his stole. Western Europe, Vedic India. Sittl, p. 132.

Useless: Gesture of throwing something behind one's back. Vulgar. France. Mitton, p. 147. Crossing the slightly cupped hand sharply across the body. The palm of the hand faces the shoulder at the beginning of the movement; at the conclusion, the palm faces outward. Spain, Lat. Am. Green, p. 85.

Vengeance: Shaking fist or drawing it back toward ear. Spain. Men. Kaulfers, p. 252. Shaking hand, palm open, thumb and fingers extended but touching, hand cupped. Spain. Women. Kaulfers, ibid. Tip of thumb and index of the right hand joined, other fingers lightly bent, hand shaking in a threatening manner. Palest. Bauer, p. 218. Fists twist and slowly pull away from each other. Colombia. (Primarily children), U.S. Saitz and Cervenka, p. 111.

Verbosity: Hand at face level, palm down, fingers move rapidly up and down from tip of thumb. Colombia, U.S. Saitz and Cervenka, p. 136.

Victory: Raising hand and shaking it. Bulwer, pp. 46-47. Hands clasped and raised above head. Colombia, U.S. Saitz and Cervenka, p. 145.

Volunteer: Hand raised. Stat., Theb.; Sittl, p. 218.

Voting: In the Roman senate since Tiberius some used the Gk. gesture of raising the right arm to vote. Sittl, p. 218.

Wait: Hand raised, palm out, fingers together. Colombia, U.S. Fingers separated, arm moving from side to side. U.S. Saitz and Cervenka, p. 146.

Warning: "shaking his hand before him in a warning manner." Dickens, Twist, p. 179. Hand(s) extended, palm facing forward. ("Stop!" "I don't want it.") French. Mitton, p. 143. Folding a corner edge of the coat to represent an ear. ("Secret

police. ") Guatemala. Kany, p. 121. "As we parted, he extended his right hand, palm upward, and shook it a few times
horizontally, to tell me 'Be careful! Look after yourself.' "
Ital. Graham, p. 26.

HAND, HAT
Anger: "he fixed his hat on his head with an indignant knock. "
Dickens, Pickw., I, p. 26. "the cabman dashed his hat upon
the ground, with a reckless disregard of his own private property..." Dickens, ibid., p. 9. " 'Now the murder's out and
damme, there's an end on it.' With these words, which he repeated with great emphasis and violence, Tom Weller dashed
his hat on the ground." Dickens, ibid., II, p. 260.
>   Defiance: Cf. s.v. HAND, Defiance.
>   Disbelief: Hat worn askew. Venezuela. Kany, p. 70.
>   Farewell: Cf. s.v. HAND, Farewell.
>   Greeting: (Cf. s.v. HAND, HEAD, Greeting.) Doffing hat
to ladies. Emperor Maximilian I, Freydal Cod. vindob. 2831.
Louis XIV never passed a woman without removing his hat, including chambermaids. How far he removed his hat depended
on the lady's rank. Hayes, p. 299. Hand placed to helmet.
Anc. Rom. military greeting. Stegmann v. Pritzwald, p. 27.
An hidalgo left Castile rather than doff his hat to another person first. Lazarillo de Tormes, ch. iii. "Put off's cap. "
Shakesp., All's Well, II, ii, 10. "Off capp'd to him. " Shakesp.,
Othello, I, i, 10. "Pipes lifting his hat, as Crabtree passed."
Smollett, Peregr. Pickle, ch. c. Lifting hat from one's head,
moving one's hand, holding the hat in the direction of the other
person, then replacing the hat on one's head. France. Mitton,
p. 142. Tipping hat by grasping crown with fingers and either
raising hat a little or removing it completely. Simultaneously
head and upper part of body move forward. Colombia. Saitz
and Cervenka, p. 67. "In Tibet a respectful salutation is made
by removing hat and lolling out the tongue." Cited from H.
Bayley, The Lost Language of Symbolism (London, 1912) by
Hayes, p. 226. Tipping hat by grasping brim, sometimes without raising hat. Also before religious shrines and churches.
Saitz and Cervenka, p. 68.
>   Insult: Cocking the hat. Mid-18th cent. London. Thomas
Burke, The Streets of London (London, 1949), p. 94, cited by
Hayes, p. 233.
>   Luck: Lifting one's hat to a chimney sweep means good
luck. England. G. L. Phillips, JAF 64 (1951), 191-196, cited
by Hayes, p. 290.
>   Marriage: On the evening before the marriage, the bridal
wreath is taken from the bride and woman's cap is put on her
head. Weise, Uberfl. Ged., II, p. 220.
>   Praise: "Some followers of mine own at lower end of the
hall hurl'd up their caps,..." Shakesp., Richard III, III, vii,
35. Applause. Shakesp., Coriol., I, i, 216.
>   Prayer: Covering the head at prayer. Priests of the
Katchin, Persians, anc. Rom., Jews. Heiler, pp. 104-105.
Baring the head at prayer. Anc. Gk., Germanic. Heiler,

p. 104. "Any man who offers prayer or explains the will of
God with anything on his head disgraces his head, and any woman who offers prayer or explains the will of God bareheaded
disgraces her head, for it is just as though she had her head
shaved." I Cor. 11, 4-6.

Respect: (Cf. s.v. HAND, Respect.) Removing hat from
head. Celestina, ix. The Chevalier de la Barre was beheaded
on July 1, 1766 partly because he failed to doff his hat to a
passing religious procession. Cited by Hayes, p. 283, from D.
Mornet, French Thought in the 18th Century (New York, 1929),
p. 52.

Reverence: "'God's will be done!' He took off his hat at
these last words." Gaskell, II, p. 17.

Sorrow: "Ne'er pull your hat upon your brows; give sorrow
words." Shakesp., Macbeth, IV, iii, 208.

Submission: Holding hat in hand. DWb, IV/2, col. 342.

HAND, HEAD

Affection: Hands laid upon someone's head in blessing is an expression of love. Boggs, p. 321. "There are twenty washed
men at the street door for you to shake hands with; and six
children in arms that you're to pat on the head...if you could
manage to kiss one of 'em, it would produce a very great im-
pression on the crowd." Dickens, Pickw., I, p. 208.

Anger: Beating the head. Anc. Gk. and Rom. Sittl, 21.
Yuquis slap back of their heads in anger and in joy. Yuqui Indians (Bolivia). Key, p. 95. "In great anger he struck his
head. Boggs, p. 321.

Approach: Head held high and protruding forward; hands at
waistlevel, palms up, fingers meeting, hand slightly curled.
Birdwhistell, Colliers (March 4, 1955). "Mrs. Tulliver rapped
the window sharply, beckoned, and shook her head,--a process
which she repeated more than once before she returned to her
chair." Eliot, p. 399.

Approval: Nodding and clapping hands. Amer. schoolchildren. Seton, p. xx. "'You're a clever boy, my dear,'
said the playful old gentleman, patting Oliver on the head approvingly." Dickens, Twist, p. 78.

Attention: "Accompanying these words with a gentle rap on
the head of the young gentleman before noticed, who, uncon-
scious of his close vicinity to the person in request, was
screaming 'Waller' with all his might." Dickens, Pickw., II,
p. 280.

Awareness: Hitting one's head at the side with flat right
hand indicates sudden awareness. Spain. Flachskampf, p. 223.

Blessing: (Cf. s.v. HAND, Blessing.) Hand placed on top
of someone's head. Ohm, p. 290.

Clairvoyance: Accompanying prognostication of events,
fingers of both hands, held at side of head with palms inward,
are pushed back and forth to and from the head. Madrid.
Green, pp. 76-77.

Concentration: "He passed his handkerchief across his forehead, took off his spectacles, wiped them, ... and his voice had

recovered its wonted softness of tone, when he said..." Dickens, Pickw., I, p. 298. " 'You stir up many thoughts,' said Donatello, pressing his hand upon his brow, 'but the multitude and the whirl of them make me dizzy.' " Hawthorne, ch. xxx. Head supported by hand, chin cupped in hand. Walter v. d. Vogelweide: "I sat upon a stone, leg crossed by leg; thereon I put my elbow up and in my hand did cup one cheek, and chin as well." Cf. also DWb, IV/2, col. 335.

Confusion: Hiding face in hands. Portug. Basto, p. 24.

Consecration: (Cf. s.v. HAND, Consecration.) Touching someone's head. Anc. Rom. Sittl, p. 369.

Cuckoldry: (Cf. s.v. HAND, Cuckoldry.) Placing thumbs against temples with indexes extended and other fingers pressed into palms. Lebanon, Syria. Semiotic. Barakat, no. 53. Tips of thumbs placed on temples, other fingers extended, palms forward, fingers wiggling. Lebanon, Syria. Semiotic. Barakat, no. 52.

Curse: Rubbing right palm down over face of another person puts a curse on that person. Libya, Saudi Arabia. Semiotic. Barakat, no. 124. Rubbing the back of the right hand on the forehead puts a curse on the person to whom the gesture is made. Usually made by women. Jordan. Semiotic. Barakat, no. 69.

Despair: Beating one's head. Anc. Gk. and Rom. Sittl, p. 21. Shakesp., Lear, I, iv, 270-273. Striking one's head with the fist. Gessner, p. 145.

Desperation: "Ma teste assez i puis debatre." Gautier de Coincy, 505, 628. Renart le Nouvel, 7352. Elbows close to body, hands raised as high as the shoulders. Right hand hits the left palm to palm. The two hands remain united and together are raised to touch the breast, then lowered. At the same time the head is shaken. Feminine and clerical. France. Mitton, p. 144.

Disappointment: Striking the forehead. Neapol. Critchley, p. 89. Scratching head. Neapol., German. De Jorio, pp. 121, 123.

Disbelief: Scratching head. Bonav. des Periers, I, p. 98. Noël du Fail, I, p. 165. "shows doubt by position of eyes (to side); hand to his mouth." Birdwhistell, Colliers (March 4, 1955), p. 56. "they shrugged their shoulders, touched their foreheads." Dickens, Pickw., I, p. 496.

Disgust: Hand, palm down, put on top of head. Colombia, U.S. (Reported 1970 as not very common among young adults in the U.S.). Saitz and Cervenka, p. 43.

Distress: Striking one's head. Anc. Rom. Ohm, p. 282.

Embarrassment: Scratching head. Mérimée, p. 146. Chronique d'Ernoul, p. 136.

Emphasis: "...bowing his head courteously in the emphasis of his discourse, gently waving his left hand to lend force to his observations..." Dickens, Pickw., II, p. 449.

Fantasy: Expressions suggesting fantasy or daydreaming may be accompanied by raising both hands, slightly clenched, spiralling upward above the level of the head. Spain, Lat. Am.

Green, p. 47.

Farewell: Hand placed to temple in military salute. Colombia, U.S. Saitz and Cervenka, p. 63.

Fear: Palm placed on back of head. Baumeister, I,
p. 588.

Forget: Slowly shake head and brush away something in
air, near forehead. Amer. schoolchildren. Seton, p. xxii.
Striking forehead with flat hand. France. Mitton, p. 146.

Good wishes (for riches): Hand is moved toward head
(hair?). Mod. Gk. Sittl, p. 115.

Greeting: Hand upright, palm inside, held at level of face,
arm half bent, moving of the tips of the fingers from forehead
outward. Aubert, p. 84. Modern military salute originated in
the 18th cent.; cf. C. Field, in Journ. of the Royal United Service Inst. 63 (1918), 42-49, cited by Hayes, p. 248. Salute.
Colombia, U.S. Saitz and Cervenka, pp. 63, 65. Hand moving
sharply from temple to side and up. Informal. Boyaca, Colombia. Ibid., p. 65. Salute in non-military context is often
humorous. Colombia, U.S. Ibid., p. 69.

Hesitation: Left arm raised, hand on head, fingers in hair.
Woodcut, Brant, p. 261.

Identification: The bride puts some yeast on her forehead
and enters the room with a jug on her head. Palest. Bauer,
p. 94.

Ignorance: Scratching head. (Response to "What happened?"
and "We can't do anything about it.") Colombia, U.S. Saitz
and Cervenka, p. 93.

Impatience: Raising hand to a position over the head, or
bringing it to rest on the back of the head. Spain. Men.
Green, pp. 89-90. Raising hand over head. The mover raises
a single hair in the rear of the head. Spain, Lat. Am. Women. Green, p. 89.

Indecision: Scratching the head. Amer. schoolchildren.
Seton, p. xxi.

Insult: Slap or blow with the hand against someone's head
or face. Anc. and mod. Gk. Not certain for anc. Rome, except as judicial usage [Brynaeus, De morte Jesu Chr., II, 5,
para. 4. 32, and Pallad., Hist. Lausiaca, 113, col. 1217 c].
Sittl, p. 109.

Intellectual: Hand, fingers extended, palm facing speaker,
is brought to side of the head and the rigid fingers are pushed
back and forth. Madrid, Lat. Am. Green, p. 75.

Joy: Yuquis slap back of their heads in anger and in joy.
Yuqui Indians (Bolivia). Key, p. 95.

Manumission: Cf. s.v. HAND, Manumission.

Memory: " 'They are here,' added the Count, tapping his
forehead significantly. 'Large book at home--full of notes--
music,...all tings.' " Dickens, Pickw., I, p. 249.

Mockery: (Cf. s.v. FINGER, HEAD, Cuckoldry.) Hands
placed slightly above temples, palms facing, fingertips forward,
thumbs pointing up. Grandes Heures of the Duke de Berry
(1409), pl. 16.

Mourning: (Cf. s.v. HAND, Mourning.) Striking one's

head. Boggs, col. 319. Anc. Gk. Men. Sittl, p. 25.

Need: "...jerk his clenched fists up and down, vigorously nodding between each inferior-superior movement of his fists." Birdwhistell, Backgr., p. 14.

Negation: A defensive movement of the hand, a despising movement of the head, in connection with which the eyebrows and eyelashes simultaneously are raised. Palest. Bauer, p. 220.

Oath: Someone taking an oath may swear by his head and, in so doing, point to it or to the most valuable part of the head, the eyes. Anc. Gk. and Rom., mod. Gk., India. Sittl, p. 139. The pater familias swears by the heads of his children, the children by the head of their father, the wife by that of her husband; in all cases, the hand of the person swearing touches the object sworn by. Anc. Gk. Sittl, p. 140. In swearing by the head of the accused, the accuser touches it. Medieval German: Reinecke Fuchs, 2171; Urk. Ludw. v. Brandenburg u. Baiern (1349), cited by Grimm, DRA, II, p. 551. Hands at sides with palms up, head tilted back. Jordan, Lebanon, Syria, Saudi Arabia. Semiotic or culture-induced. Barakat, no. 20. Palm of right hand placed on top of head. Saudi Arabia, Jordan. Semiotic. Barakat, no. 178.

Passion: Right fist moves energetically at level of chest, head thrown back, upper incisors bite lower lip, nose takes air in audibly, eyes squint. Spain. Flachskampf, p. 249.

Pensiveness: Hand against temple. Dit des rues, II, 267, 424. Scratching head. Horace, Sat. I, 10, 70. " 'So they have fired me,' said Pnin, clasping his hands and nodding his head." Nabokov, p. 170. Head resting in hand. Medieval. Haseloff, p. 307.

Perplexity: Scratching head. Godefroy de Paris, 3587, 5889.

Plea: Grasping head of a person between both hands. Anc. Gk. Sittl, p. 33.

Poverty: Accompanying the gesture for counting money (cf. s.v. FINGER, Money) with a negative head shake. Lat. Am. Kany, p. 88.

Prayer: Holding one or both hands over one's head. India. Ohm, p. 187. Putting one hand to the head. Tehuelch, Patagonia. Ohm, p. 288. "[The priest] then raises [his hands] to his face, inclines his head, and fixing his eyes upon the Sacred Host prays for the departed." Mass, p. 66.

Prohibition: Palm facing inwards, and shaking head, India. Rose, p. 313.

Punishment: A blow with hand or fist against some part of someone's head. Anc. Gk., anc. Rom. judicial usage (cf. s.v. Insult above). Sittl, p. 109. Slap. Anc. Gk., mod. Gk. Sittl, p. 109.

Regret: Hand(s) raised to side of head, palm resting on cheek or side of head. Colombia, U.S. Saitz and Cervenka, p. 101.

Reminder: Scratching one's head. Anc. Rom., Neapol. De Jorio, p. 123. Putting right hand on someone's head, turning his ear with the left. Arab. Goldziher, Zeitschr., p. 377.

Reverence: "[The priest] then joins his hands and inclines his head to the Crucifix at the sacred Name with which the blessing ends." Mass, p. 51. Hands placed palm to palm and held in front of the head. Yoga. Ohm, p. 236.

Silence: " 'Hush!' said Mrs. Maylie, laying her hand on Oliver's head." Dickens, Twist, p. 298.

Snobbishness: One hand raised, palm facing away from gesturer, head tilted, eyes half closed, lips pursed. U.S. Saitz and Cervenka, p. 128.

Sorrow: Hands hitting head. Men. Anc. Gk. Sittl, p. 25. "What dost thou mean by shaking of thy head? Why dost thou look so sadly on my son?" Shakesp., King John, III, i, 19. Cutting one's hair. Biblical. Boggs, p. 319. Strewing face and head with dust and mud. Near East. Boggs, p. 319. Hands placed on head strewn with dust. Ibid. Covering head. Odyss., Bk. viii. Applying the hand passionately to the head. Bulwer, pp. 84-85. Strewing ashes on one's head. Biblical. Ohm, p. 231.

Submission: Kissing right hand of superior and placing it on one's own head. Arab. Goldziher, Zeitschr., p. 370.

Surprise: Hitting the side of one's face with the palm of one hand, head tilted slightly to one side and eyes opened wide. Syria, Libya, Jordan, Saudi Arabia, Lebanon. Autistic. Barakat, no. 2.

Surrender: Hands held at shoulder level, palms forward, head turned slightly to one side. Libya, Lebanon, Saudi Arabia, Jordan. Semiotic. Barakat, no. 104.

Uncertainty: Scratching head. Bulwer, pp. 85-86.

Victory: Hands clasped above the head. Univ. of Calif. Berkeley. McCord, p. 290. (Cf. s.v. HAND, Victory.) Victorious warrior who pardons his enemy places his agal (rope-like circle of head-piece) over the head of the person pardoned: indicates that vanquished person belongs to the victorious warrior together with all he owns. Saudi Arabia, Kuwait, Iraq. Semiotic. Barakat, no. 175.

HAND, HEAD, KNEE

Prayer: Kneeling, face buried in hands. Michael Pacher, "Prayer of St. Wolfgang" (ca. 1483).

Sorrow: Head laid upon knees which are held by folded hands, in sitting or squatting position. Anc. Gk. and Rom. Sittl, p. 24. "...a girl throws herself upon her knees, tears her clothes and tears out her hair." Boggs, p. 319.

HAND, HEAD, SHOULDER

Uncertainty: Head is cocked to the right, the shoulders shrugged, right hand raised, thumb extended away from the body, lips puckered, eyebrows arched. "Ça...[prrrp!] je n'en sais trop rien!" Characteristically French is the sudden explosion of air between the lips, causing them to vibrate. Tongue is not involved as in the American "raspberry." Brault, p. 380.

HAND, HIP
Authority: Hand placed on hip, chest out, head held high--typical in portrayals of generals and heroes. De Jorio, p. 199.
Defiance: Cf. s.v. ARM, HAND, Defiance.
Emphasis: One or both hands placed on hips while speaking. Partic. French and Ital. women. Sittl, p. 49.
Interrogation: "The servant girl,...hands on hips, lifted her chin asking what he wanted." Wéyland, p. 24.
Oath: Servant swears to his master, son to his father, putting his hand under his thigh. Genesis 24, 2-9; 47, 29. Also Grimm, DRA, II, p. 551.
Poverty: Open hand, palm down, strikes sideways against the belt or waist. Argentina. Kany, p. 89.
Readiness: Hand on hip. Bogomil grave, Yugoslavia, 13th-14th cent. Fischer, Symbolon, p. 105.

HAND, JAW, LIP
Cruelty: Fists clenched, biting of the upper lip, forcing the lower jaw forward. Aubert, p. 120.
Hatred: Cf. s.v. Cruelty above.

HAND, KNEE
Anger: Folded hands pressed around knee, while sitting. Anc. Gk. and Rom. Sittl, p. 23.
Begging: "...for I was essaying to speak, and had, as soon as she took her dear cheeks from mine, dropt down on my knees, my hands clasped, and lifted up in a supplicating manner." Richardson, Clarissa, I, p. 100.
Calmness: Hands clasped around knee while sitting. Anc. Rom., Spain. Grimm, DRA, II, p. 375, n. 2.
Commendation: (Cf. s.v. HAND, Commendation.) Wall painting in the Tour Ferrande at Pernes shows Charles of Anjou's enfeoffment with Kingdom of Sicily by Clement IV. King with hands joined kneels before pope. Ladner, p. 259.
Despair: Folded hands pressed around someone's knee. Anc. Gk. and Rom. Sittl, p. 23.
Emphasis: "...accompanied this last sentiment with an emphatic slap on each knee." Dickens, Pickw., II, p. 172.
Farewell: Handclasp while the person remaining behind kneels. Ms. Harl. 43801, fol. 149 in Coulton, p. 98; also fol. 172b depicted in Coulton, p. 109.
Gratitude: "'You have given me life, Madam, said I, clasping my uplifted hands together, and falling on one knee." Richardson, Clarissa, I, p. 138. Falling upon one's knees and clapping hands. Protest. women in Africa. Ohm, p. 287. Cf. s.v. ARM, KNEE, Gratitude.
Greeting: Priest before ancestor's shrine clapped his hands while bending knees, as greeting of the god. Inamwanga, Tanganyika. Ohm, p. 283. Grasping a person by the knee. Anc. Gk. Ohm, p. 240. Handclasp kneeling: "Meeting of the King of France and the Duke of Brittany at Tours," Ms. Harley 4379, fol. 135b in Coulton, p. 37. Cf. also Ms. Harley 4380, fol. 40 in Coulton, pl. vi (see illustration 9).

9. "The Meeting of the King of France and the Duke of Brittany
at Tours, " Harley Ms. 4379, f.135 v., the British Library; reproduced by permission of the British Library Board (see HAND,
KNEE--Greeting).

Laziness: Clasping one's knees with both hands, head between them. Dante, Purg., c. iv.
Luck: On seeing three priests or three negroes, a girl will
scratch her knee which will bring her luck in finding a husband
soon. Colombia. Saitz and Cervenka, p. 83.
Oath: "The hero knelt before the maiden.... Then she
took, in her white hand, the oath of loyalty from him." Wolfr.
v. Eschenbach, v, 276.
Plea: One hand grasps someone's knees; performed kneeling. Anc. Gk. Sittl, pp. 163-164. "She clasped his knees and
begged for the love of God that he would have compassion, etc."
Smollett, Peregr. Pickle, I, ch. vi. Supplicant touches or embraces one or both knees of the person with whom he pleads.
If one hand is free, it is raised in supplication. Anc. Gk.
Sittl, p. 282. Kneeling on both hands or on one (right) knee,
hands extended, or one hand extended. Anc. Gk. Sittl, p. 157,
fig. 13. Cf. s.v. BEARD, HAND, Plea; HAND, Plea.
Prayer: Genuflecting, upper body resting on heels, hands
stretched upward toward deity. Anc. Egypt. Ohm, p. 358.

Genuflecting, hands raised, palms outward, elbows slightly bent.
Anc. Egypt. Brunet, pl. 174. "The knight fell doune upon his
kne, vnderneth an olyve tre, and helde up both his handes."
Syr Isenbras, I, p. 79. A portrait of Gregory X (1271-1276)
on the scarpular which he wore around his neck in the sepulcher
shows him kneeling with hands joined. Ladner, p. 253-254.
The Franciscan Pope Nicholas IV (1288-1292) is represented in
mosaics in S. Giovanni in Laterano and S. Maria Maggiore in
Rome kneeling and praying with joined hands. Ladner, p. 255.
"The portraits of Benedict XI and John XXII bring to an end, as
far as the Middle Ages are concerned, the series of images of
popes who kneel in prayer with hands joined and, almost without
exception, wear the tiara, the symbol of their plenitude of power.
The combination of the symbolisms of supreme authority and
tiara--and of surrender to God--younger prayer gesture--should
be noted." Ladner, p. 257. Kneeling on right knee, hands
palm to palm. Très Riches Heures, pl. 35. Right knee on the
ground, hands extended toward deity. Buddhist. Ohm, p. 247.
Squatting, elbows supported on knees, raised hands rubbing one
another. Advisor to a Safwa king. Ohm, p. 287. Cf. s.v.
ARM, HAND, Prayer.
     Reminder: "...now and then he knocks upon his knee with
his fist..." Palest. Bauer, p. 224.
     Reverence: "She dipped her hand in the font by the en-
trance, crossed herself, and went on to the main aisle, where
she knelt on both knees and was still for a moment. Boucher,
p. 206.
     Shame: "I fell upon my knees and spread my hands." Ez-
ra, 9, 5.
     Submission: Subject of King Savang Vatthana of Laos greets
him by kneeling on right knee while holding hands palm to palm
before his lowered head. King has hands extended before him,
palms up, hands close together, as if in request to his subject
to rise. L.A. Times (Feb. 26, 1963), p. 4. Subject greets
King Savang Vatthana of Laos by kneeling on one knee while
right hand is extended in handclasp with right hand of king.
Ibid. Laying joined hands into hands of an overlord while kneeling. Illustr. in 12th cent. Regestum of Tivoli. Ladner, p. 258,
n. 34. (Cf. s.v. HAND, Commendation, and HAND, KNEE,
Commendation.)
     Sympathy: "Hagen bent over to his friend and patted him on
his knobby knee." Nabokov, p. 168.

HAND, KNEE, LIP
Homage: Cf. s.v. HAND, Homage.
     Plea: Kneeling while kissing hand and with the left hand
touching knee of recipient of the supplication. Anc. Gk. and
Rom. Sittl, p. 169. Servants and supplicants kneel when kissing hand. Anc. Gk. and Rom. Sittl, ibid. The Romans con-
gratulated Nero upon his discovery of the Pisonian plot by kneeling and kissing his hand. Tacit. Ann.; Sittl, ibid.

HAND, LEG

Judgment: Judge signifies his function by placing right lower
leg horizontally over left knee and left hand to middle of chest.
Freiburg Cathedral. Schmidt, I, pl. 70; cf. Grimm, DRA, II
p. 375.

Reverence: Mosaic at St. Peter's in Rome shows Innocent
III (1198-1216) with slightly bent knees, arms and hands extended but not joined. Moderate proskynesis, found on numerous medieval works of art. Ladner, p. 249.

Surprise: " 'It is him!' exclaimed Sam; and having established Job's identity beyond a doubt, he smote his leg. " Dickens, Pickw., II, p. 293.

HAND, LIP

Admiration: Fingertips of right hand united and brought to the
lips. To show greater admiration, nails of the three united
fingertips are kissed and the opened hand is quickly drawn back
from the lips. Spain. Flachskampf, p. 221.

Adoration: Kissing the hand of a woman as a modest re-
quest--not gallantry! Theocritus. Sittl, p. 166.

Affection: Two lovers kiss one another's hands. Eustathios.
Sittl, p. 164. Pressing someone's hand to the lips or gently
pressing the hand as an expression of affection. Dickens, Pickw.,
I, pp. 104, 118, 119; II, pp. 241, 277. Kissing someone's
hands and lips. DWb, IV /2, col. 332. "And Joab took Amasa
by the beard with the right hand to kiss him. " II Sam. 20, 9.
Kissing of the hand, lips and eyes as a sign of affection caused
by joy or sorrow: Hartmann v. Aue, 7978. Kissing palm of
own hand, then extending hand. Used when gesticulator and
referent are at some distance from one another. Colombia.
Saitz and Cervenka, p. 79.

Congratulation: Kissing the hand. (Before Alexander this
was appropriate only to slaves.) Anc. Gk. Sittl, p. 166.

Despair: ". . . wrung his hands in secret, gnawed his nether
lip, and turned yellow with despair. " Smollett, Rod. Random,
ch. lii.

Disappointment: Arms thrown back, corners of the mouth
pulled down, lips open as if to curse. Spain. Flachskampf,
p. 228.

Etiquette: ". . . a compliment which Mr. Pickwick returned
by kissing his hand to the lady. " Dickens, Pickw., I, p. 210.

Gratitude: Kissing someone's hand. Anc. Gk. and Rom.
Sittl, pp. 167, 168, n. 7, 169. (Before Alexander this was appropriate only to slaves.) Sittl, p. 166. Kissing the back of
the right hand, then raising it, palm up. Lebanon, Saudi Arabia,
Syria. Semiotic. Barakat, no. 111. Same gesture, accompanied by raising eyes simultaneously. Saudi Arabia. Semiotic.
Barakat, no. 84. Servant kisses right hand of master and puts
it on his own hand. Oriental. Petermann, I, p. 172.

Greeting: "You told me you salute not at the court, but you
kiss your hands; that courtesy would be uncleanly if courtiers
were shepherds. " Shakesp., As you like it, III, ii, 43-45.
"Let them curtsy with their left legs, and not presume to touch

a hair of my master's horse-tail till they kiss their hands."
Shakesp., Shrew, IV, i, 80-82. "...at last, one day...Nathan-
iel Pipkin had the temerity to kiss his hand to Maria Lobbs."
Dickens, Pickw., I, p. 281. Kiss and handshake. Anc. Rom.
Sittl, p. 79. Man kisses hand of woman. Mod. Hungarian.
Révész, Univ., p. 146.

    Hesitation: Cf. s.v. LIP, Hesitation.

    Homage: Following the Persian example, the Macedonians
kissed the hand of their ruler on his deathbed. Sittl, p. 166.
Defeated princes kiss the hand of the victor. Anc. Gk. and Rom.
Sittl, ibid. Alexandrians kiss Hadrian's hand. Sittl, p. 169.
The younger Maximinus extended his hand to be kissed at audiences but was criticized for it. Sittl, p. 167. Clients kiss
hand of patron (emperor) at the salutatio. Sittl, p. 168. Gal-
lienus, upon becoming consul, had his hands kissed by matrons.
Sittl, p. 167, n. 6. Caligula and Domitian had their hands and
feet kissed by noblemen, for which they were criticized. Sittl,
p. 167. Cf. s.v. FOOT, HAND, LIP, Homage.

    Humility: Ecclesiastical officials received handkiss from
subordinates. Révész, Univ., p. 147.

    Mercy: Defeated princes kiss hands of victor in request for
mercy. Anc. Gk. and Rom. Sittl, p. 166.

    Mourning: Hand is kissed, then held out toward grave.
Anc. Gk. Sittl, p. 74.

    Pettiness: Thumb and index grasp lips, then are removed
from them and simultaneously opened. Spain. Flachskampf,
p. 233.

    Plea: Clients kiss hand of patron (emperor) at the salutatio.
Sittl, p. 168. Kissing the hand (before Alexander this was appropriate only to slaves). Anc. Gk. and Rom. Sittl, p. 166.
Supplicant for an office or patronage at the disposal of noblemen
or chamberlain kisses their hands. Anc. Gk. and Rom. Sittl,
p. 168. Kissing the back of a dignitary's hand in plea for
mercy. Saudi Arabia. Semiotic. Barakat, no. 122.

    Prayer: (Cf. HAND, Prayer.) Kissing the hand toward as-
tral deities (blowing a kiss), such as Helios, etc. Anc. Gk.
and Rom. Heiler, p. 104. Cf. Job 31, 27; also Peruvian.
Heiler, ibid. "...Odysseus was gladdened then, rejoicing in the
sight of his country, and kissed the graingiving ground, then
raised his hands in the air and spoke to the nymphs..." Odyss.,
xiii. "If my mouth hath kissed my hand." Job 31, 27. Blowing a kiss toward crucifixes and sacred images. Rural Swabia,
Styria. Heiler, p. 104; R. Fischer, p. 242.

    Respect: Ecclesiastical officials have their hands kissed by
subordinates. Révész, Univ., p. 147. Soldiers kiss the hand
of their departing general. Anc. Rom. Sittl, p. 169. "Humbly
kiss your hand." Shakesp., III Henry VI, III, iii, 61. "I kiss
his conquering hand." Shakesp., Anthony and Cleopatra, III,
xiii, 75. Kissing the nose and then the right hand of a dignitary.
Saudi Arabia. Semiotic. Barakat, no. 135.

    Silence: Laying hand on mouth. Job 29, 9; DWb, IV/2,
col. 335.

    Submission: Bowing deeply and kissing someone's hand.

Mocking: Rabener, Sat. 3, 35. Defeated princes kiss the hand of the victor. Anc. Gk. and Rom. Sittl, p. 166. Cf. s.v. HAND, Submission.

HAND, MOUTH

Apotropy: Making the sign of the cross over the open mouth while yawning. Spain. Flachskampf, p. 243. Blowing into face of convert and making sign of the cross on his forehead to exorcise evil spirits. Early Christian. Duchesne, p. 296. Placing thumb side of fist over mouth, then twisting the hand a half-turn: threat to jinn. Women. Saudi Arabia. Semiotic. Barakat, no. 226. Cf. s.v. HAND, Apotropy.

Depart: Cf. s.v. HAND, Depart.

Disappointment: Right hand makes a rapid movement from right to left in front of the mouth as if waving something off, or a fanlike folding inward of the fingers. Spain. Flachskampf, p. 235.

Discretion: Hand put to mouth, walking on toes. Anc. Rom. Baden, p. 450.

Drink: Right hand closed, thumb raised and moved to the mouth in the manner of a spigot. Spain. Flachskampf, p. 227; Green, pp. 58-59: fingers either held tightly clenched or extended at right angles to the thumb. Can also indicate drunkenness. Hand held to mouth as if grasping a glass or bottle. Southern Ital. Efron, p. 149. Amer. schoolchildren. Seton, p. xxiv. Putting cupped hand to the mouth. HDV, I, col. 321. Right thumb and small finger extended, other fingers folded into palm, the hand is moved toward the mouth several times. Lat. Am. Kany, p. 82.

Eating: Fingers of right hand curved, tips joined and repeatedly moved to the mouth. Spain. Flachskampf, p. 227; also Lat. Am. Green, pp. 57-58. Green comments that Kaulfers, failing to distinguish between Spanish and Latin American gestures, writes that "hunger, or the desire for food, is often indicated by a tapping of the lower lip with the tip of the semiclenched index finger of the right hand."

Embarrassment: "He continued to blush easily even after he was no longer fearful and tense, covering his blushes with a deprecatory smile and the placing of the fingers of one hand over his mouth, in that universal gesture of embarrassment." Kroeber, pp. 124-125.

Enthusiasm: Hands raised, fingers extended, mouth often open. Usually female, often accompanied by intake of breath. Colombia, U.S. Saitz and Cervenka, p. 49.

Excitement: Open hand covers mouth. Often in context of impending danger. Colombia, U.S. Saitz and Cervenka, p. 50.

Fatigue: Fingers extended, tapping open mouth lightly and repeatedly. Impolite in formal social context. Colombia, U.S. Saitz and Cervenka, p. 125.

Finished: Blowing over the back of the hand. Ital. De Jorio, p. 231f.

Foolishness: "If thou hast done foolishly in lifting up thyself, or if thou hast thought evil, lay thy hand upon thy mouth." Prov.

30, 32.

Frustration: Biting the palm (ball) of the hand. Palest.
Bauer, p. 218.

Greeting: Raising right hand, so that palm remains posi-
tioned toward face, hand returned to mouth, kissing fingertips
and then throwing kiss toward divine image. Anc. Gk. and Rom.
Baumeister, I, p. 592. Grasping one or both hands of someone
and occasionally kissing them. Palest. Bauer, p. 171. Between mother and son after long absence: mother rises slightly
from seat, extends her hands, which are placed together, toward
son, who places his hands (also joined) into hers and she kisses
the back of his right hand. Africa. Ohm, pp. 209-210.

Hot: Hand, fingers extended, palm down or facing mouth,
moves up and down in front of open mouth. U.S. Rare in Colombia. Refers to hot or spicy food. Saitz and Cervenka,
p. 71.

Magical: When a corpse was burned, the priest pretended
to catch its soul in his hands, then gave the soul to the dead
man's successor by throwing his hands toward him and blowing
upon him. Tabilis or Carrier Indians, N. W. America. Frazer, IV, p. 199.

Mockery: Hand put over mouth while throwing waggish
glances at someone. France. Little girls. Mitton, p. 145.

Negation: Blowing between the hands. Arab. Goldziher,
Zeitschr., p. 379.

Prayer: Laying hand or finger on mouth. Sumerian. Ohm,
p. 288.

Regret: Hand clapped over mouth quickly. Colombia, U.S.
Saitz and Cervenka, p. 102.

Respect: Kissing someone's hand. Children to fathers, be-
lievers to prophet. Anc. Gk. and Rom. Sittl, p. 168. Kissing the hand of Christian priests. Early Christian. Sittl,
p. 168.

Secrecy: Cf. s.v. HAND, Secrecy.

Silence: Putting hand to mouth. Arab. Goldziher, Ztschr.,
p. 377. Anc. Rom. Sittl, p. 213.

Sorrow: Mourning widow crouches before mummy of husband, her right hand placed over her head, lips pressed against
mummy. Mourning widow and daughter, one standing, one
kneeling, before a mummy. Both have their right hands raised
above their heads, left hands on mummy. Anc. Egypt. Dawson, pp. 86-87.

Submission: Kissing the back of someone's hand. Bulwer,
pp. 122-130.

Surprise: Hand somewhat cupped or straight, placed on
mouth. Anc. Gk. and Rom. Sittl, p. 272.

HAND, MOUTH, TONGUE, TOOTH

Calmness: Flip hand near mouth and simultaneously make a
clicking sound with tongue and teeth: to indicate that a person
is not to worry. Saudi Arabia. Semiotic. Barakat, no. 196.

HAND, NECK

Death: Drawing edge of hand across throat, head inclined.
Alas, Cajas, p. 273. Drawing swordblade quickly across one's
throat and clasping hands to show that the execution was completed. Decapitation. Damascus. Goldziher, Zeitschr.,
p. 371.

Despair: Hand grasps throat, eyes closed. ("I'm fed up
with everything.") Ital. Graham, p. 26.

Disbelief: "You simply half-close the eyes and place your
hand on your cravat, or where your cravat would be if you
wore a cravat." French. WW II. Alsop, p. 26. Index moves
lightly up and down throat several times. Often accompanied
by widening of the lips. Colombia. Saitz and Cervenka, p. 39.
Hand cupped, palm up, at neck ca. 6 in. below chin. Not usually used directly in front of the speaker who is disbelieved.
Colombia. Saitz and Cervenka, ibid.

Disgust: Hand, palm down, placed across throat. Reported 1970 as not very common among young adults in U.S.
Colombia, U.S. Saitz and Cervenka, p. 43.

Finished: Hitting the side of one's neck with right hand.
Hadhramaut. Semiotic. Barakat, no. 184.

Homosexuality: Tapping one's neck with the right hand.
Lebanon. Semiotic. Barakat, no. 56.

Invitation: Rubbing the back of one's neck with palm of
right hand: indicates that one would like to meet the woman to
whom gesture is made. Lebanon. Semiotic. Barakat, no. 51.

Jail: One hand grasps throat. Colombia. Saitz and Cervenka, p. 74.

Oath: Both hands flat, extended forward, little fingers together, then folded as if in prayer, then two fingers crossed
and one slid across throat. Children. Opie, p. 124. (Cf.
s.v. FINGER, NECK, Oath.)

Surprise: Left hand hooked around neck, left elbow pro-
jecting forward and forearm parallel to and touching left side of
face. Spain. Kaulfers, p. 253.

Threat: Stiff right index rubbed across throat, head tilted
back slightly. Usually finger is moved from left to right with
a squeaking noise accompanying the gesture. Arab. Semiotic.
Barakat, no. 91.

HAND, NOSE

Cleverness: Tapping one side of the nose ("I am no fool.")
Amer. schoolchildren. Seton, p. xxi.

Concentration: " 'How old is that horse, my friend?' enquired Mr. Pickwick, rubbing his nose with the shilling he had
reserved for the fare..." Dickens, Pickw., I, p. 7.

Cunning: " 'Mr. Warrington is in his apartment,' said the
gentleman; 'but--' and here the gentleman winked at Mr. Draper,
and laid his hand on his nose." Thackeray, Virginians, I,
p. 496.

Disbelief: Laying right index on right side of nose. ("I
smell a rat.") Amer. schoolchildren. Seton, p. 115.

Disgust: The nose is held while an imaginary lavatory chain

is pulled.   Children.   Opie, p. 319.   "placing the right hand
upon the...nose,...then a downflinging gesture of the right hand
ensues. "   French.   WW II.   Alsop, p. 28.

Flattery: Hand twists tip of nose: "Brown Nosing. "   U. S.
Saitz and Cervenka, p. 53.

Friendship: Touching tip of nose with back of right hand,
simultaneously moving head back and forth as nose is touched.
Saudi Arabia.   Semiotic.   Barakat, no. 117.

Impatience: " 'Just so, ' interposed Perker, who had accompanied this dialogue with sundry twitchings of his watch-chain,
indicative rubbings of his nose, and other symptoms of impatience... " Dickens, Pickw. , II, p. 438.

Insult: Rubbing the nose questions the ancestry of the person at whom the gesture is directed.   Ital.   Time (April 9,
1965), p. 68.

Mockery: (Cf. s. v. HAND, Mockery.)   For Shanghai Gesture see HAND, Mockery.   It is "limited to the world of childish
mockery...and even there it is scarcely common any longer. "
Does not exist in Asia or Africa, except through cultural contact
with Europe.   Röhrich, p. 24 and pl. 39.   Cf. also "cocksnook."
Davidson, p. 4; Rabelais, Garg. , Bk. I, ch. xviii; Pieter Breughel, "La Fête des fous" (1560), in Röhrich, pl. 40; Goethe,
"Lilis Park. "   Mitton observes that it is perhaps the remnant
of an ancient magic gesture.

Prayer: Hand laid to nose.   Taskodrugites.   Ohm, p. 288.

Punishment: Those found guilty of slander had to pull themselves by the nose in retracting.   Medieval German and Norman.
HDV, I, p. 322.   Pulling oneself by the nose, e. g. to indicate
that someone will be scolded by his wife.   Colombia.   Saitz and
Cervenka, p. 98.

Rejection: "nose rub among Americans is as much a sign
of rejection as the word 'No!' "   Birdwhistell, Colliers (March
4, 1955), p. 56.

Smell: Cf. s. v. HAND, Smell.

Truth: "Hookey, Hookey Walker--and 'with a hook, ' usually
accompanied by a significant upliftment of the hand and crooking
of the fore-finger, implying that what is said is a lie, or is to
be taken contrary-wise.   One tells a long-yarn-story that asks
for the disbelief of the auditory; whereupon another cries out
'Hookey Walker!' having previously shewn the sign above described, or another more elaborate still, which may be looked
upon as a counter-sign, viz. spread the fingers of both hands
wide open, apply one thumb to the tip of the nose, and the other
to the point of the little finger of the other hand--this signifies
a clincher.   History: John Walker was an out-door clerk at
Longman, Clementi, and Co. 's in Cheapside, where a great number of Persons were employed, and 'old Jack, ' who had a
crooked or hook nose, occupied also the post of spy upon their
aberrations (which were manifold).   Of course, it was for the
interests of the surveillants, to throw discredit upon all Jack's
reports to the nobs of the firm, and numbers could attest that
those reports were fabrications, however true; Jack was con-
stantly out-voted, his evidence overlaid, and of course disbe-

lieved, when his occupation ceased, but not so the fame of
'Hookey Walker.' " British, ca. 1810. Bee, p. 99.
    Understanding: " 'It's all right, Sam; quite right'--upon
which Mr. Weller struck three distinct blows upon his nose in
token of intelligence..." Dickens, Pickw., II, p. 192.

HAND, OBJECT

Apotropy: Vestal of Herero tribe rubs ashes on foreheads of
men going on dangerous trip to protect them. Frazer, II,
p. 215.
    Attention: Rising and banging on a water glass with a spoon.
Univ. of Calif. Berkeley. McCord, p. 292. Tapping table top
with ring or a glass, or tapping a glass or cup with another object, e.g. a spoon, to get waiter's attention. Colombia. Saitz
and Cervenka, p. 106.
    Blessing: The major cross made over persons or objects
with sacred object. The major Greek cross: thumb and index
united, other fingers extended, drawing "IXC" in the air. The
major Roman cross: first three fingers extended, last two
folded in toward palm, or (since the 13th cent.) all fingers extended as prescribed by Pius V. The latter form was especially
favored by the Benedictines since the 8th cent. Ohm, p. 295.
    Challenge: Knocking sand from a boy's hand by another boy:
challenge or acceptance of a challenge to fight. Syria, Saudi
Arabia. Semiotic. Barakat, no. 220.
    Claim: Cf. s.v. HAND, Claim.
    Commendation: Cf. s.v. HAND, Commendation.
    Decision: Counting beads (odd or even) before taking a trip:
to decide whether or not to take the trip or embark upon some
enterprise. Rwala Bedouin of Kuwait, Iraq, Syria, Saudi Arabia.
Semiotic. Barakat, no. 132.
    Emphasis: Cf. s.v. HAND, Emphasis.
    Farewell: Departing person takes a piece of a linen cloth,
of which the remaining person takes the other piece. Danish.
Grimm, DRA, I, p. 626. A piece is cut from the (remaining?)
woman's belt or apron. Montenegro. Grimm, ibid. "At the
close of services in a Baptist church in Moscow visited by a
group of Quakers, the congregation sang 'God be with us till we
meet again'... and while singing all the women took out their
handkerchiefs and waved them to the visitors." (Ca. 1951.)
Cited by Hayes, p. 314, from Kathleen Lonsdale, Quakers visit
Russia (London, ca.1951), p. 26.
    Friendship: Cf. s.v. HAND, Friendship.
    Gratitude: After a man dances he kneels before the musi-
cian who wipes the dancer's cheeks with his head-cloth: expression of gratitude on part of the participants. Saudi Arabia.
Semiotic. Barakat, no. 221.
    Greeting: Junior official lowered or had the fasces lowered
by his lictors in the presence of a senior or superior official.
Anc. Rom. Sittl, p. 154. Lowering fasces by the lictors.
Anc. Rom. Sittl, p. 155. In the circus the charioteer lowered
his whip before the patrons. Sittl, pp. 155-156. In accosting

each other peacefully, knights raised the visor as sign of mutual recognition. Eichler, p. 160. "He that cannot make a leg,
put off's cap, kiss his hand, and say nothing..." Shakesp., All's
Well, II, ii, 11-12. "Horatio Fizkin, Esquire, touched his hat
to the honourable Samuel Slumkey." Dickens, Pickw., I, p. 213.
Cf. also s.v. HAND, Greeting.

Joy: After departure of an enemy or when one hears of the
misfortune of an enemy, one breaks a pitcher or a pot in joy.
Palest. Bauer, p. 221. Cf. also s.v. HAND, Joy.

Luck: When a Hottentot passes a grave of Heitsi-eibeb, the
god who died several times, he throws a stone on it for good
luck. Frazer, IV, p. 3. Knocking knuckles on piece of wood
indicates that someone has had good luck or that he hopes good
luck will continue. Colombia, U.S. Saitz and Cervenka, p. 82.

Marriage: Cf. s.v. FINGER, Marriage.

Oath: (Cf. s.v. HAND, Oath.) Swearing by a pebble.
Anc. Rom. Grimm, DRA, II, p. 548. Oath sworn before the
church portal, if missal was not used, was not complete unless
swearer touched the doorpost. North Germanic. Grimm, DRA,
II, p. 557. The swearer touches an object with his right hand:
if pagan, the hilt of his sword; if Christian, a relic; if a woman, the left breast and the plait of her hair; if a cleric or
prince, right hand is laid on chest and heart. Grimm, DRA, I,
p. 194. Coachmen touched a wheel, horsemen a stirrup or
horsecollar, sailors the edge of a boat or ship, warriors a
shield or sword, messengers a spear in swearing an oath.
Grimm, DRA, II, pp. 550-551. Two persons clasp hands over
an altar. Bronze hand from Cyrenaica (Leyden, Museum).
Seligmann, II, p. 180. Touching a tree: "Glagerion (?) swore
a full great othe by oake and ashe and thorne." Percy, III,
p. 47. Christians touching an altar. Du Cange, III, col. 1608-
1609. Gregory of Tours, 5, 33: "elevatis manibus super
altarium jurare." Swearing by a sacred ring. Anc. Scand.
Poetic Edda, 248a; Eyrbygg, 10. Jews touched the torah in
swearing. Ohm, p. 244.

Ordering (wine): The classic "horns" gesture (index and
little finger extended, other fingers folded into palm). When the
hand is held vertically rather than horizontally in gesturing
toward a glass, it may mean facetiously "dos dedos de vino."
Lat. Am. Kany, p. 191.

Plea: In some medieval German courts of law (Westphalia)
it was customary that the defendant, upon pleading guilty or innocent, stuck a knife into the ground, saying "I stick the knife
into the ground for mercy," or "I stick it into the ground for
justice." Grimm, DRA, II, p. 385.

Possession: Cf. s.v. HAND, Possession.

Prayer: Touching the altar or image of the deity. Anc.
Rom. Ohm, p. 241.

Refusal: Shake coffee cup with radial motion to decline
another cup of coffee. Saudi Arabia. Semiotic or culture-
induced. Variation: place palm of right hand over cup and
shake a little. Barakat, no. 158.

Relinquishment: Throwing away a straw as symbol for the

relinquishment of a plot of land.   Salic law; Frankish, Bavarian,
Alemannic.   DWb, IV/2, col. 239.
    Remorse: Cf. s.v. HEAD, Remorse.
    Reverence: Touching clerics, relics, sacred images.
Spain.   Ohm, p. 243.   Tibet.   Ohm, p. 241.   Stroking of sacred objects.   Semitic.   Ohm, p. 244.   Cf. s.v. Prayer above.
    Royalty: "The King ascended the throne, put on his helmet
and read the following... speech."   Volkszeitung, Aug. 6, 1866.
    Sacrifice: Before serving coffee a bit of it is poured onto
the ground as sacrifice.   Rwala Bedouin of Kuwait, Iraq, Saudi
Arabia, Syria.   Semiotic or culture-induced.   Barakat, no. 160.
    Submission: Cf. s.v. HAND, Submission.
    Threat: Figure of Death holding a bone horizontally over
his head.   Woodcut, Brant, p. 256.
    Toast: " 'Perhaps a small glass of brandy to drink your
health, and success to Sammy, Sir, wouldn't be amiss.' ... and
Mr. Weller, after pulling his hair to Mr. Pickwick, and nodding
to Sam, jerked it down his capacious throat...."   Dickens,
Pickw., I, pp. 333-334.   Mary, daughter of Simon the leper,
anointed Christ's feet with scent, after which she broke the vessel which had contained it according to ancient usage which consisted in breaking a vessel from which a stranger of distinction
had been served.   Harou, XIII, p. 192.   The English do not
clink glasses but offer their compliments to each other by raising their full glasses to their lips.   Harou, ibid.   Girls break
vessels from which they have offered their betrothed a drink
from the Trevi fountain in Rome before the latter's departure on
a journey.   Harou, XIV, p. 384.   "he leaned over the bowl and
dipped the cup full and they all touched cup edges."   Hemingway,
p. 20.
    Victory: Raising the flag.   Schiller, Tell, IV, ii.   U.S.
Marines, Iwo Jima.   Life (March 26, 1945), pp. 17, 18.

HAND, SHOULDER
Anger: Pulling shoulders in and extending hand.   Anc. Rom.
Baden, p. 451.
    Approval: " 'Quite perfect,' rejoined Fagin, clapping him
on the shoulder."   Dickens, Twist, p. 398.   Also Shakesp.,
Love's Lab. Lost, V, ii, 107; Much Ado, I, i, 261.
    Assurance: " 'I know so little of the gentleman,' said Mr.
Pickwick, hesitating, 'that I--' I know you do,' interposed
Smangle, clasping Mr. Pickwick by the shoulder.   'You shall
know him better...' " Dickens, Pickw., II, p. 270.
    Attention: "Mr. Pickwick was roused... by... a touch on his
shoulder."   Dickens, Pickw., I, p. 69; II, p. 104.   "He
grasped my shoulder convulsively..."   Ibid., I, p. 48.
    Consolation: Cf. s.v. HAND, Consolation.
    Counting: Throwing stones of dates over shoulder while
eating dates: each stone indicates a camel acquired in a raid.
Rwala Bedouin of Kuwait, Iraq, Syria, Saudi Arabia.   Semiotic.
Barakat, no. 134.
    Disbelief: Shoulders hunched, face shows pain, right hand
is jiggled vigorously at approx. chin level as if burned, air is

sucked in suddenly or a quick up and down whistling sound is
made. Sometimes only the index is jiggled: "Ça, c'est un peu
fort!" French. Brault, p. 381.

Encouragement: Clapping someone on the shoulder or patting
him on the back of the hand. Bulwer, p. 78. Colombia, U.S.
Saitz and Cervenka, p. 48.

Favor: Hand brushes shoulder of gesturer: "Apple polish-
ing." Colombia. Saitz and Cervenka, p. 53.

Friendship: Hands laid on other person's shoulders. Anc.
Gk. and Rom. Sittl, pp. 36, 280. Patting another person's
shoulder with right hand: conciliatory. Lebanon, Syria, Jordan,
Saudi Arabia. Autistic or culture-induced. Barakat, no. 31.

Greeting: In the vemic court the secret jurors' greeting
was pronounced while the entering juror placed his right hand
first on his left shoulder, then on those of the other jurors.
Grimm, DRA, I, p. 194.

Helplessness: Lifting up shoulders and holding up hands at
height of head. French. Life (Sept. 16, 1946), p. 12. Lifting
shoulders, turning palms of both hands up. Physiognomic expression determines meaning. Ghetto Jews. Efron, p. 146,
fig. 34.

Ignorance: Shrugging the shoulders, shaking head, raising
right hand, palm up, to level of shoulder, inclining head to one
side. Seton, p. 114. Shrugging shoulders and raising one flat
hand. Seton, p. 105. Shoulders raised, elbows close to body,
hands raised a little to both sides, palms turned up and facing
forward from a position slightly in the rear of the body. France.
Mitton, p. 144. Shrugging shoulders, hands extended, palms up,
head tilted slightly to one side. Arab. Autistic. Barakat, no.
99.

Interrogation: Hand extended slightly, palm up, shrugging
shoulders. ("What were they supposed to do then?") French.
Life (Sept. 16, 1946), p. 12.

Kindness: Hand clapped on shoulder. Shakesp., Much Ado,
I, i, 261; Love's Lab. Lost, V, ii, 107; Troil., III, iii, 139.

Pride: "I even remember the way he imperceptibly removed
his shoulder from under the proud paternal hand, while the
proud paternal voice was saying: 'This boy has just got a Five
Plus (A+) in the Algebra examination.' " Nabokov, pp. 176-177.
Patting oneself on the shoulder with one hand. U.S. Saitz and
Cervenka, p. 97.

Resignation: "The corporal spread his hands and lifted his
shoulders in a gesture of caged resignation." Mexican. Steinbeck, p. 100. "Mr. Scoggan shrugged his shoulders and, pipe
in hand, made a gesture of resignation." Huxley, ch. xxii.

Stop: "it may be said of him that Cupid hath clapp'd him o'
th' shoulder." Shakesp., As You Like It, IV, ii, 43-44.

Submission: Subordinates in ancient Egypt placed right hand
on left shoulder, signifying peaceful intent. An extension of this
gesture was the placing of the left hand on the right shoulder also. Ohm, p. 277.

Uncertainty: Lifting hand to shoulder, palm out, head bent
slightly towards hand. French. Life (Sept. 16, 1946), p. 12.

Urgency: In urgent conversation one person puts his hand on the shoulder of the other. Anc. Gk. Sittl, p. 280.

HAND, SIDE
Jealousy: Hand(s) hit(s) side(s). Reposianus. Sittl, p. 22.

HAND, STAFF
Agreement: In old German law, a symbolic act (vadium) of handing over a staff by a debtor to a creditor establishes their relationship. Ebert, II, col. 215.

Anger: Beating the ground with a stick. Anc. Rom., early Christian. Sittl, p. 15. Dashing scepter to the ground. Odyss., Bk. ii.

Authority: Holding the staff as symbol for the power of kings, princes, judges. Grimm, DRA, I, p. 186. Court was in session as long as the judge held his staff of office; it was adjourned, as soon as he laid it down. Grimm, DRA, II, p. 372; Weisth., IV, p. 305.

Emphasis: Cf. s.v. HAND, Emphasis.

Judgment: Breaking the staff as symbol of proscription. Siuts, p. 115. Breaking of a staff symbolic of the irrevocability of a verdict; for the same reason, when judge and assessor rise for the pronouncement of the verdict, the seats are knocked over (Augsburg, 1511). Grimm, DRA, I, p. 187. Breaking of the staff over the head of the condemned, then throwing its pieces before his feet. Grimm, ibid. Breaking of the staff is mentioned sparsely in sources of the 9th to the 11th century. Siuts, p. 116. In accordance to a Würzburg-Franconian statute of the late Middle Ages, in pronouncing proscription the judge, together with the jury, is to go into the open air and, after his pronouncement, turn east with bare head, place his staff upon the earth, place his hands upon it crosswise, and pronounce the appropriate formula. Siuts, p. 119. According to the custom of the imperial court of justice at Rottweil, the judge, after pronouncing a ban, hurled his staff away if he did not want to render additional verdicts. Siuts, ibid; cf. also Grimm, Weisth., IV, p. 305. The judge broke his staff in pronouncing sentence of death. Oldest evidence of this in German territory is the Tiroler Halsgerichtsordnung of 1499 and the Carolina (1532) of Charles V, art. 96. Siuts, p. 117.

Manumission: Cf. s.v. HAND, Manumission.

Marriage: Medieval Italian painters, in depicting the marriage of Mary and Joseph represented the Entsippung of Mary by the breaking of a staff. Siuts, p. 116.

Oath: Swearing by placing a hand on the judge's staff. Grimm, DRA, II, p. 372. Touching the royal or judge's staff. Grimm, DRA, I, p. 187. Kings and judges touched their staves when they swore an oath. Anc. Gk. Grimm, DRA, II, p. 550; medieval German. Grimm, DRA, I, pp. 186-187.

Possession: Transference of ownership of land is symbolized by transference of a staff. Swiss peasants. Grimm, DRA, I, p. 185; German: Hildesh. Meierd. Stat. para. 3; cf. Grimm, DRA, I, p. 182; French: Roman de Garin, cited by Grimm,

ibid., p. 184. This symbolic act was also performed by princes
in connection with change in sovereignty over larger lands.
Grimm, DRA, I, p. 184.

Rejection: If someone wished to reject his kinship, he appeared in court and broke three or four staves over his head.
Lex Salica. Siuts, p. 116.

Relinquishment: Laying down the staff of office signifies
that the office is relinquished and vacant. Speir. Chron.,
p. 333; Grimm, DRA, I, p. 188. Breaking the staff over the
head of the condemned and casting it at his feet is an expression of the fact that he has no longer cause for hope and re-
linquishes his life. Hence also interdicting the possession of
land by casting a staff. Gulaþingslög 362-3; Grimm, DRA, II,
pp. 187-188.

Submission: Convicted rebels had to swear allegiance and
to carry a white staff the rest of their lives. German, 1576;
prisoners of war carried white staves. Medieval German.
Grimm, DRA, I, p. 185.

Surrender: Carrying a white staff as sign of surrender
German, 1504. Grimm, DRA, I, p. 185.

HAND, STONE

Condemnation: A writ of the Synod of Basel requires that after
publication of anathema, clerics and laymen assemble at the
church door and cast three stones toward the house of those who
have been excommunicated. Siuts, p. 101.

HAND, STRAW

Agreement: At the conclusion of an agreement, both parties
break a straw between them. India. Grimm, DRA, II, p. 146.

Authority: Transference to another of the authority to conduct one's case in a court of law by handing him a straw.
Marc. 1, 21: "omnes causas suas per festucam ei visus est
commendasse."

Manumission: Romans cast away a straw in freeing a slave.
Grimm, DRA, I, p. 178.

Oath: A master acting for his servant had to swear to his
good faith upon a straw. Lex Ripuar., 31 (30, 1); Grimm, DRA,
I, p. 169.

Plea: In a supplication to the king (803) that priests be ex-
empted from military service, the people declare "profitemur
omnes, stipulas dextris in manibus tenentes, easque propriis e
manibus ejicientes,...nec talia facere, nec facere volentibus
consentire." Casting straws. Grimm, DRA, I, p. 170.

Possession: In accordance to a Marculfian formula (1, 13)
the testator casts a straw into the lap of the king, who then be-
stowed the fief upon him for life and to his beneficiary after his
death. Grimm, DRA, I, p. 169. In relinquishing real property
through sale, gift, or attachment, a straw is handed to the new
owner. Grimm, DRA, I, pp. 170-175.

Rejection: A straw is handed, thrown, or grasped by the
judge or one of the participants in a case as sign of renunciation or notice of renunciation. First occurrence: Salic law,

49 (46); Grimm, DRA, I, p. 168. Charles the Simple (879-929) was publicly rejected by throwing straws. Grimm, DRA, I, p. 170.

HAND, TEMPLE (Cf. s.v. HAND, HEAD)
Despair: Hand pressed against temples. Men. Anc. Rom., Mod. Ital. Sittl, p. 22.
  Insult: Slap against temple. Suidas; Hesychius. Sittl, p. 109.
  Punishment: Cf. s.v. Insult above.

HAND, THIGH
Anger: Beating the thighs with fists. Lat. Am. Kany, p. 64. Hitting hand upon thigh. Bulwer, pp. 91-93.
  Horror: Hand slaps thigh. Anc. Gk. and Rom. Sittl, p. 21.
  Impatience: One hand slaps lightly against thigh and remains there for a moment. Often indicates imminent castigation for a child. Colombia. Saitz and Cervenka, p. 73.
  Joy: Hand repeatedly slapped against thigh. Anc. Gk. and Rom. Sittl, p. 12. Vulgar. Taylor, p. 66, n. 35. Kroll, p. 156: "He broke into a laugh, clapping his thigh." Hitting right thigh with palm of right hand. Lebanon, Jordan, Syria, Saudi Arabia. Autistic. Barakat, no. 30.
  Mourning: Beating thighs. Anc. Gk. Sittl, p. 25.
  Oath: "Put thy hand under my thigh." Gen. 24, 2.
  Shame: "I smote my thigh." Jer., 31, 19.
  Sorrow: "Smite therefore upon thy thigh." Ezek. 21, 12.
  Surprise: Hitting right thigh with palm of right hand. Lebanon, Jordan, Syria, Saudi Arabia. Autistic. Barakat, no. 30.

HAND, TONGUE
Disapproval: "Pablo made disapproving clucking noises with his tongue. He spread his hands in front of him. 'What is a man to do?' he asked. 'Is there no one to trust?' " Steinbeck, Tortilla Flat (1937), p. 22.
  Disbelief: Flip hands up and out in front of body and extend the tongue. Saudi Arabia. Semiotic, autistic, or culture-induced. Barakat, no. 210.
  Insult: Sticking out tongue and making the sign of the "fig." Hans Maler, "Christ bearing Cross," (ca. 1488-ca. 1529). Chicago Art Institute.

HAND, TOOTH
Anger: "Mr. Pott, who, stalking majestically towards him, and thrusting aside his proffered hand, ground his teeth, as if to put a sharper edge on what he was about to utter." Dickens, Pickw., I, p. 289.
  Dismay: Biting into one's hand. Pers. Baumg. 2, 18, cited in DWb, IV/2, col. 334.
  Pensiveness: Picking one's teeth. French. Latter half of 16th cent. Lommatzsch, p. 58.

HAND, TORCH
Judgment: At proscription, the judge swung a burning torch
three times. Holland. Brunner, p. 237. In pronouncing anathema or excommunication, the bishop is surrounded by twelve
priests with burning candles. After completion of the sentenc-
ing, the priests cast the candles to the ground and stepped on
them. Siuts, p. 94. The oldest collection of decretals which
mentions this ritual is Regino II, 409. Beginning with the 12th
century it is frequently mentioned in decretals and synods. According to Regino and the Heidelberg codex of the Sachsenspiegel
it was customary to break the burning candles and hurl them
away after the sentence was read. Cf. also Grimm, DRA, I,
p. 269.
   Mourning: At the funeral of an unmarried young man, a
girl walked on each side of the coffin, carrying upon a pillow a
broken candle and a mourning wreath. Teplitz. Siuts, p. 95.

HAND, WEAPON
Accolade: "As for a knight I will make you, and therewith
smote him in the neck with the sword." Malory, Bk. iii, ch.
iii. After the sword belt has been put on, there follows the
blow with the sword, the alapa militaris. This blow, administered by the knight accepting the squire into knighthood, is directed against the neck and accompanied by formal admonitions.
Schultz, I, p. 185. Priest blesses the sword, which is then
belted on the new knight by his lord. Medieval German: Mai u.
Beafl., 83, 39; Klage, 4371. At the coronation of Richard of
Cornwall in Aachen (May 17, 1257) "completo soleniter corona-
tionis officio rex regio venustratis diademate gloriosus effulgans,
in throno Caroli Magni honorifice collocatus filium suum mili-
tiae cingulo decoravit" Thom. Wykes, cited in Schultz, I, p. 182,
n. 5.
   Agreement: As symbol of an agreement to repay for dam-
age inflicted, the debtor hands over a sword to the aggrieved
party, with the understanding that, upon carrying out his part of
the agreement, he will receive it back. Early medieval Spain.
Ebert, II, col. 215. " 'Doña Elvira and Doña Sol are in your
hands, o king. Give them to whom you please and I shall be
content.' 'I thank you and all my court,' said the king. Then
arose the Princes of Carrión and kissed the hands of [the Cid] and
exchanged swords with him in the presence of King Alfonso."
Cid, ii.
   Alarm: Beating shield against chest, calling "to arms, to
arms!" Statius. Sittl, p. 215.
   Chastity: Placing sword between man and woman in bed.
Gottfr. v. Strassburg, 17407-17, cf. also 17486, 17510. Also
medieval French: Trist. 2002 and medieval English: Tristrem
3, 20-22. Similarly, when Brunhild has herself burned with the
body of Sigurd, she has a sword placed between it and her.
Poet. Edda, 225b.
      Death: Cf. s.v. ARM, NECK, Death.
      Defiance: Sword laid across knees of sitting person. Medi-
eval German: Nibelungenlied, st. 1783; Wolfr. v. Eschenb.,

Willehalm, iii, 141, 5; Alpharts Tod, 77, 4-78, 2; cf. Wynne,
pp. 104-114.

Faithfulness: Cf. s.v. HAND, Faithfulness.

Greeting: Spear was thrust into the ground, the free right
hand was raised, the shield was held with the left against an unexpected thrust. Prim. Germ. HDV, I, p. 317.

Investiture: "We here create thee the first Duke of Suffolk,
and girt thee with the sword." Shakesp., II Henry VI, I, i, 59-
60.

Joy: "Those who had been out scouting return and join
them, and their joy is so great that they fall to jousting on the
banks of the Jalón." Cid, c. ii; cf. also c. iii: "[The Cid]
heard that they were coming and swiftly spurred to meet them,
doing mock battle the while because of his great joy." Also
Nibelungenlied, st. 584, 1-3.

Judgment: Proscription was announced by the judge with
the drawn sword. Geldern. Siuts, p. 120. Public beats
weapons together at pronouncement of proscription. Germanic.
Tacitus, ch. xi. A sword on the judge's table or on the knees
of a judge symbolized his jurisdiction over capital crimes.
Medieval Europe. Siuts, p. 120.

Mourning: Soldiers turn weapons to the ground in mourning
a prince. Anc. Rom., 17th cent. German. Sittl, p. 72.
(Cf. s.v. HAND, Mourning.)

Oath: Members of the family of a murdered man and of the
family of the murderer swore upon a weapon that the royal peace
would be kept. Anglo Saxon. Grimm, Myth., I, p. 169f.;
HDA, II, col. 667. Laying down arms, helmet or hat before
kneeling and raising two fingers. Medieval. Grimm, DRA, II,
p. 556. Swearing on a sword. The customary gesture for taking an oath among German freemen. Medieval. Wigamur, 780;
Poet. Edda, 138b; Grimm, DRA, I, pp. 228-229. The Lex
Ripuar. (33, 1 and 66, 1) cites an oath which appears to require raising the sword to heaven. Grimm, Myth., I, p. 169f.
As late as the end of the 14th cent. the Saxons of Siebenbürgen
swore by sticking the bare sword into the earth. ZVK, XVIII
(1908), p. 116. "Come hither, gentlemen, and lay hands again
upon my sword: Never to speak of this that you have heard,
Swear by my sword." Shakesp., Hamlet, I, v, 142. Cf. s.v.
HAND, Oath.

Peace: Messenger takes off his sword on arrival to show
that his message is peaceful. Nibelungenlied, st. 1643, 2.

Sincerity: Hand clapped on sword to show he meant his
word. Butler, pt. I, c. 2, 681.

Superiority: The bridegroom tries to gain power over his
wife by tapping her three or seven times on the head or shoulder with his sword or dagger, or drinking first from the bowl
which he then holds for her to drink from. James, p. 61.

Surrender: The sword is taken by its point and the hilt is
extended to the victor. Voeu du paon, 108059 cited by Grimm,
DRA, I, p. 230. Walk without sword. Waltharius, 64. Sword
is handed over as symbolic for transference of land. Grimm,
DRA, I, p. 230. Laying down one's weapons. Stevenson,
p. 94. Cf. also s.v. FINGER, HAND, Surrender.

HAND, WRIST
  Capture: Captured women are led away by the wrist. Anc.
Rom. Sittl, p. 279.
  Effeminacy: The open right hand clutches the left wrist.
Lat. Am. Kany, p. 181. Left wrist seized by right hand and
moved with a circular motion. Lat. Am. Kany, p. 182.
  Jail: Right hand may seize the left wrist to suggest hand-
cuffing. Lat. Am. Kany, p. 117.
  Leading: Women and children are led by the wrist. Anc.
Gk. and Rom. Sittl, p. 280.

HEAD (Cf. s.v. FACE)
  Acknowledgment: " 'She!' said the old gentleman, with a knowing shake of the head..." Dickens, Pickw., I, p. 297. "Mr.
Pickwick bent his head very slightly in answer to these salutations..." Dickens, Pickw., II, p. 427. "...nodded his head"
in acknowledgment of an introduction. Birdwhistell, Introd.,
p. 34. " 'My name is Slurk,' said the gentleman. The land-
lord slightly inclined his head." Dickens, Pickw., II, p. 395.
  Adoration: "The people bow their heads in adoration when
the Sacred Host is elevated." Mass, p. 53. "At the name
'Jesu Christi,' the priest inclines his head toward the Crucifix."
Mass, p. 49. "I, however, crossed my arms upon my breast,
and piously inclined my head." Heine, cited in DWb IV/2, 601.
  Affection: "Here may his head lie on my throbbing breast."
II Henry VI, IV, iv, 5.
  Affirmation: Head inclined sideways left or right. Bulgaria,
Southern Yugoslavia. Röhrich, p. 14 and pl. 6b. Afghanistan.
Müller, p. 102. " 'Too true; too true, indeed,' said Mrs.
Weller, murmuring a groan and shaking her head assentingly."
Dickens, Pickw., II, p. 285. Dropping head downward and for-
ward. Arab. George, p. 320. A nod is favorable, head
thrown back has an unfavorable meaning. Onians, pp. 139-40,
n. 4. A nod indicating or emphasizing an affirmative answer.
Dickens, Pickw., II, pp. 302, 316, 338, etc. Head inclined in
direction of a pleasing object. Anc. Gk. and Rom. Sittl, p. 92.
Inclining the head and lifting it again. Probably signified originally the submission to another person's will, acc. to Mitton,
p. 141. Portug. Basto, p. 16. " 'Yes, isn't it lovely?' Jenny
replied, giving two rapid little nods." Huxley, ch. iv. Shaking
of the head from side to side. Arab. Goldziher, Zeitschr.,
p. 370. The statement that Arabs shake their heads in affirmation as we do in negation appears to have been initially made by
Petermann, I, p. 172, repeated by Wundt, I, p. 180, and disputed by George, pp. 320-323, cf. above.
  Agreement: Nodding the head. Boggs, p. 322; Colombia,
U.S. Saitz and Cervenka, p. 15; Dickens, Pickw., I, pp. 452,
etc. French. Mitton, p. 141. Anc. Gk. and Rom. Sittl,
p. 92.
  Alarm: "...backing toward the door, and shaking his head
with a kind of sober alarm." Dickens, Twist, p. 408.
  Amazement: Moving the head from side to side horizontally.
HDV, I, col. 323.

Amusement: "Sam said nothing at all. He winked, shook his head, smiled, winked again: and with an expression of countenance which seemed to denote that he was greatly amused with something or other..." Dickens, Pickw., II, p. 118.

Anger: Shaking head. Odyss., Bk. xix. Moving head from side to side horizontally. HDV, I, col. 323. Running with head against pillar. Anc. Rom. Sittl, p. 23. Head inclined forward. Agrippa v. Nettesheim, p. 236.

Antipathy: Head is thrown back on seeing or hearing something unpleasant. Gk. and Ital., Sittl, p. 82.

Apology: "He looked at her fixedly, shook his head..." Birdwhistell, Introd., p. 30.

Appreciation: " 'That 'ere young lady,' replied Sam. 'She knows wot's wot, she does...Mr. Weller closed one eye and shook his head from side to side in a manner which was highly gratifying to the personal vanity of the gentlemen in blue." Dickens, Pickw., II, p. 148.

Approval: Nodding the head. DWb, IV/2, col. 601. Dickens, Pickw., I, p. 218; II, pp. 61, 408, 471. "...said Mr. Gales, nodding his head, approvingly." Dickens, Twist, p. 255. A silent nod of approval. Wodehouse, p. 24.

Arrogance: Head turned and thrown back. Aubert, p. 119. Head raised with a certain delay. Portug. Basto, p. 27.

Assurance: "...and nodding his head again, as much as to say, he had not mistaken his man." Dickens, Twist, p. 338.

Attention: "...head and neck were cocked one eighth to the right... His eyes also were to the right; the brow was furrowed, the mouth somewhat turned down, and the chin tense." Birdwhistell, Colliers (March 4, 1955), p. 57. Turning the head. Aubert, p. 99.

Carelessness: "...she tossed her head with affected carelessness." Dickens, Twist, p. 371.

Challenge: Head turned and thrown back. Aubert, p. 119. Head lifted rapidly. Portug. Basto, p. 26.

Clarification: Moving head (from side to side?) repeatedly and slowly. Portug. Basto, p. 18.

Command: "Fagin nodded to him to take no further notice just then." Dickens, Twist, p. 418. "The old gentleman nodded; and two ragged boys...forthwith commenced climbing up two of the trees." Dickens, Pickw., I, p. 101.

Concentration: Inclining head forward. Medieval German: Graf Rudolf, p. 42, 8-10. Stroking beard, head, moustache. Krout, p. 25.

Confidence: Raising the head. Luke 21, 28; Krukenberg, p. 256.

Confirmation: "...nodding his head in a confirmatory way..." Dickens, Twist, p. 274.

Confusion: Lowering head. Portug. Basto, p. 24. Turning head aside. Ibid.

Contempt: "he eyed him with a look of ineffable contempt... and turned his head another way, in presence of the whole court." Smollett, Pickw., ch. cvi. "she tossed her head in silence with an air of ineffable contempt." Dickens, Pickw., I,

p. 129. "All they that see me laugh me to scorn...they shake the head." Ps. 22, 7. Upward snub of nose executed by throwing head upward and sideward. Women. Spain. Kaulfers, p. 254.

Cuckoldry: A circular movement of the head may indicate a bull, particularly a meek bull. Lat. Am. Kany, p. 190.

Deception: Eyelids half-closed, look to side. Brows drawn together, forced smile. Cheeks raised, wrinkling under eyes. Aubert, p. 102.

Defiance: "shook her head with an air of defiance." Dickens, Twist, p. 173.

Denial: Shaking the head. Shakesp., Much Ado, II, i, 377; Jul. Caes., I, ii, 286; Lear, IV, vi, 122. "shaking her head meanwhile, to intimate that the woman would not die so easily..." Dickens, Twist, p. 212. Also modern Indian. Rose, p. 312.

Depart: Rapid lifting of the head can be a command: "go away." Portug. Basto, p. 37. "But suddenly she closed the book...shaking her head with a backward movement as if to say 'avaunt' to floating visions." Eliot, p. 621.

Depression: Head lowered. Anc. Rom. Sittl, p. 155.

Despair: Head is moved from side to side around its axis. French. Mitton, p. 144. Dickens, Pickw., II, pp. 111, 271, etc. Running with the head against a door. Sueton., Aug. 22.

Direction: " 'She was my daughter,' said the old woman, nodding her head in the direction of the corpse." Dickens, Twist, p. 44. " 'And vere is George?' inquired the old gentleman. Mr. Pell jerked his head in the direction of a back parlour,..." Dickens, Pickw., II, p. 246. Also Portug. Basto, p. 37.

Disagreement: Shaking of the head. Shakesp., King John, III, i, 19; II Henry IV, I, i, 95. " 'That wouldn't quite fit,' replied Fagin, shaking his head." Dickens, Twist, p. 407.

Disapproval: Shaking the head. Job 16, 4, Shakesp., Much Ado, II, i, 377; King John, IV, ii, 231; Timon, II, ii, 211. Anc. Gk. and Rom., mod. Ital. (Manzoni, ch. xv.) Sittl, p. 83. Spain. Green, p. 45. " 'Hush!' said Mr. Jingle, in a stage whisper; '--large boy--dumpling face--round eyes--rascal!' Here he shook his head expressively..." Dickens, Pickw., I, p. 127. "...raised one eyebrow, nodded, moved his head slowly from one side to another." Birdwhistell, Introd., p. 34; cf. also Colliers (March 4, 1955), p. 56. "...and soon he was clucking under his breath and shaking his head every time the patriarch, after much dignified meditation, lurched forward to make a wild move [on the chessboard]" Nabokov, p. 48. Shaking the head with a grimace. Amer. schoolchildren. Seton, p. xx.

Disbelief: Shaking the head. Anc. Gk. and Rom. Sittl, pp. 82-83. " 'I doubt it, my dear young lady,' said the doctor, shaking his head." Dickens, Twist, p. 275. "...exchanging a shake of the head with a lady in the opposite shop, in which doubt and mistrust were plainly mingled..." Dickens, Twist, ch. xxvi. Shaking head. Boggs, col. 322; DWb, IV/2, col. 601. Slowly swinging head from side to side. Amer. schoolchildren.

Seton, p. xxii. Also Portug. Basto, p. 29. Head thrown
back repeatedly in excitement. Anc. Rom. Sittl, p. 82.
"Wardle measured out a regular circle of nods and winks, addressed to the other members of the company. " Dickens,
Pickw., I, p. 301. Turning head aside ("Don't come to me
with a story like that"). Portug. Basto, p. 32. While someone is speaking, turn head or back to him: implies disbelief
or unwillingness to listen further. Jordan, Lebanon, Saudi
Arabia. Autistic, semiotic or culturally determined. Barakat,
no. 5.

Disgust: Head turned away from something, eyes half
closed. Anc. Gk., Rom., early Christian. Sittl, p. 84. Head
turned, glance thrown backward, looking at the despised person
out of the corner of one's eye. Anc. Gk. Sittl, p. 83.

Dislike: Head turned away from something, eyes half
closed. Anc. Gk. and Rom., early Christian. Sittl, p. 84.
Head turned, glance thrown backwards, looking at the despised
person out of the corner of one's eye. Anc. Gk., Sittl, p. 83.
Shaking the head. Job 16, 4; Mark 15, 29.

Dismay: "Next, they switched to the usual shop talk of
European teachers abroad, sighing and shaking heads over the
'typical American college student' who does not know geogra-
phy,..." Nabokov, p. 125.

Ecstasy: Head thrown back. Women. Anc. Gk. and Rom.
Sittl, p. 27.

Effeminacy: Head inclined toward the left. Lat. Am.
Kany, p. 181.

Emphasis: " 'What do you want here?'... 'Nothing, Ma'am,
upon my honor, ' said Mr. Pickwick, nodding his head so energetically that the tassel of his night-cap danced again. " Dickens,
Pickw., I, p. 380. "Mr. Weller delivered this scientific opinion with many confirmatory frowns and nods. " Dickens, Pickw.,
II, p. 288. "Nothing will do that, sir, ' replied the man, shaking his head. " Dickens, Twist, p. 504.

Etiquette: "he would not...give the least nod of civility
when they drank to his health. " Smollett, Pickle, I, ch. ii.
"a courteous nod. " Dickens, Pickw., II, p. 202; Portug.
Basto, p. 20.

Farewell: Lowering head. Cervantes, Galatea, I, p. 57.

Fear: "You were not to be found. Pickwick looked gloomy.
Shook his head. Hoped no violence would be committed.... "
Dickens, Pickw., II, p. 169. Head turned away from supposed
location of deity encountered or addressed. Christian, Buddhist.
Ohm, pp. 177-178.

Flirting: Nods and smiles. Dickens, Pickw., II, p. 405.

Foolishness: "Sometimes the corner cowboys tapped their
heads and laughed, meaning Terry was punchy. " Schulberg,
p. 30.

Gratitude: Head bowed. Late Rom., Byzant. Sittl, p. 155.
Portug. Basto, p. 19.

Gravity: "shaking his head gravely. " Dickens, Twist,
p. 112. "Mr. Bumble shook his head with gloomy mystery. "
Ibid., p. 26.

Greeting: Removal of tip of cloak or cap from head as sign
of respect was required in the presence of Roman officials.
Anc. Rom. Sittl, p. 154. Roman officials in office did not
greet citizens by baring the head, but greeted the vestal virgins
all the more assiduously by stepping aside before them and by
lowering of the fasces on the part of the lictors. Anc. Rom.
Sittl, p. 154. Russian peasants spit on the ground three times
when they meet a cleric. v. Pritzwald, p. 24. Inclining the
head forward. DWb, IV/2, col. 601. Nod in greeting. Dickens, Pickw., I, p. 384. Portug. Basto, p. 20. Head is inclined forward, sometimes together with the upper body, in the
direction of someone. Greeting for ladies; greeting used by men
not wearing a hat. The deeper the bow, the more respectful
the greeting. France. Mitton, p. 142. Hat is lifted from the
head, and in being lifted the hand tips it in direction of someone,
then replaces it on the head. Greeting of men wearing a hat.
France. Mitton, p. 142. (Cf. s.v. HAND, HAT, Greeting.)
Mohammedans finish the ihrām on pilgrimage and at the salāt by
inclining the head to the right and to the left. Ohm, pp. 229-
230. Jews incline the head to the right and left at the end of
the Teffila. Perhaps a remnant of the turning of the body which
was part of Babylonian prayer ritual. Ohm, p. 229. Patting
someone on the head when greeting him. New Zealand. Eichler, p. 162.

Helplessness: Shaking the head. Anc. Gk. and Rom. Sittl,
p. 83.

Hesitation: Head moves slowly from right to left and back.
France. Mitton, p. 144.

Homage: Crusaders entering Jerusalem in 1099 went to the
Holy Sepulchre and offered their capitate tributum to God thus
in the best manuscripts of the Gesta Franc. The editor prefers
the reading debitum rather than tributum. (Cf. p. 206.)

Horror: Slow, repeated movement of the head from side to
side. Portug. Basto, p. 30.

Humility: Bowing the head. Shakesp., All's Well, I, ii,
43. Baring the head. Uhland, p. 362; Schiller, Räuber, II, ii.

Impatience: Shaking the head. Dickens, Twist, p. 229.

Indifference: "...and shaking her head from side to side,
with poor assumption of indifference." Dickens, Twist, p. 143.
Head moves slowly from side to side. Colombia, U.S. Saitz
and Cervenka, p. 91.

Interrogation: Backward nod of the head. Europe, India.
Rose, p. 312; Basto, p. 25.

Introduction: "...swept her head from one side to the other.
As she said the word 'all' she moved her head in a sweep up
and down from one side to the other." Birdwhistell, Introd.,
p. 30.

Irritation: Moving the head from one side to the other,
more or less accompanied by movement of the torso. Mitton,
p. 144.

Memory: Moving head repeatedly and slowly (from side to
side?) Portug. Basto, p. 18. "'Bless my dear eyes,' said
Mr. Roker, shaking his head slowly from side to side...as if

he were fondly recalling some peaceful scene of his early youth."
Dickens, Pickw., II, p. 229.

Misery: "Thus one will lean his head upon another's, the
quicker thereby to excite one's pity." Dante, Purg., c. xiii.

Mockery: "But those passing by blasphemed Him, shaking
their heads." Matth. 27, 39; Mark 15, 29.

Modesty: Head lowered, blushing. Chrétien de Troyes,
Erec 1751, Cligés 5016; Lommatzsch, p. 68.

Mourning: Head covered. Esth. 6, 12. After funeral the
relatives of the deceased return home with bowed head. Anc.
Rom. Sittl, p. 73. Anc. Frisians uncovered head before their
dead but not before the living. HDA, II, col. 850.

Negation: Head raised. Anc. Gk. and Rom. Sittl, p. 93.
Shaking of the head as reenforcement of voiced disapproval or
negation. Vergil, Manzoni (ch. xv); Sittl, p. 83. Shaking of
the head in weak or strong disapproval. Matth. 27, 39; anc.
Gk. and Rom. Sittl, pp. 82-83. Head thrown back repeatedly
in excitement. Anc. Gk. and Rom. Sittl, p. 82. Chin raised
in sudden movement, head back, eyelids half closed, eyebrows
raised. Sometimes accompanied by click of the tongue.
Southern Ital., Balkans, Greece, Albania, Southern Yugosl.,
Bulgaria, Asiatic Turkey, Iran, Iraq, Syria, Palest., Egypt.
Müller, pp. 101-102. Head raised, restricted movement of face,
neck tending to remain stationary. Arab. George, p. 320.
Nodding of the head. African, Arab. Goldziher, Zeitschr.,
pp. 370, 377ff. Shaking head from side to side several times.
Arab. Autistic or culture-induced. Barakat, no. 145. Backward jerk of the head accompanied by clicking the tongue. Near
East. Critchley, pp. 90-91. "He said nothing, only tossed his
head back twice abruptly, which was the Greek way of making a
silent but emphatic 'no!'" MacInnes, p. 184. Chin raised,
head back. Southern Ital., Southern Balkans. Röhrich, p. 14,
and pl. 6a. A nod of the head forward is favorable, the head
thrown back has unfavorable meaning. Onians, pp. 139-140,
n. 4. A click with a toss of the head. India. Rose, p. 213.
Head turned in one direction only. Semitic Ethiop., Sittl, p. 83.
Shaking the head. Ruesch and Kees, p. 33. "Mr. Grummer intimated, by a retrospective shake of the head, that he should
never forget it--" Dickens, Pickw., I, p. 405. "'No, that I
wouldn't,' said Mr. Pell; and he pursed up his lips, frowned,
and shook his head mysteriously." Dickens, Pickw., II, p. 246.
"'Commodore!' said the stranger, starting up, ...'want change
for a five--bad silver--Brummagem buttons--won't do--no go--
eh?' and he shook his head most knowingly." Dickens, Pickw.,
II, p. 12. "but God in Heaven shakes his head." Schiller,
Räuber, V, i. Head thrown back in proud negation of something. 19th cent. German. Sittl, p. 82. Head shaken once or
twice around vertical axis. ("This is wrong." "I refuse.")
France. Mitton, p. 141. Moving head from side to side rapidly. Portug. Basto, p. 29. (Cf. s.v. Affirmation above.)

Nostalgia: Expressions of nostalgia may be accompanied by
slowly lowering and raising the head. Spain, Lat. Am. Green,
p. 63. (Cf. s.v. Memory above.)

Oath: Swearing by one's head. Shakesp., Troil., II, iii, 95; Rom. and Jul., III, i, 38.

Obedience: "Mr. Phunky bowed to Mr. Pickwick with the reverence which a first client must ever awaken; and again inclined his head towards his leader." Dickens, Pickw., II, p. 34.

Penitence: Ashes on head. Uhland, p. 287.

Pensiveness: Eyes closed, head inclined forward, sometimes supported by hand. Medieval French: Roland, 139; medival German: Walther v. d. Vogelweide, miniature in Manesse Ms. Lommatzsch, pp. 45-47. "...and bore my head bowed down, like one whose mind is burdened by his thought, looking like half an archway of a bridge." Dante, Purg. c. xix. Also Schiller, Graf v. Habsb., 111.

Piety: Continuous inclination of the head forward. Palest. Bauer, p. 192.

Pity: Shaking of the head. Shakesp., Ven., 223; Merchant, III, iii, 15; King John, III, i, 19; etc.

Plea: Bowing head. Anc. Gk. and Rom. Sittl, pp. 165, 296.

Pleasure: Head inclined in direction of the pleasing object. Anc. Rom. Sittl, p. 92.

Pointing: "Mr. Pickwick happened to be looking another way at the moment, so her Ladyship nodded her head towards him, and frowned expressively." Dickens, Pickw., II, p. 122. Also extremely common in Spain and understood in Lat. Am. Green, p. 71. (Cf. s.v. Direction above.)

Prayer: Anc. Gks. uncovered head, anc. Rom. covered it. In Africa the Gk. custom predominated. Mod. Gks. and Cypriots uncover head. Sittl, p. 177. Inclining the head forward. Anc. Rom., Christian. Sittl, p. 177. Beating head against post. Anc. Rom. Sittl, p. 185. Priest bows head in prayer. Mass, pp. 21, 52. Head inclined to the side--once common, no longer favored by Christians. Ohm, p. 229.

Pride: Head thrown back in proud negation of something. German. 19th cent. Sittl, p. 82. Head held high: "But now Truth is victorious and holds her head high." Luther, cited in DWb IV/2, col. 600.

Recognition: "the knowing nod." Birdwhistell, Colliers (March 4, 1955), p. 56.

Refusal: Head thrown back. Anc. Gk. and Rom., mod. Gk. and Ital. Sittl, p. 82. Children turn head to side to refuse food or to refuse being taken on one's arm. Sittl, ibid. Shaking the head. Dickens, Pickw., II, p. 20. Head turns one or two times vertically around its axis. France. (In China, inclination of the head indicates negative, the above positive.) Mitton, p. 141. (Cf. s.v. Affirmation and Negation above.)

Regret: "The surgeon shook his head, in a manner which intimated that he feared it impossible." Dickens, Twist, p. 265.

Remorse: Putting ashes on one's head. II Sam. 13, 19; Jer. 6, 26; Job 42, 6.

Repetition: Quick jerk of the head to one side indicates that the person has not understood what has been said and that it is to be repeated. Lebanon. Semiotic or culture-induced.

Barakat, no. 245.

Reproach: "He shook his head reprovingly." Wodehouse,
p. 73.   Slow swinging movement of the head. Portug. Basto,
p. 18.

Respect: Bowing the head. Gen. 43, 28.   Removal of tip
of cloak or cap from head as sign of respect was required in
the presence of Roman officials. Anc. Rom. Sittl, p. 154.
Slave lowers his head in the presence of his master. Anc. Gk.,
Rom., Arab. Sittl, p. 155.   "Mr. Pickwick, who, as the spokes-
man of his friends, stood hat in hand, bowing with the utmost
politeness and respect." Dickens, Pickw., I, p. 414.   Turning
head aside when addressing a superior or overlord. Schilluk,
Chinese. Ohm, p. 177.

Rest: Head leaning on one palm, inclined towards one
shoulder.   To indicate sleep, one closes one's eyes, to indicate
rest, one keeps them open. Neapol. De Jorio, p. 144.

Reverence: Standing with bowed head. Mass, p. 28. "But
I held my head bowed down like one who goes reverently."
Dante, Inf., c. xv.   In China the subjects have to turn their
face away when the Emperor speaks with them, so that he will
not be contaminated.   Moses hid his face when God appeared in
the thornbush, for he feared the aspect of God. Ohm, p. 177.

Satisfaction: Nodding the head. Dickens, Pickw., II,
p. 331.   Raising the head with anticipation. Portug. Basto,
p. 28.

Secrecy: Looking in both directions before speaking.   Spain.
Green, p. 43.

Self-importance: "Does he not hold up his head, as it were,
and strut in his gait?" Shakesp., Merry Wives, I, iv, 30.

Shame: Head lowered. Chrétien de Troyes, Yvain 1785;
Dante, Purg., c. xxxi; Lommatzsch, p. 72. Portug. Basto,
p. 24.

Sorrow: "The virgins of Jerusalem hang their heads down
to the ground." Lament. 2, 10.   "And he wept as he went up,
and had his head covered, and he went barefoot." II Sam. 15,
30.   Hiding face in pillow. Stage direction, Schiller, Räuber,
II, ii.   Putting dust on one's head. Josh. 7, 6. Ashes on
head. II Sam. 13, 19.   Shaving the head. Job, 1, 20.   Head
shaken in sorrow. Anc. Gk., Rom., mod. Ital. (Manzoni, c.
xiv.) Sittl, p. 83. Shakesp., Merchant, III, iii, 15; King John,
III, i, 19; etc.   Hanging head in grief.   Shakesp., I Henry VI,
III, ii, 124; Lucr., 521.   Bowing the head. Boggs, col. 319.
"The tear...stole down the old lady's face, as she shook her
head with a melancholy smile." Dickens, Pickw., I, p. 87.
" 'My dear young lady,' rejoined the surgeon, mournfully shaking his head." Dickens, Twist, p. 265.

Submission: Mod. Gks. still bow head before the demons
in a cyclone.   Sittl, p. 177.   Fearful people passed the Grotta
di Posilippo near Naples only with bowed head. Anc. Rom.
Sittl, p. 177.   Lowering head and keeping it lowered. Portug.
Basto, p. 20.   Bared head. Schiller, Räuber, II, ii.   Uhland,
p. 362.

Surprise: Slow, repeated movement of head from side to

side. Portug. Basto, p. 30.
    Surrender: Head inclined forward. Anc. Gk. Sittl, p. 114.
    Sympathy: Shaking of the head. Dickens, Pickw., II,
pp. 409, 456.
    Threat: Head is moved rapidly laterally in threat of punish-
ment, esp. to children. Portug. Basto, p. 35.
    Uncertainty: Head sways slowly right and left, evoking
balance between two viewpoints. France. Mitton, p. 144.
    Understanding: "Sam gave a short nod of intelligence."
Dickens, Pickw., I, p. 438; II, p. 211. Sudden raising of head,
often accompanied by raising hand or index to head. Portug.
Basto, p. 28. Head raised very slowly ("Now I see.... ")
Portug. Basto, ibid.
    Warning: Slow swinging movement of the head. Portug.
Basto, p. 18.

HEAD, KNEE
    Humility: Anc. Rom. knelt before altars and images of deities,
often on the threshold of the temple, and bowed the head. Sittl,
p. 178.
    Prayer: Cf. s.v. Humility above.
    Protection: Back of head placed on knees of friend in order
to rest. Lombard, Byzant., mod. Gk., German. Sittl,
pp. 34-35.
    Sorrow: Head sinks down between knees, in sitting or
squatting position. Anc. Rom. Sittl, p. 24. Head sinks down
upon knees while sitting or squatting. Anc. Gk. and Rom.
Sittl, p. 24.

HEAD, LIP
    Apology: Kissing the top of another man's head after quarrel-
ing. Saudi Arabia. Semiotic. Barakat, no. 120.
    Contempt: "They shoot out the lip, they shake the head."
Ps. 22, 7.
    Disbelief: Lips tight, slowly widening; sometimes head
nods, accompanied, in English, by "m-hmmm." Colombia,
U.S. Saitz and Cervenka, p. 40.
    Greeting: Kiss on the head. Anc. Gk. Sittl, p. 41.
    Insolence: Head thrown back, frown, slight protrusion of
lower lip. Aubert, p. 113.
    Negation: Cf. s.v. HEAD, Negation.
    Pointing: "Chepe jerked his head toward the hut and pointed
with his lower lip. 'That's where the mosquitoes are.' " A.
Carr, The Windward Road (New York, 1956), p. 175, cited by
Hayes, p. 234. This is the usual way of pointing to objects in
Costa Rica and other Central American countries. Pointing
with the finger is tabu. In Kenya, Brit. East Africa, the lips
are similarly used for pointing. Hayes, ibid.
    Pride: Cf. s.v. Insolence above.
    Resignation: Head inclined slightly and slowly to one side,
frequently accompanied by twist of lip and clicking of the tongue.
Portug. Basto, p. 36.

Respect: Children kiss the top of their mother's head during Moslem holy days. Saudi Arabia. Semiotic. Barakat, no. 119.

HEAD, OBJECT
Oath: The Saxons of Siebenbürgen, in swearing oaths in connection with boundary disputes, swore with bare feet, loosened belt, and a clump of earth on the head. ZVK, XVIII (1908), p. 116.

HEAD, SHOULDER
Apotropy: Shrugging shoulders and shaking head: "As they sallied forth from Bivar they beheld a bird of happy augury, and as they drew nigh to Burgos, one of evil omen! But my Cid shrugged his shoulders and shook his head." Cid, c. i. (Cf. also s.v. Indifference below.)
Fear: Head drawn in between shoulders. Quintil., XI, 3, 90.
Indifference: Shrugging shoulders and shaking head. Amer. schoolchildren. Seton, xxiii. (Cf. also s.v. Apotropy above.)
Joy: "and, drawing his head and shoulders into a heap, literally hugged himself for joy." Dickens, Twist, p. 174.

HEAD, TONGUE
Negation: Clicking the tongue, head simultaneously moved back. Italy, Greece. Sittl, p. 96; Palest. Bauer, p. 220.
Resignation: Head inclined slightly and slowly to one side, frequently accompanied by a twist of the lip and clicking of the tongue. Portug. Basto, p. 36.

HEAD, TOOTH
Anger: Biting lower lip with upper teeth and shaking head from side to side. Saudi Arabia. Autistic. Barakat, no. 154.
Disapproval: Shaking head from side to side and snicking [?] teeth simultaneously. Arab. Semiotic or culture-induced. Barakat, no. 146.
Pensiveness: Cf. s.v. HAND, Pensiveness.
Vengeance: Grinding the teeth and shaking the head while raising it gradually. Palest. Bauer, p. 218.

HEAD, THIGH
Disappointment: "whereat he strikes his thigh, returns indoors, and grumbles here and there." Dante, Inf., c. xxiv.

HEEL
Contempt: Kicking with heels. Anc. Rom. Sittl, pp. 106-107.
Displeasure: Kicking seats of theater with the heels. Pollux 2, 4. 4, 19.
Mockery: Cf. s.v. Contempt above.

HIP
Copulation: Elbows held on respective hips, hips moved back and forth rapidly. Saudi Arabia. Semiotic. Barakat, no. 236.

JAW

Decisiveness: Protruding lower jaw. Krout, p. 24.

KNEE

Accolade: "Iden, kneel down...Rise up a knight." Shakesp.,
II Henry VI, V, ii, 78.

Adoption: In Gen. 30, 3 Rachel gives Bilhah to Jacob so
that she may "bear on my knees," and in Gen. 50, 23 the
children of Marchir the son of Manasseh were brought up "upon
Joseph's knees." This alludes to the custom of placing infants
on the father's knees as symbol of their adoption. Cf. also
Odyss., Bk. xix; Fischer, Antaios, II, p. 342.

Adoration: According to the Ordinal of Gregory X, the
pope, assisting at a Mass in his own chapel, first rises just
before the consecration, then, his head uncovered, kneels to
adore the sacrament. Ladner, p. 269. Pious Romans fell on
knees on the threshold of the temple and kissed it. Sittl, p. 184.
Stiff, almost military genuflection. Anc. Rom. Ohm, p. 47.
"[the priest] genuflects once more in adoration of the Precious
Blood of Christ now contained under the appearance of wine."
Mass, p. 57. In reference to the influence of Jupiter: Agrippa
v. Nettesheim, p. 236. Women kneel on both knees, men on
one. Portug. Basto, p. 9.

Attention: "turned and thrust both knees into the lateral
aspect of her left side." Desire for attention while sitting. Women. Birdwhistell. Backgr., p. 14.

Confession: "Then I confess, here on my knee, before high
heaven and you." Shakesp., All's Well, I, iii, 182-183.

Determination: "Nathaniel Pipkin went down on his knees
on the dewy grass, and declared his resolution to remain there
forever..." Dickens, Pickw., I, p. 283.

Distress: "Then down upon her knees she falls, weeps,
sobs, beats her heart, tears her hair, prays, curses..."
Shakesp., Much Ado, II, iii, 134-5.

Fear: The handwriting upon the wall so frightened Belshaz-
zar that "his knees smote one against the other." Dan. 5, 6.

Gratitude: "I will kneel to him with thanks." Shakesp.,
Anth. and Cleo., V, ii, 20. "The parson fell on his knees and
ejaculated many thanksgivings..." Fielding, Andrews, Bk. iv,
ch. 12. Women kneel on both knees, men on one. Portug.
Basto, p. 9.

Homage: Kneeling as form of homage was unknown in anc.
Greece and Rome. Euripides regards it as a curiosity in his
Phoen. Sittl, p. 156.

Humility: Kneeling. Dan. 6, 10; II Chron. 6, 13; Luke
22, 41; etc. (Cf. s.v. Prayer below.) Shakesp., II Henry VI,
I, i. Mocking humility: Mark 15, 19: "And they struck Him
on the head with a reed and spat on Him. And bending their
knees, they bowed down to Him."

Oath: "O Warwick, I do bend my knee with thine; and in
this vow do chain my soul to thine!" Shakesp., III Henry VI,

II, iii, 33-4.

Plea: (Cf. also s.v. LIP, Homage.) Matth. 17, 14; II
Kings 1, 13: "fell on his knees before Elijah and begged him."
"By my advice, all humbled on your knees, you shall ask pardon of his Majesty." Shakesp., Tit., I, i, 472-3. Bending the
knee in pleading was frequent during the Roman empire. Sittl,
p. 156. Romans knelt on one or both knees in prayer or supplication. Sittl, p. 178. Bending the knee accompanies a request for faithfulness (never a declaration of love). Tibull. 1,
9, 30. Ambassadors kneel before the Roman senate and defeated kings kneel before victorious generals. Sittl, p. 156.
Doña Elvira and Doña Sol kneel before their father, the Cid.
Cid, c. iii. Medieval German: Kaufringer, no. 1, 324-330,
no. 2, 229. "A conqueror that will pray in aid for kindness
where he for grace is kneel'd to." Shakesp., Anth. and Cleop.,
V, ii, 27-28. "I would you had kneel'd, my lord, to ask me
mercy." Shakesp., All's Well, II, i, 66. "Mrs. Grizzle...fell
upon her knees in the garden entreating her, with tears in her
eyes to resist such a pernicious appetite." Smollett, Peregr.
Pickle, I, v, vi. "Mr. Tupman had sunk upon his knees at her
feet. 'Oh, Rachel! say you love me.'" Dickens, Pickw., I,
p. 119. "Mr. Jingle fell on his knees, remained thereupon for
five minutes thereafter: and rose the accepted lover of the
spinster aunt." Dickens, Pickw., I, p. 130.

Possession: Bride is placed upon the knee of the groom.
Svenska Folkv. II, 18, 24, 167, etc. Weise, Comödienprobe,
333, 334. (Cf. s.v. Adoption above.)

Prayer: "The custom of not kneeling on the Lord's day is
symbolic of the resurrection." Irenaeus, Fragm. 7. Kneeling
in prayer. Anc. Egypt., Phoenician. (Heliodor.); Sittl, p. 178,
n. 8. The worshipper kneels and holds his hands before him,
extended downward, with fingers extended. Brunet, p. 207.
For St. Paul the expressions "to pray" and "to bend the knee"
to God are complementary. Phil. 2, 10; Eph. 3, 14. Adding
solemnity to prayer: Solomon dedicated his temple "kneeling
down in the presence of all the multitude of Israel and lifting up
his hands toward heaven." II Par. 6, 13; III Kings, 8, 54.
For other instances, cf. Hastings, Dict., p. 8; Ohm, pp. 346ff.
Anc. Gk. women fell on their knees before images of deities.
Sittl, p. 186. The anc. Gks., though maintaining the propriety
of kneeling only before gods, left this to women and children.
Sittl, p. 178. Only women and bigots among anc. Gks. knelt
in prayer. Sittl, p. 177. Romans knelt on one or both knees
in prayer or supplication. Sliding forwards on the knees in the
temple. Tibull. Sittl, p. 178. Kneeling at the threshold of
the temple. Petron. Sittl, p. 178. "The knee is made flexible
by which the offence of the Lord is mitigated, wrath appeased,
grace called forth." Ambrose, VI, ix; Hraban. II, xli. When
forgiveness of some offence is sought, Origen maintains that
kneeling is necessary. Cath. Encycl. I, col. 423-427. "Kneel,
and pray your mother's blessing." Shakesp., Winter's Tale, V,
iii, 119. Kneeling in prayer. Shakesp., Henry VIII, IV, i, 83-
85. "The innkeeper...fell upon his knees, protesting, in the

face of heaven, that he was utterly ignorant." Smollett, Peregr.
Pickle, I, ch. lviii.

Respect: Anc. Egyptians bowed the knee to Joseph. Gen.
41, 43. Women kneel on both knees, men on one. Portug.
Basto, p. 9.

Reverence: Moving on knees. Rom. Catholic; Brazil; Ohm,
p. 357. "I had knelt down." Dante, Purg., c. xix. Cf. also
Ohm, pp. 344ff. Women kneel on both knees, men on one.
Portug. Basto, p. 9.

Submission: "Mind, mind, thou bend thy knees." Dante,
Purg., c. ii. "Then jointly to the ground their knees they bow."
Shakesp., Lucr. 1846. Medieval German: Kaufringer, no. 2,
82-84, 113, 151. Kneeling on one or both knees. Anc. Gk.
and Rom. Sittl, p. 158. Proskynesis was also practiced before miracle workers. Early Christian. Sittl, p. 160. Bending the knee in pleading was frequent during Roman empire.
Slave bends knee before master. Sittl, p. 156. Proskynesis
as permanent part of court etiquette was established by Diocletian in 290; not even relatives of the emperor were exempt. It
was practiced at the court of Elagabalus, but discontinued by
Severus Alexander. It was not officially part of court ceremonial under Caligula, but was performed voluntarily; discontinued
under Claudius. Sittl, p. 159. No proskynesis in the early
Empire, except for Asiatics, Egyptians, and defeated or won-
over barbarians. Sittl, ibid. Alexander the Great insisted on
traditional proskynesis; since the Gks. regarded this as an honor
due to the gods only, Alexander declared himself a god, which
some of his successors imitated. Sittl, p. 158. Avar ambassadors knelt thrice before Justinian. Cf. three bows in Wil-
helmine German audiences with the Kaiser. This was adopted
from Roman imperial court etiquette by the papal court. Sittl,
p. 156.

Surrender: Defeated kings kneel before the emperor. Anc.
Rom. Sittl, p. 156. Ambassadors kneel before the Roman
senate and defeated kings kneel before victorious generals.
Sittl, ibid.

Victory: "Parzival brought him down and planted one knee
on his chest." Wolfr. v. Eschenbach, IV, 197.

KNEE, LIP (Cf. s.v. LIP, Homage.)
Respect: Combination of throwing a kiss and kneeling on one
knee appears to be Semitic. Sittl, p. 152. Kissing someone's
knee. Iliad, Odyss. Sittl, p. 169.

LEG
Attention: Kicking legs in desire for attention. Birdwhistell,
Backgr., p. 14.
Calmness: Crossed legs. 15th cent. French. Lommatzsch,
p. 39. 13th cent. German: Walther v. d. Vogelweide, 8, 5
and the miniature in the Heidelberg Codex C; also Oechelhäuser,
Miniat., p. 69, no. 103. Prescribed position for judges in deliberation. Grimm, DRA, II, p. 375. Comfort: Sercambi,
pp. 364-65; Mont. Fabl. I, pp. 307-308; Weissel, p. 8;

Lommatzsch, p. 35.

Concentration: Cf. s.v. BODY, Concentration.

Ecstasy: "'Ha! Ha!' roared Mr. Claypole, kicking up his legs in an ecstasy." Dickens, Twist, p. 406.

Greeting: Bending one knee, while kneeling on the other, formerly a court gesture, later taken over by the church, shows reverence or homage paid to a nobleman, ecclesiastical superior, statue or fetish. Stoebe, p. 184. "Let them curtsy with their left legs." Shakesp., Shrew, IV, i, 80.

Joy: Leaping for joy. Luke 6, 23; II Sam. 6, 16. Anc. Rom. Sittl, p. 12. Dancing for joy. Anc. Gk. Sittl, ibid. Cf. also Boggs, col. 320.

Judgment: Crossed legs prescribed for judges during deliberations. Grimm, DRA, II, p. 375 (right over left leg). Cf. also Lacroix, p. 71, Cour d'amour provençale au XIVe siécle.

Magical: Women sit cross-legged to procure good luck. Opie, p. 228. Crossing legs prevents birth as well as other processes. Anc. Rom. Meschke, ed. 336; Röhrich, p. 29.

Oath: Oaths are invalidated by the crossing of legs. Agrippa v. Nettesheim therefore says it is prohibited in deliberations of state. Röhrich, p. 29.

Prayer: Right leg hangs down to the earth, left leg is extended horizontally in front of body. Mañjustri-position. Buddhist. Ohm, p. 333. Approaching the deity by running. Anc. Egypt. Brunet, p. 560. Pious Japanese show their piousness by walking hundreds of times back and forth from the entrance to the Shinto shrine to the shrine itself. Ohm, p. 307. At the Trisaghion of Schmone Esre the Jews jump up three times; the same happens at a certain passage in the morning prayer. Probably a remnant of a primitive ritual which was taken over by early Christianity from Judaism. Heiler, p. 101.

Pride: "Why, 'a stalks up and down like a peacock." Shakesp., Troil., III, iii, 251.

Protest: "drew his legs up against the restraint of his mother's hand." Birdwhistell, Backgr., p. 14.

Recognition: "...and knocked gently at the door. It was at once opened by a woman, who dropped a curtsy of recognition." Dickens, Pickw., I, p. 361.

Respect: "Let them curtsy with their left legs." Shakesp., Shrew, IV, i, 80.

Sorrow: Pacing back and forth. Boggs, p. 319.

Surprise: Staggering backwards. Boggs, col. 321. Jumping up from a sitting position. Anc. Gk. and Rom. Sittl, p. 13.

LIP

Acceptance: Immediately after baptism, according to Hippolytus and Cyprian, the baptist and the Christians kiss the neophyte. Similarly, in antiquity a new member of a collegium was kissed by those accepting him. The custom still obtains in Russia. Ohm, p. 220.

Acknowledgment: "Many a kiss did Mr. Snodgrass waft in the air, in acknowledgment of something very like a lady's handkerchief." Dickens, Pickw., I, p. 165.

Admiration: Kiss (among men). Anc. Rom. Sittl, p. 38.
Adoration: Woman kissing Christ's feet. Luke 7, 38.
Pious Romans fell on their knees on the threshold of the temple
and kissed it. Sittl, p. 184. Deified, beautiful women were addressed with a compliment accompanied by the gesture of throwing a kiss. Anc. Gk. and Rom. Sittl, p. 183. Worshipper of
the sun god kisses the legs of the latter's horses. Sittl, p. 184.
Thresholds of churches are kissed. Early Christian. Sittl,
ibid. Wounds, bloody garments, reliques, instruments of torture connected with religious martyrdom are kissed. Early
Christian. Sittl, p. 184, also n. 7. Greek orthodox kiss
saints' images and gospels. Sittl, p. 184. Roman Catholics
kiss crucifix. Sittl, ibid. Mementos of saints are kissed.
Early Christian. Sittl, ibid. Priest kisses altar. Mass, p. 65.
Affection: "Dost thou come to kiss this child? I suffer
thee not to kiss it." Anc. Egypt. papyrus, Berlin 3027, r. 2,
1-2, containing apotropaic spells. Dawson, p. 85. "Pharaoh
perceived him, and...folded him into his arms, he placed his
mouth on his mouth, and kissed him at length in the manner in
which a man salutes his betrothed." Anc. Egypt. Maspero,
p. 261. "If I kiss her and her lips are open, I am happy..."
Anc. Egypt. love poem. Dawson, p. 84. The Ephesians kissed
Paul. Acts 20, 37. Parents kiss sons and daughters: Gen.
31, 28. 55; 48, 10; Ruth 1, 9. Brother kisses brother: Gen.
33, 4; sister kisses brother: Song of Sol. 8, 1; male cousin has
same right as brother, e.g. Jacob kisses Rachel, Gen. 29, 11;
children kiss parents: Gen. 27, 26; Joseph kisses dead father,
Gen. 50, 1. Kiss as token of love between sexes seldom mentioned in the Old Testament, plays no role in the New Testament: Song of Sol. 1, 2; Prov. 7, 13 (pejorative). Christ and
apostles kiss each other: Matth. 26, 48. "And...she laid her
left arm about his neck, longing to kiss his tender mouth."
Apoll. Rhod., I, 1236, 8. "Hence no Egyptian man or woman
will kiss a Greek on the mouth." Herodot., ii, 41. Men kiss
men. Anc. Gk. and Rom. Sittl, p. 36. Men and women kiss
each other. Anc. Rom., only in the imperial period and later.
Sittl, ibid. Kiss given to slaves. Hellenist. and Rom., Byzant.
Sittl, p. 37. Kissing while the person being kissed is being
held under the hand. Anc. Gk. Sittl, p. 39. Kissing the earth
of the land which one leaves forever. Anc. Gk. and Rom.
Sittl, p. 42. "He kiss'd the ground that he had set his foot
on." Defoe, II, p. 152. Kissing footstep of the beloved.
Hellenistic. Sittl, p. 42. Kissing address on a letter to a
friend. Hellenistic. Sittl, p. 42. Slave kisses object belonging to his master or mistress in their absence. Anc. Gk.
Sittl, p. 172. Loyal subject kisses object sent by the emperor,
such as a message. Late Gk., anc. Rom., Byzant. In mod.
Gk. orthodox and 19th cent. Turkish, the missive, after being
kissed, is held against forehead. Sittl, p. 172. Kissing vehicle
of departing husband. Anc. Gk. Sittl, p. 41. Wife kisses
ring with husbands picture. Anc. Gk. and Rom., Sittl, p. 41.
Persians kiss vehicle of Callirhoë. Anc. Gk., Sittl, ibid.
Ceres kisses spinning wheel of abducted daughter. Anc. Rom.,

Sittl, ibid. Kissing urn. Anc. Rom. Sittl, ibid. Kissing door
of the beloved. Anc. Rom. Sittl, ibid. Anc. Rom. regarded
kissing a woman in public as indecent: the elder Cato threw
Manilius out of the senate, "because, in the presence of his
daughter, and in open day, he had kissed his wife." Plut.,
Marcus Cato. A man kissing his marriageable daughter was
punishable by police. Anc. Rom. Sittl, p. 39. "He kissed
both old men affectionately." Medieval German: Kudrun, st.
474, 1. "And then he put his arms around my neck and kissed
my face." Dante, Inf., c. viii. "kindly kissed my cheek."
Shakesp., Richard III, II, ii, 24. Kissing hand at time of departure can indicate affection. Shakesp., Much Ado, IV, i, 336.
Affection for parents: Shakesp., Gent., II, iii, 28. Kiss as
token of love: Venus 18, 84, etc. Gent., I, ii, 116; Measure
IV, i, 5; Much Ado II, i, 322; etc. "Mrs. Colonel Wugsby
kissed her eldest daughter most affectionately." Dickens, Pickw.,
II, p. 123. "The worthy old gentleman pulled Arabella's ear,
kissed her without the smallest scruple, kissed his daughter also
with great affection..." Dickens, Pickw., II, 452. "He [Mr.
Tupman] jumped up, and, throwing his arm round the neck of
the spinster aunt, imprinted upon her lips numerous kisses."
Dickens, Pickw., I, p. 119. "having made clear work of it in
no time, kissed his daughter, and demanded his pipe." Ibid.,
p. 286. "if you try and kiss me again I shall box your ears."
Huxley, ch. xxix. Taking someone by the neck or the shoulders,
then putting the lips on his forehead, or on his cheeks, or on
his lips. France. Mitton, p. 141.
    Agreement: "Alan whistled. 'By Gad, I believe you're
right.'" Carr, Suicides, p. 156.
    Anger: Lips pressed together. Anc. Rom. Sittl, p. 24.
Trembling lips. Anc. Rom. Sittl, p. 15. Biting the lip.
Shakesp., Shrew, II, i, 241; Richard III, IV, ii, 27; Othello,
V, ii, 46. "'Get on!' said Mrs. Proudie, moving her foot un-
easily on the hearth-rug, and compressing her lips in a manner
that betokened much danger to the subject of their discourse."
Trollope, Barchester, ch. xxxiii. "At last, biting her thin lips,
and bridling up..." Dickens, Pickw., I, p. 129. Biting one's
lips to check the flow of words. Lat. Am. Kany, p. 64.
    Appreciation: Smacking lips. ("That tastes good.") Amer.
schoolchildren. Seton, p. xxiii.
    Approach: Master whistles to summon servant. Clement
of Alex., Paedag.; Sittl, p. 223.
    Attention: Pursing lips. Children. Krukenberg, p. 111.
    Brotherhood: Kiss among men: newly entering robber
kisses members of a robberband. Anc. Rom. Sittl, p. 38.
As token of Christian brotherhood: Rom. 16, 16; I Cor. 16, 20;
II Cor. 13, 12; I Thess. 5, 26; I Pet. 5, 14. In time this became the osculum pacis (Const. Apost., II, 57. 12; VIII, 5. 5;
Tertull., de Orat., 14), which was first given promiscuously,
later only by men to men and women to women. Hastings, Dict.,
p. 6. The confirmed kiss each other after Eucharist. Ohm,
p. 220. Men kiss men, women kiss women, entire congregation
kisses priest at Easter. Eastern Orthodox. Ohm, p. 222.

Baptist kisses neophyte after baptism.   Cyprian; Hippolyt.; Russian.   Ohm, p. 220.

Calmness: Osculum pacis.   Medieval German: Eilhart 1646, 1650; Grimm, DRA, I, p. 198.

Concentration: Pursing lips.   Krout, p. 21.   (Cf. s.v. Attention above.)

Condescension: Absalom kisses the people.   II Sam. 15, 5; 19, 39: David kisses Barzilai.   Also Schiller, Don Carlos, I, i; Piccol., II, ii.

Congratulation: Kiss among men.   Anc. Rom.   Sittl, p. 38.

Consolation: After a funeral, the relatives of the deceased kiss each other, then the other mourners form a lane through which the relatives walk in order to be kissed by the other mourners.   Palest.   Bauer, pp. 169-170.

Contempt: "All they that see me laugh me to scorn: they shoot out the lip."   Ps. 22, 7.   Spitting.   Anc. Gk.   Sittl, p. 91.   Spitting three times into bosom.   Anc. Gk. and Rom. Sittl, ibid.   Lips closed, pushed out and up.   Hellenist. and anc. Rom.   Sittl, p. 89.   "and lifting up her lip in contempt." Richardson, Clarissa, I, p. 44.

Curse: "Valachi said Genovese started talking about apples that are 'touched, not all rotten but touched.'   Finally Genovese said good night.   'He grabbed my hand and he gave me a kiss, so I gave him a kiss on the other side.'   'Is that some kind of ritual?' asked McClellan.   'No, that was a suspicious kiss. And Ralph mumbles under his breath 'Hmm, the kiss of death... An outsider like Ralph, he even was wise, so ain't I supposed to be smart?'"   Kiss of Death.   Cosa nostra.   L.A. Times (Sept. 28, 1963), p. 11.

Debauchery: Licking lips as if inebriated; belching as if replete.   Anc. Rom.   Baden, p. 455.

Deception: False kiss.   Prov. 27, 6; Luke 22, 47. 48.

Disagreement: Lips closed, pushed out and up.   Hellenist. and anc. Rom.   Sittl, p. 89.

Disappointment: Biting lower lip.   Aubert, p. 105.

Disapproval: "He hangs the lip at something."   Shakesp., Troil. III, i, 132.

Dislike: Spitting to the right and left (particularly dislike of an aroma).   Sittl, p. 91.   Lips closed, pushed up and out. Hellenist., anc. Rom.   Sittl, p. 89.   Hissing.   Isidor of Pelusium.   Sittl, p. 64.   Whistling.   Anc. Gk. and Rom.   Sittl, ibid.

Embarrassment: Licking one's lips.   Birdwhistell, Introd., p. 34.

Etiquette: Certain ranks of court officials kissed the tip of the emperor's cloak.   This probably began with Diocletian. Anc. Rom.   Sittl, p. 170.   Kissing the ground on which the emperor has trodden.   Oriental and late Rom.   Sittl, p. 171. "this is he that kiss'd his hand away in courtesy."   Shakesp., Love's Lab. Lost, V, ii, 323.   Women standing under mistletoe may be kissed.   Dickens, Pickw., I, p. 480.

Familiarity: Kissing among the sexes was permitted among relatives.   Anc. Rom.   Sittl, p. 38.   In Gaul it was still com-

mon during the late empire. Sittl, p. 39. Among men. Ibid.
Woman kisses man. The only anc. Gk. evidence: mother-in-
law kisses husband of her daughter. Quint. Smyrn. Sittl,
p. 38.

Farewell: Laban kisses sons and daughters. Gen. 31, 55.
Naomi and daughters-in-law. Ruth 1, 9. 14. Brides, upon
leaving home, kiss doors, beds, walls. Anc. Gk. and Rom.
Sittl, p. 42. Kissing the earth of the land which one leaves
forever. Anc. Gk. and Rom. Sittl, ibid. "Hagen kissed Hilde
and bowed to the king." Kudrun, st. 559, 1. "I will kiss thy
royal finger, and take leave." Shakesp., Love's Lab. Lost, V,
ii, 870. "Of many thousand kisses the poor last I lay upon thy
lips." Shakesp., Anth. and Cleop. IV, xv, 20-21.

Flattery: Kissing hem of someone's shawl or kissing cheek.
Celestina, ix, 2. Kissing the children of another. Anc. Gk.
Sittl, p. 37.

Friendship: Kiss among men. Anc. Gk. and Rom. Sittl,
p. 38. Carried from among brothers to relations outside of immediate family: Gen. 29, 13 (Laban and Jacob); I Sam. 2041
(Jonathan and David).

Gratitude: During the Roman empire actors and musicians
threw kisses at the audience at the beginning of a performance
and thanked thus for applause. Sittl, p. 171. Kissing of statues. Anc. Rom. Sittl, pp. 180-181. Reciting author threw
kiss to audience when someone called "bravo!" Martial 1, 3, 7.
Kiss among men. Anc. Gk. Sittl, p. 38. Medieval Spain:
"Still kneeling, [the Cid] kissed the king's hands, and then arose
and kissed his mouth." Cid, ii.

Greeting: Kissing a superior's hand, then placing it to one's
forehead. Egypt. Ohm, p. 211. Raquel and Vidas kiss the
hands of the Cid. Cid, i. Cid embraces Minaya Alvar Fáñez
and kisses his mouth and eyes. Cid, i. Kiss. Egypt, Persia.
Sittl, pp. 78-79; cf. also Gen. 29, 11. 13; 33. 4; Rom. 16, 16;
I Cor. 20; I Pet. 5, 14. Herodotus (i, 133) says of the Persians: "When two of them meet on the street, one can see
whether they are of the same rank: instead of greeting they
kiss each other on the mouth: if one is a little inferior to the
other, then the one kisses him on the cheek; if, however, he is
of much inferior rank, he falls to the ground and worships the
other." Cited by Ohm, p. 210. Eumaios and Penelope kiss
Telemachos' head and eyes. Odyss. Bk. xvi, xvii. Eurykleia
kisses Telemachos' head and shoulders. Odyss. Bk. xvii.
"Abengalbón smiles and embraces him, kissing him upon the
shoulder, as is the Moorish custom." Cid, ii. Persian kings
kissed only relatives and those to whom they gave that title.
Sittl, p. 79. Kissing the ground on return to homeland or on
arrival at a new homeland. Anc. Gk. and Rom., Sittl, p. 42.
In entering and leaving a temple a kiss is thrown toward the
image of the deity. Anc. Gk. and Rom. Sittl, p. 182. Tacitus criticizes slavish behavior of Otho, who threw kisses at the
cheering crowd at his ascension to the throne. Sittl, p. 171.
If the regent left the city and entered it again, he had to kiss
the senators. Anc. Rom. Sittl, p. 80. In passing the imperial

palace, a slave throws a kiss at it. Anc. Rom. Sittl, p. 171.
Philosophers threw a kiss at buildings named after classical
philosophers in passing. Marinus, Vita procli, cited by Sittl,
pp. 171-172. Beggars threw kisses at passing rich in carriages.
Juvenal. Sittl, p. 171. Kiss was used without distinction of
social class by Caligula, who kissed pantomimics. Sittl, p. 79.
In the circus the charioteer kisses the whip before the patrons.
Anc. Rom. Sittl, p. 165, n. 1. Kiss among men on returning
from journey. Anc. Rom. Sittl, p. 38. Kiss on chest as
morning salutation by the gentlemen waiting upon a nobleman.
Anc. Rom. (empire only). Sittl, p. 166. L. Verus called
Fronto into his bedroom for a kiss, in order to avoid insulting
the others present. Sittl, p. 80. Kissing someone's knee.
Late Roman. Sittl, p. 169. The guest kisses only his hostess
and those ladies of equal rank with his; sometimes also married
women of the house. Medieval German: Lanzel., 615; Schultz,
I, p. 521. Kissing on the mouth. Medieval German: Kudrun,
st. 154, 1, Orendel, 3520. Women permitted to receive equal
or higher ranking guests with a kiss: Medieval German:
Nibelungenlied, st. 297, 3; 1652, 3. "My lady, the gracious
king wishes to receive you here. Whomever I tell you to kiss
let this be done: you are not to greet all Etzel's men equally."
Nibelungenlied, st. 1348, 2-4. "Mr. Pickwick kissed the young
ladies--we were going to say, as if they were his own daughter,
only as he might possibly have infused a little more warmth into
the salutation, the comparison would not be quite appropriate."
Dickens, Pickw., I, p. 165. "The kiss at the altar [priest kissing altarstone] is expressive also of a greeting to Christ, the
Bridegroom who is represented by the altar, on the part of His
Bride, the Church." Mass, p. 19. Kissing both cheeks in
greeting after long absence. Palest. Bauer, p. 169. "...kiss-
ing ritual among Spanish women of all ages. One of the two
women permits herself--by design or by accident--to be kissed
by the other woman... The gesture often consists simply of brushing the other woman's cheek--almost always both--with the lips
...American women are rarely observed kissing both cheeks of
their women friends... Throwing kisses and pointing to the area
to be kissed are movements common to both cultures..." Spain,
Lat. Am. Green, p. 39. A kiss at Christmas is a customary
greeting. Swift's Pol. Conv., p. 175. Women (friends or related) kiss one another when meeting and departing. Mod. West.
Cont. Europe. Révész, Univ., p. 146. Men (friends or related) kiss one another on both cheeks in greeting. Russia,
pre-20th cent. Révész, Univ., p. 146. Two men kiss quickly
on the lips in greeting. Lebanon, Saudi Arabia, Syria. Semiotic. Barakat, no. 140. "She smiled at him, lips pulled back
from clenched teeth.... She smiled toothily again...pointed to
the guest with her lips...pursed her lips." Birdwhistell, Introd.,
p. 30.

Hesitation: To pull or stroke lip or lips. France. Mitton,
p. 146.

Homage: (Cf. s.v. KNEE, Plea.) Falling to the ground
and kissing the earth before a person of importance. Anc. Egypt.

Eichler, p. 95. "Minaya and Pedro Bermúdez rise forward and
dismount and kneel before King Alfonso. They kiss the earth
and his feet." Cid, c. ii. "Then [the Cid] casts himself upon
the ground and plucks a mouthful of grass, weeping in his great
joy. Thus he pays homage to King Alfonso, his lord, and falls
at his feet." Cid, c. ii. "Sub-sheiks in the Near East kiss
the hand and dagger, the latter in a holster, of the Chief Sheik."
Hayes, p. 262. Kissing the foot. Shakesp., Temp. II, ii, 142.

Honor: "...and here my bluest veins to kiss--a hand that
kings have lipp'd, and trembled kissing." Cleop. to messenger.
Shakesp., Anth. and Cleop., II, v, 28-30.

Humility: Since the beginning of Christian sculpture, the
feet of saints' statues were kissed. Sittl, p. 181. The only
occurrence of kissing feet of a deity in anc. Gk. literature is
Chariton 1, 1, 7. 8, 8, 15. Cf. Sittl, p. 181. Anc. Rom.
kissed feet of statues in the temple. Sittl, ibid.

Identification: Judas' betrayal of Christ. Matth. 26, 49;
Mark 14, 45.

Indifference: Lower lips move forward, expulsion of air re-
sults in noise made with upper lip. Spain, Portug. Flachskampf, p. 228.

Insult: Air is forced through pursed lips to make a noise.
"Raspberry." Children. Opie, p. 319.

Investiture: Lord kisses vassal in investing him with fief.
Grimm, DRA, I, p. 197.

Joy: Smiling. Boggs, p. 320. In Christianity the smile
is the outer expression of the happiness which fills the believer
at the thought of salvation and God's beauty. In Buddhism the
smile on the face of Buddha indicates that he has overcome the
world and has achieved inner peace. Ohm, pp. 195-196.

Luck: Tossing a kiss or lifting one's hat to a chimney
sweep, or having the bride kissed by a sweep at the wedding
means good luck. England. Cited by Hayes, p. 290 from G.
L. Phillips, JAF, LXIV (1951), pp. 191-196.

Mourning: Kissing the departed. Gen. 50, 1. Anc. Gk.
and Rom. Sittl, p. 72. Kissing the urn containing the ashes
of the deceased. Anc. Rom. Sittl, p. 74. Kissing forehead
and hand of the departed by relatives in church. Goar, pp. 435-
436.

Nervousness: Biting lips. Krout, p. 22.

Oath: Kissing "the book" in swearing an oath. Shakesp.,
Temp., II, ii, 132. Kissing the Bible is required in many
states of the United States before testimony in court can be legal. In the South some communities have two Bibles in court:
one for whites and the other for negroes. Hayes, p. 268.

Peace: Kiss of peace. Osculum pacis. Early Christian.
Cf. Sittl, p. 39, and s. v. Brotherhood above, Union below.

Plea: Daughter of the king pleads with her father and kisses
the ground before him. Erotokritos. Sittl, p. 171, n. 1.
Doña Ximena kneels before her husband, the Cid, and attempts
to kiss his hands. Cid, c. i. Kissing someone's knee. Iliad,
Odyss., Sittl, p. 169.

Pleasure: " 'Good stuff that,' observed Mr. Claypole,

smacking his lips." Dickens, Twist, p. 397.

Pointing: Lips protruded. Movimas do not accompany this
with quick thrust of the head as the Tacana and Ayorco do, but
instead they thrust their hand straight out with palm held sideways. Bolivian Indians. Key, p. 94. Extending lower lip to
point at another person. Portug. Basto, p. 38. Lips pursed
and moved in direction of object intended to be pointed at. For
nearby people and objects. Colombia. Saitz and Cervenka,
p. 33.

Prayer: Before beginning and after concluding a journey one
kisses the Mezuzah over or at the side of one's door. During
worship one kisses the Torah when it is taken from the Ark and
carried by the community. While praying the third paragraph of
the Schema in the morning prayer, one kisses the Tsitzith on
the Tallis. Jewish. Ohm, p. 213. The Canaanites kissed the
idols of the ba'alim. I Kings 19, 18; Hos., 13, 2; Heiler,
p. 103; Hastings, Dict., p. 9 suggests comparison to kissing of
the black stone in the Ka'ba at Mecca. Mohammedan. Semitic
adoration of unreachable heavenly bodies. Job 31, 26-27. To
honor Ge without throwing oneself on the ground one could throw
her a kiss. Anc. Gk. Sittl, p. 182. A kiss was part of the
adoration of Helios and Silene as well as the gods of the wind
and the Gk. Adrasteia-Nemesis. Sittl, p. 181. The anc. Gks.
kissed the sacred oak of Zeus at Aegina. Ovid, Metam., vii,
631. Throwing kiss. St. Jerome. Sittl, p. 183. Christian
page throws kiss toward crucifix. Sittl, p. 182. Romans kissed
feet of statues in temples. Sittl, p. 181. Kissing thresholds of
churches. Early Christians. Sittl, p. 184. Sulla kissed his
statuette of Apollo which he carried with him. Sittl, ibid.
Kissing sacred trees, cup and healing potion, threshold of house.
Anc. Gk. and Rom. Sittl, ibid. Kissing the graves of martyrs.
Early Christian. Heiler, p. 104. Kissing crucifix. Catholic.
Sittl, p. 184. Throwing kiss at saints' images. Neapol. De
Jorio, p. 67. Since the beginning of Christian sculpture the
feet of saints' statues have been kissed. Sittl, p. 181. Kissing
mementos of saints. Early Christian. Sittl, p. 184. Wounds,
bloody garments, reliques, instruments of torture connected with
religious martyrdom are kissed. Early Christian. Sittl, p. 184
and n. 7. Anc. Arabs kissed the images of domestic deities
when entering or leaving their houses as well as the black stone
in the Ka'aba at Mecca. Heiler, p. 103. "The priest bends and
kisses the altar as if to salute Jesus Christ..." Mass, p. 39.

Reconciliation: Kiss. Gen. 45, 15; II Sam. 14, 33; Luke
15, 20. Also anc. Rom. Sittl, p. 38, and as formal reconciliation of prizefighters after bout. Sittl, ibid. Medieval German:
Kudrun, st. 159, 1.

Respect: Moses kisses his father-in-law. Ex. 18, 7; cf.
also I Sam. 10, 1; Prov. 24, 26; Luke 7, 38. 45. Vitellius
kissed the shoe of the empress. Sittl, p. 172, n. 4. The
slave kisses objects belonging to his master or mistress in their
absence. Anc. Gk. Sittl, p. 172. Throwing kiss at sacred objects, such as altars, sacred stones, graves, statues. (Cf.
s.v. Prayer above.) Anc. Gk. and Rom. Sittl, p. 182. Early

Christians kissed the threshold of the church--presumably in imitation of anc. Rom., who kissed the thresholds of temples--al-
tars, dying people and dead people. Kissing of the dead was
prohibited by the Council of Auxerre, 585. Ohm, p. 215. Kissing a priest's stole at departure after mass. Celestina, ix.
Respect and love for parents is shown by a kiss. Kissing one's
hand in token of respect to another: "it had been better you had
not kiss'd your three fingers so oft, which now again you are
most apt to play the sir in." Shakesp., Othello II, i, 171-72.
"To see him walk before a lady and to bear her fan! To see
him kiss his hand, and how most sweetly 'a will swear!"
Shakesp. Love's Lab. Lost, IV, i, 138-9; I Henry VI, V, iii,
47-49: "For I will touch thee but with reverent hands; I kiss
these fingers for eternal peace, and lay them gently on thy
tender side." Kissing the ground before someone. Burton, III,
p. 218. Kissing someone's hand. Schiller, Fiesko, IV, xii,
14. Bride kisses groom's hand, which she then puts against
her forehead (cf. s.v. Greeting above). Palest. Bauer, p. 94.
Modern Egyptians (1890) kiss hand of superior and then put it
against their forehead. When friends meet they first shake hands
and then kiss their own hand or bring their hand to the lips or
forehead or at least lift it close to the forehead (cf. s.v. Greeting above). Ohm, p. 211.
    Reverence: "Let the men that sacrifice kiss the calves."
Hos. 13, 2. Egyptian priests kissed the earth before the image
of a deity. Kissing of idols' hands, feet, clothing or earth on
which they stood was common in anc. Egypt, Sumer, Babylon,
Assyria, Syria, Persia. In the cult of Baal the statue of the
god was kissed. Anc. Arabs kissed the stone fetish in the
Ka'aba at Mecca. The anc. Gks. and Romans also knew the
sacred kiss. The latter kissed hands, feet of idols, the threshold of temples, sacred trees and other objects. The Shites kiss
the Koran when they take it in their hands. Ohm, p. 213. Anc.
Peruvians threw kisses to the sun, anc. Semites threw kisses
to sun and moon (Job 31, 27), the anc. Gks. worshipped the
rising sun and other astral deities by throwing kisses, and the
Hittites and Babylonians also used the gesture. Anc. Romans
threw kisses to the deities when they passed their statues and
temples or on entering a temple. Similarly, Catholics use the
gesture to statues, crosses and pictures. Ohm, pp. 217-218.
Kissing the foot of pharaoh or emperor. Anc. Egypt., Rom.,
Byzant. Ohm, p. 216. Kissing the foot of pope or bishop.
Ohm, ibid. Deacon kisses knee of bishop before reading gospel.
Early Christian. Ohm, 216-217. In joining the mourning community around a coffin, the Russian orthodox made the sign of
the cross, then kissed the icons standing on the coffin or on the
grave. Today one kisses the icons which replace these, i.e.
those in church. Russians kiss the ground before the icono-
stasis, then the icons. Pilgrims to Santiago de Compostela in
the late 17th cent. kissed the image of the saint on the main
altar three times and put on its head the hat they were wearing.
d'Aulnoy, p. 76. Monk kisses snuffbox he received as gift.
Sterne, ch. xi. "The priest...inclines a little, and kisses [the

Missal] where he signed it at the beginning, to show his love
and veneration for the Divine Word." Mass, p. 30.

Silence: Pressing lips together. Anc. Rom. Sittl, p. 214.

Submission: Kissing someone's feet. Oriental in origin.
(Cf. s.v. Reverence above.) Ohm, p. 215f. Samuel anointed
Saul and kissed him. I Sam. 10, 1. Moses kisses his father-
in-law. Ex. 18, 7. "went out into the way of the king and up
to his chariot and kissed his knees and clasped them." Odyss.,
Bk. xiv. Kissing someone's shoulder. Odyss. (Cf. s.v. Greeting above.) The defeated army kisses the ground before the
emperor. Anc. Rom. Sittl, p. 171, n. 1. At the coronation
of Emperor Henry VI, April 15, 1191, the emperor elect, empress and his barons and clerics kiss the pope's feet and swear
allegiance to him. Thereafter the pope asks him whether he
desires peace with the Church, which Henry affirms thrice and
the pope agrees to "give you peace as the Lord gave it to his
disciples." He kisses his forehead, chin, both cheeks, then
the mouth. Then the pope rises and asks him thrice whether he
wants to be a son of the Church, which Henry affirms thrice
whereupon the pope, replying "and I accept you as son," takes
him under his cloak and Henry kisses the chest of the pope,
taking his right hand, while his chamberlain supports the pope
on the left. Schultz, II, p. 659. Kissing the rod. Shakesp.,
Gentlemen, I, ii, 59. Kissing the earth. Shakesp., Macb. V,
viii, 28. Kissing the foot of the sultan. Book of Accomplishments, Topkapi Palace Mus., Istanbul (cf. s.v. Respect above).
Penitent Syrian woman kisses ground before bishop. Sittl,
p. 171, n. 1.

Surprise: Biting lower lip. Aubert, p. 105. "Alan
whistled. 'By gad, I believe you're right!'" Carr, Suicides,
p. 156.

Threat: "having picked up the pieces and put them into
three separate pockets, folded his arms, bit his lips, and looked
in a threatening manner at the bland features of Mr. Pickwick."
Dickens, Pickw., II, p. 337.

Union: Osculum sanctum or Osculum pacis. The early
Christian Church took the kiss over from paganism. Achelis,
p. 229f. In the Roman liturgy the kiss of peace became common before communion, as provided by Innocent I. Originally
all Christians kissed each other, later the priests kissed the
bishop, the men other men, the women other women. In the
13th century the osculum pacis as a popular custom disappeared
under the influence of the Franciscans and was replaced by the
kiss of the osculatorium, which in turn has disappeared. Ohm,
pp. 220-221. In Russian Orthodox churches the kiss of peace is
common at Easter, when the men kiss the men, the women kiss
the women. The Swedish Protestants use the osculum sanctum
at the consecration of a bishop, the Hungarians at the ordination
of a pastor. It is also used at the reception of novices into the
Zentraldiakonissenhaus Bethanien, Berlin. Ohm, p. 222.

Warning: Puckering lips and blowing: "Secret police."
Lat. Am. Kany, p. 121.

LIP, NECK
Affection: Kiss on neck (sensuous as well as paternal). Anc.
Rom. Sittl, p. 41.

LIP, NOSE
Disgust: Sneering. Krukenberg, p. 257.

LIP, SHOULDER
Greeting: (Cf. s. v. LIP, Greeting, Submission.) During the
Hadj (pilgrimage) one may kiss only on the shoulders in greeting.
Saudi Arabia. Semiotic. Barakat, no. 179. Parents of a recently deceased son or daughter may kiss only on the shoulders
in greeting. Bahrein, Saudi Arabia. Semiotic. Barakat, no.
180.
    Homage: Kissing right shoulder of a dignitary as sign of
respect or show of homage. Kuwait, Saudi Arabia. Semiotic.
Barakat, no. 238.

LIP, TONGUE
Affection: Kiss and simultaneous projection of tongue into the
other's mouth. Anc. Rom. Sittl, p. 43. Tongue protrudes
slightly and moves slowly along lips. Primarily adolescent men.
Request for a kiss. U.S., Colombia. Saitz and Cervenka,
p. 79.
    Apology: Kissing the nose of a person with whom one has
fought. Saudi Arabia. Semiotic. Barakat, no. 242.
    Contempt: Whistling and clicking the tongue. Anc. Gk.
Sittl, p. 96.

LIP, TOOTH
Affection: Kiss and simultaneous bite. Anc. Gk. and Rom.
Sittl, p. 42.
    Anger: Biting lower lip indicates more intense rage than
that manifested by gnashing teeth. Anc. Gk. (Odyss., Bk. xx),
anc. Rom., Ital. Sittl, p. 16; de Jorio, p. 265. "The king is
angry; see, he gnaws his lip. " Shakesp., Richard III, IV, ii,
27. Biting the moustache. Mod. Gk. Sittl, p. 16, n. 4.
    Embarrassment: Biting lip. Anc. Gk. Sittl, p. 17.
    Envy: Biting lip. Anc. Gk. Sittl, p. 17.
    Excitement: Biting lips. Krukenberg, p. 212.
    Mockery: Upper lip lifted to bare canine. Anc. Gk., Rom.,
Ital. Sittl, p. 89.
    Pain: Biting lip to suppress pain. Early Christian. Sittl,
p. 17.
    Perplexity: " 'Nothing can be done, Madam, I must pre-
sume to say, if this gentleman's address be the end. ' She
looked upon my uncle, who bit his lip; and looked upon Mr.
Solmes, who rubbed his neck. " Richardson, Clarissa, II,
p. 225.
    Regret: Tongue protrudes over upper lip; often accompanied
by a finger flap. Colombia. Saitz and Cervenka, p. 101.
    Self-discipline: "his hollow eyes flashing fire, and biting
his under lip, to show he could be manly. " Richardson,

Clarissa, II, p. 235. Cf. also Krout, p. 21.
    Sorrow: Biting lip. Mod. Gk. Sittl, p. 17.

MOUTH
    Adoration: Spitting in the direction of a deity. Zulu, Ovambo,
Shinto, Buddhist. Ohm, pp. 224-225.
    Affection: A high whistle produced between the teeth. Used
between lovers to attract the affection of the other. Neapol.
De Jorio, p. 161.
    Anger: Chewing on one's moustache. Boggs, p. 321.
    Apotropy: (Cf. s.v. Magical below.) To protect oneself
against the evil eye or the evil glance of an insane person or
epileptic one spits once or thrice into the folds of one's garment. Anc. Gk. Sittl, p. 120. Patients suffering from an
illness thought to come from the gods are spat on, e.g. epilep-
tics or the insane. Anc. Rom. Sittl, p. 119. Those watching
over children spit on them to protect them against the evil eye,
particularly if the child is asleep and a stranger present. Anc.
Rom. Sittl, p. 118. Spitting on someone or oneself as protection against the evil eye appears in Italy only during the empire. Sittl, p. 120. Nurse spits three times on child entrusted
to her in order to protect it against the evil eye and envy. Anc.
Rom. Seligmann, p. 207. In Hungary "a child is never to be
praised or admired. If one looks at a child for a while in admiration, he should then spit on it three times." Temesvary,
p. 75. Mother must spit thrice upon the spot where her child
has fallen, so that no adverse consequences may result from
the fall. Palest. Bauer, p. 195. Spitting three times as protection against spirits when a dog howls or a cat meows. Mod.
Germ. Sittl, p. 118. Someone handing medicine to a sick person spits on floor or out of the window as protection of patient
against demons. Sardinia. Sittl, p. 118. When one yawns evil
spirits enter the body; therefore one makes the sign of the cross
in the name of the Holy Trinity when one opens the mouth.
Tirol. HDA, III, col. 254. Spitting into one's bosom after
praising something to protect it against the evil eye--for whoever has the evil eye harms by means of praise. Old women.
Mod. Gk. Sittl, p. 120. "A friend may spit in a baby's face
to prove he has no 'evil eye' intentions." Cited from M. L.
de Benedekfalva, Folklore, LII (1941), 101-119, by Hayes,
p. 227. A close relative spits in the face of an adult to protect him against the evil eye. Anc. and Mod. Gk. Sittl,
p. 118. Tribes in southern Africa spit to avert the evil omen
when they see a shooting star. Frazer, IV, p. 61. Spitting
into one's bosom lest one has aroused jealousy through self-
praise. Lucian, Navig. 15; Theocrit., vi, 39; Juvenal, vii,
153. One also spat at one's breast if one praised someone else,
in order to protect him from harm. Seligmann, II, pp. 208-209.
Slaves spat over their shoulder as protection against magic.
Anc. Rom. Sittl, p. 118, n. 1; Ohm, p. 227. Use of saliva

in healing. Mark 7, 33; 8, 23. Early Christians spat against
the devil at baptism. In the Orthodox and Armenian church the
neophyte spits out the devil toward the West or other direction
deemed to be toward the devil. Ohm, p. 227. Women in India
spit three times to frighten a demon when they see a falling
star. Frazer, IV, p. 62. Spitting over the left shoulder at
the devil. Mohammedan. Ohm, p. 227. Priest applies saliva
to ears and nose of neophyte at baptism (Chrism). Roman rite.
Ohm, p. 227. Breating on a cat. Meschke, col. 333.

   Approach: Hissing as form of beckoning. Isaiah 5, 26;
7, 18; Zech. 10, 8.

   Approval: Belching as a sign that one has enjoyed a meal.
Jordan, Lebanon, Kuwait, Syria, Saudi Arabia, Egypt. Semiotic or culture-induced. Barakat, no. 244.

   Attention: "and announced her presence by a slight cough:
the which being disregarded, was followed by a louder one."
Dickens, Pickw., II, p. 409; cf. also I, p. 127; II, p. 388.
Short hiss to call waiter. Colombia. Saitz and Cervenka,
p. 107. (Cf. s.v. Approach above.)

   Blessing: The Dinka (nilotic Sudan) in blessing his son,
spits on his head and strokes his head with his hand into which
he has spit before. Ohm, p. 226. The Lāma spits at the
morning worship, while saying the Mantras. Hindu. Ohm,
p. 226.

   Boredom: Yawn, deliberate or involuntary. If deliberate,
it is a signal that one wants to leave. U.S. and Colombia.
Saitz and Cervenka, p. 25.

   Contempt: Spitting into someone's face. Num. 12, 14;
Job 30, 10. "Wouldst thou not spit at me and spurn at me."
Shakesp., Com. of Errors, II, ii, 133. "This amendment drew
bitter invective from an ultra-Orthodox Knesset member, Rabbi
Manahem Porush, who at one point spat on a prayer book of the
Reform movement and hurled it to the floor." L.A. Times
(March 12, 1970), p. 18. "and spit upon my Jewish gaberdine"
Shakesp., Merchant, I, ii, 3. Spitting at someone or in some-
one's face. Anc. Gk. and Rom., Ital., Span. Sittl, p. 105.
Spitting at someone or in someone's face as judicial punishment.
Jewish. Sittl, p. 106. Spitting prohibited in a temple. Arrian,
Epict. 4, 11, 32. Spitting on the threshold of one who has
broken the laws of hospitality. Sardinia. Bresciani, II, p. 202.
Corsica. Merimée Mat. Falc.; Sittl, p. 106. Mouth in the act
of spitting, directed at the face of the other person. Highest
expression of contempt. Neapol. De Jorio, p. 131. Mouth
in the act of spitting, directed towards the ground. Intense degree of contempt. A sudden puff of air, with a little upward
movement of the head and expression of contempt. Mild contempt. Neapol. De Jorio, p. 130. Mouth open, air suddenly
exhaled, or blowing air out. Anc. Rom. Sittl, p. 97. Hissing.
I Kings 9, 8; Job 27, 23; Jer. 18, 16, etc. Whistling. Neapol.
De Jorio, p. 164. One corner of the mouth as if smiling, the
other drawn down, eyelids slightly drooping. Aubert, p. 108.
Corner of mouth pulled back. Plaut., Mil. 94.

   Copulation: Gently blowing smoke into a woman's face indicates desire for that woman. Northern Syria. Semiotic. Barakat, no. 4.

Debauchery: Belch. Anc. Rom. Baden, p. 455.

Decisiveness: Tightly closed mouth. Krukenberg, p. 212.

Defiance: "but as she spit in his face, so she defied him." Shakesp., Measure, II, i, 80-81; "I do defy him, and I spit at him" Shakesp., Richard II, I, i, 60.

Disagreement: One corner of mouth smiling, the other drawn down, eyelids drooping. Aubert, p. 108.

Disapproval: Hissing. Krout, p. 23.

Dislike: One corner of mouth pulled back. Anc. Rom. Sittl, p. 89. Both corners of mouth pulled down. Anc. Rom., 19th cent. Ital. children. Sittl, p. 89.

Dissatisfaction: Grunting. Krout, p. 23. "Letting the mouth hang," i.e. corners of the mouth hang down. Schuppius cited in DWb, IV/2, col. 450. Exhale very slowly. Saudi Arabia, Syria. Autistic. Barakat, no. 205.

Embarrassment: "and several of the beholders tried to cough down their emotions." Dickens, Pickw., II, p. 79.

Enmity: Spitting. Palest. Bauer, p. 200.

Etiquette: When the coffee is ready, the host tastes a little of it in order to show that all is as it should be. Palest. Bauer, p. 183. A little wine is poured first into the glass of the host so that he may make sure that the wine is not "corked," before the guests are served. This is only done in restaurants. At his own table, a host does not serve himself first, since he has opened the wine first and therefore knows that the cork has not deteriorated and affected the wine. Lichine, Encycl. of Wines and Spirits, p. 13. The Japanese smile is not necessarily a spontaneous expression of amusement, but a law of etiquette. Ruesch and Kees, p. 22.

Exasperation: "The face expresses annoyance and exhaustion, the shoulders sag, the knees buckle, and air is audibly forced out of the lungs; occasionally the right hand appears to be limply tossing something over the right shoulder, or the thumb is jerked in that general direction: 'J'en ai marre.'" Brault, p. 377.

Expectancy: "licking his chops." Panchatantra, V, 12.

Fatigue: Yawning. Krout, p. 26.

Flirting: Men make slurping sound in flirting with woman. Lebanon. Semiotic. Barakat, no. 247.

Foolishness: Mouth open. Krukenberg, p. 134.

Friendship: South African tribe spits at seeing shooting star as sign of friendliness toward dead chief, whom the shooting star is felt to represent. Frazer, IV, p. 65.

Greeting: Spitting upon the other person. Dyurs (Nile). Ohm, p. 226. With saliva one gives part of one's strength to the other. Ohm, p. 226.

Humility: In early and medieval Christianity carefree laughter was thought of as unbecoming. St. Chrysostom justifies this by the example of Christ, who never laughed nor smiled.

Hunger: Mouth open as far as possible, eyes animated. Head moving repeatedly from left to right. Neapol. De Jorio, p. 149.

Insult: Spitting in someone's face. Deut. 25, 9; Job 30,
10. Spitting at someone. Matth. 27, 30; Persius, Sat. iv, 35.
Catull. 50, 19. Spitting at some other person's feet or in his
face. Lebanon, Bahrein, Saudi Arabia. Semiotic. Barakat,
no. 185. "if you had but look'd big and spit at him, he'd have
run." Shakespear, Winter's Tale, IV, iii, 101-102.

Magical: (Cf. also s.v. Apotropy above.) The face of a
believer in a magical process is spit at once or three times.
Anc. Rom. Sittl, p. 119. One who praises a child or its
beauty is requested to spit on it. Anc. Rom., mod. Gk. Sittl,
p. 118. The dug-up vampire spits burning saliva at his supposed
betrayer. Anc. Gk. Sittl, pp. 119-120. Egyptian magician
spits Gks. in the face, causing them to look like the dead during the day. Anc. Gk. Sittl, p. 119. Spitting back at someone destroys the power of prophecy. Anc. Gk. and Rom. Sittl,
ibid. Whoever wants to see devils must let his mouth be spit
into. Byzant. Sittl, ibid. Murderer spits the victim's blood
out three times to protect himself against avenging spirits. Anc.
Gk. Sittl, p. 117. Spitting out three times as part of an in-
cantation. Anc. Rom. Sittl, ibid. Old women spit on and blow
on their charges. Hellenist. Sittl, p. 121. Blowing as a
means of driving evil spirits away--a consequence of the description of the devil as malus spiritus in the New Testament.
Early Christian. Sittl, ibid. Mother spits after someone who
has praised her child. Sardinia. Sittl, p. 118. Owner of a
horse spits on it after it has been praised. Sardinia. Sittl,
ibid. A finished piece of work is spat on. German. Sittl,
p. 118. Visitor of a sick person spits on his threshold to protect the patient against demons. Sardinia. Sittl, ibid. Spitting
once or thrice while urinating so that the insulted spirit of the
place does not persecute the offender. Mod. Gk. (Thrace).
Sittle, pp. 117-118. Spitting over one's shoulder (thrice?) to
protect oneself against magic. Slavic. Sittl, p. 118. Spitting
into someone's mouth gives him magical wish-power. Mod. Gk.
Sittl, p. 119. Shepherds spit on newborn lambs and their
mothers. Sardinia. Sittl, ibid. A dervish, in transferring his
duties to another, moistens a piece of sugar with saliva and
gives it to his successor, who takes it with closed eyes, then
blows his breath into his mouth. Palest. Bauer, p. 11. One
exhales at cats. German. Sittl, p. 121; Meschke, col. 333.

Medico-magical: Mother spits on and makes the sign of the
cross over child who has cramps. Sardinia. Sittl, p. 128.
Breathing into the mouth of sick people. Palest. Bauer, p. 11.

Mockery: Spitting at someone or into someone's face. Anc.
Gk. and Rom., Ital., Span. Sittl, p. 105. Also Matth. 26, 67;
27, 30; Mark 10, 34; 14, 65; 15, 19.

Nervousness: Twitching mouth. Krout, p. 26.

Prayer: Ritual laughter. Hindu women in ascending the
stake; anc. Sardinians, in sacrificing their old people; Phoeni-
cians in sacrificing their children; Thracians at the death of one
of them; at the ritual of the celebration of Hera the priestess
had to tear the veil of the idol and break into laughter; at the
Roman festival of the Lupercalia the priest, after sacrificing

goats, touched the forehead of two young men with the bloody
knife, wiping the blood off with wool, whereupon the two men
(the "laughers") broke into laughter. Ohm, pp. 191-192.
Parthians hide mouth behind cloth while praying. Heiler, p. 105.
The Safwa chew, while praying, the leaves of the Spaneba tree
and then spit them out. Ohm, p. 224. When a Dschajga comes
out of his hut in the morning he looks up to the sky and, asking
for blessing, spits three times. Ohm, ibid. Pious Shintoists
and Buddhists in Japan spit at statues and images of certain
gods in an effort of having their prayers heard. This custom is
limited to apply to those deities which, according to popular belief, grant health. If the worshipper's concern is for his eyes,
he spits at the eyes of the deity, thus facilitating the deity's
taking over his illness. The worshipper is healed if a piece of
paper, spat out, hits the eye of the deity. Ohm, p. 225. The
Ni-ō are spit at in the belief that one receives strength from
the upper arm of the deities if a paper, spat at the deity's arm,
sticks there. Ohm, ibid.

 Reconciliation: Spitting into a vessel is a symbol of reconciliation. Prose Edda. Ohm, p. 226.

 Rejection: "All my fond love thus do I blow to heaven.
'Tis gone." Shakesp., Othello, III, iv, 449-450.

 Relief: Sighing. Krout, p. 25.

 Reverence: Spitting was common in the Sabazius-cult. Anc.
Gk. Ohm, p. 225.

 Sarcasm: One corner of mouth as if smiling, the other
drawn down, eyelids slightly drooping. Aubert, p. 108.

 Sorrow: Screaming, sobbing, sighing, groaning. Boggs,
p. 319.

 Submission: " 'How does thy honor? Let me lick thy
shoe.' " Shakesp., Tempest, III, ii, 22.

 Surprise: Opening the mouth. Boggs, p. 321; Krout, p. 23.

MOUTH, TONGUE

Disbelief: Moving tongue in and out of mouth rapidly. Saudi
Arabia. Semiotic. Barakat, no. 156.

 Pain: "He twisted up his mouth, and like an ox that licks
his nose, stuck out his loathsome tongue." Dante, Inf., c. xvii.

MOUTH, TOOTH

Anger: (Cf. s.v. TOOTH, Anger.) Gnashing teeth. Acts 7,
54.

 Contempt: Hissing and gnashing teeth. Lament. 2, 16.

 Mockery: (Cf. s.v. TOOTH, Anger.) Gnashing teeth. Ps.
35, 16.

NECK

Affection: Falling on someone's neck. Gen. 45, 14; Acts 20,
37.

 Curiosity: Stretching one's neck. "Ye other few who lifted
up your heads betimes." Dante, Par. c. ii.

Greeting: Falling on someone's neck. Gen. 33, 4; Luke 15, 20.

Obstinacy: Making a stiff neck. Jer. 17, 23.

Plea: Falling about someone's neck. "With his strong arms he fastened on my neck." Shakesp., Lear, V, iii, 212; Othello, IV, i, 140.

Shame: "bending down his corrigible neck, his face subdu'd to penetrative shame." Shakesp., Anth. and Cleop., IV, xiv, 73-75.

Submission: Marinus, brother of Peter Damian, offered himself as serf at the altar of the Virgin with a rope round his neck. Petrus Damiani, PL, CXXXXV, col. 566. St. Odilo offered himself as a serf to the Virgin, with the token offering of serfdom hung round his neck. Vita Sti. Odilonis, in PL, CXXXXII, cols. 915-916. St. Gerard of Brogne went to Rome every other year with 10 shillings hanging from his neck to offer himself as a serf to his Lord. Odo of Cluny, Vita Sti. Geraldi, in PL CXXXIII, col. 680.

Superciliousness: Walking with stretched-forth necks. Isaiah 3, 16.

NOSE

Affection: Father of the house "kissed" the newborn infant or the child returned from a journey three times by sniffing it. Anc. Ind., anc. Egypt. Ohm, p. 212. Rubbing of nose on nose. New Zealand, Lappland. Krukenberg, p. 111; Malay. Sittl, p. 36 citing Mantegazza, p. 227.

Amusement: Wrinkled nose, air drawn in through nose and expelled, accompanied by a dull sound. (Hidden amusement.) Sittl, p. 88.

Anger: Distended nose. Anc. Gk. Sittl, p. 15. Wrinkled nose. Anc. Rom. Sittl, p. 14. Desire to pull the nose as outlet for frustrated anger. Dickens, Pickw., I, p. 52; II, p. 44.

Contempt: Turning up one's nose. ODP, p. 677.

Curiosity: Nostrils drawing in air abruptly and repeatedly. Head forward, moving from right to left, eyes lively, lips pursed. Imitating sniffing dog. Neapol. De Jorio, p. 124.

Defiance: "There was a general nose-in-the-air, defiant kind of aspect." OED, s.v. Nose, 6a.

Disapproval: "Lady Constance had a high, arched nose, admirably adapted for sniffing. She used it now to the limits of its power." Wodehouse, p. 24. Wrinkling nose. Anc. Rom. Sittl, p. 87. Colombia, U.S. Saitz and Cervenka, p. 38.

Disgust: "Heaven stops the nose at it." Shakesp., Othello, IV, ii, 79; also Anthony and Cleop., III, xiii, 39. Wrinkling nose. Anc. Rom. Sittl, p. 87.

Dislike: Wrinkling nose. Krout, p. 26. Nose wrinkled, air drawn in through nose and forcefully expelled. Hellenist., anc. Rom. Sittl, p. 88.

Farewell: "One or two of them then took my hand and smelt it, making rather a noise about it, which is here a very courteous and respectful method of salutation and farewell."

Fiji. Johnson, p. 302. Salutation by nose contact has been recorded also in Malaya, southern India, Mongolia, Lappland, and
among certain African tribes. Dawson, p. 89.

Friendship: Joining noses. Hawaii. J. Cook, Bk. v, ch.
iii.

Greeting: "Geb rejoices at thy approach; he extends his hand
to thee; he kisses thee; he fondles thee." The term used for
"kiss" is anc. Egypt "sn," i.e. "smell" and has as determina-
tive two noses, tip to tip. Pyramid text from the pyramid of
Teti. Dawson, p. 83. Cf. also the pillar from Karnak, depicting Sesostris I touching noses with the god Ptah. Cairo Museum.
Ibid. Sniffing without joining noses as salute was customary in
the Fiji Islands, Malaya, Burma, Nicobar Islands, Melanesia.
Dawson, pp. 88-89. In Melanesia this gesture is applied principally to children. Rubbing noses is practised in the Polynesian
settlement. Codrington, p. 354, cited by Dawson, p. 88.
Among the Maoris of New Zealand nose-pressing was the kiss of
welcome, as well as of mourning and sympathy. Dawson, p. 87.
Polynesians, Lapps and Eskimos rub noses together as sign of
affection and greeting. Eichler, p. 161. Two men touch noses
three times, then smack lips in greeting. Saudi Arabia (Bedouin). Semiotic. Barakat, no. 136. Bedouin touch noses three
times in greeting. Saudi Arabia. Semiotic. Barakat, no. 116.

Hesitation: Nose is scratched with one or more fingers.
France. Mitton, p. 146.

Laziness: "A jailer stood reclining against the dock-rail,
tapping his nose listlessly with a large key." Dickens, Twist,
p. 410.

Penitence: "had been for some seconds scratching his nose
with the brim of his hat in a penitent manner." Dickens, Pickw.,
II, p. 322.

Superciliousness: Nostrils somewhat distended. Appears in
anc. Rome under Augustus. Sittl, pp. 87-88. "She tossed her
nose in disdain. Smollett, Clinker, letter of Melford, May 24.
"she observed, with a toss of her nose, that Brown was a civil
fellow enough, considering the lowness of his origin." Smollett,
ibid., letter of Melford, Sept. 21.

RING

Engagement: "Here, take my ring; my house, mine honour, yea,
my life, be thine, and I'll be bid by thee." Shakesp., All's
Well, IV, ii, 52, 54. Cf. also Kudrun, st. 1649-50; Wigamur
4633; Heinr. v. Freiberg, Tristan 654.

Marriage: Bridegroom's presentation of ring to the bride
sanctioned by Talmudic authority. Hastings, Dict. p. 271. Anc.
Rom., medieval German. Grimm, DRA, pp. 244-245.

Possession: Transference of property symbolized by gift of
ring. Medieval. Grimm, DRA, I, p. 246; Du Cange, III, col.
1528; Vilkinasaga, c. 378. Cf. Investiture by ring and staff.

SHIELD (Cf. s.v. HAND, WEAPON.)
  Mourning: Knight carrying his shield upside-down signifies his
  mourning for the death of his lord. Wolfr. v. Eschenbach, II,
  80.
    Negotiation: Setting down the shield before one's feet indi-
  cates a readiness to negotiate. Nibelungenlied, st. 2254, 2.

SHOE
  Engagement: Bridegroom brings bride a shoe; as soon as she
  has put it on, she is considered to be subject to his authority.
  Gregory of Tours, Vit. patr. xvi; Vilkinasaga, cap. 61.
    Refusal: Relinquishment of property is symbolized by taking
  off a shoe. Grimm, DRA, I, p. 215. Also anc. Israel: Ruth
  4, 7; Deut. 25, 9.
    Submission: Shoes sent by one king to another, less power-
  ful king had to be put on by the latter as sign of submission.
  Norwegian. Du Cange, s.v. calceamenta; Grimm, DRA, I,
  p. 215.

SHOULDER
  Contempt: Rapid shrugging of the shoulders once or twice, often accompanied by sighs and raising of the eyes to the sky.
  Feminine. Regarded by the English as typically French. Mitton, p. 144.
    Copulate: (Cf. s.v. ARM, HAND, Copulate.) Shrug of the
  shoulders. Lat. Am. Kany, p. 187. Extended forearms and
  fists jerked backward and downward toward the body. Venezuela.
  Kany, ibid.
    Doubt: Shrug of the shoulders. Boggs, p. 322. "having
  misplaced their confidence once... so they looked wise as they
  could, shrugged their shoulders." Dickens, Pickw., I, p. 496.
  "Lieutenant Tappleton turned round to his friend Doctor Slam-
  mer, with scarcely perceptible shrug of the shoulder, as if implying some doubt of the accuracy of his recollection." Dickens,
  Pickw., I, p. 50.
    Frustration: Shoulders raised and lowered rapidly once or
  twice. Often reenforced by a sigh, eyes directed upward.
  Mainly feminine. Called "typically French" by the English.
  Mitton, p. 144.
    Helplessness: Shrugging shoulders. Ariosto, 42, 27.
    Ignorance: Shoulders slightly raised, lips pursed. Colom-
  bia, U.S. Saitz and Cervenka, p. 93.
    Impatience: "Mrs. Colonel Wugsby would shrug up her
  shoulders, and cough, as much as to say she wondered whether
  he ever would begin." Dickens, Pickw., II, p. 124. "Sikes
  shrugged his shoulders impatiently." Dickens, Twist, p. 173.
    Indifference: Shrugging shoulders. Krout, p. 25. Spain.
  Flachskampf, p. 229. "'and suppose the verdict is against
  me?' said Mr. Pickwick. Mr. Perker smiled... shrugged his
  shoulders and remained expressively silent." Dickens, Pickw.,
  II, p. 27. "'Has Mr. Pickwick a strong case?' The attorney
  shrugged his shoulders." Dickens, ibid., p. 31. Cf. also
  McCord, p. 292; and Seton, p. xxiii. If used in Colombia by a

child to an older person, it is deemed to be very impolite. Also occurs in U.S. Saitz and Cervenka, p. 43.

Negation: " 'Eh! I am selfish: but am I more selfish than the rest of the world?' asks my Lord, with a French shrug of his shoulders, and a pinch out of his box." Thackeray, Virginians, II, ch. xxiv, p. 262. Quick jerk of left shoulder. African. Ohm, p. 44.

Resignation: Shrugging shoulders. Boccaccio, 2, 8. "he shrugged up his shoulders, and, with a peculiar grimace in his countenance, said, he was sorry for my misfortunes; but there was no remedy like patience." Smollett, Random, ch. xliii. Also Folengo, 3, 33.

Submission: Shoulders raised in acceptance of an unpleasant situation. Anc. Rom. (not before Augustan period); early Christian. Sittl, p. 113.

Truth: "Actress Russell, humped up and hipped out till she resembles a super-annuated ostrich, encompasses...the standard repertory of Jewish gesture--the delicately deprecating shrug that says: I don't mean to offend, but a fact is a fact,..." Time (Jan. 19, 1962), p. 55.

TONGUE

Affection: Sticking out one's tongue at someone. Plaut. Asin. 795.

Anticipation: Tongue extended ca. 1/4 in., moving slowly along lips. Eyes widen. Colombia, U.S. Saitz and Cervenka, p. 18.

Apotropy: Sticking out tongue against evil spirits and enemies; hence the gargoyles of medieval cathedrals, of gate towers of medieval castles, and gorgonheads at the eaves of temples in antiquity. Also in late medieval depictions of the Passion of Christ. Röhrich, pp. 22, 26. Old women lick children's forehead with tongue to protect them against the evil eye. Byzant. Sittl, p. 120. Sticking tongue out against cats at night (= demons). Mod. Ital. Children. Sittl, p. 117.

Applause: Smacking the tongue. Anc. Gk., Austral. aborigines, Eskimos. Sittl, p. 61.

Approach: Master clicks tongue to summon servant, muledriver to hurry mules. Hellenist. Sittl, p. 223.

Copulation: Tongue protruded slowly. Invitation to a prostitute. Colombia. Saitz and Cervenka, p. 117. Wagging tongue from one side of mouth to the other without extending the tongue fully from the mouth: proposition by man to woman. Lebanon. Semiotic. Barakat, no. 107.

Defiance: Tongue is stuck out in the direction of someone. French. Childish. Mitton, p. 150.

Disbelief: "Duncan clucked his tongue thoughtfully." Carr, Suicides, p. 102.

Disdain: Sticking out the tongue. Meschke, col. 337.

Drink: Tongue protrudes over lower lip. Often comic. U.S. Saitz and Cervenka, p. 44.

Greeting: (Cf. s.v. FINGER, TONGUE and HAND, HAT, Greeting.) Sticking out the tongue. Polynesia. Röhrich, p. 13.

Insult: Sticking out tongue at someone. Children and, joking, adults. Colombia, U.S. Saitz and Cervenka, p. 76. Europe. Ohm, p. 45. Krout, p. 24. HDA, I, col. 323. Childish. Mitton, p. 150. Amer. schoolchildren. Seton, p. xxi.

Mockery: Sticking out the tongue. Meschke, col. 337. The "Lallekönig" of Basle, who mocked the German Empire across the Rhine. Röhrich, pl. 21. Childish. Mitton, p. 150. "The Prentice speaks his Disrespect by an extended finger, and the Porter by sticking out his Tongue." Spectator, no. 354 (Apr. 16, 1712). Sticking out the tongue, according to Sittl, pp. 90-91, was known to the ancient Gks. only as signifying bloodthirstiness, and he deems it probable that the Romans borrowed it as signifying mockery from Gaul. Cf. also Taylor, p. 17. Sticking out the tongue. Isaiah 57, 4. Jan Polack, "Ecce Homo" (1492)--in combination with the "Schabab"-gesture of crossing one index with the other and rubbing it along the lower index. Cf. s.v. FINGER, Mockery ("Rübenschaben"). Tongue stuck out of the corner of the mouth. Ital. Besciani, Edm., vii, 144. Tongue stuck out frontally. Children. 19th cent. German. Sittl, p. 90.

Negation: Clicking the tongue. Italy, Greece. Sittl, p. 96.

Respect: Sticking out the tongue. Tibet. Ohm, p. 45.

Reverence: "lick up the dust off your feet." Isaiah 49, 23.

Submission: "They shall lick the dust like a snake." Micah 7, 17; Ps. 72, 9.

Teasing: Tongue extended from open mouth. Jordan, Lebanon, Kuwait, Syria, Saudi Arabia, Iraq. Semiotic. Barakat, no. 70.

TONGUE, TOOTH

Anger: "So York must sit and fret and bite his tongue." Shakesp., II Henry VI, I, ii, 225.

Disbelief: Snicking teeth with tongue, simultaneously lifting head quickly: "No, never," "perhaps," "I don't believe you." Arab. Semiotic or culture-induced. Barakat, no. 144.

Embarrassment: Biting tongue. Anc. Gk. Sittl, p. 17. French. Rousseau, Emile, v.

Pain: "and they gnawed their tongues for pain." Rev. 16, 10.

TOOTH

Anger: Gnashing of teeth. Anc. Gk. and Rom., predominantly Rom. Sittl, p. 44, cf. also p. 16. Boggs, p. 321. Krout, p. 23. Gritting one's teeth as indication of extreme anger or rage. Ruesch and Kees, p. 36. Biting into moustache. Mod. Gk. Sittl, p. 17.

Apotropy: Gnashing teeth against cats at night (= demons). Mod. Ital. children. Sittl, p. 117; Meschke, col. 337. Show-

ing teeth to a person suspected of having the evil eye.   Ital.
Seligmann, II, p. 287.

Chagrin: "grinding his teeth together, with a look that
baffles all description. " Smollett, Peregr. Pickle, ch. lxix.

Despair: "There shall be weeping and gnashing of teeth. "
Matth. 8, 12; 13, 42. 50; etc.

Determination: Gritting teeth. Boys. Opie, p. 230.

Ecstasy: Gnashing of teeth in orgiastic ecstasy.   Anc. Gk.
Sittl, p. 27.

Greeting: Cutting oneself with shark's teeth and wailing as
a form of receiving a friend or showing joy at his arrival.
Tahiti.   Ellis, II, p. 337.

Hatred: Gnashing of teeth.   Pausanias 10, 28, 7; Dante,
Inf. c. v; De Jorio, p. 265; Manzoni, ch. xi.   Early Christian.
Sittl, p. 44.

Mockery: Gnashing of teeth and laughing.   Anc. Rom.
Sittl, p. 98. Hissing and gnashing of teeth. Lam. 2, 16; Ps.
35, 16.

Submission: Biting the grass. Cid, 2022.

Threat: Gnashing teeth. Pausanias 10. 28, 7; Devil in the
Tomba dell' Orco of Tarquinius (Etruscan); Dante, Inf., c. v.
"Our Eastern Shore Virginians are again beginning to growl and
to show their teeth. " Simms, 30.

INDEX OF SIGNIFICANCES

Absence: Hand.

Acceptance: Finger; Hand; Lip.

Accolade: Hand; Hand, weapon; Knee.

Accompaniment: Hand.

Accusation: Arm, finger; Arm, hand.

Acknowledgment: Hand; Head; Lip.

Address (Passionate): Hand.

Admiration: Cheek, eyebrow, head, mouth; Cheek, finger; Cheek, forehead, mouth; Chin, finger, head, nose; Eye, finger; Finger; Finger, lip; Finger, mouth; Hand; Hand, lip; Lip.

Admonition: Finger; Hand.

Adoption: Beard, hand; Hand; Knee.

Adoration: Arm; Arm, breast; Body; Body, face; Eye, hand, leg; Face, hand, knee; Foot; Foot, lip; Hand; Hand, lip; Head; Knee; Lip; Mouth.

Affection: Arm; Arm, breast; Arm, lip; Arm, neck; Arm, shoulder; Beard, hand; Beard, lip; Breast, hand; Breast, hand, head; Breast, lip, shoulder; Cheek, eyebrow, head, mouth; Cheek, finger; Cheek, hand; Cheek, hand, lip; Cheek, nose; Chin, hand; Ear, eye, hand, lip; Ear, hand, lip; Eye, hand; Eye, mouth; Face; Face, hand, knee; Finger; Finger, lip; Finger, mouth; Forehead, hand; Forehead, lip; Hair, hand; Hair, lip; Hand; Hand, head; Hand, lip; Head; Lip; Lip, tongue; Lip, tooth; Mouth; Neck; Nose; Tongue.

Affirmation: Arm, fingers, hand; Breast, hand; Eyebrow; Finger; Hand; Head.

Age: Hair, hand.

Agreement: Eyebrow, head, shoulder; Finger; Hand; Hand, staff; Hand, straw; Hand, weapon; Head; Lip.

Alarm: Arm, breast; Breast, hand; Hand; Hand, weapon; Head.

Amazement: Cheek, hand; Ear, hand; Eye, hand; Eyebrow, mouth, shoulder; Finger, nose; Hand; Head.

231

Amusement: Arm; Head; Nose.

Anger: Abdomen; Arm; Arm, finger, hand; Arm, hand; Beard,
     hand; Breast, hand; Cheek; Cheek, hand; Ear, hand; Eye,
     eyebrow, fist; Eye, finger; Eye, hand; Eye, mouth; Eyebrow;
     Face; Face, hand; Finger; Finger, hand; Finger, tooth;
     Fingernail, tooth; Foot; Forehead, hand; Forehead, lip; Hand;
     Hand, hat; Hand, head; Hand, knee; Hand, shoulder; Hand,
     staff; Hand, thigh; Hand, tooth; Head; Head, tooth; Lip; Lip,
     tooth; Mouth; Mouth, tooth; Nose; Tongue, tooth; Tooth.

Anticipation: Eyebrow; Hand; Tongue.

Antipathy: Hand; Head.

Apology: Arm, hand; Body; Finger; Finger, tooth; Hand; Head;
     Head, lip; Lip, tongue.

Apotropy: Arm; Breast, forehead, hand, mouth; Breast, hand;
     Buttocks; Eye; Eye, finger; Face; Face, hand; Finger; Finger,
     hand; Finger, hand, mouth; Finger, head; Foot; Genitals;
     Hand; Hand, mouth; Hand, object; Head, shoulder; Mouth;
     Tongue; Tooth.

Appeasement: Hand.

Appetite: Eyebrow, head, lip.

Applause: Body; Breast, foot, hand, lip; Finger; Hand; Tongue.

Appreciation: Abdomen, hand; Hand; Head; Lip.

Approach: Arm; Arm, finger, hand; Cheek, nose; Finger; Finger,
     hand; Hand; Hand, head; Lip; Mouth; Tongue.

Approval: Cheek, finger; Ear, finger; Eye; Eye, finger; Finger;
     Finger, hand; Finger, lip; Foot; Hair, hand; Hand; Hand,
     head; Hand, shoulder; Head; Mouth.

Arrogance: Body, head, lip; Eyebrow; Hand; Head; Nose.

Assistance: Arm; Arm, finger; Arm, hand; Breast, hand; Chin,
     finger; Finger; Hand.

Assurance: Finger, hand; Forehead, head; Hand; Hand, shoulder;
     Head.

Astonishment: Hand.

Attention: Arm; Body; Elbow, rib; Eye; Eye, finger; Eye, head;
     Finger; Finger, hand; Finger, lip; Finger, nose; Foot; Hand;
     Hand, head; Hand, object; Hand, shoulder; Head; Knee; Leg;
     Lip; Mouth.

Authority: Arm; Arm, hand; Body; Hand; Hand, hip; Hand, staff;
     Hand, straw.

Avarice: Elbow; Elbow, hand; Finger; Hand.

Awaken: Eye.

Awareness: Eye, finger; Forehead, hand; Hand, head.

Baby: Arm.

Bargain: Hair, hand.

Begging: Finger; Hand; Hand, knee.

Begin: Arm, finger, hand.

Betting: Finger; Hand.

Blessing: Arm; Arm, finger, hand; Body; Eye, hand; Finger; Finger, hand; Foot; Foot, hand; Hand; Hand, head; Hand, object; Mouth.

Boredom: Beard, hand; Cheek, finger; Cheek, hand; Chin, hand; Eyebrow, jaw; Finger; Hand; Mouth.

Bravery: Finger; Finger, hand.

Bribery: Finger; Hand.

Brotherhood: Lip.

Buxom: Breast, hand.

Calmness: Beard, hand; Finger, hand; Glove (gauntlet); Hand; Hand, knee; Hand, mouth, tongue, tooth; Leg; Lip.

Capture: Hand, wrist.

Carelessness: Hand; Head.

Censure: Eye, finger; Eye, hand; Finger.

Chagrin: Finger, tooth; Fingernail, tooth; Tooth.

Challenge: Chin, finger; Finger; Glove, gauntlet; Hand; Hand, object; Head.

Change: Hand.

Chastity: Hand, weapon.

Cheating: Finger, hand.

Christ: Finger.

Cigarette: Finger, hand.

Claim: Hand; Hand, object.

Clairvoyance: Hand, head.

Clarification: Finger; Head.

Cleansing: Finger; Hand.

Cleverness: Eye, finger; Finger, forehead; Finger, nose; Hand, nose.

Cold: Arm, hand; Hand.

Collect: Hand.

Command: Arm, finger, hand; Eyelid; Finger; Head.

Commendation: Hand; Hand, knee; Hand, object.

Complaint: Cheek, head, lip.

Complication: Hand.

Concentration: Body; Cheek, tongue; Chin, hand; Ear, hand; Eye;
    Eye, eyebrow, jaw; Eye, hand; Eye, head; Eyebrow; Eyebrow,
    jaw; Face, hand; Finger; Finger, head; Fingernail, tooth;
    Forehead; Forehead, hand; Hands; Hand, head; Hand, nose;
    Head; Lip.

Condemnation: Hand, stone.

Condescension: Lip.

Confession: Arm; Knee.

Confidence: Body; Eye, hand; Finger; Hand; Head.

Confirmation: Cheek, hand; Hand; Head.

Confusion: Arm, head; Eyebrow, foot, head, mouth; Face, hand;
    Forehead, hand; Hand, head; Head.

Congratulation: Arm; Back, hand; Breast, hand; Hand; Hand, lip;
    Lip.

Consecration: Hand; Hand, head.

Consolation: Arm, hand; Arm, hand, shoulder; Back, hand; Hand;
    Hand, shoulder; Lip.

Contempt: Arm, wrist; Back; Buttocks, hand; Cheek, tongue; Chin,
    finger; Chin, foot, hand; Eye; Eye, tongue; Face; Finger;
    Finger, hand; Finger, tooth; Foot; Genitals; Hand; Head; Head,
    lip; Heels; Lip; Lip, tongue; Mouth; Mouth, tooth; Nose;
    Shoulder.

Conviviality: Eye.

Copulation: Arm, hand; Finger; Finger, hand; Finger, nose; Hand;
    Hip; Mouth; Shoulder; Tongue.

Counting: Finger; Finger, hand; Hand, shoulder.

Creation: Hand.

Crowd: Arm, hand.

Cruelty: Hand, jaw, lip.

Cuckoldry: Ear, finger; Finger; Finger, forehead; Finger, hand;
    Finger, head; Hand; Hand, head; Head.

Cunning: Cheek, finger; Eye, mouth; Finger; Finger, nose; Hand,
    nose.

Curiosity: Eye, hand, head; Eye, head; Neck; Nose.

Curse: Breast, hand; Face, hand; Finger; Hand; Hand, head; Lip.

Dance: Finger.

Deafness: Finger.

Death: Arm; Arm, neck; Finger; Finger, neck; Hand; Hand, neck.

Debauchery: Ear, finger, mouth; Lip; Mouth.

Deception: Eye, eyebrow, jaw; Finger; Finger, mouth; Hand; Head; Lip.

Decision: Finger; Hand, object.

Decisiveness: Finger, forehead; Jaw; Mouth.

Dedication: Breast, hand; Hand.

Defiance: Arm; Arm, breast; Arm, hand; Arm, head; Body; Finger; Finger, hand; Finger, nose; Hand; Hand, weapon; Head; Mouth; Nose; Tongue.

Delicacy: Arm, hand.

Denial: Arm, finger; Hand; Head.

Depart: Arm, hand; Finger; Finger, hand; Foot; Hand; Head.

Depravity: Eye, jaw; Eyebrow, jaw.

Depression: Head.

Derangement: Finger; Finger, temple.

Desire: Eyebrow, head, lip; Fingernail, tooth.

Despair: Beard, hand; Body; Breast, hand; Cheek, hand; Clothing, hand; Eyebrow, head; Face, hand; Forehead, hand; Hair, hand; Hand; Hand, head; Hand, knee; Hand, lip; Hand, neck; Hand, temple; Head; Tooth.

Desperation: Eyebrow, jaw; Finger; Fingernail; Hand; Hand, head.

Destruction: Finger; Hand.

Determination: Clothing, hand; Eye, eyebrow, jaw; Foot; Foot, leg; Hand; Knee; Tooth.

Dignity: Eyebrow, head; Hand.

Direction: Arm, finger, hand; Eye; Finger; Finger, hand; Hand; Head.

Disagreement: Arm, hand; Finger; Hand; Head; Lip; Mouth.

Disappearance: Finger.

Disappointment: Breast, hand; Chin, finger; Eyebrow, jaw; Finger, mouth; Finger, nose; Hand; Hand, head; Hand, lip; Hand, mouth; Head, thigh; Lip.

Disapproval: Cheek, forehead, mouth; Clothing, hand; Eye, head; Eyebrow; Eyebrow, finger, nose; Face; Finger; Forehead; Hand; Hand, tongue; Head; Head, tooth; Mouth; Nose.

Disbelief: Abdomen, hand; Arm; Arm, hand; Arm, hand, head; Arm, head; Beard, hand; Cheek, eye, mouth; Cheek, finger; Clothing, hand; Ear, hand; Eye; Eye, finger; Eye, hand; Eye, hand, mouth; Eyebrow; Eyebrow, mouth; Finger; Finger, head; Finger, head, nose; Finger, mouth; Finger, nose; Finger, temple; Hand; Hand, hat; Hand, head; Hand, neck; Hand, nose; Hand, shoulder; Hand, tongue; Head; Head, lip; Mouth, tongue; Tongue; Tongue, tooth.

Discord: Finger.

Discouragement: Eye, head, mouth, nose; Eyebrow, head, lip; Hand.

Discretion: Hand, mouth.

Disdain: Eyebrow; Tongue.

Disgust: Body; Breast, hand; Eye, head, mouth, nose; Eye, lip, nose; Face, hand; Hand; Hand, head; Hand, neck; Hand, nose; Head; Lip, nose; Nose.

Dislike: Ear, hand; Eye; Face, hand; Finger; Head; Lip; Mouth; Nose.

Dismay: Forehead, hand; Hand; Hand, tooth; Head.

Dismissal: Hand.

Displeasure: Ear, hand; Eye, hand; Eyebrow; Heels.

Dissatisfaction: Finger, nose; Mouth.

Distress: Breast, hand; Eye, hand; Hand; Hand, head; Knee.

Distrust: Eye, finger; Eye, head, mouth, nose.

Doubt: Hand; Shoulder.

Down: Hand.

Drink: Finger; Finger, hand, mouth; Finger, lip; Finger, mouth; Finger, neck; Finger, nose; Hand; Hand, mouth; Tongue.

Dropping: Finger.

Drunkenness: Hand.

Duality: Hand.

Eating: Abdomen, hand; Finger, hand, mouth; Finger, mouth; Hand; Hand, mouth.

Ecstasy: Eye, eyebrow, head, jaw; Head; Leg; Tooth.

Effeminacy: Arm, hand; Cheek, finger; Chin, finger; Hand; Hand, wrist; Head.

Egotism: Arm, finger.

Embarrassment: Beard, hand; Cheek, eye; Cheek, finger; Cheek, hand; Eye; Eye, finger; Face, hand; Finger; Finger, head; Finger, lip; Finger, mouth; Finger, tooth; Fingernail, tooth; Foot; Hand, head; Hand, mouth; Lip; Lip, tooth; Mouth; Tongue, tooth.

Emphasis: Arm; Breast, hand; Elbow, rib; Eye; Finger; Finger, hand; Finger, nose; Foot; Forehead, hand; Hair, hand; Hand;

Hand, head; Hand, hip; Hand, knee; Hand, staff; Head.

Encouragement: Arm; Arm, elbow; Buttocks, hand; Finger; Finger, hand; Finger, mouth; Hand; Hand, shoulder.

Engagement: Hand; Ring; Shoe.

Enlightenment: Finger, forehead.

Enmity: Arm, finger; Eye; Finger; Hand; Mouth.

Enthusiasm: Arm; Arm, hand; Body; Ear, finger; Finger; Hand; Hand, mouth.

Envy: Lip, tooth.

Equality: Finger; Hand.

Etiquette: Arm; Arm, hand; Body; Body, hand; Finger; Finger, nose; Foot; Hand; Hand, lip; Head; Lip; Mouth.

Exasperation: Mouth.

Exchange: Finger.

Excitement: Hand; Hand, mouth; Lip, tooth.

Exclamation: Eye, jaw.

Expectancy: Hand; Mouth.

Exquisiteness: Hand.

Extreme: Hand.

Facetiousness: Eye; Finger, nose.

Facility: Hand.

Faithfulness: Hand.

Familiarity: Finger, nose; Lip.

Fantasy: Hand, head.

Farewell: Arm; Arm, hand; Body; Cheek, hand; Cloth, hand; Finger; Finger, lip; Hand; Hand, head; Hand, knee; Hand, object; Head; Lip; Nose.

Fatigue: Cheek, eye, hand; Cheek, hand; Chin, hand; Eye; Eye, finger; Eye, hand; Eye, hand, head; Face, hand; Finger; Finger, forehead; Foot; Hand, mouth; Mouth.

Favor: Hand, shoulder.

Fear: Arm; Beard, hand; Body; Body, face; Cheek, hand; Chin; Chin, hand; Eye, forehead; Face, hand; Finger; Foot; Hand; Hand, head; Head; Head, shoulder; Knee.

Fervor: Hand.

Fight: Hand.

Finished: Arm, finger, hand; Arm, hand; Body, hand; Finger; Foot; Hand; Hand, mouth; Hand, neck.

Flattery: Arm; Finger; Hand; Hand, nose; Lip.

Flirting: Eye; Eyebrow; Eyebrow, head, lip; Finger, tooth; Foot, leg; Head; Mouth.

Foolishness: Elbow, finger; Elbow, hand; Finger, forehead; Finger, head; Finger, lip; Hand; Hand, mouth; Head; Mouth.

Forget: Hand, head.

Forgetfulness: Fingernail, tooth.

Forgiveness: Hand.

Forwardness: Hand.

Friendship: Arm; Arm, hand; Arm, hand, shoulder; Finger; Hand; Hand, nose; Hand, shoulder; Lip; Mouth; Nose.

Frustration: Abdomen, hand; Arm, hand, shoulder; Eye, lip, tooth; Frustration; Finger, tooth; Hair, hand; Hand; Hand, mouth; Shoulder.

Gently: Hand.

Goad: Arm, hand.

Gone: Hand.

Good wishes: Hand, head.

Gossip: Ear, hand; Finger; Finger, tongue; Hand.

Graft: Hand.

Gratitude: Arm; Arm, knee; Body; Body, face; Body, hand; Breast, hand; Breast, hand, head; Eye; Finger, forehead; Finger, hand, mouth; Foot, lip; Hair, hand; Hand; Hand, knee; Hand, lip; Hand, object; Head; Knee; Lip.

Gravity: Head.

Greed: Arm, finger; Hand.

Greeting: Abdomen, hand; Arm; Arm, hand; Arm, lip; Back, hand; Body; Body, face; Body, hand; Breast, forehead, hand, mouth; Breast, forehead, lip; Breast, hand; Breast, hand, head; Cheek, hand, lip; Clothing, hand; Ear, hand; Eye; Eye, finger; Eye, head; Eyebrow, head, lip; Finger; Finger, hand; Finger, hand, mouth; Finger, head; Finger, nose; Finger, tongue; Finger, wrist; Foot; Foot, hand, head; Foot, lip; Forehead, hand; Forehead, lip; Hand; Hand, hat; Hand, head; Hand, knee; Hand, lip; Hand, mouth; Hand, object; Hand, shoulder; Hand, weapon; Head; Head, lip; Leg; Lip; Lip, shoulder; Mouth; Neck; Nose; Tongue; Tooth.

Guilt: Arm, finger; Hand.

Gunshot: Finger.

Hanging: Finger, neck.

Hard times: Hand.

Harmony: Hand.

Hatred: Hand; Hand, jaw, lip; Tooth.

Health: Finger.

Helplessness: Eye, hand; Hand; Hand, shoulder; Head; Shoulder.

Hesitation: Arm, finger; Chin; Chin, hand; Finger, head; Hand;
    Hand, head; Head; Lip; Nose.

Hitchhiking: Finger, hand.

Homage: Body; Finger, hand; Foot, lip; Foot, hand, lip; Forehead;
    Hand; Hand, lip; Head; Knee; Lip; Lip, shoulder.

Homosexuality: Arm, hand; Eyebrow, finger; Finger; Hand; Hand,
    neck.

Honor: Lip.

Horror: Eye, hand; Eye, jaw; Face, hand; Hand; Head; Hand,
    thigh; Head.

Hot: Finger; Forehead, hand; Hand, mouth.

Humiliation: Finger, nose.

Humility: Arm, breast; Body; Body, hand, head; Breast, hand;
    Breast, hand, head; Cheek, head, mouth; Eye; Finger; Hand;
    Hand, lip; Head; Head, knee; Knee; Lip; Mouth.

Hunger: Abdomen, hand; Hand; Mouth.

Hurry: Finger, nose, tongue; Hand.

Hypocrisy: Eyelid.

Idea: Finger

Idealism: Finger; Finger, head.

Identification: Breast, hand; Finger; Hand; Hand, head; Lip.

Idleness: Finger; Hand.

Ignorance: Eyebrow; Eyebrow, mouth, shoulder; Face, hand;
    Finger; Finger, nose; Hand; Hand, head; Hand, shoulder;
    Shoulder.

Impatience: Cheek, hand; Eyebrow; Finger; Foot; Hand; Hand,
    head; Hand, nose; Hand, thigh; Head; Shoulder.

Impossibility: Finger, hand.

Impulsiveness: Hand.

Indecision: Cheek; Ear, hand; Finger; Finger, tongue; Hand, head.

Indifference: Arm, hand, shoulder; Chin, finger; Chin, hand;
    Finger; Hand; Head; Head, shoulder; Lip; Shoulder.

Infidel: Finger.

Influence: Ear, finger; Hand.

Innocence: Abdomen, chest, hand; Arm; Hand.

Insolence: Head, lip.

Insult: Abdomen, finger; Arm, hand; Beard, hand; Breast, hand;
Buttocks; Buttocks, hand; Cheek, hand; Chin, hand; Ear,
finger; Ear, hand; Eye, finger; Finger; Finger, hand; Finger,
hand, tongue; Finger, head; Finger, mouth; Finger, neck;
Finger, nose; Finger, tooth; Fingernail; Foot; Forehead, hand,
neck, nose; Genitals; Hand; Hand, hat; Hand, head; Hand,
nose; Hand, temple; Hand, tongue; Lip; Mouth; Tongue.

Intellectual: Hand, head.

Intelligence: Finger, head; Forehead, hand.

Interest: Eyebrow, head, jaw.

Interrogation: Arm; Arm, hand; Chin; Ear, finger; Eye, head;
Eyebrow; Finger, hand; Hand; Hand, hip; Hand, shoulder;
Head.

Introduction: Hand; Head.

Investiture: Foot; Hand; Hand, weapon; Lip.

Invitation: Arm, hand; Cloth, hand; Finger; Finger, hand; Hand;
Hand, neck.

Irritation: Head.

Jail: Face, hand; Finger; Hand; Hand, neck; Hand, wrist.

Jealousy: Eye, finger; Fingernail, tooth; Hand; Hand, side.

Joke: Finger, nose.

Joy: Arm; Cheek, forehead, mouth; Clothing, hand; Eye; Foot;
Foot, hand; Foot, leg; Hand; Hand, head; Hand, object; Hand,
thigh; Hand, weapon; Head, shoulder; Leg; Lip.

Judgment: Arm; Body; Clothing, hand; Document, hand; Finger;
Hand; Hand, leg; Hand, staff; Hand, torch; Hand, weapon;
Leg.

Kill: Finger; Hand.

Kindness: Cheek, hand; Hand, shoulder.

Laziness: Glove; Hand; Hand, knee; Nose.

Leading: Arm, hand; Hand, wrist.

Leniency: Eye, finger.

Liberty: Hand.

Life: Finger.

Limits: Finger.

Look: Hand.

Louder: Ear, hand.

Luck: Clothing, hand; Finger; Finger, tooth; Hand; Hand, hat; Hand, knee; Hand, object; Lip.

Magical: Body; Buttocks; Ear, finger, mouth; Eye; Eye, finger; Finger; Finger, hand; Foot; Hand; Hand, mouth; Leg; Mouth.

Magnanimity: Finger.

Magnitude: Arm; Cheek, hand; Eye, hand; Eye, mouth; Finger; Finger, hand; Hand.

Manumission: Hand; Hand, head; Hand, staff; Hand, straw.

Marriage: Arm; Cloth, hand; Finger; Hand; Hand, hat; Hand, staff; Ring.

Masculinity: Finger, hand.

Masturbation: Hand.

Medico-magical: Abdomen, hand; Arm; Arm, finger; Finger; Finger, hand; Finger, hand, mouth; Finger, tooth; Foot; Foot, hand; Genitals; Hand; Mouth.

Mediocre: Hand.

Meditation: Beard, hand; Buttocks, hand; Finger, head.

Melancholy: Arm.

Memory: Hand, head; Head.

Mercy: Finger; Hand, lip.

Minimization of difficulties: Finger; Hand.

Misery: Head.

Mistake: Eye, eyebrow; Finger, head; Finger, neck.

Mockery: Arm, finger; Arm, finger, hand; Arm, hand, mouth; Beard, hand; Buttocks; Buttocks, hand, tongue; Cheek, finger; Cheek, hand; Chin, finger; Clothing, hand; Ear, hand; Eye; Eye, finger, mouth, tongue; Eye, head; Face; Finger; Finger, forehead; Finger, hand; Finger, hand, nose; Finger, lip; Finger, mouth; Finger, mouth, tongue; Finger, nose; Finger, nose, tongue; Finger, shoulder; Genitals; Hand; Hand, head; Hand, mouth; Hand, nose; Head; Heels; Lip, tooth; Mouth; Mouth, tooth; Tongue; Tooth.

Modesty: Arm, head, shoulder; Eye; Eye, head; Head.

Money: Arm, finger; Arm, hand; Finger; Finger, hand; Hand.

Moot: Hand.

Mourning: Arm; Arm, hand; Arm, shoulder; Beard, hand; Body;
    Body, hand; Breast, cheek, hair, hand; Breast, eye, hair,
    hand; Breast, hair, hand; Breast, hand; Breast, hand, head;
    Cheek, finger; Cheek, hand; Clothing, hand; Eye; Eye, hand;
    Face; Face, hand; Finger; Finger, hand; Finger, neck; Fin-
    ger, tooth; Foot; Hair, hand; Hand; Hand, head; Hand, lip;
    Hand, thigh; Hand, torch; Hand, weapon; Head; Lip; Shield.

Mysterious: Finger, lip.

Need: Hand, head.

Negation: Arm; Arm, finger, hand; Arm, shoulder; Chin, finger;
    Chin, hand; Eyebrow; Eyelid; Finger; Finger, hand; Finger,
    mouth; Finger, neck; Finger, tooth; Fingernail, tooth; Hand;
    Hand, head; Hand, mouth; Head; Head, lip; Head, tongue;
    Shoulder; Tongue.

Negotiation: Shield.

Negro: Finger, hand; Finger, head.

Nervousness: Beard, hand; Face, hand; Finger; Foot, leg; Hand;
    Lip; Mouth.

Nostalgia: Head.

Nothing: Arm, hand; Chin, hand; Eye, finger; Finger; Finger,
    tooth; Fingernail, tooth; Hand.

Oath: Animal, hand; Arm; Arm, breast; Arm, breast, shoulder;
    Arm, hand; Arm, hand, shoulder; Arm, knee; Beard, hand;
    Breast, hand; Cheek, hand; Chin, hand; Clothing, hand; Eye,
    hand; Eyelid, finger; Finger; Finger, hand; Finger, head;
    Finger, knee; Finger, lip; Finger, mouth; Finger, neck;
    Finger, tooth; Fingernail, tooth; Foot; Hair, hand; Hand;
    Hand, head; Hand, hip; Hand, knee; Hand, neck; Hand, ob-
    ject; Hand, staff; Hand, straw; Hand, thigh; Hand, weapon;
    Head; Head, object; Knee; Leg; Lip.

Obedience: Breast, hand; Finger; Hand; Head.

Obstinacy: Neck.

Oppression: Finger; Hand.

Order: Hand.

Ordering (wine): Finger; Hand, object.

Overburdened: Hand.

Overcoming obstacles: Finger, hand.

Pacification: Arm; Hand.

Pain: Cheek, hand; Eye, eyebrow, head, lip; Finger; Finger, tooth; Foot; Forehead, hand; Hand; Lip, tooth; Mouth, tongue; Tongue, tooth.

Pardon: Hand.

Passion: Arm, breast; Arm, hand; Eye; Hand, head.

Past: Finger.

Pay: Finger; Finger, hand; Hand.

Peace: Finger; Hand; Hand, weapon; Lip.

Pederasty: Ear, hand; Hand.

Penitence: Breast, hand; Head; Nose.

Pensiveness: Arm, hand, head; Beard, hand; Cheek, hand; Chin, finger; Chin, finger, head, nose; Chin, forehead, hand, leg; Chin, hand; Chin, hand, knee; Ear, hand; Finger; Finger, hand; Finger, hand, mouth; Finger, lip; Finger, mouth; Hand; Hand, head; Hand, tooth; Head.

Perfection: Finger; Finger, lip.

Permission: Glove.

Perplexity: Eyebrow, hand, head; Eyebrow, head, lip; Finger, forehead; Hand, head; Lip, tooth.

Pettiness: Hand, lip.

Piety: Hand; Head.

Pity: Hand; Head.

Placation: Hand.

Plea: Arm; Arm, breast; Arm, hand; Arm, knee; Beard, hand; Body; Body, face; Breast, hand; Breast, lip; Cheek, finger; Cheek, hand, knee; Cheek, head, lip; Chin, hand; Chin, hand, knee; Eye; Finger, forehead; Finger, hand; Finger, hand, mouth; Foot, lip; Forehead, hand; Hand; Hand, head; Hand, knee; Hand, knee, lip; Hand, lip; Hand, object; Hand, straw; Head; Knee; Lip; Neck.

Pleasure: Chin; Ear, finger; Eye, head, lip, tooth; Finger; Hand; Head; Lip.

Pledge: Glove.

Plenty: Finger; Finger, hand.

Pointing: Arm; Arm, finger; Arm, hand; Chin; Eye, head; Finger; Finger, head, mouth; Finger, shoulder; Hand; Head; Head, lip; Lip.

Possession: Arm, hand; Body, hand; Foot; Glove; Hand; Hand, staff; Hand, straw; Knee; Ring.

Possibility: Hand.

Poverty: Clothing, hand; Ear, hand; Eye; Finger; Finger, mouth; Finger, neck; Finger, nose; Finger, throat; Finger, tooth;

Fingernail, tooth; Hand; Hand, head; Hand, hip.

Praise: Arm; Clothing, hand; Finger; Finger, hand; Hand; Hand, hat.

Prayer: Arm; Arm, breast; Arm, breast, knee; Arm, face; Arm, finger, hand; Arm, hand; Arm, knee; Back, hand; Body; Body, face; Body, foot; Body, hand; Breast, forehead, hand mouth; Breast, forehead, hand, shoulder; Breast, hand; Buttocks, hand; Chin, hand; Eye; Eye, hand; Eye, navel; Eye, nose; Face, hand; Finger; Finger, hand; Finger, nose; Foot; Foot, leg; Forehead, knee; Hair, hand; Hand; Hand, hat; Hand, head; Hand, head, knee; Hand, knee; Hand, lip; Hand, mouth; Hand, nose; Hand, object; Head; Head, knee; Knee; Leg; Lip; Mouth.

Precision: Finger.

Pregnancy: Abdomen, hand; Arm; Clothing, hand; Hand.

Preparedness: Hand.

Pride: Arm; Arm, finger; Arm, hand; Body, finger, mouth; Body, Head; Hand; Hand, shoulder; Head; Hand; Head, lip; Leg.

Probably: Finger.

Prohibition: Eye; Eyebrow; Eyelid; Hand; Hand, head.

Promise: Body, head, lip; Breast, finger; Chin, hand; Finger; Finger, forehead; Finger, nose; Hand.

Proof: Hand.

Proscription: Glove.

Prosperity: Cheek, eyebrow, head, mouth.

Prostitute: Finger; Hand.

Protection: Arm; Hand; Head, knee.

Protest: Breast, hand; Leg.

Proxy: Eyelid, finger.

Punishment: Cheek, hand; Ear, hand; Hand; Hand, head; Hand, nose; Hand, temple.

Quickly: Finger; Hand.

Readiness: Eye, finger; Hand; Hand, hip.

Recognition: Body; Eye; Eye, hand; Head; Leg.

Reconciliation: Finger; Finger, hand; Forehead, hand; Hand; Lip; Mouth.

Redemption: Finger.

Refusal: Arm; Arm, hand; Finger; Finger, nose; Hand; Hand,

object; Head; Shoe.

Regret: Breast, hand; Cheek, hand; Finger, hand; Finger, lip; Finger, tooth; Hand; Hand, head; Hand, mouth; Head; Lip, tooth.

Rejection: Arm; Chin, hand; Eye, hand; Face; Finger, hand; Foot; Hand; Hand, nose; Hand, staff; Hand, straw; Mouth.

Relief: Breast, hand; Eye, lip; Forehead, hand; Mouth.

Relinquishment: Hand, object; Hand, staff.

Reminder: Elbow, rib; Finger; Finger, forehead; Finger, mouth; Finger, tooth; Forehead, hand; Hand, head; Hand, knee.

Remorse: Breast, hand; Eyebrow, hand, head; Hand, object; Head.

Repetition: Finger; Head.

Reproach: Cheek, head, lip; Finger; Hand; Head.

Request: Finger, hand; Hand.

Resignation: Arm; Breast, hand; Finger, hand; Hand; Head, lip; Head, tongue; Hand, shoulder; Head, lip; Head, shoulder; Shoulder.

Respect: Back, breast, hand, head; Body; Body, face; Breast, hand, lip; Chin, finger; Finger, head; Finger, lip; Foot; Foot, lip; Forehead, lip; Hair, hand; Hand; Hand, hat; Hand, lip; Hand, mouth; Head; Head, lip; Knee; Knee, lip; Leg; Lip; Tongue.

Rest: Arm; Head.

Result: Finger; Finger, hand.

Retraction: Finger, nose.

Retreat: Finger; Hand.

Reverence: Arm, hand; Body, eye, hand; Body, face; Body, hand, head; Hand; Hand, hat; Hand, head; Hand, knee; Hand, leg; Hand, object; Head; Knee; Lip; Mouth; Tongue.

Review: Hand.

Revulsion: Finger, nose.

Rise: Finger, hand; Hand.

Royalty: Finger; Hand; Hand, object.

Sacrifice: Animal, hand; Breast, hand; Hand; Hand, object.

Salvation: Hand.

Sanctuary: Finger.

Sarcasm: Mouth.

Satisfaction: Abdomen, hand; Arm; Beard, hand; Breast, hand; Cheek, eyebrow, head, mouth; Hand; Head.

Secrecy: Eye; Finger, nose; Finger, tooth; Hand; Head.

Seduction: Arm, lip.

Seeking: Finger.

Seize: Hand.

Self-acknowledgment: Hand.

Self-discipline: Lip, tooth.

Self-gratitude: Eye, hand.

Self-importance: Body; Breast; Cheek, head, mouth; Head.

Self-irony: Finger, hand.

Self-satisfaction: Fingernail; Hand.

Sensibility: Cheek, forehead, mouth.

Separation: Finger; Hand.

Series: Arm; Arm, hand; Hand.

Shame: Buttocks; Chin, finger; Eye; Eyebrow, finger; Face; Face, hand; Finger; Hair, hand; Hand; Hand, knee; Hand, thigh; Head; Neck.

Shock: Face, hand; Hand.

Shyness: Cheek, finger; Cheek, hand; Finger; Hand.

Sick: Abdomen, hand; Face, hand.

Silence: Chin, hand; Ear, finger; Eye, lip, tooth; Finger; Finger, hand, mouth; Finger, lip; Finger, mouth; Finger, nose; Hand; Hand, head; Hand, lip; Hand, mouth; Lip.

Sincerity: Arm; Breast, hand; Hand; Hand, weapon.

Sit down: Hand.

Skepticism: Eyebrow.

Smell: Hand.

Snobbishness: Chin; Hand, head.

Solemnity: Body; Finger, nose.

Sorrow: Arm; Arm, breast; Arm, hand; Beard; Beard, hand; Body; Body, cheek, hand; Body, face; Body, forehead, mouth; Body, hand, head; Breast; Breast, hand; Cheek, finger; Cheek, forehead, mouth; Cheek, hand; Chin, hand; Elbow, eye; Eye; Eye, finger; Eye, hand; Eye, mouth; Eyebrow, jaw; Eyebrow, lip; Face; Face, hand; Face, hand, knee; Finger; Finger, forehead; Finger, hand; Fingernail, tooth; Hair, hand; Hair, hand, mouth; Hand; Hand, hat; Hand, head; Hand, head, knee; Hand, mouth; Hand, thigh; Head; Head, knee; Leg; Lip, tooth; Mouth.

Speaking: Finger, mouth.

Speed: Hand.

Stand: Hand.

Stealing: Finger; Finger, hand; Hand.

Stop: Arm; Arm, hand; Finger; Finger, hand; Hand; Hand, shoulder.

Strength: Arm; Arm, hand; Breast, hand.

Strike: Body, hand; Hand.

Stupidity: Forehead, hand.

Submission: Arm; Arm, breast; Arm, hand; Body; Body, forehead; Body, head; Cheek; Chin; Face; Foot; Foot, hand; Foot, lip; Forehead; Hand; Hand, hat; Hand, head; Hand, knee; Hand, lip; Hand, mouth; Hand, shoulder; Hand, staff; Head; Knee; Lip; Mouth; Neck; Shoe; Shoulders; Tongue; Tooth.

Success: Finger, tongue.

Suffering: Eye, eyebrow, head, lip; Hand.

Superciliousness: Nose.

Superiority: Body; Finger; Hand; Hand, weapon.

Superlative: Finger; Finger, lip.

Surprise: Arm; Cheek, eyebrow; Cheek, finger; Cheek, hand; Eye; Eye, finger; Eye, hand; Eye, head; Eyebrow; Eyebrow, hand, mouth; Eyebrow, head; Eyebrow, mouth; Finger; Finger, lip; Forehead, hand; Hand; Hand, head; Hand, leg; Hand, mouth; Hand, neck; Hand, thigh; Head; Leg; Lip; Mouth.

Surrender: Arm; Arm, hand; Arm, neck; Finger; Finger, hand; Finger, mouth; Hair, hand; Hand; Hand, head; Hand, staff; Hand, weapon; Head; Knee.

Suspicion: Eye, finger; Finger, nose.

Sustain: Hand.

Sympathy: Eye; Hand, knee; Head.

Sympathy (false): Arm, hand.

Taste: Finger; Finger, tongue.

"Teach me": Hand.

Teasing: Arm, hand; Breast, hand; Ear, finger; Eyebrow; Finger; Finger, hand; Finger, lip; Finger, nose, tongue; Hand; Tongue.

Telephone: Ear, hand; Hand.

Thief: Cheek, hand.

Threat: Arm, finger; Arm, hand; Arm, hand, shoulder; Body, finger; Body, head; Cheek, finger; Chin, finger; Chin, hand; Ear, finger; Elbow, hand; Eyebrow; Finger; Finger, forehead; Finger, hand; Finger, nose; Finger, tooth; Genitals; Hand;

Hand, neck; Hand, object; Head; Lip; Tooth.

Time: Eye, hand; Finger, hand.

Toast: Hand, object.

Tomorrow: Finger.

Tortuousness: Finger.

Treaty: Hand.

Trivia: Hand.

Trust: Hand.

Truth: Breast, hand; Finger; Finger, hand; Hand; Hand, nose; Shoulder.

Uncertainty: Cheek, eye, mouth; Eye, head; Eyebrow, mouth, shoulder; Hand; Hand, head; Hand, head, shoulder; Hand, shoulder; Head.

Understanding: Arm; Eye; Eye, hand; Eye, head; Finger; Finger, forehead; Finger, nose; Finger, temple; Hand; Hand, nose; Head.

Undetermined (future): Finger.

Union: Finger; Finger, hand; Hand; Lip.

Urgency: Hand, shoulder.

Useless: Body, hand; Finger; Finger, nose; Hand.

Vanity: Foot.

Vengeance: Arm, mouth; Finger; Finger, hand; Hand.

Verbosity: Hand.

Victory: Arm; Arm, hand; Beard, hand; Finger; Foot; Hand; Hand, head; Hand, object; Knee.

Virility: Arm; Body, hand.

Volunteer: Arm, hand; Hand.

Voting: Arm, hand; Hand.

Wait: Hand.

Warning: Arm, elbow; Arm, hand; Cheek, finger; Ear, hand; Eye, finger; Eye, hand; Eye, mouth; Finger; Finger, head; Finger, tooth; Hand; Head; Lip.

Weakmindedness: Eyebrow, jaw.

Welcome: Arm.

Wisdom: Chin, finger.

Wish: Finger; Finger, hand.
Withdraw: Finger, hand.